Reading Autobiography

Reading Autobiography

A Guide for Interpreting Life Narratives

Sidonie Smith and Julia Watson

Second Edition

University of Minnesota Press
Minneapolis
London

The section on "Space" in chapter 2 is excerpted from Julia Watson, "The Spaces of Auto-biographical Narrative," *Räume des Selbst. Selbstzeugnisforschung transkulturell*. Chapter 5 is an expanded version of Sidonie Smith and Julia Watson, "New Genres, New Subjects: Women, Gender, and Autobiography after 2000," *Revista Canaria de Estudios Ingleses* 58 (April 2009): 13–40. The section on human rights narratives in chapter 5 is adapted from Kay Schaffer and Sidonie Smith, *Human Rights and Narrated Lives: The Ethics of Recognition* (New York: Pal-grave Macmillan, 2004), and from Kay Schaffer and Sidonie Smith, "Human Rights, Story-telling, and the Position of the Beneficiary: Antjie Krog's *Country of My Skull*," *PMLA* 121, no. 3 (2006): 1577–84. Pages 173–79 of chapter 6 were excerpted from Sidonie Smith and Julia Watson, "Introduction: Mapping Women's Self-Representation at Visual/Textual Interfaces," in *Interfaces: Women/Autobiography/Image/Performance* (Ann Arbor: University of Michigan Press, 2002), 1–46, and Sidonie Smith and Julia Watson, "The Rumpled Bed of Autobiography: Extravagant Lives, Extravagant Questions," *Biography* 24, no. 1 (Winter 2001): 1–14. Portions of chapter 7 have been excerpted, with revision, from chapter 1 of Sidonie Smith, *A Poetics of Women's Autobiography: Marginality and the Fictions of Self-Representation* (Bloomington: Indiana University Press, 1987), and from chapter 3 of Sidonie Smith, *Subjectivity, Identity, and the Body: Women's Autobiographical Practices in the Twentieth Century* (Bloomington: Indiana University Press, 1993).

Copyright 2010 by the Regents of the University of Minnesota

First edition published in 2001 by the University of Minnesota Press

Published by the University of Minnesota Press
111 Third Avenue South, Suite 290
Minneapolis, MN 55401-2520
http://www.upress.umn.edu

Library of Congress Cataloging-in-Publication Data

Smith, Sidonie.
    Reading autobiography : a guide for interpreting life narratives / Sidonie Smith and Julia Watson. — 2nd ed.
        p.   cm.
    Includes bibliographical references and index.
    ISBN 978-0-8166-6985-1 (hc : alk. paper) — ISBN 978-0-8166-6986-8 (pb : alk. paper)
    1. Autobiography.   I. Watson, Julia.   II. Title.
    CT25.S595 2010
    808'.06692—dc22

                                                                                        2010011471

Printed in the United States of America on acid-free paper

The University of Minnesota is an equal-opportunity educator and employer.

18 17 16 15 14 13 12 11 10   10 9 8 7 6 5 4 3 2 1

*To our inspirational colleagues around the world
in the International Auto/Biography Association*

Contents

Preface

This second edition of *Reading Autobiography: A Guide for Interpreting Life Narratives* is both a comprehensive critical introduction and a theoretical approach to life writing, the wide-ranging field of autobiographical texts, practices, and acts. As a guide it is organized to address advanced undergraduate and graduate students, as well as scholars in the humanities, social sciences, and arts who are interested in the burgeoning field of life writing. We hope that general readers will also find it user-friendly and accessible.

What's new in this version of *Reading Autobiography*? If, according to Timothy Dow Adams, the first edition was the "Whole Earth Catalog" of autobiography studies, the second edition aims to track a field that, in the wake of the memoir boom, has become virtually intergalactic. The nine substantive chapters explore the building blocks and components of autobiographical acts, review the history of life writing and life writing criticism, and offer a "tool kit" of pertinent questions for twenty-four key concepts. There are two entirely new chapters: one on new genres and new subjects, surveying the innovative forms of life writing that have emerged since 2001, and the other on life narrative in exemplary visual and virtual modes, such as autographics and online blogs, that are reshaping the discursive terms and audience expectations that traditionally defined the field. Two chapters on the history of autobiographical criticism have been revised to encompass new kinds of scholarly work in the past decade. Sections of other chapters have been updated—for example, the discussions of memory and agency in chapter 2. As in the first edition, each chapter has clearly labeled sections to facilitate classroom use. Finally, there are three appendixes: an overview of key terms and modes; a set of suggested classroom activities to engage students in innovative ways with the process of life writing; and a list of international print journals, selected online resources, and bibliographies of primary and secondary texts. Although the chapters reference one another, each can be used independently, enabling users to tailor information to specific needs.

Who will find *Reading Autobiography* of interest? For instructors in departments of literature, history, American studies, African American studies, women's studies, ethnic and cultural studies, and other fields that examine the autobiographical in texts, discourses, and visual and online practices, it will be a helpful guide and a spur to theoretical and historical exploration. At the graduate level, *Reading Autobiography* offers a comprehensive introduction for students engaging primary texts or doing intensive theoretical work in the field. At the undergraduate level it is a handbook to accompany survey, period, or multicultural courses on life writing and memoir, as well as literary history more broadly. We hope that general readers fascinated by the memoir boom of the past two decades will find *Reading Autobiography* a helpful introduction and guide to this exciting, wide-ranging, and ever-growing field.

Acknowledgments

Revising a book completed nearly a decade ago was a daunting prospect—
like raising a child twice. As the field of life writing expanded exponentially
in the intervening years, our own ambitions for a second edition grew, yet
we were concerned to keep the book concise, affordable, and user friendly.
How could the burgeoning sites of life writing in digital and visual media,
the innovative forms of memoir writing, and the welter of new theoretical
approaches to autobiographical practices that have emerged in the past
decade be encompassed in a single volume?

Our task was not made easier, though much enriched, by the imaginative and often witty suggestions sent by colleagues around the world to
add more terms and subfields. We became aware of our own evolving understanding of life writing by examining some of the assumptions we had
asserted a decade ago. How do constraints on agency and the contours of
memory structure self-presentation? How should the situating of selves
in space be conceptualized, and the compelling particularity of autobiographical voices be theorized? How might we develop theories of audience
and think about the apparent binary between narrated and narrating "I"s?
And, crucially, what is in fact the relationship of life writing to life narrative, and both to the tradition of autobiography? On this last point, as
on much else, G. Thomas Couser has been a stimulating and resourceful
colleague. His queries, grounded in classroom experience with *Reading
Autobiography* as well as his prolific research, have offered insights and
proposed shifts in emphasis, and we are grateful for his attentive support.

We appreciate the continuing support of the University of Minnesota
Press over two decades. Douglas Armato, Richard Morrison, Adam Brun-
ner, and Laura Westlund, and before them Biodun Iginla, have encouraged the project as a wide-ranging investigation into life narrative and
guided its successive stages. Our copy editors (for the first edition, Therese
Boyd, and for this edition, Louisa Castner) graciously accommodated our
editorial needs. Our trusted indexer, Suzanne Aboulfadl, again lent her

expertise. We owe special gratitude to Sidonie's research assistants at the University of Michigan: Bethany Davila, Hannah Dickinson, Brett Griffiths, Andromeda Hartwick, and Randall Pinder kept us on track, checked our sources, constructed bibliographies, and shared in the intellectual excitement and research labor of revising and expanding this book.

Our conceptual debts are also numerous. We are enduringly indebted to Mary Louise Pratt for prodding us to address the exclusionary implications of the term *autobiography*. Her comparative theorizing, like that of other postcolonial critics such as Françoise Lionnet, remains influential for engaging the diverse meanings and consequences of telling a life story. Timothy Dow Adams contributed his critical acumen and ready wit to our thinking in both editions, particularly during the West Virginia University Summer Seminar in Literature and Cultural Studies he invited us to lead in 1998. The trenchant questions about the breadth and diversity of life writing that Susanna Egan provided in our initial draft continued to guide us in expanding the scope of this second edition. We continue to benefit from the sage counsel of William L. Andrews, who has supported our work for more than twenty years. The probing readings raised by Leigh Gilmore and Gillian Whitlock, our intrepid collaborators in an upcoming project, have prompted us to rethink in the second edition some assumptions of the first. Kay Schaffer, Sidonie's collaborator on *Human Rights and Narrated Lives,* influenced our view of the importance of human rights storytelling and issues of trauma, testimony, and acts of witnessing.

We also acknowledge less direct contributions of scholars in the field whose work sustains and enriches our own. The theoretical interventions and formal experimentation of Nancy K. Miller, as critic and practitioner of life writing, have been inspirational for more than three decades. The forays of Paul John Eakin into how life writing intersects with such fields as neuroscience and the social sciences have both complemented and stimulated our own inquiries. Julie Rak's invigorating questions at conferences, in correspondence, and in her essays often have prompted our reconceptualization of the social and material contexts and networks of life narrative. James Phelan's theorizing of issues of voice and intended audience, as well as the ethics of narration, prompted a new section in this book that rethinks key theoretical concepts. We are sustained by the extraordinary efforts of Craig Howes, editor of the journal *Biography* and manager of the International Auto/Biography Association listserv. His fresh insights, wealth of scholarly expertise, and intellectual generosity have unflaggingly nurtured and supported our work and that of our colleagues in autobiography studies.

This list of acknowledgments would be incomplete without recognition of the formative influence on autobiography studies of two foundational scholars. We owe a particular debt of gratitude to James Olney. Independently, each of us benefited from his support of our work at an early stage and found his generosity sustaining. James's profound engagement with questions at the heart of self-referential discourse, his commitment to the field of autobiography studies, and his generosity with younger scholars have been inspirational. Similarly, Philippe Lejeune's remarkable body of work on autobiography and diary and his leadership of a network of autobiography enthusiasts in France exemplify the everyday uses of life writing and a mode of collaborative scholarship joining academia and the publics of life writing. His dedication to and delight in the work of autobiography studies, evident at conferences, is a model of passionate engagement.

As ever, our thinking has been informed, shaped, and enriched by regular interactions (on the International Auto/Biography Association listserv and at its conferences, and in oral and written dialogues) with our colleagues in the Auto/Biography Society of the United States. An intrepid band of scholars with whom we have worked to bring academic legitimacy to the field of life narrative, they have challenged, cajoled, and consoled one another for more than two decades. In particular, Jon Alexander, O.P., William Boelhower, Bella Brodzki, Robert Folkenflik, Cynthia Franklin, Joseph Hogan, Rebecca Hogan, Alfred Hornung, Margaretta Jolly, Roseanne Kennedy, Jeremy Popkin, and Roger Porter shared their insights, readings, and probing questions with us. As this revision expanded our inquiry into life narrative to the arenas of visual and online forms, we learned from and relied on the work of scholars in two vast interdisciplinary areas. In visual and graphic media, as well as performance and self-portraiture, the advice of our colleagues Julie Codell, Lesley Ferris, Jared Gardner, and Kathleen McHugh led us to issues of automediality in self-representation. In digital forms, established and emerging scholars mining the proliferating modes of online lives (among them Brian Rotman and Laurie McNeill) have called our attention to theoretical implications of digital subjectivity. We also recognize here the perceptive observations of our undergraduate students, whose facility with navigating the Web always amazes, and the insights of our graduate students, whose energy for theorizing diverse media regularly dazzles.

In addition to several societies for whose support we expressed gratitude in the first edition, we now thank societies that supported our work during this past decade. Julia thanks the University of California Humanities Research Institute on Autobiography in the Americas for its residency grant and its members for their congenial conversations, and the Camargo Foundation for its residency grant with an inspirational group of artists and scholars. Sidonie thanks the Humanities Centre and its fellows at the Australian National University in Canberra, and the faculty in Arts and Sciences at Curtin University in Perth, especially Barbara Milech, for their generous fellowships and productive conversations.

As our networks expanded over the past decade, each of us also encountered other communities working with aspects of life writing. Julia learned from stimulating exchanges with researchers at several sites: the Ludwig Boltzmann Institute for the History and Theory of Biography in Vienna, and the gender studies programs there and at the University of Klagenfurt, Austria; Gabriele Jancke and others of the DFG Research Group on self-documents in transcultural perspective at the Free University, Berlin; Deborah Madsen in American studies at the University of Geneva and the Society of Swiss Americanists; and Renata Jambresiç Kirin and her colleagues at the Institute for Ethnology and Folklore of the University of Zagreb. We both participated in rewarding dialogues with the American studies faculty in Istanbul, Turkey, particularly Oya Berk and Sirma Soran at Haliç University, and Hülya Adak at Sabanci University.

Julia is appreciative of the resources made available by The Ohio State University and the insights of her colleagues in comparative studies; Sidonie, of resources made available by the University of Michigan.

As always, we recognize the understanding and good-humored tolerance of the usual suspects. They know who they are.

Finally, we acknowledge the schooling in wisdom of self-reflexive writers. Studying autobiographical work is, if nothing else, an enduring lesson in humility. As Montaigne observed in "Of Experience": "There is no use our mounting on stilts, for on stilts we must still walk on our own legs. And on the loftiest throne in the world we are still sitting only on our own rump."

Life Narrative: Definitions and Distinctions

My life is history, politics, geography. It is religion and metaphysics. It is music and language.

Paula Gunn Allen, "The Autobiography of a Confluence"

Defining Kinds of Life Narrative

What could be simpler to understand than the act of people representing what they know best, their own lives? Yet this act is anything but simple, for the teller of his or her own story becomes, in the act of narration, both the observing subject and the object of investigation, remembrance, and contemplation. We might best approach life narrative, then, as a moving target, a set of shifting self-referential practices that, in engaging the past, reflect on identity in the present. We intend in this book to complicate ordinary understandings of the concept and practices of self-referential narrative. A first step is to define terms and draw distinctions between autobiographical self-representation and other closely related kinds of life writing.

In Greek, *autos* denotes "self," *bios* "life," and *graphe* "writing."[1] Taken together in this order, the words *self life writing* offer a brief definition of *autobiography*. British poet and critic Stephen Spender cites the dictionary definition of *autobiography* as "the story of one's life written by himself" but notes its inadequacy to the "world that each is to himself" (115). French theorist Philippe Lejeune expanded that definition in a pronouncement many would call definitive: "We call autobiography the retrospective narrative in prose that someone makes of his own existence when he puts the principal accent upon his life, especially upon the story of his own personality."[2] But if *life* is expanded to include *how* one has become who he or she is at a given moment in an ongoing process of reflection, the concept of the autobiographical as a story requires more contextualizing. We here offer some historical, geographic, and generic contexts for the term.

In English the term *autobiography* first appeared in the review of Isaac D'Israeli's *Miscellanies* by William Taylor of Norwich in the *Monthly Review*

(1797). Its first use, however, is often ascribed to Robert Southey's anglicizing of the three Greek words in 1809.[3] In his extensive survey of the term *autobiography*, Robert Folkenflik specifies the exact dates of the word's emergence in the West: "The term *autobiography* and its synonym *self-biography*," "having never been used in earlier periods, appeared in the late eighteenth century in several forms, in isolated instances in the seventies, eighties, and nineties in both England and Germany with no sign that one use influenced another" (5). Folkenflik also notes that until the twentieth century the word *memoirs* (in French *les mémoires*) was commonly used to designate "self life writing."

Autobiography, now the most commonly used term for life writing, thus describes writing being produced at a particular historical juncture, the period prior to the Enlightenment in the West. Central to that movement was the concept of the self-interested individual of property who was intent on assessing the status of the soul or the meaning of public achievement. By the eighteenth century, notions of self-interest, self-consciousness, and self-knowledge informed the figure of the "Enlightened individual" described by philosophers and social and political theorists. And "autobiographies" as studies in self-interest were sought by a growing reading public with access to affordable printed books (see Krailsheimer, Weintraub, and Sturrock).

But the relatively recent coinage of the term *autobiography* does not mean that the practice of self-referential writing began only in the later eighteenth century. In earlier centuries, terms such as *memoir* (Madame de Staël, Glückel of Hameln) or *the life* (Teresa of Avila) or *the book of my life* (Cardano) or *confessions* (Augustine, Rousseau) or *essays of myself* (Montaigne) signaled the writer's focus on self-reference through speculations about history, politics, religion, science, and culture, and often involved developing a method of and vocabulary for self-study. Moreover, since the end of the eighteenth century a host of terms, such as *testimonio*, *autoethnography*, and *psychobiography*, have been coined to designate new kinds and contexts of self-referential writing. This rich and diverse history of self-referential modes requires that we make some crucial distinctions among key terms—*autobiography, memoir, life writing, life narrative*—that may seem to imply the same thing.

Autobiography, as we have seen, became the term for a particular generic practice that emerged in the Enlightenment and subsequently became definitive for life writing in the West. It remains the widely used and most generally understood term. But because the term privileges the autonomous individual and the universalizing life story as the definitive achievement of life writing, it has been vigorously challenged in the wake of postmodern and postcolonial critiques of the Enlightenment subject. Early twentieth-century theorists installed this master narrative of "the sovereign self" as an institution of literature and culture, and identified a canon of representative self life writings. Implicit in this canonization, however, is the assumption that many other kinds of life writings produced at the same time have lesser value and were not "true" autobiography—the slave narrative, narratives of women's domestic lives, coming-of-age and travel narratives, among others.

Thus, many postmodern and postcolonial theorists contend that the term *autobiography* is inadequate to describe the extensive historical range and the diverse genres and practices of life writing not only in the West but around the globe. Indeed, these critics contend, the concept of autobiography, celebrated by an earlier generation of scholars such as Georges Gusdorf and Karl Joachim Weintraub as the highest achievement of individuality in western civilization, has been defined against many coexistent forms of life writing. Thus, its politics is one of exclusion. Other critics, among them Julie Rak and Leigh Gilmore, address this troubling, exclusionary aspect of autobiography by shifting the term of reference to autobiographical discourse, that is, to discursive formations of truth-telling "sustained by the trappings of identification that have underwritten what the self is and how it has been seen in much of the Western World" (Rak, *Negotiated Memory* ix). This shift from genre to discourse opens to the scenes of autobiographical inscription beyond the printed life story. It also attends to the aspects of power inherent in acts of autobiographical inscription and recognizes that those whose identities, experiences, and histories remain marginal, invalidated, invisible, and partial negotiate and alter normative or traditional frames of identity in their differences (Rak, *Negotiated* ix).

At this moment, another term has gained currency in popular and scholarly arenas. Predating the term *autobiography, memoir* is now the word used by publishing houses to describe various practices and genres of self life writing. Historically, memoir was understood as *mémoire (les mémoires),* recollections by the publicly prominent who chronicled their social accomplishments (see Quinby). These recollections often bracketed one moment or period of experience rather than an entire life span and offered reflections on its significance for the writer's previous status or self-understanding. Rak suggests that memoir has long been attached to popular forms of life writing and used as a nominal marker to distinguish stories about unacknowledged aspects of people's lives, sometimes considered scandalous or titillating, and often written by the socially marginal (*Negotiated* 316–20). In contemporary writing, the categorization of memoir often signals autobiographical works characterized by density of language and self-reflexivity about the writing process, yoking the author's standing as a professional writer with the work's status as an aesthetic object. For Nancy K. Miller the term *memoir* captures a dynamic postmodernism in its movement between the "private and the public, subject and object" (*Bequest* 2). The term *memoir*, then, seems more malleable than the term *autobiography*, foregrounding historical shifts and intersecting cultural formations; and so when a narrative emphasizes its mode as memoir, as in Maxine Hong Kingston's *The Woman Warrior: Memoirs of a Girlhood among Ghosts*, readers are invited to think about the significance of that choice and the kind of reading it invites.

In this book, we have chosen to use the term *autobiography* only to refer to the traditional Western mode of the retrospective life narrative. We have chosen not to use the more common term *memoir*. We often use the adjective *autobiographical* to designate self-referential writing. And throughout we use the terms *life writing* and *life narrative* as more inclusive of the heterogeneity of self-referential practices. We understand *life writing* as a general term for writing that takes a life, one's own or another's, as its subject. Such writing can be biographical, novelistic, historical, or explicitly self-referential and therefore autobiographical. The autobiographical mode of life writing might more precisely be called *self life writing*, but we employ this phrase only for occasional emphasis because of its clumsiness. Both memoir and autobiography are encompassed in the term *life writing*. We understand *life narrative*, by contrast, as a general term for acts of self-presentation of all kinds and in diverse media that take the producer's life as their subject, whether written, performative, visual, filmic, or digital.[4] In other words, we employ the term *life writing* for written forms of the autobiographical, and *life narrative* to refer to autobiographical acts of any sort.[5] As G. Thomas Couser has noted recently, "the use of the terms 'life writing' and 'life narrative' does not deny generic distinctions but rather reflects an impulse toward catholicity and toward reconsideration of traditional definitions and distinctions" ("Genre Matters" 126). Furthermore, by shifting from *autobiography* and *memoir* to *life writing* and *life narrative,* we suggest the terms in which a new, globalized history of the field might be imagined, although the scholarship for undertaking such an encyclopedic project is still emerging, much of it not yet available to the English-speaking reader.

The preliminary distinctions clarified here are developed throughout the book. Chapter 2 explores in detail the components of autobiographical subjects: memory, experience, identity, space, embodiment, and agency. Chapter 3 elaborates the narrative features of particular autobiographical acts in their multiple contexts. These two chapters suggest the processes, formal options, and rhetorical addresses that, taken together, comprise the resources on which life narrators draw and the diverse contexts they negotiate and mobilize. Chapter 4 offers a brief historical survey of the many kinds of life writing that have emerged in the West over the past two thousand years, many of them by subordinated subjects, and chapters 5 and 6 track aspects of contemporary life narrative in many media. Chapter 7 tracks the history of autobiography studies to the 1990s; and Chapter 8 tracks key concepts that inform contemporary theorizing in the field. And chapter 9 is a "tool kit" offering twenty-four sets of questions for engaging concepts central to life narrative.

Now let us turn to distinctions between autobiographical writing and the practices of related kinds of life writing, namely, biography, the novel, and history writing.

Life Writing and Biography

While life writing and biography are both modes of narrating a life, they are not interchangeable. To be sure, bookstores shelve both in the biography section, and people may think of autobiography as the biography someone writes about him- or herself, as Nigel Hamilton suggests in his often admirable *Biography: A Brief History,* but there are crucial distinctions in *how* these forms narrate a life.[6] In biography, scholars of other people's lives document and interpret those lives from a point of view external to the subject. In life writing, subjects write about their own lives predominantly, even if they write about themselves in the second or third person, or as a member of a community. And they write simultaneously from externalized and internal points of view, taking themselves as both subject and object, or thematizing that distinction. Moreover, as Louis

Menand observes, "all biographies are retrospective in the same sense. Though they read chronologically forward, they are composed essentially backward" (66). That is, the events the subject becomes renowned for determine what the biographer selects to interpret as formative. By contrast, in self life writing the interpreter often recognizes that her or his choices of what to narrate as formative are subjective and idiosyncratic.

These kinds of life writing are fundamentally different. But what is the significance of that difference? Stephen Spender suggested that the life writer confronts not one life but two. One is the self that others see—the social, historical person, with achievements, personal appearance, social relationships. These are "real" attributes of a person living in the world. But there is also the self experienced only by that person, the self felt from the inside that the writer can never get "outside of." The "inside," or personally experienced, self has a history. While it may not be meaningful as an objective "history of the times," it is a record of self-observation, not a history observed by others. Spender writes that "we are seen from the outside by our neighbors; but we remain always at the back of our eyes and our senses, situated in our bodies, like a driver in the front seat of a car seeing the other cars coming toward him. A single person . . . is one consciousness within one machine, confronting all the other traffic" (116). To continue Spender's metaphor of driving the automobile, the biographer can circle the car with the driver in it to record the history, character, and motivations of the driver, the traffic, the vehicle, and the facts of transportation. But only the life narrator knows the experience of traffic rushing toward her and composes an interpretation of that situation, that is, writes her subjectivity.

Matters of time and timing also differentiate biography and life writing. For a biographer the death of the subject is not definitive. A biography can be written either during the life or after the death of the person being written about. In fact, biographies offering different interpretations of particular historical figures may appear periodically over many centuries, as have biographies of Caesar, Galileo, Michelangelo, and Byron. For the life writer, on the other hand, death is the end of the matter. While self life writing can be, and often is, written over a long span of time, as is the case with the multiple narratives of Edward Gibbon and Maya Angelou, it must be written during the writer's life span—or be published posthumously "as is."

In writing a life, the life narrator and the biographer also engage different kinds of evidence. Most biographers incorporate multiple forms of evidence, including historical documents, interviews, and family archives, which they evaluate for validity. Relatively few biographers use their personal memories of their subject as reliable evidence, unless they had a personal relationship to the subject of the biography (as a relative, child, friend, or colleague). For life narrators, by contrast, personal memories are the primary archival source. They may have recourse to other kinds of sources—letters, journals, photographs, conversations—and to their knowledge of a historical moment. But the usefulness of such evidence for their stories lies in the ways in which they employ that evidence to support, supplement, or offer commentary on their idiosyncratic acts of remembering. In autobiographical narratives, imaginative acts of remembering always intersect with such rhetorical acts as assertion, justification, judgment, conviction, and interrogation. That is, life narrators address readers whom they want to persuade of their version of experience. And, as we will see in chapter 2, memory is a subjective form of evidence that cannot be fully verified externally; rather, it is asserted on the subject's authority.

The biographer almost invariably writes about the object of his or her study in the third person, while the life narrator usually employs the first person. Certainly, there are autobiographical narrators who present their subjects in the second and/or third person. In *The Education of Henry Adams: An Autobiography,* Henry Adams refers to himself as "Henry Adams," "he," and "him." But readers understand that this is Adams's convention for presenting himself and that the teller and protagonist of the narrative are one and the same. "Henry Adams" appears as both subject and author on the title page. The biographer, however, cannot present his or her subject in the first person—except when quoting statements or letters or books written by that person.

Of course, there are texts that combine biographical and autobiographical modes of narration. As early as the second century B.C.E., Plutarch wove his own ethical observations and judgments into his parallel *Lives of the Noble Grecians and Romans.* In the seventeenth century, aristocratic women in England such as Anne, Lady Halkett, and Margaret Cavendish, Duchess of Newcastle, appended brief narratives of their lives to the adulatory biographies they wrote of their husbands. More recently, life narrators have blurred the boundary separating autobiographical and biographical modes by embedding their versions of the life of a family member in their own personal narratives, as does Kim Chernin in *In My*

Mother's House: A Daughter's Story, John Edgar Wideman in *Brothers and Keepers,* and Drusilla Modjeska in *Poppy*; or they entwine the case history of a patient with the writer's own self-analysis, as Annie G. Rogers does in *A Shining Affliction: A Story of Harm and Healing in Psychotherapy* or Kay Redfield Jamison in *An Unquiet Mind.* As much as we have argued for distinguishing life writing and biography, contemporary practices increasingly blend them into a hybrid, suggesting that life narrative indeed is a moving target and an ever-changing practice without absolute rules.

In the past two decades innovative forms of biographical writing have emerged that shuttle between the fictive and the autobiographical. Writers— professional biographers, novelists, literary critics—have adapted the form of biography to new kinds of stories that make critical interventions in conventions of biographical narration. "The new biography"[7] is a phrase employed by such literary critics as Ramón Saldívar, whose *The Borderlands of Culture: Américo Paredes and the Transnational Imaginary* entwines a study of the Mexican American author and scholar with the development and growth of Chicano studies as a field attentive to border identities and transnational imaginaries and implicitly with his own identity formation as a scholar in this field.[8] Carolyn Steedman's *Landscape for a Good Woman* could also be considered a form of "new biography." In it she considers her mother, the "good woman" of the title, as a working-class woman with middle-class aspirations, and tells the story of frustrated ambition in a protofeminist moment rarely considered by historians of social class. That story is combined with the biography Steedman largely omits of a father who abandoned them. And this case study of the Lancaster working class is joined to her obliquely autobiographical narrative of education and movement into the professional class where she achieves the status that eluded her mother.

Edmund Morris's *Dutch* was also heralded as a "new biography" of President Ronald Reagan. In a mode of telling that is subjective, speculative, and buoyantly playful, Morris employs fictive characters, including a version of himself as biographer and gossip columnist making droll comments on the inscrutable President Reagan.[9] In a quite different register, W. G. Sebald in *The Emigrants* uses biography to undermine its premises and show the deep personal investment people have in this apparently objective form. Sebald's conflation of the storytelling tactics of biography and autobiography is fully exploited in *Austerlitz,* where the unnamed narrator describes becoming a biographer of someone he meets in a railway carriage who is eventually persuaded to narrate his story of growing up in

World War II–era Europe, experiencing arrest and incarceration in There-sienstadt and becoming a stateless exile of an identity both indeterminate and overdetermined. Sebald's struggle to find a form adequate to narrat-ing the traumatic events and aftermath of the Holocaust incorporates fab-ricated biographical documentation and conflates events of an individual life with the historical panorama of mass memory dispersed in archives of many sorts. *New biography*, then, signals many kinds of practices that exploit the boundaries drawn between biography and fiction at particular moments and seeks innovative modes adequate to the complexity of nar-rating a life at various moments of paradigm shift.

While recognizing distinctions between autobiographical and bio-graphical forms, we note, in conclusion, the popularity of biography as a contemporary form of life writing as well as its capaciousness, variety, and experimentation. Biographies of founding fathers continue to fly off the shelves and top best-seller lists, as did David McCullough's *John Adams* and Walter Isaacson's *Benjamin Franklin*. Writing Abraham Lincoln biogra-phies might be considered an industry, and celebrity biographies fill mega-stores across the Western world. Always in demand are biographies on television (such as the Arts & Entertainment series in the United States) and filmic biographies of sports figures and musicians. What scholars call the "biopic" has become an innovative and ubiquitous mode for telling a life.[10] Some biopics offer straightforward chronological narratives of their subjects as heroes, villains, or innovators; others offer complex explora-tions of a life and its moment, as does Raoul Peck's *Lumumba* and Olivier Dahan's rendering of the life of French chanteuse Edith Piaf, *La Vie en Rose*.[11] Todd Haynes's biopic on Bob Dylan, *I'm Not There*, employs six ac-tors less to impersonate Dylan than to stand in for aspects of his protean presence at various moments in his career. With each episode narrated through a different genre and visual style, the ensemble interrogates the notion that a "life," especially one so diverse and creative, can be told as a single story.

Life Writing and the Novel

People often confuse life writing and fiction. Typically, they call autobio-graphical texts "novels," though they rarely call novels "autobiographies." An autobiography, however, is not a novel, and calling life writing "non-fiction," which is usually done, confuses rather than resolves the issue. Life writing and the novel share features we ascribe to fictional writing: plot, dialogue, setting, characterization, and so on. But they are distinguished by their relationship to and claims about a referential world. We might helpfully think of what fiction represents as "*a* world," and what life writing refers to as "*the* world." Further complicating matters, many contemporary writers deliberately blur the boundary between life writing and the kinds of stories told in the first-person novel that some call "faction," others "autofiction" (see Rachel Toor). Yet differences that have historically arisen between these forms are crucial to understanding the distinct practices, audiences, truth claims, and traditions of autobiographical writing.

In the nineteenth century many novels were presented as autobiographical narratives, the life stories of fictional characters. Think of Charles Dickens's *David Copperfield*, Charlotte Brontë's *Jane Eyre*, Johann Wolfgang von Goethe's *Wilhelm Meister's Apprenticeship*, and Fyodor Dostoyevsky's *Notes from Underground*. The narrators of these texts employ the intimate first person as protagonists confiding their personal histories and attempting to understand how their past experiences formed them as social subjects. Such narratives and the traditions from which they emerged are part of the development of the bildungsroman, a form that German scholar Wilhelm Dilthey defined as the story of an individual's struggle to become a social subject who "becomes aware of his purpose in the world" (cited in Burt 105). The individual's potential, thwarted by circumstances of birth and repressive social convention, by constraints of class and gender, is discovered in the extended process of becoming educated; and that education involves encounters with mentors, apprenticeship, and eventual renunciation of errant idealism followed by adherence to social conventions and structures.

Many twentieth-century novels are also narrated as first-person autobiographies, for example, Rainer Maria Rilke's *The Notebooks of Malte Laurids Brigge*, J. D. Salinger's *Catcher in the Rye*, Thomas Wolfe's *Look Homeward, Angel*, and Jamaica Kincaid's *Autobiography of My Mother*. But, as Raymond L. Burt suggests, the teleology of the bildungsroman collapses throughout the twentieth century (105). The great modernists, Thomas Mann, Marcel Proust, Virginia Woolf, and Robert Musil, invoke its tropes of individuation to also show the fragmentation of selfhood and the constructed nature of the social. The fractured selves and inhospitable sociality of the twentieth-century bildungsroman find a parallel in many of the century's autobiographical works, making distinctions between the two modes increasingly tenuous. Nonetheless, first-person novels continue to signal readers in various ways that they are reading a novel and not an autobiographical narrative. Most obviously, the author's name on the title page differs from the name of the character narrating the tale. That is, Malte is the named narrator of Rainer Maria Rilke's *The Notebooks of Malte Laurids Brigge* and Holden Caulfield the named narrator of *Catcher in the Rye*. Readers of such narratives are challenged to observe the biases and fantasies of these young protagonists and discover discrepancies between how each views himself at various moments and how we, as readers, regard the limitations or the blind spots of their knowledge.

The identification of authorial signature with the narrator, by contrast, is a distinguishing mark of autobiography, argues Philippe Lejeune in his seminal essay "The Autobiographical Pact." Lejeune usefully defines the relationship between author and reader in autobiographical writing as a contract: "What defines autobiography for the one who is reading is above all a contract of identity that is sealed by the proper name. And this is true also for the one who is writing the text" (19).[12] For Lejeune, two things indisputably distinguish autobiography and, by implication, a wide range of life narratives, from the novel: the "vital statistics" of the author, such as date and place of birth and education, are identical to those of the narrator; and an implicit contract exists between author and publisher attesting to the truth of the "signature" on the cover and title page (21). When we recognize the person who claims authorship of the narrative as its protagonist or central figure—that is, we believe them to be the same person—we read the text written by the author to whom it refers as self-reflexive or autobiographical. With this recognition of the autobiographical pact, Lejeune argues, we read differently and assess the narrative as making truth claims of a sort that are suspended in fictional forms such as the novel.

There is also a temporal distinction between a novel and an autobiographical text. Novelists are not bound by historical time. They can situate their narratives at any time in the past, present, or future. This does not mean that life narrators only and simply offer a retrospective narrative in chronological order about the life lived to the point of its writing. They can return to the past, even the cultural past before the writer's birth, or offer an imaginative journey into a fantasized future. The narrator of Thomas De Quincey's *Confessions of an English Opium Eater*, for example, is stimulated by opium to transport his life to other centuries and continents; yet corporeally he remains located in nineteenth-century London, increasingly the victim of his addiction. Unlike novelists, life narrators have to anchor their narratives in the world of their own temporal, geographical, and cultural milieu.

Novelists are bound only by the reader's expectation of internal consistency in the world of verisimilitude created within the novel. They are not bound by rules of evidence that link the world of the narrative with a historical world outside the narrative. As Samuel Taylor Coleridge famously observed, we practice a "suspension of disbelief" when engaging fictional or poetic worlds. In contrast, life narrators inevitably refer to the world beyond the text, the world that is the ground of the narrator's lived experience, even if that ground is in part composed of cultural myths, dreams, fantasies, and subjective memories or problematized by the mode of its telling, as in Georges Perec's *W, or the Memory of Childhood*. Audre Lorde may subtitle *Zami: A New Spelling of My Name* a "biomythography," thereby emphasizing the mythic resonance of her story of growing up as an African American child of a woman from Carriacou, Grenada; but the struggles of her young self are embedded in the New York of the 1950s, no matter how the myth of Carriacou women's friendship lets her valorize and explore the differences of lesbian identity. Moreover, autobiographical narrators are expected to remain faithful to their personal memory archives while novelists need not observe this constraint (Eakin, *Touching the World* 28).

Of course, the boundary between the autobiographical and the novelistic is, like the boundary between biography and life narrative, sometimes exceedingly hard to fix. Many life writers take liberties with the novelistic mode in order to negotiate their own struggles with the past and with the complexities of identities forged in the present. This fluid boundary has particularly characterized narratives by writers exploring the decolonization of subjectivity forged in the aftermath of colonial oppression. Such writers as Michelle Cliff in *Abeng: A Novel* (Jamaica), Tsitsi Dangarembga in *Nervous Conditions* (Zimbabwe), Maryse Condé in *Hérémakhonon: A Novel* (Guadeloupe), Myriam Warner-Vieyra in *Juletane* (Guadeloupe-Senegal), and Camara Laye in *The Dark Child* (Guinea) create hybrid forms tied to local histories of struggle and claim the novel as a translation of their experience to distance themselves from autobiography's alliance with colonial regimes. As Françoise Lionnet notes of her decision to treat such narratives as self-referential texts, they function to illuminate the processes of identity formation through a subjectively rendered consciousness ("Of Mangoes and Maroons" 321–23).

Life Writing and History

Sometimes people read autobiographical narratives as historical documents, sources of evidence for the analysis of historical movements, events, or persons. From this perspective, autobiographical narrative and history writing might seem to be synonymous. Although it can be read as a history of the writing/speaking subject, however, life narrative cannot be reduced to or understood only as historical record. While autobiographical narratives may contain information regarded as "facts," they are not factual history about a particular time, person, or event. Rather, they incorporate usable facts into subjective "truth," a concept we take up in the next section.

When life narrators write to chronicle an event, to explore a certain time period, or to enshrine a community, they are making "history" in a sense. But they are also performing several rhetorical acts: justifying their own perceptions, upholding their reputations, disputing the accounts of others, settling scores, conveying cultural information, and inventing desirable futures, among others. The complexity of autobiographical texts requires reading practices that engage the narrative tropes, sociocultural contexts, rhetorical aims, and narrative shifts within the historical or chronological trajectory of the text. To reduce autobiographical narration to facticity is to strip it of the densities of rhetorical, literary, ethical, political, and cultural dimensions.

Jeremy D. Popkin, a historian interested in both the parallels and the differences between autobiographical writing and history, points to a distinction between the modes of life narrative and history writing in terms of temporality. Life writing, Popkin suggests, "privilege[s] a temporal framework based on the individual author's lifespan, whereas historical narrative takes place in collective time." The "arbitrary and concrete" personal time of experience in life writing does not have to engage the moments of shared experience that historians identify as significant in the collective time of an era, nation, or culture, or present the "big picture" expected of a historian (727).[13]

Now, it is true that historians, like life narrators, "tell a story" about the past, as Hayden White so persuasively argues, proposing the "truth" of the past through a narrativization of events that "is always a figurative account" (48). Like life writing, history writing is replete with literary tropes (metaphor and metonymy, for instance) and intelligible plots (a rise and fall, for instance). But historians, attentive to the norms of the discipline, place themselves outside or at the margin of the historical picture, even as they remain present in the discourses they mobilize, the very words they use, the shaping of the story they tell.[14] They preserve the professional norm of objectivity and the truthfulness it pledges by establishing distance from their material and typically removing or qualifying any reference to themselves in the narrative. Autobiographical narrators, in contrast, place themselves at the center of the stories they assemble and are interested in the meaning of larger forces, or conditions, or events for their *own* stories.

The power of Sally Morgan's *My Place,* at once the narrative of a young woman coming to claim her identity as an Aboriginal Australian and an exposé of the effects on the older generations of her family of colonial practices of forceful removal and assimilation, resides in its acknowledgment of an official history of the Australian nation. Morgan insists on inserting the history of indigenous Australians into the national narrative. The power of William Apess's "A Son of the Forest" and "The Experience of Five Christian Indians of the Pequot Tribe" derives from the way in which Apess situates himself as an agent of American history, negotiating his status as Native American in his relationships to a series of white people and to literacy in the new republic. In the details and the immediacy of the lived lives of such autobiographical narrators, the political and cultural contexts of the historical past become vivid and memorable.

In summary, autobiographical narrators establish for their readers a different set of expectations from those established in either the verisimilitude or suspension of disbelief of the novel or the verifiable evidence and professional norms of biography and history writing. Even this rudimentary set of distinctions among the novel, biography, history, and autobiography, however, is tentative. For example, *Summertime,* the third volume of Nobel laureate J. M. Coetzee's extended engagement with his past (here, his thirties), blurs any easy distinction between the fictional and the autobiographical. Confounding the norms of genre, Coetzee's work is a novel about a writer assembling the biography of the deceased writer "John Coetzee." The biographer, as part of his research, interviews characters who knew the young "Coetzee" and cites their critical points of view on him. The pseudo-archive mobilized by the biographer becomes a route of self-investigation for the novelist and life writer to examine the meanings of memory, obligation, and vulnerability. In an intriguing riff on the conventional relationship between the authorial signature and the narrator of the story, Coetzee appears on the cover as the author and in the narrative as the object of biographical representation. Thus Lejeune's concept of the autobiographical pact as the negotiated relationship of author, reader, and publisher is fractured. Frank Kermode aptly reviewed Coetzee's narrative as "fictioneering," a metatextual reflection that situates writing as fundamentally self-reflexive, regardless of its declared genre.

Autobiographical Truth

In trying to differentiate autobiographical narrative from biography, the novel, and history writing, we encounter a fundamental question: what is the truth status of autobiographical disclosure? How do we know whether and when a narrator is telling the truth or lying? And what difference would that difference make? These questions often perplex readers of autobiographical texts. For example, a life narrator may narrate his history as a young person full of illusions subsequently lost by the adult narrator, as does the young immigrant Edward William Bok in *The Americanization of Edward Bok: The Autobiography of a Dutch Boy Fifty Years After.* Life narrators may present inconsistent or shifting views of themselves. They may even perpetrate acts of deliberate deceit to test the reader or to hint at the paradoxical "truth" of experience itself, as Timothy Dow Adams suggests of strategic decisions to deceive in literary life writing (*Telling Lies* 14–16). Is autobiographical writing then only a species of "damned lies," to paraphrase Mark Twain?

We might respond by asking what we expect life narrators to tell the truth about. Are we expecting fidelity to the facts of their biographies, to lived experience, to self-understanding, to the historical moment, to social community, to prevailing beliefs about diverse identities, to the norms of autobiography as a literary genre itself? And truth for whom and for what? Other readers, a loved one, the narrating I, or for the coherent person we imagine ourselves to be?

John Sturrock has pithily noted, "It is impossible for an autobiographer not to be autobiographical" (52). More recently, Stanley Fish has observed that "autobiographers cannot lie because anything they say, however mendacious, is the truth about themselves, whether they know it or not" (A19). Any utterance in an autobiographical text, even if inaccurate or distorted, is a characterization of its writer. Thus, when one is both the narrator and the protagonist of the narrative, as in life writing, the truth of the narrative becomes undecidable; it can be neither fully verified nor fully discredited. We need, then, to adjust our expectations of the truth told in self-referential writing.

Of course, autobiographical claims such as date of birth can be verified or discounted by recourse to documentation outside the text. But autobiographical truth is a different matter. Even the author of a life narrative is not an authority on it, for life writing requires an audience to both confirm the writer's existence in time and mark his or her lived specificity, distinctiveness, and location. Thus autobiographical truth resides in the intersubjective exchange between narrator and reader aimed at producing a shared understanding of the meaning of a life. Susanna Egan's concept of "mirror talk" captures the refractive interplay of such dialogic exchange between life narrator and reader (or viewer). The multifacetedness inherent in autobiographical writing produces a polyphonic site of indeterminacy rather than a single, stable truth: "Neither the person nor the text can reveal any single or final truth, but both can provide activities of interpretation in which the reader is compelled to join" (*Mirror Talk* 326).

In *The Autobiography of W. E. B. Du Bois: A Soliloquy on Viewing My Life from the Last Decade of Its First Century*, Du Bois acknowledges that "autobiographies do not form indisputable authorities." This insight motivates him to reflect on the difficulties of telling his story "frank and fair":

> Memory fails especially in small details, so that it becomes finally but a theory of my life, with much forgotten and misconceived, with valuable testimony but often less than absolutely true, despite my intention. . . . This book then is the Soliloquy of an old man on what he dreams his life has been as he sees it slowly drifting away; and what he would like others to believe. (12–13)

Refiguring his narrative as a "soliloquy" addressed to "others," Du Bois accepts the impossibility of recording only factual truth and turns to the compensations of an intersubjective truth—partly dream, partly promissory belief—that invites our confirmation of its interpretation. The authority of the autobiographical, then, neither confirms nor invalidates notions of objective truth; rather, it tracks the previously uncharted truths of particular lives.

If we approach such self-referential writing as an intersubjective process that occurs within a dialogic exchange between writer and reader/

viewer rather than as a story to be proved or falsified, the emphasis of reading shifts from assessing and verifying knowledge to observing processes of communicative exchange and understanding. It redefines the terms of what we call "truth": autobiographical writing cannot be read solely as either factual truth or simple fact. As an intersubjective mode, it resides outside a logical or juridical model of truth and falsehood, as models of the paradoxical status of self-reference have suggested, from Epimenides of Crete to contemporary language philosophers.[15]

But having asserted the special case of intersubjective discourse in life writing with some confidence in the first edition of *Reading Autobiography*, we find ourselves, like many readers and critics, both fascinated and confused by the range of autobiographical hoaxes that always existed but have come to global prominence in the past decade. Both an increase in the kinds of autobiographical fakery and intensified attention to their exposure have gained cultural attention. We have elsewhere articulated a taxonomy that offers critical distinctions, generic scripts, and ethical implications of the problematic of hoaxes ("Say It Isn't So"). To summarize, hoaxed life writing may be of several kinds: enhanced or exaggerated experience á la James Frey's *A Million Little Pieces*; ethnic impersonation; fantasized alternative lives; lives plagiarized from another's text; lives fabricated at the boundary of documentary history and fiction; and false witnessing to human rights abuses or trauma.

Probing these manifestations of autobiographical hoaxes raises questions about the cultural anxieties provoked through the scandal hoaxes create. How flexible is the autobiographical pact between writer and reader, and does it have limits? What are our ethical investments in the "truth" of increasingly fragmented lives? Does media exploitation of celebrity self-narrators, in print and on reality television or online, render obsolete the notion of the real? We also observe new or heightened characteristics of readers in this Information Age: their desire to participate vicariously in the suffering of others at a moment of global commodification of narratives of suffering and survival; their impetus to self-reimagining through alternative identities; and their thirst for authenticity in a moment of ersatz authenticity. This is to say, even scandalous hoaxes on the one hand and, on the other, charges of fabrication used to discredit certain witnesses expose truths about the commodification of storytelling, the politics of readerly desires, and the social action that constitutes the construction and consumption of lives.

"Tell me your life story" as a readerly expectation is a bid not just for entertaining distraction but for insight and the possibility of wisdom gained, not least from the recognition of folly. At this cultural moment audiences look to the ethos of a narrator able not just to confess spectacular transgressions or harms but to reflect on, interrogate, and recognize something gained in the struggle to sort out the detritus of the everyday, the ever-faster pace of change, and the myriad personae or "lives" we all must perform. Commitment to self-narration, not as an act for calculated gain in fortune or fame but as an epistemological act of thinking through what one as a subject knows to be or not to be, remains a basis of both writerly tact and readerly trust. It does not rule out the use of the found, the fabricated, the strategic, the consciously invented. But it asks that "my experiments with truth," Mahatma Gandhi's fine title for his autobiography, be in the service of a project larger than personal gain, opportunism, an overt political agenda, or a desire to obfuscate and impress. If indeed intersubjective truth, always tentative and provisional, emerges in autobiographical acts, its nurturance is a project requiring the care and active engagement of both readers and writers.

Conclusion

Our working definition of *self life writing* assumes that it is not a single unitary genre or form, "autobiography." Rather, the historically situated practices of self-representation may take many guises as narrators selectively engage their lived experience and situate their social identities through personal storytelling. Located in specific times and places, narrators are at the same time in dialogue with the processes and archives of memory and the expectations of disparate others. Ever constrained by occasion and convention, and ever contingent, adaptable, fluid, and dynamic (Couser, "Genre Matters" 125), self life writing shares features with the novel, biography, and history. It can employ the dialogue, plot, setting, and density of language of the novel. It may incorporate biographies of others in its representations of family, friends, historical or religious figures. It projects multiple histories—of communities, families, nations, movements. Even as it does so, however, it maintains its distinctive relationship to the referential world in its temporality.

Our notion of autobiographical practice thus may parallel Carolyn R. Miller's concept of genre not as fixed form but as social action.[16] "Mediating," in Miller's words, "private intentions and social exigence" (31), autobiographical acts join form to human agency, history, location, and the dynamics of communicative exchange.[17] From this perspective, the auto-biographical might be read, as Couser suggests, for what it does, not what it is. Rather than being simply the story of an individual life, self life writing "encode[s] or reinforce[s] particular values in ways that may shape culture and history" ("Genre Matters" 129–30).

With this working definition in mind, let us turn to the components that comprise autobiographical acts.

Autobiographical Subjects

For lack of a natural memory, I make one of paper.

Michel de Montaigne, *Essays*

It is funny this knowing being a genius, everything is funny. And identity is funny being yourself is funny as you are never yourself to yourself except as you remember yourself and then of course you do not believe yourself. That is really the trouble with an autobiography you do not of course you do not really believe yourself why should you, you know so well so very well that it is not yourself, it could not be yourself because you cannot remember right and if you do remember right it does not sound right and of course it does not sound right because it is not right. You are of course never yourself.

Gertrude Stein, *Everybody's Autobiography*

The question of the spontaneity of the I belongs in a very different, a (biological?) context.

Walter Benjamin, *Gesammelte Schriften*

I got this rig that runs on memories.

Leonard Cohen, "I Can't Forget"

Life writing, as act and text, seems transparently simple. Yet it is intriguingly complex. In what follows we explore a set of concepts helpful for understanding the sources and dynamic processes of autobiographical subjectivity:

- Memory
- Experience
- Identity
- Space

- Embodiment
- Agency

Memory

The life narrator depends on access to memory to narrate the past in such a way as to situate that experiential history within the present. Memory is thus the source, authenticator, and destabilizer of autobiographical acts. But what is memory and how does it work?

Memory as Meaning-Making

As memory researchers from fields as diverse as neuroscience, cognitive psychology, and philosophy have argued, remembering involves a re-interpretation of the past in the present. The process is not a passive one of mere retrieval from a memory bank. Rather, the remembering subject actively creates the meaning of the past in the act of remembering (Rose). Thus, narrated memory is an interpretation of a past that can never be fully recovered. As Daniel L. Schacter has suggested, "memories are records of how we have experienced events, not replicas of the events themselves" (6). He goes on to explore how "we construct our autobiographies from fragments of experience that change over time" (9). That is, we inevitably organize or form fragments of memory into complex constructions that become the changing stories of our lives.

According to researchers in developmental psychology, we learn early in childhood what people around us and, by extension, our culture expect us to remember (Nelson 12). We learn techniques for remembering. We learn something about who is charged with remembering and what kinds of memories they are charged with keeping. And we learn the cultural uses of remembering, how certain ways of remembering are elicited, acknowledged, valued. For instance, in the United States public rituals of remembering include such occasions as Memorial Day parades, Veterans' Day marches, and religious holidays. Private rituals include the preservation of objects such as heirlooms and family Bibles, and the continuation of family reunions where people gather to remember, reenact, and reaffirm the family's collective past. Such rituals may be part of the texture of memory evoked in life narrative, but narrators may also struggle with or resist collective forms of cultural remembering, finding other meanings in these moments and activities.

Memory and History

In the early twenty-first century (in the United States at least), memory is organized by such artifacts as the scrapbook and the videotape. But at other historical moments, cultures have used different means or "technologies" of memory.[1] Early Romans carried the *lares,* urns filled with ancestral remains, to their new homes to be honored as household deities and sites of remembering. During the early modern period "memory theaters" became aids to memory. As Frances A. Yates has shown, the memory theater was a mnemonic device for mentally placing and organizing large amounts of material. The material to be remembered was imagined as a set of rooms or places in a palace through which the rememberer moved, remembering items by their place.

James Olney has distinguished two models of memory at work in Augustine's fourth-century *Confessions,* the archaeological and the processual. The archaeological model of memory is spatial, "a site where . . . [he] can dig down through layer after layer of deposits to recover what he seeks"; memories so recovered will be unchanged, if decaying over time (*Memory and Narrative* 19). In contrast, the processual model for memory is temporal, "bring[ing] forth ever different memorial configurations and an ever newly shaped self." This kind of remembering is imagined as a process of weaving that makes new forms from memorial strands that are also in flux (20–21).

As these examples indicate, techniques and practices of remembering change. How people remember, what they remember, and who does the remembering are historically specific. A culture's understanding of memory at a particular moment of its history shapes the life narrator's process of remembering. Often a historical moment itself comprises multiple, competing practices of remembering. Narrators at the crossroads of conflicting understandings of memory, such as the contemporary Native American writer Leslie Marmon Silko, may explore these competing practices of memory and interrogate the cultural stakes of remembering by juxtaposing a dominant modern mode and an alternative indigenous mode. In *Storyteller,* Silko interweaves personal narratives with stories not strictly her own, photographs, and the poems and traditional stories of the Laguna Pueblo. Through joining the personal and the social, she remembers Pueblo cultural practices and situates herself as a creative and reverential voice bridging multiple cultures.

Memory as Contextual

If remembering is a historically inflected phenomenon, it is also contextual (see Engel's *Context Is Everything: The Nature of Memory*). Acts of remembering take place at particular sites and in particular circumstances. We remember the history of a relationship in the context of sexual intimacy or as we celebrate anniversaries. We remember our history as national citizens in the context of parades and national holidays. Similarly, the memory invoked in autobiographical narrative is specific to the time of writing and the contexts of telling. It is never isolatable fact, but situated association. In *Family Secrets: Acts of Memory and Imagination,* Annette Kuhn explores her past identity as a working-class child in Britain by rereading her family album and reconstructing the secrets hidden in the camera's official snapshots of familiality. She also rereads public documents of the 1953 coronation of Queen Elizabeth II as forms of remembering that create for the nation a "family drama" generating desire for belonging in that larger "family" of Britain.

The Politics of Remembering

Contexts are charged politically. What is remembered and what is forgotten, and why, change over time. Thus, remembering has a politics. There are struggles over who is authorized to remember and what they are authorized to remember, struggles over what is forgotten, both personally and collectively. For instance, under National Socialism, Germans in the 1930s were schooled (literally and figuratively) to remember the past of the nation as an Aryan past. After World War II the two Germanys were taught to remember different and competing versions of the war and the Holocaust and highly selective versions of the national past, depending on whether they lived in the socialist East or the liberal-democratic West. Since 1989, German autobiographical writing has been negotiating these different versions of national memory, as the formerly East German writers Christa Wolf and Jana Hensel suggest.

In the United States in the past two decades, we have seen fierce struggles over how the American past is to be remembered at such crucial junctures as the Civil War, the civil rights movement, and the Vietnam War era. Those who celebrate the nineteenth century as a century of America's Manifest Destiny have strongly differing versions of the meanings of westward expansion from those of the descendants of Native Americans displaced across the western plains. Sherman Alexie, a member of the Spokane/Coeur d'Alene tribe, explores the necessity of remembering differently with condensed wit in an autobiographical fragment of diary entries he includes in *First Indian on the Moon*. For the May entry, Alexie imagines Moses, who "wanted to memorialize every Indian who died in war" by capturing a swallow in his mouth and "breath[ing] out the names" of the men, women, and children killed: "Moses worked for years. After he was finished, Moses released the swallows into the air over the reservation, millions of them. Millions" (12).

These examples suggest how the politics of remembering—what is recollected and what is obscured—is central to the cultural production of knowledge about the past, and thus to the terms of an individual's self-knowledge. Autobiographical narratives, as we will see, signal and invite reading in terms of larger cultural issues and may also be productively read against the ideological grain.

Collective Remembering

If we think about remembering not as an entirely privatized activity but as an activity situated in cultural politics, we can appreciate to what degree remembering is a collective activity. On a daily basis we move in and out of various communities of memory—religious, racial, ethnic, gendered, familial. Communities develop their own occasions, rituals, archives, and practices of remembering. They establish specific sites for remembering. Furthermore, particular communities are aided in their acts of remembering by different technologies: the memory theaters of the early modern period, writing, movable type, the digital code of online networks. These become systems of "artificial" memory—not in the sense that the memories are fabricated or false but in the sense that the technologies, as aids to preserving and passing on memories, shape the memories conveyed and the selves those memories construct.

Frequently, life narrators incorporate multiple modes and archives of remembering in their narratives. Some of these sources are personal (dreams, family albums, photos, objects, family stories, genealogy). Some are public (documents, historical events, collective rituals). One way of accessing memory may dominate because it is critical to a narrator's project, his sense of the audience for the narrative, or her purpose for making the story public. For example, in *Maus: A Survivor's Tale,* Art Spiegelman includes many forms of documentary evidence from the death camps to authenticate his father's story of deportation to Auschwitz before his own birth. And in *Vibration Cooking; or, The Travel Notes of a Geechee Girl,* Vertamae Smart-Grosvenor embeds the recipes of African American relatives and friends into stories of communities held together through the senses, rituals, and the "vibrations" of memory. For such life narrators, public, shared memories can reconstitute fragmented communities, or mark and mourn their loss.

Acts of remembering extend beyond the acknowledgment of collective sites of memory, historical documents, and oral traditions. They engage motives for remembering and question on whose behalf one remembers. Precisely because acts of remembering are relational, they are implicated in how people understand the past and make claims about their versions of the past. Thus memory is an inescapably intersubjective act, as W. J. T. Mitchell insightfully suggests: "Memory is an intersubjective phenomenon, a practice not only of recollection of a past *by* a subject, but of recollection *for* another subject" (193 n. 17). Memory is a means of "passing on," of sharing a social past that may have been obscured, thereby activating its potential for reshaping a future of and for other subjects. In sum, acts of personal remembering are fundamentally social and collective.

The concept of collective memory helps explain how societies develop notions of shared national history and even how individuals acquire their own memories related to the social frameworks of family, religion, and social class, according to Maurice Halbwachs (cited in Landsberg 7). Pierre Nora, in his monumental study *Les Lieux de mémoire,* theorized that in the nineteenth century there developed a new form of collective public memory related to national feeling that attaches to particular places or sites. Alison Landsberg extends earlier theorizing of collective memory by arguing that because of its mass technologies and massive historical events, modernity requires a different concept of collective memory, which she calls "prosthetic memory." Forms of mass culture, such as film, television, and, now, the Internet, make specific memories available to large groups, creating "imagined communities" across differences of nation, ethnicity, and geography (8). Such communities share memories to which the people in them have no experiential connection. In Landsberg's scheme, mass media "construct arenas—. . . *transferential spaces* in the Freudian sense—in which people might have an experience through which they did not live" and "take on 'prosthetic memories' as bodily symptoms" that both tie them to the dead (as in the Holocaust or a war) and suture possibilities of political engagement (23–24). Landsberg argues that the advent of mass culture technologies produces collective memories that are individually felt and may evoke empathy and reorient people politically, though not necessarily in progressive or ethical ways. As forms of life narrative increasingly engage how self-narrators construct themselves through a relation to global phenomena, there is a need for an articulated theory of collective memory, such as Landsberg's, in the conditions of modernity and, indeed, global capital. Approaching life writing as a project of linking organic memories to, or replacing them by, prosthetic memory is a provocative possibility.

Memory and Materiality

Memory, apparently so immaterial, personal, and elusive, is always implicated in materiality, whether it be the materiality of sound, stone, text, garment, integrated circuits and circuit boards, or the materiality of our very bodies—the synapses and electrons of our brains and our nervous systems. Memory is evoked by the senses—smell, taste, touch, sight, sound—and encoded in objects or events with particular meaning for the narrator. In the *Confessions,* Augustine's memory of stealing pears from a tree is imbued with the sense-awakening qualities of the pears that momentarily overcome him in writing that moment. In the early twentieth century, the aroma of the madeleine stirs Marcel Proust's narrator as an olfactory conduit imaginatively returning him to a scene of his past. And later in the century Vladimir Nabokov exercises a fiercely aestheticized mode of visualizing memory in mnemonic images of the past of his childhood in Russia. In *Speak, Memory: A Memoir,* Nabokov links his fascination with entomology and butterflies to his art of remembering in pictures and words.

Memory and Trauma

Life writers often struggle to remember and tell histories of violence and suffering. They do so in narratives of genocide, torture, sexual abuse, AIDS, and disability, among others. In such stories of victimhood and survival the problematic of memory often comes to the fore. For some narrators, the problem of recalling and re-creating a past life involves organizing the inescapable but often disabling force of memory and negotiating its fragmentary intrusions with increasing, if partial, understanding. For some, language fails to capture, or engage, or mediate the horrors of the past and the aftereffects of survival.

In her ten-part autobiographical poem *A Poem without a Hero,* for instance, Russian poet Anna Akhmatova narrates her husband's and son's arrest during 1935–40 (the four years of Stalin's regime of terror) and links her son's imprisonment to the larger tragedy of state-sponsored murder. The subjective *I* breaks down midway through the cycle as she confesses her struggle with the pain of memory and the forgetting offered by madness. Negotiating this break, the narrator moves toward a transpersonal identification with those who suffered. Its testimony to political trauma in both her family and the state makes *A Poem without a Hero* not just an autobiographical poem but also a call to collective Russian conscience.

For Holocaust survivors such as Charlotte Delbo in *Auschwitz and After,* Elie Wiesel in *Night,* and Primo Levi in *Survival in Auschwitz: The Nazi Assault on Humanity,* the struggle with memories of the Holocaust necessitates the return again and again to those incomprehensible moments in the past. Levi, for instance, struggles to exorcise memories of a regime of existence whose logic destroyed all the bases of humanity, including the metaphorical and literal dimensions of language itself. And in Spiegelman's doubly autobiographical *Maus,* the distortions and omissions of the father Vladek's memory are a partial amnesia compelling the telling of his son Art's story of the legacies of what Marianne Hirsch calls postmemory, particularly the inaccessible memory of his dead mother.[2]

Narrators suffering from traumatic or obsessional memory may see the act of telling as therapeutic in resolving troubled memories, acknowledging how the process of writing has changed the narrator and the life story itself. In her story of traumatic childhood sexual abuse, *My Father's House: A Memoir of Incest and Healing,* Canadian writer Sylvia Fraser marks the break between the historically situated and the imaginary modes of narrating with different fonts. In this way, the daughter of the father/lover can shuttle between recollection/commentary and fantasy, using writing to engage "the anxiety and rage against a spectral patriarch who is everywhere and nowhere—whose nefarious deeds are hidden in the recesses of the unconscious, and whose authoritarian presence his daughter can never escape" (Henke, 129). The two modes of self-narrating are mutually enabling, as Fraser seeks to capture the multiple modes in which trauma is scripted and exorcised. In her profoundly disturbing and daring account of child sexual abuse titled *Don't: A Woman's Word,* Canadian writer

Elly Danica pieces together, in a mode of diaristic dailiness, the disjoint-
ed memories from a reservoir of horrific abuse. Her Dantesque progress
requires translation into "a woman's word" as a narrative of descent into
a private hell and ascent toward that moment when she can write: "The
sentence has changed. Once I could not remember. Now I cannot forget"
(101). Suzette Henke calls such responses to trauma "scriptotherapy" to
signify the process of speaking or writing about trauma in order to find
words to give voice to previously repressed memories.

Some narrators engage traumatic remembering around a world-
historical event, such as the Holocaust, the Rwandan genocide, or the New
York World Trade Center attacks on 9/11. Other narrators shift attention to
effects in everyday life of inequality and suffering. They tell stories of self,
family, or community that illuminate the legacies of larger historical formations, such as processes of racialization, which emerged out of and secured specific conditions of oppression, colonialism, and neocolonialism.
Registering the effects of racialization as lived historical legacy in the present, they relocate trauma in everyday life and relations. Such narratives
of legacy, lived both as personal history and collective history, often encompass multigenerational family history. Sally Morgan's *My Place*, mentioned earlier, tracks the story of her mother and grandmother back two
generations in order to comprehend the costs of the brutal family policies of the Australian state (separation of mixed-race children from their
mothers and communities) and the sexual and economic exploitation of
Aboriginal women. Morgan's attempt to recover the past that was erased
in official policies designed to assimilate and "disappear" Aboriginality
and in personal refusals of indigenous identification becomes a way to
understand the untold stories of Australian nationalism and the counter-
narratives of indigenous Australians.

Several generations of indigenous Australians have written or told
their stories of a "stolen generation" over the past two decades, in print, in
as-told-to narratives, before the Australian Human Rights Commission,
and in film. *Rabbit-Proof Fence*, by Doris Pilkington (Nugi Garimara),
is the story of Pilkington's mother and aunt, who with another child in
the 1930s escaped from the Moore River Settlement in Perth where they
had been forcibly relocated for education and training and trekked a
thousand miles to their communities in northwest Australia. Reimagining the achievement of that trek, the daughter/niece registers the struggles
of that earlier generation, emphasizes their survival and survival skills,
and honors their reconstitution of community in the midst of policies of

forced assimilation. Pilkington also reenlivens that earlier generation and its culture by registering different knowledges of time: "Consistent with Aboriginal storytelling style, seasonal time and the features of the natural environment are more important to recounting this journey than are the western notions of time and distance. I have though worked to synthesise these different forms of knowledge to give readers the fullest insight into this historic journey" (xiv). Intergenerational life writing of this kind captures the ways in which generations carry different histories and explores those histories of everyday trauma that are embodied in the next generations. It also offers stories that position those who have suffered not only as victims of violent events but as survivors with imagination, energy, and resilience. The traumas of everyday life are thus remembered as collective and systemic.

Reading for Memory

When we read or listen to an autobiographical narrative, then, we listen for and attend to the role of remembering—and conscious forgetting—in the act of making meaning out of the past and the present. We may notice an emphasis on particular acts of remembering or particular moods and voices identified with certain memories. We may glimpse the triggering devices that stimulate certain memories. Then, too, narrators themselves may make the act of remembering a significant theme within the narrative. That is, they may be self-reflexive about the problem of remembering and the value of particular kinds of remembering, as are, for example, St. Augustine in *The Confessions,* Mary McCarthy at the beginning of *Memories of a Catholic Girlhood,* Richard Rodriguez in *Hunger of Memory: The Education of Richard Rodriguez, an Autobiography,* and Alison Bechdel in *Fun Home: A Family Tragicomic.* They may call attention to things forgotten, times irretrievable, and to the personal, familial, and communal stakes of that forgetting. Life narratives, through the memories they construct, are records of acts of interpretation by subjects inescapably in historical time, and in relation to their own ever-moving pasts.

Experience

Experience. We have it. It is ours. The intimacy and immediacy and palpability of our memories tell us so. But what does it mean to say we have an experience? While the experience represented in an autobiographical narrative seems merely personal, it is anything but that. Mediated through memory and language, "experience" is already an interpretation of the past and of our place in a culturally and historically specific present.

Experience as Constitutive of the Subject

A provocative exploration of the phenomenon we call experience can be found in Joan W. Scott's essay "Experience." Scott challenges the foundational status of experience as a ground of analysis and a ground of knowledge about the world and ourselves. She cautions that talking about experience as either internal to an individual (expressive of an individual's consciousness—what we have inside us) or external to the individual ("the material upon which consciousness works"—what happens to us from outside) "leads us to take the existence of individuals for granted" (27). This taken-for-grantedness of the relationship between individual experience and the claim to unique individuality is what Scott calls into question because it obscures how our notion of meaningful experience is socially produced. How do we know what we know about ourselves? How do we know who we are?

Taking the analysis of Teresa de Lauretis as a point of departure, Scott defines "experience" as "a process . . . by which subjectivity is constructed" (27). "Through that process," de Lauretis writes, "one places oneself or is placed in social reality and so perceives and comprehends as subjective (referring to, originating in oneself) those relations—material, economic, and interpersonal—which are in fact social, and, in a larger perspective, historical" (*Alice Doesn't* 159). Experience, then, is the very process through which a person becomes a certain kind of subject owning certain identities in the social realm, identities constituted through material, cultural, economic, and psychic relations. "It is not individuals who have experience," Scott claims, "but subjects who are constituted through experience." Autobiographical subjects do not predate experience. In effect, autobiographical subjects know themselves as subjects of particular kinds of experience attached to their social statuses and identities. They know themselves to be a "woman" or "child" or "heterosexual," a "worker" or "Native American" because these identity categories come to seem natural, "given characteristics of persons" (27).

Experience as Discursive

Subjects know themselves in language because experience is discursive, embedded in the languages of everyday life and the knowledge produced at everyday sites. For instance, through the "discourse" of medical institutions (the language, images, metaphors, and narratives through which medical institutions produce and circulate knowledge about persons) people learn to understand themselves—"experience" themselves—as "patients" in need of healing or as "diseased" or "insufficient" bodies in need of surgical intervention and repair. This medical discourse also becomes the language through which doctors understand themselves as "scientists" or "healers." Of course, this is only one example of how we understand what has happened or is happening to us, and thus how we know ourselves through what Michel Foucault analyzed as discursive regimes. Every day we know ourselves, or experience ourselves, through multiple domains of discourse, domains that serve as cultural registers for what counts as experience and who counts as an experiencing subject. But since discourses are historically specific, what counts as experience changes over time with broader cultural transformations of collective history.

At the same time that we say that experience is discursive, we recognize that there are human experiences outside discursive frames—feelings of the body, feelings of spirituality, powerful sensory memories of events and images. Every day, all day long, the material universe affects us, literally as well as discursively. Bodies bleed. They manifest illnesses. They get hurt. They feel hunger, thirst, and desire. These are among the material events in our lives. But in making meaning of these events, we make that meaning, or the "experience" of those events, discursively, in language and as narrative. Thus, we retrospectively make experience and convey a sense of it to others through storytelling; and as we tell our stories, discursive patterns both guide and compel us to tell stories about ourselves in particular ways.

Experience as Interpretation

The discursive nature of experience requires us to be self-reflexive about what we understand as "our experience" or what we think we mean when we say things like "That's just my experience!" or "I'm a man." That is, what seems "ours" or "mine" has been formed and has changed over time, and we can investigate this process of change. This thing called "experience is," as Scott cautions, "at once always already an interpretation *and* is in need of interpretation" (37).

In autobiographical acts, narrators become readers of their experiential histories, bringing discursive schema that are culturally available to them to bear on what has happened. The multiple autobiographical narratives of Giacomo Casanova, Frederick Douglass, Mary McCarthy, Marguerite Duras, Buchi Emecheta, and Maya Angelou, for example, offer fascinating glimpses into life narrators' successive interpretations or revisions of the past. These versions, written at different points in their lives and, in Douglass's case, retelling the "same" story divergently in two subsequent narratives, invite readers to question whether different readings of an experience signal stages of, or changes in, the overall pattern of beliefs encoded in the autobiographical story. Or do changes from one text to its "sequel" or "prequel" signal larger cultural transformations affecting how people know themselves through stories tellable (and discourses available) to them at particular historical moments?

Experience as Authoritative

It is important to theorize what we call experience because the narrator's lived experience is the primary kind of evidence asserted in autobiographical acts, the basis on which readers are invited to consider the narrator a uniquely qualified authority. Thus, a narrator's investment in the "authority" of experience serves a variety of rhetorical purposes. It invites or compels the reader's belief in the story and the veracity of the narrator; it persuades the reader of the narrative's authenticity; it validates certain claims as truthful; and it justifies writing and publicizing the life story.

In their autobiographical acts, narrators claim the "authority of experience" both explicitly and implicitly. Implicit claims can be as unobtrusive as the appearance of the autobiographer's name on the title page. This is the case for people who are public figures and celebrities whose names on the front cover announce credibility: Eric Clapton or Sammy Sosa or Mahatma Gandhi or Nelson Mandela or Mumia Abu-Jamal or Queen Latifah or Hillary Rodham Clinton or Sarah Palin. The name itself—well known or notorious—is a kind of guarantee. It assures the reader of the authority of the writer to tell his or her story and aims to make the story a credible disclosure to its audience.

In the case of persons outside the dominant culture, persons unknown and marginalized by virtue of their lack of public status, appeals to the authority of experience may be explicit. Such appeals may be made on the basis of sexual, or ethnic, or racial, or religious, or national identity claims. In other words, identity confers political and communal credibility. In such cases, a previously "voiceless" narrator from a community not culturally authorized to speak—the slave, the nonliterate, the child, the inmate of a mental hospital, the formerly colonized, for instance—finds in identification the means and the impetus to speak publicly. Richard Wright, for example, in narrating his autobiography *Black Boy (American Hunger): A Record of Childhood and Youth,* explicitly situates himself vis-à-vis racialized communities, both black and white, inviting his reader to accept his narrative as authoritatively representative of the life script of an African American "boy." Similarly, James Baldwin negotiates his identity as a "native son" in *Notes of a Native Son.*

As the cases of Wright and Baldwin suggest, not all "experience" is accorded social and cultural recognition or legitimacy. Whereas the names of the celebrities cited above bestow the "authority" of experience on the narrator (even in cases where the narratives are ghostwritten), in other narratives the authority to narrate is hard-won in a constant engagement with readers posited as skeptical, unbelieving, resistant, and even hostile. Thus the instability of something called the authority of experience suggests how the category of experience itself is socially, culturally, historically, and politically negotiated.

Experience and the Reader

Because issues of authority can be crucial to autobiographical acts, life writers have much at stake in gaining the reader's belief in the experiences they narrate and thus having the "truth" of the narrative validated. Persuasion to belief is fundamental to the intersubjective exchange of, or "mirror talk" between, narrator and reader. Appeals to the authority of experience bring to the fore issues of trust in autobiographical narrating, since the autobiographical relationship depends on the narrator's winning and keeping the reader's trust in the plausibility of the narrated experience and the credibility of the narrator. In some life writing this makes for a complex relationship between narrator and reader.

Consider the position of Susanna Kaysen in *Girl, Interrupted.* Kaysen appeals to the reader with the authority of her experience as a young woman who was incarcerated in a mental institution for two years in the 1960s. That experience is "documented" in one sense by her inclusion of twelve documents concerning her admission, treatment, and release. Her experiential history as a resident of McLean Hospital (outside Boston) assures the reader that she knows whereof she speaks. But her project is a politically motivated one, not just an occasion to tell a lively and engaging story of "crazy" young women in the 1960s. The adult narrator provides a pointed critique of how medical and psychological discourses have assigned her the status of "crazy." The critique involves her challenge to the either/or differentiation of the worlds of the sane and the crazy, a binary mode of thinking that led doctors and nurses to label her "borderline." But in order to convince the reader of the legitimacy of her claim to having been misidentified as a borderline personality, Kaysen must persuade the reader that, although she was unstable and at times self-destructive, she reliably knows herself and thus is more authoritative than either those promoting the cultural norm she is judged by or readers who adhere uncritically to societal norms. This example suggests that securing the authority of some experiences is a tricky rhetorical process of speaking credibly and ethically about a dehumanizing and self-alienating past.

Or consider the case of a slave narrative such as *Incidents in the Life of a Slave Girl: Written by Herself* by Harriet A. Jacobs, published in 1861. Defenders of slavery were fiercely invested in debunking the authenticity of narratives about life in the slave system. And certain conventions of slave narratives provided grounds for alleging that these stories were fictionalized. Fugitive or former slaves often gave fictional names to the people in their narratives to maintain secrecy about escapes and to protect people left behind. Often the narratives were "edited," and in the process rearranged and changed, by Northern abolitionists, many of whom helped fugitive slaves to write their narratives and get them published. Given such circumstances, Southern pro-slavery apologists found grounds on which to challenge the credibility and veracity of the narratives and thus the whole enterprise of abolitionism. Jacobs's *Incidents* was drawn into this maelstrom of debatable authenticity and authorship. Jacobs fictionalized the names of people in her narrative, including her own, and depended on the editorial help of abolitionist Lydia Maria Child in revising her text. Soon after publication the narrative was dismissed as a fraud and a fiction. More than a century later, scholar Jean Fagan Yellin documented its historical veracity, which helped move *Incidents* from the status of forgotten fiction to much-taught slave narrative. It became evident that its narrative of brutalization, attempted rape, and imprisonment has a truth value beyond the accuracy of particular facts. The example of *Incidents,* therefore, suggests how narratives, and the authority of experience asserted in them, enter a public arena where issues of verifiability and authenticity are fiercely contested by interested groups and where changing norms of the "truth" of experience lead to reevaluation.

Readers have expectations about who has the cultural authority to tell a particular kind of life story. They also have expectations about what stories derived from direct, personal knowledge should assert. For instance, readers expect the slave narrative to be written by an ex-slave, or the Holocaust narrative to be written by a survivor or survivor-descendant, or the narrative of nationalization or exile to be written by an immigrant. Readers also accept the authority of the near-and-dear to entwine the biography of a loved one with an autobiographical reflection that is mediated through the account of the loved one. In *The Woman Warrior: Memoirs of a Girlhood among Ghosts* Maxine Hong Kingston braids her stories with the stories of her ancestor No-Name Woman, her mother Brave Orchid, and her aunt Moon Orchid. And Barack Obama juxtaposes stories of growing up with his Kansas-born white mother and her family in Hawaii to the African father he seeks and Kenyan extended family he discovers in *Dreams from My Father.*

The case of Gertrude Stein's *The Autobiography of Alice B. Toklas* offers a more extreme case of the issue of who claims the authority to tell the story of a loved one. Stein, writing in the voice of her lifelong partner and friend Alice, primarily celebrates the brilliance and accomplishments of Stein and their expatriate circle in Paris of the 1920s and 1930s. Is this, as critics have suggested, fraudulent, an act of ventriloquism in Alice's voice? Is it parasitic, an act of appropriating Alice's experience? Or is it an act of dedicated speaking through the other that commingles the boundaries of separate identities into a shared subject? For Stein, whose response to publishers' requests for her autobiography was "Not possibly," writing "that autobiography" in which "I" and "you," "eye" and "other" become indistinguishable, seems to authorize a subject that is irreducible to either "Gertrude" or "Alice."

Some life writing, however, seeks to misrepresent the identity of the writer and to persuade readers that the experience of fictive protagonists in fact occurred. This undermining of readerly expectations about the authenticity of experience suggests why autobiographical hoaxes are so troubling. The story of Wanda Koolmatrie is a case in point. In 1994 an autobiographical narrative titled *My Own Sweet Time* was published in Australia as the first work of Wanda Koolmatrie, an indigenous woman. It narrated Wanda's peripatetic journey from her hometown of Adelaide to the urban landscape of Melbourne. A youthful, hip, urbanized narrative, *My Own Sweet Time* was heralded as capturing the spirit of a new generation of indigenous Australian writers, alienated from traditional Aboriginal community but at home in the multicultural maze of the city. A year later, when the publishing house asked to meet Wanda Koolmatrie after giving the book a literary award, a hoax was discovered. The publisher revealed that Wanda Koolmatrie was really a young white man named Leon Carmen who was cashing in on the popular appeal of the personal narratives of indigenous people because, in his view, white men could no longer get published in Australia. Or take the example of Binjamin Wilkomirski's *Fragments: Memories of a Wartime Childhood,* the purported memoir of a Latvian Jew's struggles as an orphan in two concentration camps during World War II. *Fragments* garnered much international publicity as it was first declared a fraud and then withdrawn from circulation by its German publisher, Suhrkamp Verlag, after it had received such honors as the National Jewish Book Award in the United States. Even when confronted with documentary proof of his identity as a Swiss citizen adopted by a middle-class couple named Dössekker, the author declared, "I am Binjamin Wilkomirski."[3]

Charges of autobiographical bad faith or hoaxing reveal how complex questions of the authenticity of experience and the integrity of identity can become, how critical they are to the central notion of the relationship between life writer and reader.[4] Through the text the life narrator claims that the memories and experiences are those of the author named on the cover. Readers ascribe these memories and experiences to a flesh-and-blood person and assume that publication acts as an ethical guarantee by publishers and agents. Certainly we allow that memories, and the experience made out of memories, can be inconsistent (as they are in much life writing), probably because we experience our own as inconsistent. We understand that the source text—the memories of the author—is not accessible or verifiable in any literal sense. But we are far less willing to accept intentional duping. The situation of fiction is radically different: a hoax is unimaginable, unless one person claims to have written a fictional narrative actually written by another person. In the case of life writing, however, the hoax is a potent and politically charged possibility.

Identity

Autobiographical acts involve narrators in "identifying" themselves to the reader. That is, writers make themselves known by acts of identification and, by implication, differentiation.

Identity as Difference and Commonality

Identities materialize within collectivities and out of the culturally marked differences that permeate symbolic interactions within and between collectivities.[5] One is a "woman" in relation to a "man." One is a "disabled" person in relation to someone who is seen as "able." Identities are marked in terms of many categories: gender, race, ethnicity, sexuality, nationality, class, generation, family genealogy, religious belief, and political ideologies, to list the most obvious. These are differences that, at least for now, have meaning in the material and symbolic structures that organize human societies. But identity as difference implies also identity as likeness. As Susan Stanford Friedman notes, "an identity affirms some form of commonality, some shared ground" (*Mappings* 19). In *The Sweeter the Juice: A Family Memoir in Black and White,* for instance, Shirlee Taylor Haizlip explores how "black" and "white" identities in the United States are far more fluid than many suspect as she traces a family history that includes the passing of certain aunts and uncles as "white." Reconstructing family trees, Haizlip reconsiders the basis on which racial identities are founded and flounder and exposes the "dark secrets people have in their white souls" (238).

But social organizations and symbolic interactions are always in flux; therefore, identities are provisional. What may be a meaningful identity, on one day or in one context, may not be culturally and personally meaningful at another moment or in another context. Think, for instance, of how many identities you cycle through in the course of a day, identities linked to gender, national citizenship, work status, sexuality, class location, generational location, ethnicity, and family constellation. And notice the potential for conflict between or among these different identities. Because of this constant placement and displacement of "who" we are, we can think of identities as multiple and as "contextual, contested, and contingent" (Scott 36).

Identities as Discursive

As Scott argued for experience, so for identities. They are constructed. They are in language. They are discursive. They are not essential—born, inherited, or natural—though much in social organization leads us to regard identity as given and fixed. The Russian theorist M. M. Bakhtin argued that consciousness—which also implies identity as a category of consciousness—is dialogical. That is, it is always implicated in the processes of social exchange. Since social groups have their languages, each member of the group becomes conscious in and through that language. Thus autobiographical narrators come to consciousness of who they are, of what identifications and differences they are assigned, or what identities they might adopt through the discourses that surround them. And because of what Bakhtin calls "heteroglossia" in the social realm, the multiplicity of languages, words, and meanings that "mutually supplement one another, contradict one another and [are] interrelated dialogically" (292), the subject comes to consciousness through multiple identities and multiple voices. This is why, as Stuart Hall argues, identity is "a 'production' which is never complete, always in process, and always constituted within, not outside, representation" (392).

Identities as Historically Specific Models

Cultural identities, according to Hall, are "the unstable points of identification or suture, which are made, within the discourses of history and culture" (395). Thus they are marked by time and place. There are models of identity culturally available to life narrators at any particular historical moment that influence what is included and what is excluded from an autobiographical narrative. Some models of identity culturally available in the United States over the past three hundred years have included the sinful Puritan seeking the signs of salvation, the self-made man, the struggling and suffering soul, the innocent seeker, the "bad" girl or boy, the adventurer, and the trickster.

Life writers incorporate and reproduce models of identity in their narratives as ways to represent themselves to the reader. Consider the single identities announced in the titles of the following life narratives: *Kaffir Boy: The True Story of a Black Youth's Coming of Age in Apartheid South Africa* by Mark Mathabane, *Autobiography of a Face* by Lucy Grealy, *When I Was Puerto Rican* by Esmeralda Santiago, *Teacher* by Sylvia Ashton-Warner, *Bad as I Wanna Be* by Dennis Rodman, *The Lieutenant Nun: Memoirs of a Basque Transvestite in the New World* by Catalina de Erauso, *Made in Detroit* by Paul Clemens. The titles announce a limit of identity that the narratives explore, exploit, and explode. In *Rivethead: Tales from the Assembly Line,* for instance, Ben Hamper reimagines himself as Rivethead, a figure of renegade agency in the monotonous assembly-line life of General Motors. The Rivethead speaks Hamper's fears of fading into the emasculated catatonia of alcohol and mechanized routine and his desire to resist the orders of faceless bureaucrats. As the narrator writes of his alter ego, Rivethead is the "thoroughbred of all thoroughbreds, the quickest trigger-man this side of the River Rouge" (119).

Autobiographers often incorporate several models of identity in succession or in alternation to tell a story of serial development. In *Confessions,* Jean-Jacques Rousseau presents himself as an eager schoolboy, "a man of very strong passions" (33), a wicked sensualist, a thief, a true philosopher, and "an old dotard" (9). In *The Autobiography of Malcolm X* the narrator presents himself in successive chapters as Mascot, Home-Boy, Harlemite, Detroit Red, Hustler, Satan, Minister Malcolm X, Icarus, and El-Hajj Malik El-Shabazz. These apprenticeships in different models of identity are put on for particular occasions but, when cast off, leave traces that may conflict with other models.

The stuff of autobiographical storytelling, then, is drawn from multiple, disparate, and discontinuous experiences and the multiple identities constructed from and constituting those experiences. Often these models of identity are conflictual, as in the cases of Rousseau and Malcolm X. Some life writers are aware of the conflicts and contradictions, some not. Some narrators thematize the conflictual nature of identity in the narrative, while others do not. Some narrators explicitly resist certain identities; others obsessively work to conform their self-representation to particular identity frames. We can read for these tensions and contradictions in the gaps, inconsistencies, and boundaries breached within autobiographical narratives.

For example, in *Boyhood: Scenes from Provincial Life,* J. M. Coetzee narrates in the third person a memoir of his childhood in the apartheid nation of South Africa in the late 1940s. Refusing his Afrikaner heritage, identifying as English, aligning intellectually with Soviet Russia, and erotically drawn to the "Coloured boys" marginalized by the official identity assigned them by the state, Coetzee explores identity vectors as multiply constructed, in tension, and shifting with political conditions. While boyhood was a fixed time in his life, it was also a time that the narrator reads retrospectively as both facilitating try-outs of possible identities and undermining their realization in the repressive apartheid state. And in the sequel, *Youth: Scenes from Provincial Life II,* situated primarily in England, Coetzee's narrator revises his earlier provisional identity as London, the metropolis of empire, makes him uncomfortably aware of his marginal status as an exilic outsider, aspiring poet-writer, and awkward lover.

Identities as Intersectional

We cannot, however, just add the effects of one identity to those of another to understand the position from which someone speaks, for effects of a multiplicity of identities are not additive but intersectional. To speak autobiographically as a black woman is not to speak as a "woman" and as a "black." It is to speak as a black woman. To speak as an Australian indigenous man is not to speak as a "man" plus as an "Australian" plus as an "Aboriginal." There is no universal identity of "man" or "woman" outside specificities of historical and cultural location.

The South Asian Canadian writer Michael Ondaatje captures this amorphous intersectionality when he maps for the reader his return to the familial and now postcolonial geography of the "Ceylon" of his childhood. *Running in the Family* traces the return home of the migrant writer to a realm of family and myth. Shuttling across identities—Ceylonese, migrant Sri Lankan, Canadian, Commonwealth expatriate—Ondaatje mixes time past and time present to conjure up the past he describes as "frozen opera" (22) in order to understand his identity as multiply positioned and continuously mobile.

In her "biomythography," *Zami: A New Spelling of My Name,* Audre Lorde captures this intersectional aspect of identity and difference when she writes of herself and her friends in Greenwich Village in the 1950s:

> Being women together was not enough. We were different. Being gay-girls together was not enough. We were different. Being Black together was not enough. We were different. Being Black women

together was not enough. We were different. Being Black dykes together was not enough. We were different. . . . It was awhile before
we came to realize our place was the very house of difference rather
than the security of any one particular difference. (226)

Like Lorde in *Zami,* Gloria Anzaldúa in *Borderlands/La Frontera: The
New Mestiza* effectively traces the hybridity of her own identity in a way
that suggests how multiple and intersectional identities can be. The very
title both differentiates English from Spanish and joins them at the border
of the slash. The "I"/eye moves back and forth across the border, just as
Anzaldúa writes of navigating the intersections of sexuality, ethnicity, gender, and nationality at the constructed borderland of Texas and Mexico.
And Barack Obama's *Dreams* shuttles between his racialized identities as
both black and white and neither solely black nor white. His narrative of
becoming a man is traced in his shifting locations as a citizen of Hawaii,
Indonesia, and Kenya, a student in California and in New York, a political organizer in Chicago, and an aspirant to a global citizenship of the
future. Postcolonial writers have coined different terms to characterize inextricably mixed identities forged from histories of oppression. Among
these terms are *mixed-race, marginal, migratory, diasporic, multicultural,
minoritized, mestiza,* and *nomadic.* All of these terms indicate the fluidity of identities in movement through time and across political and geographical spaces.

Space

We as subjects are bodies inhabiting space; but more important, we are
positioned subjects, in and of place. Emplacement, as the juncture from
which self-articulation issues, foregrounds the notions of location and
subject position, both concepts that are inescapably spatial. The concept
of location emphasizes geographical situatedness; but it is not just geographical site. It includes the national, ethnic, racial, gendered, sexual, social, and life-cycle coordinates in which narrators are embedded by virtue
of their experiential histories and from which they speak. Location expands to include what Susan Stanford Friedman terms "the geopolitics of
identity within differing communal spaces of being and becoming" (*Mappings* 3).[6] The concept of subject position, by contrast, implies the ideological stances—multiple and heteroglossic rather than single and unified—

adopted by a narrator toward self and others. It also signals the kind of subject a narrator becomes by employing particular forms of autobiographical narration. The focus on both the *location* and the *position* of a narrator has importantly reshaped thinking about life writing.

Space as Material Surround or Place

Although we think of *place* geographically as region or immediate material surround, the sense of place is, as Lawrence Buell argues, necessarily always a social product, not simply an unmarked, unmediated space (*Environmental Imagination* 21). For the natural environment cannot be articulated on its own terms, outside the history of cartographies that have assigned it place-names and boundary markers (77). Thus "felt space" is "space humanized, rather than the material world taken on its own terms" (253). Space becomes place, according to Buell, when one is conscious of where one lives and develops a "sense of place" as a subject inhabiting a specific locale.

As an example, Kathleen A. Boardman and Gioia Woods assert that "one marker of autobiography produced in and about the North American West is a preoccupation with place, along with a focus on identity issues directly related to place: rootedness, anxiety, nostalgia, restlessness" (3). They observe the performance of identity at the intersection of three kinds of location—physical, rhetorical, and political—vectors not reducible simply to geography (19); and they note that "for some autobiographers place is a problem to be solved; for others, it is the basis (or 'ground') for a claim to authenticity" (3). The location of life writing may be a space as vast as the American West, where landscape becomes a horizon against and through which subjectivity is defined. It may also be a small, even minuscule space. Consider the centrality to the scene of narration of such domestic spaces as the writing desk or word processor, the intimate space of the bedroom or bath, the sociality of the dining room table, of gendered spaces such as the kitchen and the garage/workroom, and that prized space of postmodern self-reflection, the automobile. Or it may be interstitial spaces. Indeed, much modern travel writing turns on the encounter with material space by way of a mode of transportation—train, plane, or an earlier form of conveyance. Sidonie Smith has observed that "the travel narrator negotiates the dynamics of and contradictions in the drift of identity and reveals the ways in which modes of mobility—engines of temporality, spatiality, progression, and destination—are (un)defining" (*Moving Lives* 27).

For multitudes of urban peoples in the twenty-first century—in post-Katrina New Orleans, in Beirut and Baghdad, Grozny and Mogadishu—a new formation, the "tragic mobility of space" in the wounded city, is discernible (Yaeger 10). The city, traditionally viewed as both "shelter and economic flow," is now often a site of crisis, marked by migration and production zones that both structure and disrupt daily life. Thinking about the space of the city, as Patricia Yaeger asks us to do, not as an autonomous metropolis but as the intersection of multiple populations, the site of multiple modernities, and the juxtaposition of the local and the global (the glocal), requires us to rethink the impact of new globalized spaces on the kinds of diasporan identity articulated now in much life writing.

Social Spaces, Spaces of Sociality

Autobiographical narratives are also organized around *spaces of sociality,* that is, relationships and actions that are formalized in communicative interaction and ritualized or identified by gesture and bodily positioning, as Erving Goffman has suggested *(Gender Advertisements).* In life writing, actors may be situated discursively vis-à-vis others who are present explicitly, as is the host to the traveler, or implicitly, as is the warden in a prison, or a divinity to the religious. In such narratives, negotiations occur across boundaries—differences of rank, nation, ethnicity, religion, and gender—that are both constructed and redefined in such an encounter. As critics attend to these spaces of the self, their dynamics, and the fluctuating positions actors take up within them, they may assign more specific coordinates to what has often been discussed as "relationality" in life writing. That is, they can explore how a subject's narration of her or his life is implicated in and impinges on the lives of others and may encapsulate their biographies.

For example, John Edgar Wideman in *Brothers and Keepers* takes the story of his brother Robby, who as a youth was convicted of murder on the streets of Pittsburgh and imprisoned for life, and refracts it through his own quite different career trajectory as a writer, to create what he calls a "mix of memory, imagination, feeling, and fact" that characterizes the experience of urban space for many African American men (1). Art historian Jennifer González and cultural critic Mieke Bal have argued that some contemporary visual life narrative is "autotopography" (see González). Defined as "a spatial, local and situational 'writing' of the self's life in visual art," autotopography situates an artist's self-presentation within a surround of cultural objects that reference specific times, places, and networks of the past (Bal n. 42, 163).

Consider also the explicit use of an in-between space that may link artist and viewer in art installations by an African American autobiographical artist such as Adrian Piper. Piper employs a range of official identity documents in her installation *Cornered* that contradictorily identify her as white and as black in order to confront the audience with the arbitrary practices of racialization in the United States.[7] This visualization of social relations as a space of antagonistic difference inflected by the history of racial struggle has implications for both artists and viewers, calling for uncomfortable self-reflection, sustained by differential sociocultural locations (see Drake).

Geopolitical Space and Spatial Rhetorics

While social relations are of course situated within geographic space, sometimes *geopolitical space* is explicitly foregrounded, as transnational cultural studies asserts. For subjects located in complex spaces of citizenship, or multiculturally across nations with histories of conflict, questions of migration and the negotiation of borders or points of transition engage contradictions of geopolitical space.

For example, Esmeralda Santiago's *When I Was Puerto Rican* not only contrasts her experience of coming of age in 1950s San Juan and its countryside with her teenaged years as an immigrant in working-class Brooklyn. The narrative also situates her family story as emblematic of the ambiguous status in the United States of Puerto Ricans, who are citizens for the purpose of military service and the rule of law but who cannot vote. Puerto Ricans are racialized as a Spanglish-speaking, impoverished minority and stereotyped as an ethnic other in the dominant American narrative. Interrogating the space of the watery border between the island of Puerto Rico and the continental United States, as well as the less palpable internal borders of its New York neighborhoods, Santiago emphasizes the shifting valences of particular locations and the irreducibility of these heterogeneous sites to a monolithic place called "America."

North American theorizing of geographic borders also employs spatial terms to signal both location and dislocation. Gloria Anzaldúa proposes the concept of *la frontera* or borderlands as a site of encounter between different cultures that configures local inhabitants as "aliens" in both. Acts of crossing, translating, and inventing new hybrid languages and practices, seen as "linguistic terrorism," are strategies for navigating a geopolitical space that can never be "home" (58 ff.). And in the aftermath of September 11, 2001, the focus on policing national borders as a means of marking ideological contests has tracked historical contestations about citizenship.

While Anglo-American and Australian theorists of settler colonialism have emphasized encounters across borders, postcolonial theory has importantly emphasized another sense of the location of colonized subjects as the "third space," in Homi Bhabha's term. For Bhabha the third space is a zone or "place of hybridity" produced at the moment of colonial encounter, a site at which communication, negotiation, and cross-translation may occur; in the third space, "the construction of a political object that is new, *neither the one nor the other,*" produces a changed form of recognition (Bhabha 25). Both colonizer and colonized are implicated in the dynamics of this encounter, which may enable the colonized to claim a new political identity through mimicry and innovation, if not always to produce change, at the location of in-between spaces. The concept of situatedness in a third space becomes crucial in theorizing postcolonial life narratives by such writer-critics as Jamaica Kincaid, Maryse Condé, Wole Soyinka, and Manthia Diawara. In such stories the "I" is often representative of a larger group's experience at powerful moments of social change and an articulation of the desire for transformation as a social group. Similarly, locations of diaspora around the globe can be read as shifting political spaces, as Michael Keith and Steve Pile observe: "Spatiality needs to be seen as the modality through which contradictions are normalized, naturalized and neutralized. . . . Spatialities represent both the spaces between multiple identities and the contradictions within identities" (*Place and the Politics of Identity* 224 ff). Hence the geopolitical may be understood as a space both of negotiation and of erasure.

In thinking about geopolitical space, Wendy S. Hesford has employed the concept of "spatial rhetorics" to discuss how some human rights documentaries about rape in the Balkan conflicts of the 1990s created "a rhetorical space of intersubjectivity" that filmmakers used to engage visual narratives that bear witness to violence and violation, and to elicit a situation of "transnational rhetorical witnessing" (Hesford, "Documenting" 121). Similarly, Theresa Kulbaga has employed the notion of "spatial rhetorics of memory" to discuss tropes of "memory as both temporally (historically) and geographically (politically) located" in, for example, Eva Hoffman's treatment of her Jewish family's post-Holocaust immigration, first to Canada and then to the United States, in *Lost in Translation*. In a different way, German filmmaker Ursula Biemann's documentary film *Performing the Border* represents the United States–Mexico border as a performative space, realized in embodied acts of crossing by women workers that are constitutive of unstable, conflictual spatial surrounds vulnerable to manipulation by nations, by transnational corporations, and by violent outlaw practices (as in the hundreds of unsolved Ciudad Juárez murders of young women). These theorists redefine spatial rhetoric to present autobiographical subjects as migratory and transnationally situated, rather than defined by a stable national identity. Reading life writing as foregrounding spatial dynamics across geographic borders and forging new alliances with readers suggests how new hybrid identities and global practices are transacted or contested in geopolitical space.

Spatial Tropes and Topoi of Interiority

We may also think about how space is invoked in life writing through tropes and topoi that represent self-relationship. In his *Essais,* Montaigne, for example, often uses a metaphorics of dynamic space to characterize his self-experience. In *Of Presumption* (II, 17) the phrase *je me contreroulle* (653) (I roll around in myself, Frame 499) spatially describes the capaciousness and intensity of his self-study. In *Of Solitude* (I, 39) Montaigne asserts that his creative process occurs in the *arriereboutique* (241) or back room of his mind (Frame 177), a solitary space that he opens to the reader.[8] In a different way Virginia Woolf in "A Sketch of the Past" characterizes the prelinguistic dimension of the relationship to her infant self through spatial metaphor. She says she has "the feeling, as I describe it sometimes to myself, of lying in a grape and seeing through a film of semi-transparent yellow" (65). And later she writes, "I am hardly aware of myself, but only of the sensation. I am only the container of the feeling of ecstasy, of the feeling of rapture" (67). In the fluidity of this "grape" subjectivity, the preegoic body is a locus of sensation in immediate contact with the world, coexisting as undemarcated (see Smith *Subjectivity,* 95 ff.).

An entire autobiographical genre may be established around a spatial metaphor, as with the "interior landscape" that spiritual life narrators from Teresa of Avila to Thomas Merton, from Christianity to Buddhism, draw on. Such narratives conduct self-examination according to protocols of mystic practice for developing a space within. The spiritual autobiographer often retreats from a hostile external world and creates a verbal landscape as the site for expressing devotion to an otherworldly being or idea. Another kind of life writing, the apology, often uses the courtroom as a spatial metaphor, imagining the setting of a trial at which arguments for and against the speaker are rehearsed and the reader acts as a jury rendering the verdict. Spatial contexts are similarly implied in the confessional narratives of Augustine and Rousseau, which juxtapose sites of self-exposure and contrition with scenes of flagrant sinning in intimate back rooms.

Memory and Spatialization

Life narratives, as we discussed in the section on memory, may serve as repositories for preserving memory against the erosion of time and the rewriting of new generations of historians. Consider how in sites such as Germany, Ireland, Palestine, and South Africa over the past century geopolitical space is linked to national self-definition. In Jana Hensel's *Zonenkinder,* for example, the ideological shift that East Germans experienced after the demise of the Deutsche Demokratische Republik (DDR) invites self-relocation. The view of the world she grew up with is now erased except in memory. Artifacts such as her Pioneer photos and membership cards, included in her narrative as photographs, and her recollections of "Ossie" clothing, holidays, and education, comprised material life in the East "Zone," now only a zone of memory in her personal archive. This space of memory is already unavailable to the following generation, born after the 1989 demise of the Wall but who will be "Wessie" subjects. Her generation, Hensel suggests, is located in a liminal space of irreconcilable conflict between the former East and a merged nation that has occluded their collective past, a space of nowhere.

Reading for Space

Space as a concept is used in life writing not only as literal surround, scene of narration, and sense of place. It also can have geopolitical resonance for transnational subjects and delineate the psychic terrain of reflection for writers shuttling between social and private worlds or present-day locations and erased pasts. We may even think of life writing as itself an arti-fact in the space of publication and circulation, its paratextual surround, a topic discussed in chapter 3. Life narrative inevitably ensues from and is situated in spaces of many kinds.

Embodiment

It is easy to think that subjectivity and life writing have little to do with the material body. But the body is a site of autobiographical knowledge be-cause memory itself is embodied. And life narrative is a site of embodied knowledge (a textual surface on which a person's experience is inscribed) because autobiographical narrators are embodied subjects. Here we ex-plore how memory is embodied, the relationship of embodiment to loca-tion, the "some body memoir," and reading for the body.

Embodied Memory

Life narrative inextricably links memory, subjectivity, and the materiality of the body. As Paul John Eakin argues in *How Our Lives Become Stories: Making Selves,* "our lives in and as bodies profoundly shape our sense of identity" (xi). The ability to recover memories, in fact, depends on the ma-terial body. There must be a somatic body that perceives and internalizes the images, sensations, and experiences of the external world. Subjectivity is impossible unless the subject recognizes her location in the materiality of an ever-present body (Damasio 239). Moreover, the embodied materi-ality of memory and consciousness is grounded in neurological, physio-logical, and biochemical systems.

In those with Alzheimer's or dementia, memory slips away bit by bit, and others sense that the person is increasingly remote from, lost to, them. In *Elegy for Iris,* John Bayley charts how his wife, British writer and phi-losopher Iris Murdoch, was changed by the onset of the disease and offers a relational portrait of the couple. Thomas DeBaggio's *Losing My Mind: An Intimate Look at Life with Alzheimer's,* written by a man experiencing the early stages of the disease, charts how the progression of the disease enters his everyday life and records memories threatened with extinction. And death promises the limit of materiality. In her autobiographical poem cycle *The Father,* for example, Sharon Olds observes her dying father through an ethics of description. The poet seeks to know this remote and silent father through the materiality of his body as it shuts down before her. Invoking metaphors of pregnancy and mothering, she imagines her own body full with the body of the father. Hers is an embodied mode of remembering, knowing, and mourning an unloving father and expressing her filial resentment across a generational divide.

Embodiment and Location

Cultural discourses determine which aspects of bodies become meaning-ful—what parts of the body are there for people to see. They determine when the body becomes visible, how it becomes visible, and what that visibility means. That is, life narrators are multiply embodied: in the body as a neurochemical system; in the anatomical body; in, as Elizabeth Grosz notes, the "imaginary anatomy" that "reflects social and familial beliefs about the body more than it does the body's organic nature" (39–40). There is also the sociopolitical body, a set of cultural attitudes and dis-courses encoding the public meanings of bodies that have for centuries underwritten relationships of power.

In *Loving in the War Years: Lo que nunca pasó por sus labios* Chicana writer and activist Cherríe Moraga directs attention to the very material-ity of her skin as a source of her political consciousness. In this way she joins skin to the body politic, observing the different significations of "light" and "dark" in different communities. Taking her body as a narra-tive point of departure, she elaborates, through multiple modes of address, her complex cultural position as lesbian, biracial Chicana, and daughter of working-class parents. A very different kind of body is narrated into shape in Annie Dillard's *An American Childhood*. Repeatedly invoking the specificities of "skin" to mark the meeting point of the internal and exter-nal worlds, Dillard explores the way in which she learned to fit (and some-times failed to fit) the skin of her white middle-class identity to America's Pittsburgh. If Dillard tells a story of fitting into the skin of middle-class identity, Richard Rodriguez meditates on his failure to fit into the skin of Americanized masculinity in *Hunger of Memory*. Figuring himself as an upwardly mobile "scholarship boy," Rodriguez exposes the cost of the poli-tics of skin color that associates darkness with poverty and silence at the same time that he uses this dynamic of marginalization to mask his own homosexual desire. In his embrace of middle-class intellectual masculin-ity, he writes eloquently of his failure to find acceptance from the Mexican *braceros*/manual workers with whom he works one summer. In shifting modes of masculinity, the younger Rodriguez shifts skins of identity. In all these examples, the body—its skin, anatomy, chemistry—resonates as both a locus of identity and a register of the similarities and differences that inflect social identities.

Narratives of the Body

The cultural meanings assigned particular bodies affect the kinds of stories people can tell, an aspect of life writing sometimes neglected by critics who assert misleadingly that the body did not figure in life writing in the West until relatively recently. For instance, respectable middle-class women up through the nineteenth century could not, and would not, tell explicitly sexual stories about their bodies because the cultural meanings assigned to those bodies had to do with myths of the corrupt nature of female sexuality. To speak sex was to shame or pollute oneself. Women who wrote confessional narratives about sexual adventures, such as religious women telling life stories of shameful desire seeking absolution in a spiritual bridegroom, usually gave their narratives to their male confessors, who did not publish them. Teresa of Avila and Sor Juana Inés de la Cruz were exceptions. Women such as Charlotte Charke and Laetitia Pilkington, who published memoirs in the eighteenth century, incited condemnation of both their narratives and their lives. Interestingly, within their "scandalous" narratives, as Felicity A. Nussbaum has noted, such female narrators mapped their own topography of sexuality, "relegat[ing] unlicensed sexuality to the lower classes" (179). Thus, even as they spoke of sexual desire, these life narrators reproduced the identification of sexual license with lower-class status. While seeming to violate the norms of female self-disclosure, they reproduced the prevailing norms.

Many men, though not all, well into the nineteenth century also remained silent and self-censoring about their bodies and male embodiment generally, reproducing the identification of the male autobiographer with rationality, objectivity, and the mind. But generations of critics have also approached autobiographical narration from this Cartesian mind-set, overlooking the prominence of the body in the life writing of Rousseau, Casanova, Goethe, and others. Montaigne, at one point characterizing his *Essays* as "some excrements of an aged mind, now hard, now loose, and always undigested" (III, 9, "Of Vanity" 721), suggests how the mind-body binary fails to attend to the "consubstantial" embodiment of language and materiality. Studying how male embodiment is presented or concealed in life narratives is a rich prospect for future research. Ken Plummer's *Telling Sexual Stories: Power, Change, and Social Worlds,* Martin A. Danahay's *A Community of One: Masculine Autobiography and Autonomy in Nineteenth-Century Britain,* and Trev Lynn Broughton's *Men of Letters, Writing Lives: Masculinity and Literary Auto/Biography in the Late-Victorian Period* explore texts, tropes, and critical lenses for critiquing models of masculinity. David Jackson's *Unmasking Masculinity: A Critical Autobiography* performs the dual labor of critiquing forms of masculinity and relating his discovery of the social construction of his gendered and sexual identity. Many coming-out life narratives of gay men similarly indict enforced social norms of heterosexual masculinity and might be read more comprehensively within the project of situating male embodiment at a nexus of categories of identity. They range from Reinaldo Arenas's *Before Night Falls* to Kenny Fries's *Body, Remember: A Memoir,* and other life narratives in the Living Out: Gay and Lesbian Autobiography series of the University of Wisconsin Press, for example. The prolific publication of gay life writing has transformed both consciousness and social practice.

Now, in the twenty-first century, sexual confessions have become standard fare of daytime television, blogs, and published narratives in the West. In the United States, Kathryn Harrison in *The Kiss: A Secret Life* and Michael Ryan in *Secret Life: An Autobiography* went public with autobiographical narratives of sexual abuse inflicted on them in childhood. In *Shame,* Annie Ernaux narrates her witnessing at age twelve of a violent encounter between her parents as a primal scene, replacing a Freudian sexual imaginary with rape and violence as the stain that marked her childhood. In much of the developing world, writing about sexual experience, especially by women, is still prohibited and punished. For some this has come at the cost of incarceration, persecution, and exile. Feminists such as Nawal El Saadawi in Egypt and Ken Bugul in Senegal have defied prohibition by publishing narratives of sexed and gendered bodies. The discredited narrative *Burned Alive* by the pseudonymous author Souad tells a story of a young Palestinian woman's sexual desire, illicit affair, and the honor-killing her family subsequently attempted by burning her alive. But as Thérèse Taylor and Gillian Whitlock *(Soft Weapons)* have argued, there are ample grounds for reading this narrative as a hoax motivated by right-wing ideologues. Stories of the body, then, can be deployed in struggles around the politics of sexuality and the "war on terror."

Life writing about the body has also enabled people to confront the destiny of the ill or impaired body, their own or someone else's. G. Thomas Couser helpfully explains how memoirs focused on the body have been categorized as "nobody" memoirs that explore the experience of being situated in a particular body. He draws on book reviewer Lorraine Adams's definition of the "some body memoir" as that of someone known before its publication. Couser, however, complicates Adams's argument by noting that a "nobody" memoir is of some *body* because it explores a particular embodiment. Couser concludes that the common drive of many kinds of "some body memoir" is "the fundamental endeavor to destigmatize various anomalous bodily conditions or certain kinds of eros" ("Introduction: The Some Body Memoir"). Such writers, he notes, remind us of our own embodiment and push the potential of life narrative to capture lived experience through all the senses and sensibilities of writing subjects.

In *Autobiography of a Face,* for example, Lucy Grealy concentrates on how both she and others see her face differently as her face changes over the course of many reconstructive surgeries. In the wake of the disability, women's, and gay rights movements in the past quarter-century, life writing on the body with illness or impairment has produced a considerable literature in much of the developed world. In a succession of essays Nancy Mairs tracks the physical and psychological losses of/in a body becoming increasingly disabled by multiple sclerosis. She writes candidly about her sexual desires in order to claim full humanity for herself and for people with disabilities. In memoirs of living and dying with AIDS, David Wojnarowicz, Harold Brodkey, and Paul Monette explore the conjunction of desire, danger, and disease in the male body at a moment of moral panic about the AIDS pandemic. In *Close to the Knives: A Memoir of Disintegration,* Wojnarowicz refuses the fixed cultural identities of "queer" or "gay man" as he writes "close" to the body and its desires. Immersed in the visuality of memory, Wojnarowicz re-creates the specificity of desire and embodiedness as an "I" who has always "lived with the sensations of being an observer of my own life as it occurs" (149). It is this distance, this imagination of observing himself, that the photographer taps to re-create sensory experience. In this way he tries to counter cultural practices that render invisible "any kind of sexual imagery other than straight white male erotic fantasies" (119). These and other narratives of bodily centered crisis and trauma underscore the centrality of embodiment to the telling of lives.

Reading for the Body

In summary, the body has always been there in life writing as the source and site of autobiographical utterance, and critical readings can tease out the encoded forms in which it is presented. By exploring the body and embodiment as sites of knowledge and knowledge production, life writers do several things. They negotiate cultural norms determining the proper uses of bodies. They engage, contest, and revise laws and norms determining the relationship of bodies to specific sites, behaviors, and destinies, exposing, and sometimes queering, as they do so, the workings of compulsory heterosexuality and of what philosopher Namita Goswami describes as compulsory heteroimperial masculinity (344). And they reproduce, mix, or interrogate cultural discourses defining and distinguishing the cultural norms of embodiment.

Agency

We like to think of human beings as agents of or actors in their own lives rather than passive subjects of social structures or unconscious transmitters of cultural scripts and models of identity. Consequently, we tend to read autobiographical narratives as acts and thus proofs of human agency. They are at once sites of agentic narration where people control the interpretation of their lives and stories, telling of individual destinies and expressing "true" selves. In fact, traditional forms of autobiography have often been read as narratives of agency, evidence that subjects can live and interpret their lives freely as transcendental, universal "enlightenment" subjects. But we must recognize that the issue of how subjects claim, exercise, and narrate agency is far from simply a matter of free will and individual autonomy.

There are many ways in which the liberal notion of human agency might be challenged. From a Freudian or psychoanalytic perspective, we might point to the uncontrollable workings of the unconscious and desire. Or we might, after French philosopher Jacques Derrida, point to the ways in which meanings in language are never fixed, but in process, deferred.

Or we might note that discursive systems and social structures shape the operations of memory, experience, identity, space, and embodiment, as we have done above. We also have to consider the many ways that agency is conceptualized: as changing the terms of one's social relations, as an oppositional tactic of resistance, as self-empowerment, as public visibility and participation. To understand the complexities of questions of agency, we turn to contemporary investigations by a sampling of theorists who have redefined its possibilities and practices.

Theories of Agency

Theorists of agency have found the work of Louis Althusser helpful in thinking through ideological contradictions of the Enlightenment notion of human agency. Althusser argues that the subject is a subject of ideology—not in the narrow sense of propaganda but in the broad sense of the pervasive cultural formations of the dominant class. Althusser recognizes the power of coercive state institutions to conform subjects to particular behaviors, beliefs, and identities—institutions such as the military and the police. He also recognizes that there are less overtly coercive institutions—social services, educational institutions, the family, literary and artistic formations—that "hail" subjects who enter them. By *hailing* Althusser means the process through which subjects become interpellated, become what institutional discourses and practices make of them. They are "subjected." Most important, individuals understand themselves to be "naturally" self-produced because the power of ideology to hail the subject is hidden, obscured by the very practices of the institution. In this way, people are invested in and mystified by their own production as subjects, by their own "subjection." That is, they have "false consciousness": they collude in their own lack of agency by believing that they have it. It is not enough, then, to say that people exercise free will. The concept of "free will" is itself embedded in a discourse about the Enlightenment individual, a historically specific discourse through which subjects understand themselves as intellectually mature and free to make their own choices. To claim that all humans have something called "free will" in this way is to misunderstand an ideological concept as a "natural" aspect of existence. The enlightenment "individual" is itself an effect of ideology.

The theories of Michel Foucault also challenge the Enlightenment concept of the agentic liberal subject as free, rational, and autonomous. Where

Althusser emphasizes power that is centripetally concentrated in official and unofficial institutions that interpellate subjects, Foucault argues that there is no "outside" to power, that power is capillary, pervasive, inescapable, centrifugally dispersed across microlocations. Power activates through discourses, the languages of everyday life through which knowledge and regimes of truth are produced and distributed. It is through discursive "technologies of self" that subjects come to know themselves, and to surveil themselves. Thus autobiographical narration functions as a technology of self that constitutes the cultural meanings of experience, as Joan Scott argues. Discursive regimes determine who can tell their stories, what kinds of stories they can tell, and the forms those stories will take. People tell stories of their lives through the cultural scripts available to them, and they are governed by cultural strictures about self-presentation in public. In this sense, then, there is no autonomous, agentic subject outside of discourse, and no freely interpreted or fully controlled self-narration.

Other theorists have taken these challenges to the liberal notion of human agency as starting points from which to rethink its possibilities. The recurrent themes of these redefinitions circle around the terms *creativity, heterogeneity, multiplicity, dynamic reconfiguration, excess,* and *ethics.*

Political theorist Elizabeth Wingrove rereads Althusser, arguing that "agents change, and change their world, by virtue of the systemic operation of multiple ideologies." Key here is the multiplicity of ideologies through which the subject is hailed. These multiple ideologies "expose both the subject and the system to perpetual reconfiguration" (871). In reconfiguration, new possibilities emerge for knowing oneself as a subject and for understanding a system. (See also Catherine Belsey on subject construction.) Such reconfigurations, prompted by densities in ideologies and subject positions, gain momentum and intensity in times of great mobility. Changes in social, economic, and political formations, for instance, bring attendant disruptions of identities, behaviors, and interpretations of experiential history as traditional social arrangements and self-understandings are rearranged and revalued in new locations.

French sociologist and theorist Michel de Certeau locates agency in what he terms "transverse tactics." Individuals and groups deploy such tactics to manipulate the spaces in which they are constrained, such as the workplace or the housing project. For instance, a factory worker may superimpose another system (of language or culture) onto the system imposed on him in the factory. Combining systems, he can create "a space in which he can find ways of using the constraining order of the place or of the language" to establish "a degree of plurality and creativity." Such modes of "re-use," then, are interventions that open a space of agency within constrained systems (29–30). Another way of understanding re-use might be to think of the ways that people living in conditions of extremity—in revolutionary times or times of radical violence and trauma—redefine and/or resite the symbolic valences of material, behavioral, or linguistic markers of identification.

Two influential theorists look to the dynamics through which individuals construct their worlds. For the French theorist Jean-François Lyotard, the flexible and uncontrollable networks of language through which people construct their worlds spawn unexpected moves and countermoves. As a result language itself holds strategic potential for the formation of new sociopolitical subjects. For postcolonial theorist Arjun Appadurai, agency in this particular historical moment of global capitalism resides in imagination mobilized as "an organized field of social practices" (327). Imagination negotiates between "sites of agency," namely, the imagined communities in which we participate, and "globally defined fields of possibility" (327). Situated amid multiple forms of imagined worlds, individuals as sites of agency deploy their imaginations as both a social fact and a kind of work to navigate the disjunctures of global flows that create radically different self-understandings. Appadurai's discussion of imagination suggests that agency takes distinct historical forms and operates in distinct geopolitical and geographical contexts.

Feminist theorist Teresa de Lauretis turns to the unconscious as a potential source of agency. The unconscious is a psychic domain of disidentification, a repository of all the experiences and desires that have to be repressed in order for the subject to conform to socially enforced norms ("Eccentric Subjects" 125–27). As such, it lies at the intersection of the psychic and the social. A repository of the repressed, the unconscious is also a potential site of agency; its excess is a source of resistance to socially enforced calls to fixed identities.

Anthropologist Sherry B. Ortner situates agency in the capacities people bring when they play the "games" of culture—with their rules and structures. For Ortner, sociocultural structures are always partial rather than total. And thus there is always the possibility of changing the rules—although not of escaping rules altogether. It is the individual's wit and intelligence that influence his or her potential for pressuring the rules of the games.

In her early work, Judith Butler situated agency in what she calls the "performativity" of subjectivity. According to Butler, identity is enacted daily through socially enforced norms that surround us. Thus it is through our reenactment of the norms of, say, masculinity or femininity that we know ourselves to be "a heterosexual man" or "a woman." But this enforcement of norms cannot be totally effective. Individuals fail to conform fully to them because of the multiplicity of norms we are called on to reenact in our everyday lives. The failure to conform signals the "possibility of a variation" of "the rules that govern intelligible identity." And with failure come reconfigurations or changes of identities (*Gender Trouble* 145).

More recently, Butler has focused on the opaqueness of the "I" to itself (*Giving an Account* 19). Invoking the late writings of Foucault, she argues that the self's founding condition of being is vulnerability, its embeddedness in its social conditions and its engagement with others: "The 'I' cannot knowingly fully recover what impels it, since its formation remains prior to its elaboration as reflexive self-knowledge. . . . conscious experience is only one dimension of psychic life and . . . we cannot achieve by consciousness or language a full mastery over those primary relations of dependency and impressionability that form and constitute us in persistent and obscure ways" (58). Moreover, in telling a story of itself, the "I" enters a scene of narration that externalizes the self: "The 'I' who begins to tell its story can tell it only according to recognizable norms of life narration . . . to the extent that the 'I' agrees, from the start, to narrate itself through those norms, it agrees to circuit its narration through an externality, and so to disorient itself in the telling through modes of speech that have an impersonal nature" (52).

Autobiographical subjects, then, are multiply vulnerable: to their own opaqueness, to their relationality to others, and to the norms through which they tell of themselves. And yet Butler situates ethical agency in the willingness of the "I" to give an account of itself as opaque and vulnerable to the other. In such an offering of narration, "nonviolence may well follow from living the persistent challenge to egoic mastery that our obligations to others induce and require" (64). Agency, then, might be said to derive from our willingness to narrate our opacity, our fragmentation, our limits of knowability, to narrate, that is, "the way in which we are constituted in relationality: implicated, beholden, derived, sustained by a social world that is beyond us and before us" (64). Butler here shifts the idea of agency from the exercise of control over one's interpretation of one's life to openness to the self's opacity and its ethical obligation to the other.

We have briefly surveyed recent theorizing of agency as located in transverse tactics and modes of disuse; the flexible network of language; the navigation of imagined communities; performativity; psychic disidentification; play with the games of culture; and an ethics of vulnerability. These concepts offer critical frameworks for considering how people, in the act of narrating their lives, might understand their addressees, change the stories they tell, gain access to other cultural scripts, and come to understand themselves differently. They might, that is, exercise not something called free will or autonomy, but "agency."

The Politics of Agency

The question arises: What about formerly colonized peoples who have been educated as subject populations in the colonizers' language, beliefs, and values (interpellated as "colonized"), while their indigenous culture has been repressed, often brutally? Such subjects are inheritors of the legacies of a colonial history that rendered them less than fully human. For them, autobiographical writing has at times served as a tactic of intervention in colonial repression.

When people have encountered representations of themselves as the objects of the surveyor's gaze—the "exotic" native Other of anthropology and the racialized laborer or slave of imperialism—how do they begin to assert cultural agency, especially while using the terms and the medium of the colonizer? To think about the uses of life narrative in postcolonial writing is to encounter these conundrums. As, historically, a master narrative of Western hegemony in its celebration of the sovereign individual, traditional autobiography would seem inimical to people whose modes of expression were formerly oral and collective. Yet its reinterpretation in a range of what Caren Kaplan calls "out-law genres"—such as autoethnography, *testimonio,* and prison memoir—has been an important means of asserting cultural agency for postcolonial subjects in many parts of Africa, Asia, and the Americas. For Kaplan an out-law genre "mix[es] two conventionally 'unmixible' elements—autobiography criticism and autobiography as thing itself." The result of this mixing is a textual "politics of location," a specific context in which the text is produced and the self-narrator situated ("Resisting Autobiography" 208).

Employing autobiographical discourse and available generic forms to assert their cultural difference and their subjectivity, postcolonial autoethnographers have both engaged and challenged the Western tradition of individualist life narrative. Senegalese writer Ken Bugul (Mariétou M'baye), for example, narrates how she came to consciousness of her separate self in Europe, in *The Abandoned Baobab: The Autobiography of a Senegalese Woman*. She tells how, as a student in Brussels, she is confronted by the desirous looks of Europeans who exoticize her as an African female Other in the midst of white Europe. The education and the "privilege" held out to the young woman—a "child" of colonial Francophone Africa studying in Europe—to "agentify" her have the opposite effect, making her more keenly aware of her interpellation as a subject of neocolonial practices. But this crisis of individuation is also one in which her memory of African tradition intervenes to enable her to return to African soil and identity, to remember herself in the possibility of a future—as yet neocolonial—African "home." As a subject of the French "empire," Bugul adopts an autobiographical discourse of alienated selfhood (as a child of the West and its modes of self-knowing); yet as an autoethnographer deploying an out-law genre, she critiques the ground of knowing on which she stands. While the narrator could not be called an agentified subject at the end of her narrative, her quest for an African home that is as yet virtual suggests that reconstructing her life, from village to metropole, has reoriented her from colonized subject to a critically aware subject in process.

In such instances, writing becomes a means of re-forming (or deforming) the former empire and its enforced symbolic interactions. But the deferral of the achievement of agency suggests that gaining it in such a situation is complex. For the language of writing, the means of publication—publishing house, editor, distribution markets—and even the tropes and formulas of individualizing an autobiographical "I" are associated with colonial domination.

Consider the case of *I, Rigoberta Menchú: An Indian Woman in Guatemala*. As Mary Louise Pratt notes, Menchú's narrative, as told to Elisabeth Burgos-Debray, interweaves multiple discourses of identity: ethnographic ritual, parody, political manifesto, familial chronicle, and a tragic personal narrative of loss and renunciation ("Me llamo Rigoberta Menchú"). Throughout, Menchú shuttles between cultures (Quiché, Ladino, and Western European), languages (Spanish and Quiché), and positionings (teacher, political activist, daughter, Catholic acolyte, worker, woman) as she communicates an urgent testimony of the suffering of her people and the injustice done to them. In concluding this *testimonio,* Menchú vows to keep some aspects of her identity secret, thereby resisting the reader's desire to possess the truth about the survival of this indigenous culture. In her insistence on keeping secrets, Menchú positions herself at once as dutiful daughter, political leader, and social critic of a Western middle-class readership (see Sommer). She also subverts the comfortable cultural assumption of readers that we can "know" the life narrator by reading the narrative. In her testimony to the resiliency of disenfranchised indigenous Guatemalan people, Menchú seeks to change consciousness, enabling herself and her readers to resist an oppressive regime and assert human rights. Her testimony, then, attests to a process of exercising agency both in telling and in withholding cultural stories.

Conclusion

Readers often conceive of autobiographical narrators as telling unified stories of their lives, as creating or discovering coherent selves. But both the unified story and the coherent self are myths of identity. For there is no coherent "self" that predates stories about identity, about "who" one is. Nor is there a unified, stable, immutable self that can remember everything that has happened in the past. We are always fragmented in time, taking a particular or provisional perspective on the moving target of our pasts, addressing multiple and disparate audiences. Perhaps, then, it is more helpful to approach autobiographical telling as a performative act.

To theorize memory, experience, identity, space, embodiment, and agency is to begin to understand the complexities of autobiographical subjectivity and its performative nature. In chapter 4 we will frame that subjectivity by exploring the historical interplay of autobiographical texts and changing concepts of personhood. Now we turn to the complexities of specific autobiographical acts in order to think more deeply about what happens locally, at the intersection of text and context.

3

Autobiographical Acts

Language is not a neutral medium that passes freely and easily into the private property of the speaker's intentions; it is populated— overpopulated—with the intentions of others.

M. M. Bakhtin, Discourse in the Novel

All these people—producers, coaxers, consumers—are engaged in assembling life story actions around lives, events, and happenings— although they cannot grasp the actual life. At the centre of much of this action emerge the story products: the objects which harbour the meanings that have to be handled through interaction. These congeal or freeze already preconstituted moments of a life from the story teller and the coaxer and await the handling of a reader or consumer.

Ken Plummer, Telling Sexual Stories

We recognize that memory, experience, identity, spatial location, embodiment, and agency are not separable constituents of autobiographical subjectivity. They are all implicated in one another. But disentangling them in chapter 2, however artificially, allowed us to frame the psychic, the temporal, the spatial, the material, and the transformative dimensions of autobiographical subjectivity. Moreover, the concepts of memory, experience, identity, spatiality, embodiment, and agency enable us to begin probing the complexity of what happens in a particular autobiographical act.

Let's situate the autobiographical act in a story, a story in time and place. This situatedness is especially crucial since life narratives are always symbolic interactions in the world. They are culturally and historically specific. They are rhetorical in the broadest sense of the word. That is, they are addressed to an audience/reader; they are engaged in an argument about identity; and they are inevitably fractured by the play of meaning (see Leith and Myerson). Autobiographical acts, then, are anything but simple or transparent.

In *Telling Sexual Stories,* sociologist Ken Plummer, considering autobiographical stories through the lens of a "pragmatic symbolic interactionist ethnography," differentiates three kinds of people who contribute to every story action (xi). There is the producer or teller of the story—what we call the autobiographical narrator. There is the coaxer, the person or persons, or the institution, that elicits the story from the speaker. There are the consumers, readers, or audiences who interpret the story (20–21). While we take Plummer's tripartite schema as a starting point in the following discussion, we complicate it by introducing other situational and interactional features of autobiographical acts.

The components of autobiographical acts include the following:

- Coaxers/occasions
- Sites
- Producers of the story, autobiographical "I"s
- The Others of autobiographical "I"s
- Voice
- Addressees
- Structuring modes of self-inquiry
- Patterns of emplotment
- Media
- Consumers/audiences
- Paratextual frames

Coaxers, Coaches, and Coercers

Every day we are called on to tell pieces of our life stories. Think of autobiographical acts, then, as occasions when people are coaxed or coerced into "getting a life." The coaxer/coercer, in Plummer's terms, is any person or institution or set of cultural imperatives that solicits or provokes people to tell their stories (21). Telling may occur in intimate situations when someone solicits a personal narrative—for example, that intimate exchange between lovers who seek to enhance desire by giving the gift of their memories to one another. Requests for personal narratives may come in letters or e-mail messages from friends and family members: "Tell me what's been happening to you. I haven't heard from you for so long." Compulsions to confess may be coaxed by our internalization of religious values and practices—the voiced confession of the Catholic Church, prayerful confession in silence in Protestant services, the Jewish Day of Atonement. Compulsions to confession may also be of a commercial kind, commodified in daytime talk shows that package the obsessions of popular culture in neat segments on "loving too much" or "secret eating." Publishers may invite celebrity figures to tell life narratives to a public hungry for vicarious fame. Friends and colleagues of distinguished people may urge them to tell stories exemplary of public and professional life on formal occasions.

Coaxers and coercers are everywhere. Think of these everyday situations in which people's stories about themselves are elicited in the contexts of social institutions:[1]

- In political speeches candidates often tell compelling personal narratives that may project "character" and "values" or situate them in the major wars and movements of the time or attach them to specific religious, ethnic, or vocational communities.
- In the communal confessions of self-help groups participants conform their life stories to the narrative model, for example, the Alcoholics Anonymous format, required of them to make progress in recovery.
- In family gatherings, individuals participate in the shared communal recollection of the family's stories as rituals that reinforce familial history and the very idea of the family itself.
- In hospital waiting rooms, people fill out forms requesting stories of their bodies. Often their body narratives rematerialize on film in mammography, ultrasonography, and MRI scans that make their futures readable in signs of disease or bodily abnormality.
- Every day people fill out standardized forms to get food stamps or housing vouchers, driver's licenses or passports. In each of these institutional settings, personal narratives are conformed to particular routines, bureaucratic imperatives, and identities appropriate to the occasion.
- Through the bold-faced headings of personal ads, people advertise their current fantasies, their sexual histories, and their desires.
- The conventions of the employment résumé require presenting packaged credentials to prospective employers, condensing long years of experience into job skills that signify more than they state: the status of the institutions attended or the career path.

- Every day people present themselves to the scrutiny of members of groups they seek to join—neighborhood associations, churches, veterans' organizations, fraternities, or sororities. Through these narratives they announce their qualifications for membership.
- Raising their hands in court to "tell the truth," people before the bar become implicated in "crime and punishment." Legal testimony requires stipulating the facts of a verifiable identity. When competing truth claims are presented, their adjudication may require further personal revelations, sometimes against the will of the witness.
- And now, as personal information travels in digital code, millions of Web pages carry personalized visual and verbal narratives around the world in microseconds.

This list could go on and on, taking us through cultural institutions, state bureaucracies, nonstate organizations, friendships, cross-cultural encounters, communities, media, virtual reality. Global culture multiplies the possibilities for both coaxing and coercing life stories.

Although the autobiographical narratives of published writers may, in their highly crafted aesthetics, seem far removed from such everyday sites, the coaxing to which they respond shares a number of concerns and features with the kinds of autobiographical presentations we've described, or that people might engage, in telling parts of their own stories.

Some coaxing is explicit. In his *Confessions* Augustine projects a coaxing God needful of his confession. In the section of his autobiography begun in 1788, Benjamin Franklin includes several letters from friends setting out various reasons all Americans would benefit from reading his life story. The "Benjamin Franklin" friends want to coax from him is, of course, a particular version of Franklin, the statesman, social benefactor, and moral guide. In a comparable way, slave narrators were urged to recite their narratives of slavery's degradations in the setting of abolitionist meetings and for the abolitionist press.

But coaxing is also more broadly diffused throughout a culture. Successive generations of immigrants in the United States, for example, have responded to the need to affirm for other Americans their legitimate membership in the nation by telling stories of assimilation. Some autobiographers publish their life stories in order to defend or justify their past choices, to "set the record straight." In writing his apologia, *In Retrospect: The Tragedy and Lessons of Vietnam,* Robert S. McNamara responded to the continuing widespread debate in the United States about the Vietnam War and the role of government officials in waging it.

Coaxing is an integral part of the life writing process when more than one person is directly involved in producing the story. It can take several forms. In doubled autobiographical narratives, two (or more) people offer their versions of shared events or experiences, as do Mary Barnes and Joseph Berke in *Mary Barnes: Two Accounts of a Journey through Madness,* in which patient and therapist reconstruct their versions of the journey. In as-told-to or ghostwritten narratives, multiple levels of coaxing take place, including those of the ghostwriter or cowriter, whose prompting questions, translations of the autobiographer's oral speech, and revisions are often invisible in the final text, as is the case with Alex Haley in *The Autobiography of Malcolm X* or Ida Pruitt in *A Daughter of Han: The Autobiography of a Chinese Working Woman,* based on the narrative of Ning Lao T'ai-t'ai. Yet another case of invisible intervention is the publisher who requires that the celebrity or recovery autobiography be rewritten and shaped for special audiences.

In collaborative life writing, we think of two people as involved in producing the story: one is the investigator, who does the interviewing and assembles a narrative from the primary materials given; the second is the informant, who tells a story through interviews or informal conversations. But with collaborative narratives of Native Americans and indigenous colonized people, the situation is in fact often triangulated among three or more parties. Someone must undertake the translation and transcription from the indigenous language for the person who finally "edits" the narrative into a metropolitan language, such as English, and a culturally familiar story form, such as traditional autobiography or the ethnographic "life." This complex nexus of telling, translating, and editing introduces a set of issues about the process of appropriating and overwriting the original oral narrative. The case of *Black Elk Speaks: Being the Life Story of a Holy Man of the Ogalala Sioux as Told to John G. Neihardt,* G. Thomas Couser argues, is one in which a native informant in a transcultural interview situation may "speak with forked tongue" ("Black Elk"). Couser thus calls attention to the difficulty of translating what was suggested indirectly or *not* said by an informant. Arnold Krupat has considered another complexity, the "invented" English into which such narratives were often cast. But while the transcription-translation process often effaced characteristics of an Indian language, Krupat argues, a text such as *Black Hawk: An Autobiography* might be reconsidered as a collaborative effort to create a "hybrid or creolized language *based on* English" that nonetheless seeks to convey an Indian mode of language through linguistic invention ("Introduction" 7). A third kind of complexity is suggested by the publication history of *I, Rigoberta Menchú*. Menchú has protested that the intervention of the editor, Elisabeth Burgos-Debray, effaced suggested versions of its narrative by its translators, thus controlling the pattern of meaning of the narrative (see Canby).

This politics of coproduction may be mediated differently when life narrators who are deaf or otherwise prevented from directly recording their life stories depend on someone to transcribe their stories into a standard language such as English. Use of American Sign Language, for example, mediates the life writing differently from the way it is when signing to an interpreter who then "translates" the text to a recorder-editor, as H-Dirksen L. Bauman has shown ("'Voicing'"). All these cases suggest that collaborative life writing, as a multilingual, transcultural process, can be a situation of coercion and editorial control presented in the name of preserving the voice, the experience, and the culture of the life narrator.

Editorial exercise of censorship is a final example of coercion in the name of coproduction at the point of publishing the life narrative. Zora Neale Hurston's *Dust Tracks on a Road: An Autobiography* is a life narrative in which the publisher, concerned about literary propriety for a 1940s white reading public, excised certain phrases and folkloric turns of speech from Hurston's manuscript and omitted altogether some "sexy" stories she wanted to tell, as Claudine Raynaud has discussed ("Rubbing a Paragraph with a Soft Cloth?").

As we see in all these cases, the role of a coaxer in assembling a life narrative can be more coercive than collaborative. Complicated ethical issues arise when one or more people exercise cultural authority over assembling and organizing a life narrative (Couser, "Making, Taking, and Faking Lives"). In giving thematic shape to life writing by virtue of decisions about what is included or excluded, a coaxer can subordinate the narrator's modes and choices of storytelling to another idea of how a life story should read and how its subject should speak appropriately. Although this editorial coaxer often effaces his or her role in producing the narrative, a preface "describing" the working relationship between editor/transcriber and narrating subject may try to control the audience's reading, as Peter Canby suggests in his account of the Menchú controversy.

What is a critical reader to do in engaging the complexities of collaborative texts? All of the examples discussed here argue, first, for specifying the roles of various coaxers in making the autobiographical text, and, second, for relinquishing the widespread notion that indigenous texts produce a kind of unmediated authenticity. The stimulating debates of anthropologists about participant observation, of historians about the authority of primary documents, and of cultural studies theorists about autoethnography offer critics of life writing sites and tools for situating it as a mode of cultural production in which various voices and versions contest, and contend for, authority.

Sites of Storytelling

The examples we have considered suggest the degree to which coaxing/coercing occurs at particular sites of narration. Think of sites as both occasional, that is, specific to an occasion, and locational, that is, emergent in a specific mise-en-scène or context of narration. The site is, first, a literal place, a talk show, perhaps, or a social service agency, an airplane, or, as in the case of Carolina Maria de Jesus in *Child of the Dark: The Diary of Carolina de Jesus,* the desperate *favelas* (slums) of São Paolo, Brazil. But the site of narration is also a moment in history, a sociopolitical space. So we might want to think about how particular sites of narration perform cultural work, how they organize the personal storytelling on which they rely. And we might think about what kinds of narratives seem "credible" and "real" at particular sites of narration.

The appropriateness of personal narratives for particular sites is a crucial consideration. Sites establish expectations about the kinds of stories that will be told and will be intelligible to others. The autobiographical presentation you make on a Web site, for example, would not be appropriate in a legal setting and might cause real problems there. So the needs, practices, and purposes of institutions that seek to manage some aspects of our lives might be very different from our own needs and intentions in telling stories to others in intimate settings, or the ideal self-image we would like others to know and believe from our more public self-presentations.

Occasional and locational, sites are multilayered matrices at which coaxing and narrating take place. They may be predominantly personal, institutional, or geographical, though to some extent these three levels often overlap. Let's return to the example of a family gathering. Autobiographical acts in the context of a family reunion might have a lot to do with a specific coaxer—an uncle asking a niece to recall what it was like to spend time with her grandmother. But where the coaxer might be specific—an uncle—the site would have far broader import, for family reunions are occasions at which the ideology of familiality is enacted and reproduced. In order to appreciate the meaning of autobiographical acts in such contexts, then, we would need to consider the role of family reunions in a family's life, the ways in which storytelling within an extended family binds a group of disparate individuals together, the kinds of stories that are appropriate to such occasions, and the kinds that would be seen as violating codes of familiality. In an autobiographical narrative primarily concerned with family relations, such as Mary McCarthy's *Memories of a Catholic Girlhood,* family houses and rituals are primary sites of narration.

Another institutional site is the prison cell. Here the locational norm is forced incarceration, and with it the monotonous and deindividuating routine of daily discipline. Within this context of state coercion, autobiographical narrative can become a site of enabling self-reconstruction and self-determination in its insistence on imagining forms of resistance to those deindividuating routines. This was certainly the case with Eldridge Cleaver as he wrote his manifesto *Soul on Ice,* or Jacobo Timerman in *Prisoner without a Name, Cell without a Number.* Earlier it was the case with Albertine Sarrazin in "Journal de prison, 1959." In her journal, this young French vagabond writes against the cultural construction of the female prisoner as defeminized by imagining (and at least momentarily freeing) herself through writing the libidinal economy of heterosexual love and desire.

In many narratives, the geographical location strongly inflects the story being told. Jane Addams's Hull House is both a social institution and a location of impoverished immigrant Chicago in the early twentieth century. Autobiographies as diverse as Edward William Bok's *The Americanization of Edward Bok: The Autobiography of a Dutch Boy Fifty Years After,* Audre Lorde's *Zami: A New Spelling of My Name,* Vivian Gornick's *Fierce Attachments: A Memoir,* and David Sedaris's *Naked,* all situated in New York City, establish richly textured portrayals of its streets, bars, apartments, and urban scene. In the vast and heterogeneous space of the city, stories of lives engage its particular locations as well as the complexity of urban life for various kinds of subjects to produce not "New York City" but diverse stories of the highly charged, dense, sensorily saturated, and often jarring, hostile world of the city. This aspect of life narrative, as yet rarely studied by critics who tend to see the site as a backdrop, shapes the contexts of both autobiographical subjectivity and the kinds of stories that can be told. Conversely, narratives steeped in the specifics of rural place or wilderness—Kathleen Norris's *Dakota: A Spiritual Geography,* Terry Tempest Williams's *Refuge: An Unnatural History of Family and Place,* Michael Ondaatje's *Running in the Family*—are also sociocultural sites in which struggles about environmental, familial, national, and cultural politics intersect as "layers" of narrative location. Site, then, more actively than notions of place or setting, speaks to the situatedness of autobiographical narration.

The Producer of the Autobiographical "I"

Now let's turn to the producer of the story, the autobiographical "I." What do we encounter as readers/listeners when we come to an "I" on a page or hear an "I" in a story told to us? We know from the discussion in chapter 2 that this "I" is not a flesh-and-blood author, whom we cannot know, but a speaker or narrator who refers to him- or herself. But much more is involved in this marker of self-referentiality. While this speaker has one name, the "I" who seems to be speaking—sometimes through a published text or an intimate letter, sometimes in person or on screen—is composed of multiple "I"s.

Often critics analyzing autobiographical acts distinguish between the "I"-now and the "I"-then, the narrating "I" who speaks and the narrated "I" who is spoken about. This differentiation assumes that the "I"-now inhabits a stable present in reading the "I"-then. It also assumes a normative notion of life narrative as a retrospective narrative about a separable and isolatable past that is fully past. But, as our discussion of processes of autobiographical subjectivity revealed, this is too limited an understanding of life narrative. It cannot account for the complexities of self-narrating or the heterogeneous array of autobiographical modes. Nor does it adequately capture the complexity of the "I" in even the most traditional of autobiographies. We need to think more critically about the producer of the life narrative.

We propose complicating this autobiographical "I" beyond the "I"-then and the "I"-now framework by attending to the multiple "I"-thens, to the ideologies spoken through the "I," to the multiple "I"-nows, and to the flesh-and-blood author. Thus we can differentiate the following "I"s:

The "real" or historical "I"
The narrating "I"
The narrated "I"
The ideological "I"

The "Real" or Historical "I"

Obviously an authorial "I" is assumed from the signature on the title page—the person producing the autobiographical "I"—whose life is far more diverse and dispersed than the story that is being told of it. This is the "I" as historical person, a flesh-and-blood person located in a particular time and place. This "I," as Chantal Mouffe notes, can be understood as "the articulation of an ensemble of subject positions, corresponding to the multiplicity of social relations in which it is inscribed" (376). This "I" lives or lived in the world, going about his or her business in everyday life.

Because there are traces of this historical person in various kinds of records in the archives of government bureaucracies, churches, family albums, and the memories of others, we can verify the existence of this "I." We can hear her voice, if she is still alive. But this "I" is unknown and unknowable by readers and is not the "I" that we gain access to in an autobiographical narrative.

The Narrating "I"

The "I" available to readers is the "I" who tells the autobiographical narrative. This "I" we will call the narrator or the narrating "I." This is a persona of the historical person who wants to tell, or is coerced into telling, a story about the self. While the historical "I" has a broad experiential history extending a lifetime back into the past, the narrating "I" calls forth only that part of the experiential history linked to the story he is telling. This narrating "I" usually, though not universally, uses the first-person referent in this act.

The Narrated "I"

It is crucial to observe that, and how, the narrating "I" is distinguished from the narrated "I." As Françoise Lionnet suggests, the narrated "I" is the subject of history whereas the narrating "I" is the agent of discourse (*Autobiographical Voices* 193). The narrated "I" is the object "I," the protagonist of the narrative, the version of the self that the narrating "I" chooses to constitute through recollection for the reader.

For example, a narrator may begin her narrative with memories of childhood. She conjures herself up at the age of five or eight or ten. She sets that child version in the world as she remembers her. She may even give that younger "I" a remembered or reimagined consciousness of the experience of being five or eight or ten as voiced through dialogue or interior monologue. That child, however, is an objectified and remembered "I," the memory of a younger version of a self. The child is not doing the remembering or the narrating of the story. Nor is that narrated "I" directly experiencing that past at the time of writing the narrative or its telling. The narrating "I" confronting the blank page or the computer screen or a live audience is the remembering agent who creates the story. And that narrating "I," as we will see, must be further theorized as occupying multiple, at times contradictory, subject positions.

Complicating the Narrating "I"–Narrated "I" Distinction

Although we have offered a schematic framework for distinguishing the narrating "I" and the narrated "I" of autobiographical narration and self-presentation, that distinction is not sufficient when reading a particular autobiographical work. The schema may be a helpful first step in engaging autobiographical narrative, but its neat, binaristic logic needs to be complicated and understood as a starting point from which to explore how the "I" is encoded, represented, and engaged. To that end, we offer the following considerations that qualify the "I" and suggest its inherent mobility.

First, there are times when the narrating "I" is situated in the second or third person or first-person plural instead of the more common singular pronoun. Narratives as disparate as those of Edward William Bok, Henry Adams, and J. M. Coetzee are presented through the third-person pronoun. African American artist Faith Ringgold uses the second-person "you" of self-reference in *The Change Series: Faith Ringgold's 100-Pound*

Weight-Loss Quilt, where she writes of herself as the "you" of disorderly eating habits. Christa Wolf often uses the second person in *Patterns of Childhood* to distance a past "I" of the Hitler years. We might speculate that the effect of deploying the third-person pronoun is to disrupt the expectation of first-person intimacy, to create a sense of self-alienation through objectification, and to open a gap between the narrating "I" and an implicit narrating "he" or "she." By contrast, the effect of using the second-person pronoun is to reroute the expected address between narrator and reader to an unexpected intimacy of exchange between the narrating "I" and narrated "I." In either case, we as readers become aware of the elastic effect of conventions of distance and intimacy in life writing.

Second, the narrating "I" is an effect composed of multiple voices, a heteroglossia attached to multiple and mobile subject positions, because the narrating "I" is neither unified nor stable. It is split, fragmented, provisional, multiple, a subject always in the process of coming together and of dispersing. We can read, or "hear," this fragmentation in the multiple voices through which the narrator speaks in the text. These voices might include the voice of publicly acknowledged authority, the voice of innocence and wonder, the voice of cynicism, the voice of postconversion certainty, the voice of suffering and victimization, and so on. For instance, the narrating "I" of *The Autobiography of Malcolm X* speaks in several voices: as an angry black man challenging the racism of the United States, a religious devotee of Islam, a husband and father, a person betrayed, a prophet of hope, among others. Thus, the narrating "I" is a composite of speaking voices. The "I" can be seen as a sign marking the site of multiple voices that can be disentangled to a greater or lesser degree, rather than a single, unified monolithic "I." We develop this point in more detail later in this chapter (see the section on voice).

Third, the narrated "I" can be conspicuously fractured and fragmented as a thematic project. In *How I Grew,* Mary McCarthy writes of posing for a poor artist whom she met in Seattle. "Canvas cost a lot," she writes. "So I, who was not yet 'I,' had been painted over or given a coat of whitewash, maybe two or three times, till I was only a bumpiness, an extra thickness of canvas" (161). Here McCarthy differentiates her earlier girl selves from the writer she would become, "I." But those old selves are visible as a palimpsest, a bumpy textual surface that leaves its trace in the layers of covering wash. McCarthy's narrative is a good instance of our larger point: while we use a single "I" as a pronoun to refer to the autobiographical speaker in the text, not only the narrated "I" of earlier times but also the narrating "I" in the temporal present is multiple, fragmented, and heterogeneous; the utterance is in time, mobile.

Fourth, the existence of serial autobiography, either as chapters within a single volume or as multiple texts, challenges any simplistic dichotomy between narrating and narrated "I"s. As one narrative, and its narrative moment and occasion, displaces another, stories from the past may be rerouted through different narrating "I"s, who assign different meanings, affective valences, and effects to events, stages in life, conflicts, and traumas. The narrated "I" returns, to be put under a new definition, given new identities, set in a new relation to history. Serializing the "I," then, asserts the condition of mobility, as one version follows another.

Fifth, there are certain narratives in which the narrating "I" produces a narrated "I" that then becomes his or her agent of narration. This narrating "I" can, for instance, be cast as the voice of a younger version of the writer. In such narratives, it remains the case that the older narrator with greater knowledge, narrative experience, and linguistic competence controls the recourse to simplistic vocabulary, to truncated phrases, to sensory description, all associated with the youthful narrating "I." The child narrating "I" of the storytelling is an "I" constructed by the experienced narrating "I" to represent the meaning of that narrated child's experience. For example, in his best-selling memoir *Angela's Ashes,* Frank McCourt deploys the narrative voice of his younger self to tell a story of growing up in the rough streets and violent homes of Limerick, Ireland, and in New York City. The intimacy of the narrating "I"'s voice comes through McCourt's attempt to imagine and capture a sense of what that experience might have been like.

As an aside, we note that some narratologists would posit a third term to complicate the narrating "I"/narrated "I" schema: the implied author. Narrative theorist James Phelan, for instance, suggests that the narrating in *Angela's Ashes* is being done by the implied author rather than a narrating "I." The implied author in life writing is, according to Phelan, "the knowable agent . . . who determines which voices the narrator adopts on which occasions—and . . . provides some guidance about how we should respond to those voices" (*Living to Tell about It* 69).[2] A shaping, invisible agent—who cannot be a flesh-and-blood author—the implied author performs the functions of editing, arranging, and shaping the experience that a narrating "I" reconstructs of a narrated "I."

In our view of autobiographical narration, however, the narrating "I"'s voice is in fact the vocalization of the narrated "I"'s story as an oral presence. The narrating and narrated "I"s are temporally too interlinked to both be effects of an implied author, and the project of self-narration is too involved with its own process of reading and interpretation to sustain, or require, this third term. It is, however, crucial to insist on the mobility of the narrating and narrated "I"s. Phelan's model of positing a triangular situation (with narrating "I," narrated "I," and implied author) seems to depend on a narrating "I" fixed in one temporal plane. We would argue that the dynamism of much autobiographical work, its ability to put the narrative situation into play, makes such a category redundant.

The Ideological "I"

Thus far, we have discussed the "I" as a site of self-relation but not as grounded in any historical location or belief system. But, of course, the "I" is neither a transparent subject nor a free agent. Rather, it is, as Louis Althusser insists, steeped in ideology, in all the institutional discourses through which people come to understand themselves and to place themselves in the world, or as Althusser terms it, through which people are interpellated as certain kinds of subjects. Through discourses people come to know themselves and their experiences in ways that seem normal and natural. While Althusser's dismissal of agency in the face of pervasive ideological interpellation may be too hasty, as the occasional, partial, and imperfectly enabling force of testimonial discourse in autobiographical projects indicates, his focus on the many routes of interpellation influence the subsequent theorizing of subject positions, and thus of the mobile positionalities of the "I."

The concept of ideological interpellation also illuminates the importance of cultural notions of "I"-ness. The ideological "I" is the concept of personhood culturally available to the narrator when he tells his story (Paul Smith 105). Historical and ideological notions of the person provide cultural ways of understanding several things: the material location of subjectivity; the relationship of the person to particular others and to a collectivity of others; the nature of time and life course; the importance of social location; the motivations for human actions; the presence of evil, violent, and self-destructive forces and acts; even the metaphysical meaning of the universe. Because every autobiographical narrator is historically and culturally situated, each is a product of his or her particular time and place. A narrator, then, needs to be situated in the historical notion of personhood and the meaning of lives at the time of writing.

The ideological "I" is at once everywhere and nowhere in autobiographical acts, in the sense that the notion of personhood and the ideologies of identity constitutive of it are so internalized (personally and culturally) that they seem "natural" and "universal" characteristics of persons. Yet changing notions of personhood affect autobiographical acts and practices; so do the competing ideological notions of personhood coexisting at any historical moment. For the ideological "I" is also multiple and thus potentially conflictual. At any historical moment, there are heterogeneous identities culturally available to a narrator (identities marked through embodiment and through culture; gender, ethnicity, generation, family, sexuality, religion, among others). Some narrators emphasize their ideological complexity (Gloria Anzaldúa, Jean-Jacques Rousseau), while others may bend aspects of the story to support a prevailing ideology, as in narratives of religious conversion. But the ground of the ideological "I" is only apparently stable and the possibilities for tension, adjustment, refixing, and unfixing are ever present.

For instance, in "A True History of the Captivity and Restoration of Mrs. Mary Rowlandson," the seventeenth-century Puritan Mary Rowlandson remembers her captivity by the Narragansett Indians. Rowlandson is at a "remove" from her sustaining Puritan belief system and subjected to unfamiliar practices and values that seem incoherent to her. But her experience among the Narragansett also subtly shakes the foundations of that Puritan ideology as she comes to identify with its unsaved, savage Other. Despite her return to the community, she now sees its beliefs as one set of values rather than how the world "is" and hence struggles with reoccupying the ideological "I" from which she was forcibly removed.

In the early twentieth century the Russian revolutionary Alexandra Kollontai negotiates, in her 1926 *Autobiography of a Sexually Emancipated Communist Woman,* the call for a revolutionary "new womanhood" and the cultural force of what she calls "the given model" of normative femininity. Throughout her narrative the residual imprint of the given model persists even as she insists on the transformation to a new ideological model.

The ideological "I" occupies a different and complex location in Gloria Anzaldúa's *Borderlands/La Frontera.* The narrator is critical of a political ideology of American expansionism that has appropriated Mexican lands and oppressed its people. To counter that prevailing ideology, in which she has been schooled and which has judged her as marginal, she counterposes an indigenous mythology of Mexican figures as a foundation for reorienting Chicanas ideologically toward the "new Mestiza." This figure of hybridity also contests ideologies of the gendered subordination of women and of heteronormativity. Anzaldúa wages her critique across multiple borders, including the linguistic frontier of Spanish-English. In so extensively mapping pressure points of resistance to an imposed ideological "I," she defamiliarizes its naturalness. Her posing of Mexican goddess figures, queer identification, and activist woman-of-color feminism gives these countervailing beliefs new ideological force.

Ideological "I"s, then, are possible positions for autobiographical narrators to occupy, contest, revise, and mobilize against one another at specific historical moments. Only apparently a "choice," they are nonetheless multiple, mobile, and mutating.

Reading the "I"

As we read life narratives, we need to attend to these four "I"s or, rather, to the three that are available in the autobiographical act before us—the narrating, the narrated, and the ideological. We can look for places where the narrator addresses readers directly or where he calls attention to the act of narrating itself, to problems of remembering and forgetting, to a sense of the inadequacy of any narrative to get at the truth of his life as he is defining it. We can watch how the narrator organizes the times of past, present, and future in the telling of the story as a way of teasing out narrated versions of the "I" presented and the ideological stakes of those representations in the present of narration.

Sometimes the narrating "I" produces an apparently continuous chronology from birth to adolescence to adulthood. Sometimes she produces an explicitly discontinuous narrative, beginning "in the middle" and using flashbacks or flash-forwards. Sometimes exactness of chronology is of little importance to the narrator. Always there are moments in the text when that impression of narrative coherence breaks down, in digressions, omissions, gaps, and silences about certain things, in contradiction. While we may read the narrator's recitation to us as one long, continuous narrative, the text signals discontinuities that will not bear out our own fiction of coherence.

As one example, consider how, in *The Education of Henry Adams*, Henry Adams omits the story of his wife Clover's suicide. Just at the chronological moment of her suicide, the narrative breaks into two parts. Reading for this gap, we can explore how our knowledge of the silence resonates with the split structure, undermining the illusion of narrative coherence Adams's narrator seems to project. We construct a coherent "Henry Adams," or other ideologically coherent "I"s, only by underreading the ways in which the narrative calls attention to its own fissures.

Voice in Autobiographical Writing

When we read autobiographical texts, they often seem to be "speaking" to us. We "hear" a narrative voice distinctive in its emphasis and tone, its rhythms and syntax, its lexicon and affect. But theorizing voice as a construct in life writing has not yet been the focus of sustained critical attention.[3] How might we understand our attribution of a particular "voice" to life writing? And how do we theorize the relationship of voice to autobiographical acts? This section considers how voice arises at the conjunction of narrating, narrated, and ideological "I"s and distinguishes it from the spoken voice of the historical "I."

Although life writing is published as words on a page, readers experience those words as the narrator talking to them, to persuade or demand, to confess or confide, to mourn or celebrate. James Phelan suggests that the concept of "voice" can be understood as "a metaphor, in which writing gets treated as speech." But, he observes, voice is more than metaphor; it is "a learnable kind of synesthesia: as we see words on a page we can hear sounds" ("Teaching Voice" 2). In those "sounds" we have an impression of a subject's interiority, its intimacy and rhythms of self-reflexivity.[4] Voice as an attribute of the narrating "I," then, is a metaphor for the reader's felt experience of the narrator's personhood, and a marker of the relationship between a narrating "I" and his or her experiential history.

Inflected with distinctive rhythms or cadences, idioms, tone, and styles of speech, and shaped by rhetorical strategies, voice has a charge that calls the reader to some kind of relationship with the story and the narrator. In life writing, as opposed to the novel, readers may uncritically ascribe the voice of the narrative to the author. That is, the metaphor of "voice" attached to the narrating "I" may influence us to think of life writing as monovocal, told by a single individual who controls the telling of the story and its meanings. The syncopations of self-telling, however, are rarely unitary, for the narrating "I" of an autobiographical text is often polyvocal, an ensemble of voices. Autobiographical narration may shift through a register of voices that are all aspects of the narrating persona. These voices may be attached to particular identities and subject positions that the narrator takes up in telling the story: for example, the voice of the parent or the politician, the survivor or the confessor, the renegade or the celebrity, the subaltern or the conqueror. Although the text unfolds through an ensemble of voices, we as readers ascribe a distinct voice to that ensemble, with a way of organizing experience, a rhetoric of address, a particular register of affect, and an ideological inflection that is attached to the subject's history.

Autobiographical narrators also incorporate the voices of others within their archives of memory and reference. Most prominent among these others is the narrated "I," the voice attached to that remembered version of oneself whose interiority is represented through its distinct syntax, rhetorical address, style, and worldview and re-presented through reconstructed dialogue or internal monologue. The complex relationship of the voices of the narrating and narrated "I"s involves what Phelan describes as questions of distance ("Teaching Voice" 3). In coming-of-age narratives, for instance, the narrating "I" can expand the distance between him- or herself at the time of narration and the earlier version of him- or herself who struggles toward the present, making the voices of the narrating and narrated "I" markedly distinct.[5] In other narratives, the distance is contracted and the self-commentary may be less ironic, detached, bemused, or censuring. Phelan suggests a useful set of differentiations for the kinds of distance that affect the play of voices across narrating and narrated "I"s, including "temporal, intellectual, emotional, physical, psychological, ideological, and ethical" gaps (3).

Autobiographical narration is also populated with external voices. The voices of literal others may be incorporated through citation of dialogue or the use of free indirect discourse (in which the narrating "I" projects another's subjectivity by imagining his or her interiority of thought and affect). The narrating "I" can embed, for instance, an imagined interiority in the voice of a parent or sibling, a lover or friend. The voices of literal others may be less individuated or specific than those of loved ones and constitute the voice of a community or other kind of collectivity. The narrating "I" may draw in a web of voices from the oral life of a culture, voices that may be conflicting or in relative harmony. Critics use the terms *poly-vocality* or *polyphony* for the evocation of multiple conflicting or harmonious voices in a text.[6] Finally, the voice of another may enter through the narratee within the autobiographical text (the imagined addressee of the narrative), the reader to whom the story and its mode and texture of storytelling are directed. (See the sections on relationality and addressees below for an elaboration on these sites of exterior voicing in life writing.)

The conjunction of interiority and exteriority in a text produces the "internal dialogism of the word," a concept developed by Russian theorist Mikhail Bakhtin (282). For Bakhtin, language is the medium of consciousness. Because language registers play, as noted earlier, subjectivity itself is dialogical; it is always an effect of "the process of social interaction" (Voloshinov et al. 11). All of us become conscious of ourselves through the languages available to us in the social groups to which we belong. An individual's language is thus permeated by other people's words; and those words combine as various discourses in the sociocultural field that are multiple, contradictory, and, in Bakhtin's term, heteroglossic. The voices of the narrating "I" and the narrated "I" are permeated by a dialogism through which heterogeneous discourses of identity are dispersed. These discursive fragments affect the ways we narrate the past and the tropes through which we route its meanings. Françoise Lionnet uses the term *métissage* for the braiding of voices that issue from diverse languages and ethnic groups in postcolonial life writing. She attends to how narrators mix indigenous, often oral, dialects with colonial or metropolitan languages: "The search for past connections must be a thorough reinterpretation of the texts of the other 'noisy' voices of history" (*Autobiographical Voices* 23). This dialogism of the word, to which we are all subject, suggests that the autobiographical voice is inevitably inflected by such ideological formations as national and/or regional identity, gender, ethnic origin, class, and age. Mae Gwendolyn Henderson, for example, developed the concept of "glossolalia" to particularize African American women's enunciation of a discourse in dialogue with complex otherness (22).[7]

Consider an example. Sean O'Casey's *I Knock at the Door,* the first book in his remarkable six-volume autobiography of his life as an Irish playwright and politician, captures the interplay of interiorized and exteriorized voices.[8] In this narrative the adult narrator represents his childhood as a time of coming to his distinctive artistic voice through hearing and imaginatively rescripting both the language and the interior monologues of others, showing how his voice arose from the interplay of theirs. Troubled by diseased eyes, the young O'Casey, in a Dublin family immersed in poverty and hardship, listened to their articulations of a social world that became a source for self-reflection and a provocation to his own creativity.

The polyvocal voices populating the narrative capture the heteroglossic texture of Irish everyday life in rooms and on the streets of Dublin in a Joycean incantatory mixture of fragments. In addition to the boy's voice—O'Casey initially refers to himself in the third person and later as Johnny—an unnamed narrator adopts the rhythmic, repetitive phrasing of an oral storyteller, as in the following passage:

> And all this was seen, not then, but after many years when the
> dancing charm and pulsing vigour of youthful life had passed
> her by, and left her moving a little stiffly, but still with charm and
> still with vigour, among those whose view of the light of life had
> dimmed and was mingling more and more with a spreading dark-
> ness; and vividly again, and with an agonized power, when she was
> calmly listening to the last few age-worn beats of her own dying
> heart. (11–12)

O'Casey's musical prose with its onomatopoetic lilt interweaves the cadences of oral speech that are distanced from the overview of the storyteller.

O'Casey uses interior monologue to capture a character's thoughts as voice, as James Joyce did with Molly Bloom. When Sean's elder sister Ella is married, the narrator refracts her subjectivity through the cadence of her interior voice:

> . . . as we go up the aisle facin' the altar to be reverently an' dis-
> creetly an' advisedly buckled together for ever an' ever till death
> do us part from that day forward for better'n worse an' richer or
> poorer in sickness or health to love an' to cherish to hate an' to
> perish, me Ma says if I marry him, for he's rough and uncouth, but
> the love of a good woman'll make him gentle an' meek an' mild, an'
> even if all the gilt an' braid an' swingin' tassels are hidin' ignorance,
> after we've been married a day or two, a lesson a night for a year'll
> learn him more than a swift way of picking out the coloured letters
> of the alphabet. . . . (73)

Here the turns of speech and the rhythm of breath create a lilting voice that both discloses the sister's ambivalence and shows her marital illusions in a way her younger brother would not then have known. Other characters are also depicted in their interior voices, for example, the clergyman at the funeral (53–54) whose thoughts swing between bodily discomfort in the cold to a fantasy of being home and the things he must do that week.

The crowd itself becomes a collective voice in the telling of public events: "But the vigour of the lusty singing voices was pushed down to a murmur by a low humming boo from the crowd, growing louder and deeper till it silenced the song and shook itself into a menacing roar of anger. A crash of splintered glass was heard, and pieces of a broken college window fell tinkling on to the pavement below" (182). Rather than quoted dialogue, narrative voices, both exterior and interior, texture what O'Casey is narrating as speech and not mere reportage of events. Weaving together snatches of dialogue and song heard on the street, repeated proverbs and clichés, he assembles a pastiche of voices that turn what we think of as *written* life narrative into a lyrical polyvocal song. Voice is dialogically produced yet is not just the sum of other people's voices, a set of citations, or the dialogue of multiple protagonists in a novel. O'Casey's heteroglossic narrative, in which his own voice arises amid and against others', is an extreme example that suggests how we might read the textured interplay of voices giving rise to subjectivity in life writing.

Linking the concept of dialogism to the constitution of a subjective voice is productive for understanding the complexities of autobiographical acts. There are other concepts also helpful to describe voice in life writing. Consider three examples of what Nancy K. Miller has called extreme genre, in which a compelling, unique, textual voice emerges in the act of articulating a personally or politically unspeakable event ("Closing Comments"). In Joan Didion's *The Year of Magical Thinking* the narrator chronicles a year in which she tries to comprehend the sudden death of her husband, writer John Gregory Dunne, and the mysterious illness of their daughter Quintana. Much of Didion's narrative employs a dry, flat reporting voice, attentive to details of medical procedure, which seems obsessive in its concern with the material—autopsy details, clothing, food, the passage of days. Another self-reflexive voice tentatively questions her own mental status and juxtaposes citations from other writers about mortality that she references but cannot engage. Throughout her memoir, she refuses a voice of grief and mourning, the expected way of telling and "overcoming" a story of loss and shock. The process of coming to "speak" the irreversibility of death to herself emerges tentatively, if at all, in a counterpoint of speech and silence.

In a different way, Kathryn Harrison's *The Kiss* uses an unexpected voice to chronicle her father's long-term sexual violation of her, disclosing details in a haunting voice tinged with erotic ambivalence. The narrator refuses the abject position of one confessing victimization and crafts a voice at once intimate and nonjudgmental for her disturbing story of father-daughter relationship. In Frederick Douglass's *Narrative of the Life of Frederick Douglass,* by contrast, the narrating "I" shapes a voice both authoritative and stirring to tell the story of his illiterate voiceless life as a slave. It is the voice of the public abolitionist that Douglass became, mixing the cadences of classical oratory with the preacher's exhortations. As each sentence unfolds, its cadences resonate with a critique of slavery, contrasting exemplary stories of the stunted humanity he observed in both master and slave with the rhetorician's command of persuasive periodic sentences that ring with conviction.

In attending to voice, then, we may be led to aspects of life writing that raise questions about the relationship of narrative performance to the experiential life of the "real" historical "I." While we are reluctant to posit an implied author, the urgency and intensity of lived experience in these examples of extreme genre inflect the narration in a way that a performative theory of life writing does not adequately address. Crafting a textual voice out of such experience raises the stakes of life writing and asks that readers grant a different kind of authority to the narrators of such struggles, particularly when their voices are multifarious and ambivalent.

In many texts published in the past three decades, *voice* took on a second meaning as a metaphor for speaking the formerly unspeakable, a thematics of speech and silence. During the 1970s and 1980s, feminist activists and critics called for women to speak out and invoked the trope of "coming to voice" in calls for women to participate in consciousness-raising and express feelings that had been repressed in the patriarchically organized home. Voice became associated with the political agenda of changing women's lives, bringing them into the public sphere as actors, and calling attention to women's experiential histories, stories, and traditions of storytelling. Psychologist Carol Gilligan posited that women spoke "in a different voice" (the title of her book on the subject), grounded in a different ethical development. "Coming to voice" meant articulating an emergent subjectivity outside or against the repressive constraints of asymmetrical gender relationships.

Incited by the slogan "the personal is political," the Second Wave feminist movement turned to life writing as a discursive mode and a self-reflexive genre through which women could find, claim, and deploy a "liberated" voice in becoming agents and actors. The voicing of socially unsanctioned critique continues, literally and metaphorically, in life writing from the developing world by writers such as Assia Djebar. In "Forbidden Gaze, Severed Sound" (in *Women of Algiers in Their Apartment*), she crafts a narrative voice from those of women in the harem under imperialism to enunciate a silenced group in "fragments of ancient murmuring" (Djebar, "Forbidden Gaze" 342). Similarly, other historical and contemporary witnesses and activists—among them those in abolitionist and antislavery movements in England, Canada, the Caribbean, and the United States in the nineteenth century and anticolonial movements in Africa, Asia, Australia, and Latin America in the past century—have framed their testimonies of oppression through voice, as in Domitila Barrios de Chungara's *Let Me Speak!* Bearing witness publicly thus involves several acts: coming to voice, claiming social space, and insisting on the authority of one's previously unacknowledged experiential history. More recent testimonial narratives continue to be characterized by the call for witnesses to come forward to attest to injustice, oppression, and violations of human rights through voicing their stories, sometimes in interlocutory situations where someone records them (such as truth commissions).

Lest we too easily hail the metaphorics of coming to voice as a self-liberating gesture, we might keep in mind that testimony also involves telling stories that put the narrator in jeopardy because what is told is in some sense publicly "unspeakable" in its political context. That is, the personal experience out of which a narrator "speaks truth to power" is fraught with risk: public condemnation and ostracism or threats to family members. Acts of witness also risk psychic injury. Acts of telling can trigger re-traumatization, invite shaming in public exposure, address unsympathetic listeners. Moreover, contexts of witnessing such as truth commissions and the markets for stories of suffering influence and constrain whose story can be heard and what kind of story can be told.

Relationality and the Others of Autobiographical "I"s

The self-inquiry and self-knowing of many autobiographical acts is relational, routed through others, as Adriana Cavarero *(Relating Narratives: Storytelling and Selfhood)*, G. Thomas Couser *(Recovering Bodies)*, Paul John Eakin *(How Our Lives Become Stories* 43–98), Nancy K. Miller ("Representing Others"), and Sidonie Smith and Julia Watson ("Introduction: Situating Subjectivity") in different ways have argued. This concept of relationality, implying that one's story is bound up with that of another, suggests that the boundaries of an "I" are often shifting and permeable. Relationality invites us to think about the different kinds of textual others— historical, contingent, or significant—through which an "I" narrates the formation or modification of self-consciousness. These include historical others, the identifiable figures of a collective past such as political leaders. In some autobiographies a narrator reads his or her "I" as having engaged such figures as models or ideals. For example, the idea of American presidents, as well as his contact with actual former presidents, drives Bok's narrative of self-formation as an ambitious assimilated American. Such historical others often serve as generic models of identity culturally available to the narrator, which we have already discussed in chapter 2.

There are also contingent others who populate the text as actors in the narrator's script of meaning but are not deeply reflected on. And there are what we might call significant others, those whose stories are deeply implicated in the narrator's and through whom the narrator understands her or his own self-formation, as is the case in Edmund Gosse's *Father and Son: A Study of Two Temperaments* and Abraham Verghese's *My Own Country: A Doctor's Story of a Town and Its People in the Age of AIDS*. Significant others appear in narratives of several kinds. Relational narratives incorporate extensive stories of related others that are embedded within the context of an autobiographical narrative. As noted earlier, in *Brothers and Keepers,* John Edgar Wideman focuses on the story of his brother Robby, who became a street criminal while Wideman became a writer and college professor. In his effort to understand their different lives and to memorialize his brother, Wideman interweaves his own story, not just of growing up together but of deeply felt emotions about African American manhood. In *In My Mother's House: A Daughter's Story,* Kim Chernin weaves the narrative of her mother, and her mother's voice, into her story of a complex filiality among several generations of mothers and daughters.

Traditional stories of empowered women as well as communal proverbs and family histories of devalued women transmitted through generations and in contexts of immigration and cultural change also form the core of Maxine Hong Kingston's autobiographical narrative *The Woman Warrior.*

A relational narrative of a different sort is at the center of Paul Monette's life narrative *Borrowed Time: An AIDS Memoir.* The partner of Roger Horwitz, a gay man who died of AIDS, Monette remembers a partner and a relationship in a text that, as Couser notes, blurs the line between autobiography and biography. Monette struggles to narrate several stories simultaneously—a chronological journal of illness and death, a romantic love story that contests popular representations of gay men, an AIDS story of cultural crisis in that community, a narrative of rereading and revising a crisis in the gay community, and a narrative of rereading and revising a journal's gaps and emotions (Couser, *Recovering Bodies* 155–60). Monette's second memoir, *Becoming a Man: Half a Life Story,* is a prequel of his life that ends with meeting Horwitz and realizing that his previous life, alone and in the closet, was one of being "bodiless" (38) and "frozen" (173), without a life. While family members, spouses, or lovers are not always the focus of narratives of significant others, they are understandably prominent forms of deeply felt relationship (*Recovering Bodies* 160–63).

Another form of significant other to whom a narrative may be addressed and in whom it may invest special meaning is the idealized absent Other, whether secular or divine. Such narratives cannot "tell" the Other because of the profundity and inextricability of the relationship, but allusions to it as central to self-understanding resonate throughout the narrator's telling of a narrated "I." In his *Confessions,* for example, Augustine rereads his experience before conversion through a language transformed by conversion and his implicit dialogue with God. For Montaigne, his friend La Boétie, who died young, is the significant other whose absence underwrites the *Essays.* While Montaigne praises La Boétie as a "brother" and has La Boétie's essay "Of Voluntary Servitude" published posthumously, he does not embed this "brother's" biography in his own narrative. Rather, in "Of Friendship" Montaigne asserts the impossibility of differentiating his friend from himself: "Our souls mingle and blend with each other so completely that they efface the seam that joined them" (1:28, 139). Similarly, in his collaborative narrative *Black Elk Speaks,* the Lakota shaman incorporates the voices of multiple others as he tells his story through the dreams, visions, and voices of other spiritual leaders. Doing so, Black Elk secures the authority of his own visions by situating himself in a genealogy of visionaries.

Yet another textual model of the significant other organizing autobiographical discourse is the subject Other, the other internal to every autobiographical subject. As Jacques Lacan has argued in *The Language of the Self: The Function of Language in Psychoanalysis,* the illusion of a whole self acquired in the mirror stage is an identification taking place in "the imaginary." The infant is both captivated and trapped in an image of self, an alienation on which the ego constituted at this stage maintains a false appearance of coherence and integrity. Life narrators by definition cannot address the subject Other that in a sense speaks them. But critics can perform Lacanian readings of the fissures and gaps of texts, as, for example, Shari Benstock does with Virginia Woolf's *Moments of Being.* Or the gap can be read in the tensions of narrative strategies. In *The Lover,* for instance, Marguerite Duras's narrator shifts between the confessional mode of first-person narrative and the novelistic mode of third-person narrative. Duras, according to Suzanne Chester, "undermines the objectification to which she was subjected . . . [and] appropriates the masculine position of the observer" (445). Here the narrator exploits the otherness of her identity as a young white woman in colonial Indochina to undermine the stability of a colonizer and a colonized "I."

These multiple others—historical, contingent, significant, idealized but absent, and subject Others—suggest the range of relational others evoked and mobilized within life writing for the purposes of self-narrating and self-knowing. The routing of a self known through its relational others undermines the understanding of life narrative as a bounded story of the unique, individuated narrating subject. What these examples suggest is that no "I" speaks except as and through its others.

Next we need to look more closely at the explicit textual other addressed within the text, the other to whom the narrator tells his story. For, as narrative theory suggests, a text's narrator constructs an implied reader to whom the narrative is addressed, even if never named.

The Addressee

The narrator of necessity tells his story to someone. That someone might be in the same room, if the narrator's story is told orally. But even in the case of a written or published narrative, the narrator is addressing someone. Sometimes, as in a diary, that someone might even be another version of himself. We call this someone "the addressee," although we note here that scholars of narratology (the study of narrative structures) differentiate the "narratee" from the "implied reader." "The narratee," notes Shlomith Rimmon-Kenan, "is the agent which is at the very least implicitly addressed by the narrator. A narratee of this kind is always implied, even when the narrator becomes his own narratee" (89). Although narratologists differ in their understanding of the relationship of narratee to implied reader, they concur on the importance of the ways in which narratives depend on addressees in the process of storytelling.

The implied reader is a particularly interesting addressee. The self-narrator whose story is published cannot know who in fact her readers (or, in Plummer's schema, consumers) will be. But she cannot tell her story without imagining a reader.

The implied readers to which self-referential modes are addressed vary across time, cultures, and purposes. Some speakers imagine an addressee as an intimate, as Glückel of Hameln does as she addresses her children in her 1690–91 "Memoirs in Seven Little Books" (5), or as the Englishwoman Frances Anne Kemble does when she addresses her journal entries describing her sojourn in the Georgia Sea Islands in the late 1830s as letters to her friend "Elizabeth." Others imagine an addressee at some distance. Spiritual life narrators may identify "God" as the implied reader. Still others idealize an addressee, as Anne Frank does in constructing the implied reader of her diary as a sympathetic friend whom she names "Kitty." And, of course, letter writers who employ the opportunities the form offers to engage in self-reflection, social or political critique, and philosophical speculation in condensed form address their letters to particular persons who are at once specific and universalized, as is the case with the letters of the Indonesian writer and activist Raden Adjeng Kartini, whose *Letters of a Javanese Princess* includes letters written from 1899 to 1904. Sometimes the narrator addresses a universalized implied reader directly, as Susanna Kaysen does in *Girl, Interrupted*. "Do you believe him or me?" (71–72), she challenges her addressee as she contests the power of the doctor who labeled her personality disordered and sent her to McLean Hospital as a teenager in the late 1960s. Or this implied reader can be a category of people—the white Northerners whom Frederick Douglass addresses in the first of his three autobiographies, or the white Northern "sisters" whom Harriet Jacobs addresses explicitly in her *Incidents in the Life of a Slave Girl*.

Addressees can be imagined and addressed directly in the text or indirectly through the text. And often there are multiple addressees in the narrative, narratees and implied readers addressed simultaneously or in sequence. For instance, when the medieval mystic Margery Kempe dictated her narrative to an amanuensis, she addressed a multiplicity of interlocutors: the God to whom she would manifest her purity of soul; the amanuensis on whom she depended for the preservation of her story; the Church fathers who threatened her with excommunication, perhaps even death; the community of Christians before whom she would claim her rightful membership as a true believer and thereby secure her social status.

Narrator and addressee(s), then, are engaged in a communicative action that is fundamental to autobiographical acts and the kinds of intersubjective truth they construct. Attending to the addressee or implied reader of a life narrative allows us to observe subtle shifts in narrative intent. That attention also allows us to consider the kind of reader the text asks us to be as we respond to such rhetorics of intent.

Structuring Modes of Self-Inquiry

Autobiographical acts are investigations into and processes of self-knowing. But both the modes of inquiry and the self-knowledge gained or produced change over time and with cultural locations. Thus there is a history to presentations of self-knowledge. How one knows oneself today is very different from how one would have known oneself in a Socratic dialogue or in the *Imitatio Christi* of Thomas à Kempis in the early modern period. Or in the ritual Dreaming through which contemporary indigenous Australians in traditional communities understand their place within a system of totem and kinship and through which they enact their systems of values, beliefs, and relationships.

Some life narrators formalize schemes of self-investigation through a method. And these have varied dramatically. In *The Autobiography of Benjamin Franklin,* Franklin produces self-knowledge through his "Project of arriving at Moral Perfection." John Donne produces his through relentlessly self-questioning sermons; Montaigne through the self-tryouts of his *Essays*; William Butler Yeats through the mythical system of *A Vision*; Saint Teresa through the topography of "interior landscape"; Robert Burton through the anatomy as a physiological and systemic metaphor. Each narrator developed and improvised on a particular structure of self-knowing.

Some well-known patterns for presenting processes of self-knowing are linked to other genres of literature, such as the novel, and provide templates for autobiographical storytelling. Among them are the bildungsroman or narrative of social development, the *künstlerroman* or narrative of artistic growth, the confession, memoir, conversion narrative, *testimonio,* and quest for lost identity or a lost homeland or family. The bildungsroman, for instance, unfolds as a narrative of education through encounters with mentors, apprenticeship, renunciation of youthful folly, and eventual integration into society. The conversion narrative develops through a linear pattern—descent into darkness, struggle, moment of crisis, conversion to new beliefs and worldview, and consolidation of a new communal identity. In the quest or adventure narrative, a hero/heroine alienated from family or home or birthright sets forth on a mission to achieve elsewhere an integration of self that is impossible within the constraints (political, sexual, emotional, economic) imposed in a repressive world and to return triumphant. The *testimonio* unfolds through the fashioning of an exemplary protagonist whose narrative bears witness to collective suffering, politicized struggle, and communal survival.

Conventions that are culturally and historically specific govern storytelling options, narrative plotting, and the uses of remembering. And those conventions have histories: that is, at certain historical moments and in specific milieu, certain stories become intelligible and normative. Yet such stories stretch and change, gain cultural prominence or lose their hold over time. Think, for instance, of the genre of feel-good narratives that have become dominant in contemporary American cultural life. Conventions can also be displaced by newly emergent ones. For instance, autobiographical narratives published in the late twentieth century—at least those by women and people of color—radically altered the inherited conventions of life narrative by their reworking of the bildungsroman to account for the lives of formerly subordinated subjects.

And so, when we read or listen to autobiographical narratives, we need to attend to methods of self-examination, introspection, and remembering encoded in them through generic conventions. Sometimes the narrator turns his method upon particular kinds of experiences, such as dreams, and particular kinds of knowledge, such as intuitive, irrational, supernatural, mystical, or symbolic knowledge. Sometimes the narrator interrogates cultural forms of knowledge valued at the historical moment of writing. Sometimes he establishes complex linkages between knowledge of the world/others and self-knowledge. Sometimes she imagines alternative knowledges. And sometimes she refuses the very possibility of self-knowing, as is the case with the avant-garde narrators of works by Michel Leiris and Roland Barthes.

Patterns of Emplotment

The expanded concept of autobiographical acts that this study proposes leads us to review narrative plots or patterns from the perspective of a theory centered in narrative modalities. We might broadly frame these as of two kinds, although in practice these kinds are always mixed: temporally based patterns, which concern the organization of narrative times; and spatially based patterns, what might be termed, in the phrase of Susan Stanford Friedman, the "geographics" of narrative subjectivity *(Mappings).*[9]

We are subjects in time: the time of our bodies, its rhythms and cycles; the time of our everyday lives, the sense of their unfolding, the sense of succession, of one moment turning into another moment, the accumulation of our personal past; the time of history, our era, our place in a larger narrative. When we tell autobiographical stories, we engage these multiple temporalities. There is the time of our writing, the moment in life when we tell our story, the moment of history. But even the time of our writing can extend over a long period of time, and its historical moment can change radically. And then there is the time of the past under narration, a past that may be long or short, expanded or condensed.

It may seem as if there is a strict division between time-past and time-now in narration; but time in narration is always elastic. Thus there are temporal patterns both *of* the narrator's telling and *in* the telling. Some narrators tell their stories from a relatively fixed moment of their lives, as does, for instance, Isak Dinesen in *Out of Africa.* In this haunting memorial return, Dinesen reflects, after returning to Europe, on her years in Kenya as irretrievably lost. But many narratives seem to have been written at different times. Franklin's *Autobiography,* for example, identifies the narrator at different ages and in various professions rereading his past. His autobiographical "I"s are serial, multiple, and heterogeneous, in part because of the long life span over which he narrated his life.

Autobiographical narratives can be plotted strictly by chronology, with the narrator looking back on the life course and organizing the segments of telling according to the movement of historical time. It may seem that chronology is an obvious way to organize time, but it is only one way. Time can be scrambled; it can be rendered cyclical or discontinuous, as in postmodern texts. Thus a strict linear organization of narrative can be and often is displaced by achronological modes of emplotment. A narrator may employ a scheme of associational, or digressive, or fragmented remembering told through multiple flashbacks and flash-forwards, as does, for example, Janet Campbell Hale in *Bloodlines: Odyssey of a Native Daughter.* Such a pattern is multidirectional rather than linear-progressive.

Ultimately, time unfolds through no stipulated measure (see Brockmeier). The time-past of the autobiographical subject can be expanded. It can also be compressed, fragmented, or repetitive. It can be belated, as it may be for those surviving traumatic events and their aftereffects. And the time of narration can expand when an autobiographical narrator reflects on the process of writing his or her story. Moreover, time-now and time-past can interpenetrate in ways that confuse the relationship of one time to another, as our discussion of Rowlandson's captivity narrative noted. And since a narrative cannot recount all time of experience, its gaps as well as its articulated times produce meaning. Since autobiographical narration gestures toward the future, the time of the past and the present of writing are also triangulated with time future, as imagined and projected by the narrator.

Temporality intersects as well with the spatiality of autobiographical narration. Friedman suggests, in invoking a "geographics" of subjectivity that the spatial mapping of identities and differences is distinct from the chronological tracking of identity. "The new geographics," she suggests, "figures identity as a historically embedded site, a positionality, a location, a standpoint, a terrain, an intersection, a network, a crossroads of multiply situated knowledges" (*Mappings* 19). In *The Words to Say It: An Autobiographical Novel,* for instance, Marie Cardinal locates the struggle with her female body in the context of the Algerian struggle for liberation from colonialism. Mapping the intersections of political oppression and psychological repression of colonialism and sexism, the agony of Algeria and the agony of her mother, Cardinal enacts the revolutionary potential of a psychoanalysis that links the psychological to the sociopolitical. Similarly, in contemporary Australia, narratives such as Elsie Roughsey Labumore's *An Aboriginal Mother Tells of the Old and the New* and Ruby Langford Ginibi's *Don't Take Your Love to Town* map the diverse geographies of individual struggles within collective histories of physical displacement, cultural dislocation, and state forms of oppression affecting indigenous peoples.

A pastiche of textual memories may layer the narrative by incorporating multiple forms of self-inquiry, borrowed from such genres as the lyric sequence, fable, essay, diary, meditation, or public testimony. Life narrative may also incorporate multiple media—graphic images, photographs, tables, or charts—that juxtapose other geographic sites to that of the verbal story. Narratives composed of heterogeneous modes and media of self-inquiry and achronologically organized enable us to see more clearly how narrated "I"s are indeed multiple.

The conscious diffraction of times of telling and the fragmentation of chronological sequence are narrative means of emphasizing that a subject is not unified or coherent. That is, different modes of emplotment and different media of self-presentation offer possibilities for and constraints on the kind of "I" that can be narrated. Let us briefly consider some narrative genres that have provided occasions for autobiographical acts. The fable presents the narrated "I" as an allegorical type enacting human aspiration, as in, for example, John Bunyan's *Grace Abounding to the Chief of Sinners*. The meditation presents the stages of a narrated "I"'s reflections, with increasing understanding or momentary glimpses of the meaning of her spiritual history, as occurs in *The Shewings of Julian of Norwich,* Teresa of Avila's *Interior Castle,* and Thomas Merton's *The Seven-Storey Mountain.* A secular narrative, such as Robert Burton's *Anatomy of Melancholy* or Loren C. Eiseley's *The Star Thrower,* also can perform a meditative exploration occasioned by situating a life within the context of a system of thought. The lyric sequence may present the narrating "I" as a subject charting its own moments of intense emotion and rereading the narrated "I"s of previous poems as an increasingly complex structure of self-reflection, as do the sonnet sequences of French Renaissance poet Louise Labé and, in quite different ways, American poets Robert Lowell in *Notebook 1967–68* and *Life Studies* and James McMichael in *Four Good Things,* for example. The sketch (or way of life) presents the narrated "I" as a subject enmeshed in a way of life that may be recalled precisely because it is a time now past, as happens in Mark Twain's *Life on the Mississippi.*

The emplotment of autobiographical narratives, then, can be described as a dense and multilayered intersection of the temporal and the geographic. By teasing out the complex ways in which life narratives are organized, readers may discover the cultural, or historic, or generic specificities of these emplotments. As autobiographical acts increasingly innovate modalities of self-representation, critics are called on to inventively contextualize the host of strategies that these texts employ.

The Medium

While we normally think about self life writing as an extended narrative in written form, it is possible to enact self-presentation in many media, as we discuss more extensively in chapter 6. The kinds of media that can be used to tell an autobiographical story include short feature and documentary films; theater pieces; installations; performance art in music, dance, and monologue; the painted or sculpted self-portrait; quilts, collages, and mosaics; body art; murals; comics; and cyber art. As Plummer suggests, storytellers "even and more complexly can perform their stories—not just in words and scripts but as emotionally charged bodies in action" (21).

Examples of the uses of mixed media for projects of autobiographical telling abound in the twenty-first century. In such story quilts as The French Collection series, Faith Ringgold chronicles, as a *künstlerroman*, the life of a black woman artist in Paris and in America. Quilt, painting, text on cloth, the story quilts present, through a fictionalized narrative of African American woman artist Willia Marie, Ringgold's struggle to find her place "in the picture" of Western art history and to make a place in that history for the aesthetics of her African American quilting heritage. The performance pieces of such artists as Laurie Anderson, Alina Troyano (Carmelita Tropicana), Rachel Rosenthal, Guillermo Gómez-Peña, Coco Fusco, and Bob Flanagan become occasions for staging ethnically, racially, and sexually marked bodies, and for remembering and dismembering the psychic costs of identity, cultural visibility, and the social construction of difference. Since the Renaissance, artists' self-portraits have powerfully imaged the social milieu, virtuosity, and cultural myths of mastery through which the artist has claimed the authority of his or her professional status.

Of course, the medium that comes most readily to mind in self-representation is photography. Because photos individually or in family albums seem literally to memorialize identity, they often accompany written life narratives. Photographs accompany the autobiographical works of Mark Twain and August Strindberg, and are a focal point of narratives such as Roland Barthes's *Camera Lucida,* Norma Elia Cantú's *Canícula:*

Snapshots of a Girlhood en la Frontera, Donna Williams's *Nobody Nowhere: The Extraordinary Autobiography of an Autistic,* and Sheila Ortiz Taylor and Sandra Ortiz Taylor's *Imaginary Parents: A Family Autobiography.* Photographer Joanne Leonard, in her recent *Being in Pictures,* reverses the direction of the relation of photograph and autobiographical narrative, juxtaposing a narrative of her professional development as an artist and her personal experience of motherhood with a retrospective of her life's experimentation with the image as feminist consciousness. But there are separate conventions in visual and verbal media. Photographs never simply illustrate a written narrative. Each photo tells a separate story, and taken together they form a separate, often conflicting, system of meaning. Stories in photographs may support, or be in tension with, or contradict the claims of the verbal text. To read these multimedia texts we need to develop familiarity with the narrative and generic conventions of visual compositions. This power of the photograph to "tell a story" of subjectivity has become a fascinating focus of theorizing about life writing, as studies by Marianne Hirsch *(Family Frames),* Linda Haverty Rugg, and Timothy Dow Adams *(Light Writing and Life Writing)* suggest.

Finally, media may be assembled into what might be described as an ensemble text of life narrative. This is the case with Kate Bornstein's *Gender Outlaw: On Men, Women, and the Rest of Us.* Bornstein takes her experience as a male-to-female transsexual as a starting point for critiquing the binary social construction of gender and gendered desire. Her strategy of engaging the reader in actively interpreting gendered experience produces a hybrid text, composed of photographs, a play, interviews, the analyses of social critics and scholars, and a dispersed, nonchronological personal narrative. No one medium or generic mode suffices for this ensemble narration, and her cut-and-pasted text suggests both the suturing of body parts and social networks, and the subversion of the system of gender identity that its collage method achieves.

As the example of Bornstein's narrative suggests, the media for self-narrating are and have always been multiple, although critics until recently have not often emphasized the autobiographical dimension of genres other than published texts.

The Consumer

We have seen how life writing is addressed to one or more narratees and the implied reader within the text. Both addressees are implicit in autobiographical acts. But there are also actual readers of, and listeners to, personal stories. Plummer calls these readers and listeners the "consumers" in the tripartite symbolic interaction that is personal storytelling. Most literary critics call them audiences (or flesh-and-blood readers).

When someone tells his life story before a "live" audience, that audience is palpably there, soliciting, assessing, even judging the story being told. Thus the audience directly influences the presentation of identity. It shapes the inclusion of certain identity contents and the exclusion of others. It has an effect on which narrative itineraries or intentionalities are incorporated and which are silenced. And it may persuade the narrator to adopt certain autobiographical voices and mute others. In a sense, then, orally performing an autobiographical act minimizes the distances between the narrator and the narratee, the implied audience, and the consumer when the story is addressed to a live audience that, to an extent, immediately and audibly responds.

But reading audiences are not such homogeneous communities. They are heterogeneous collectives for whom certain discourses of identity, certain stories, certain truths make sense at various moments. Although they come to their readings of an autobiographical text with expectations about the kinds of narrative that conform relatively comfortably to criteria of intelligibility, they come from different experiential histories and geopolitical spaces. There are, then, constraints on the kind of "reading" such audiences will take away from, or give to, an autobiographical narration.

Distances of both space and time further complicate our understanding of the responses of audiences to life writing. Scholars of the history of the book try to discover, through research into the material conditions of publication, who constituted "reading publics," the historical consumers of life narratives at various times. They analyze what meanings reading publics assigned a given text in order to understand the cultural meanings it acquired at and since its first publication. And they assess the investments that religious, juridical, political, and/or cultural institutions may have had in the reproduction—or suppression—of genres of life writing or in a particular personal narrative.

How published narratives are produced and circulated among reading publics, what routes they take through various institutions before they get into people's hands, are issues that affect the ways in which life writing achieves its ongoing effects in social interactions. And because readers "consume" narratives along with other stories from elite as well as popular culture, their responses to life writing are influenced by other kinds of stories in general circulation—in families, communities, regions, nations, diasporas.

Consider two examples of popular American life writing that circulated among reading publics throughout, and beyond, the nineteenth century: Barbary Coast pirate narratives and Mary Jemison's captivity narrative. A fascinating subgenre of captivity narrative, the Barbary captive narratives (both English and American, authored by Anglo and African writers) were usually told by mariners captured by pirates and held in North Africa. These tales were widely read as popular exploration and adventure stories. But in the United States in the nineteenth century they were also read as cautionary tales, warning of the vulnerability of the new nation to its European trading partners, all of whom sought wealth in Africa (Baepler 25). These tales mobilized divisions in American discourses of race at a key moment in the early nineteenth century when the slave trade had greatly intensified and slave narratives were circulating. A captive such as African American Robert Adams, who told his story to a white editor in 1816, was read as "white," "Arab," or "negro" by readers whose interpretations of his narrative varied wildly according to their locations and politics (21). A female Barbary captive, Eliza Bradley, wrote "an authentic narrative," published in 1820 as the true and harrowing tale of a white English woman who, in captivity, was sheltered and never the victim of sexual advances (247). This narrative, borrowing large parts of its story from a best-selling adventure narrative of its time, captivated readers with its contradictory notions of fragile and independent white womanhood. Barbary Coast narratives traded on exoticizing Africa as a land of extremes in bizarre stories of grotesque spectacles. Both rationalizing and critiquing slavery in the United States, they inaugurated a public taste for Barbary captive narratives in print and into the twentieth century on the stage and screen (50–51).

A different aspect of reading publics is evident in the changing responses to the narrative of Mary Jemison, popularly known as "the white woman of the Genesee," told to James E. Seaver. Jemison was captured in 1755 by the Seneca Indians in what is now upstate New York and stayed voluntarily for life with her captors, raising a large family. Her narrative, first published in 1824, was so popular it went through twenty-seven printings and twenty-three editions that ranged in size from 32 to 483 pages. In these editions the story was reshaped as, at various moments, an ethnographic record of life among the Seneca and Iroquois; a "true history" of captive experience; a document attesting to settler stamina; a nostalgic mourning for the decline of Indian life; a site for displaying photos of the new sites and monuments of western New York; and a popular children's book (Namias 4–6). In examining its successive editions, we can trace shifts in reading tastes by observing the modifications of content and presentation of the versions over time.

To date, the study of audiences for autobiographical narratives is not a developed field. More scholarly work needs to be done on how popular narratives are received and internationally transmitted, and on the shifts in content and emphasis that occur from edition to edition in response to changing public tastes. In sum, changes in reading publics can be signaled by subtle changes in the material production of the book (in print size; the use of illustrations, introductions, and appendixes; and in the framing of the narrative for readers whose interpretative schema have shifted dramatically from those of an earlier time). Since narratives are riddled with the play of meaning beyond any fixed referentiality, reading publics—or consumers—become cocreators of the text by remaking the story through the social codes and psychic needs of their times. Umberto Eco aptly captures this dynamism of publics for narrative by titling a section of his 1979 book, *The Role of the Reader: Explorations in the Semiotics of Texts,* "How to Produce Texts by Reading Them" (3). And reading publics are not the only groups influential in changing the shape and contents of life writing. We now turn to how reception is also shaped by publishing conglomerates, international markets, and online practices in our times.

Paratextual Apparatuses

Autobiographical acts and texts are situated in a *paratextual surround,* what we might think of as the framing produced by their publication, reception, and circulation. The concept of the paratext is identified with Gérard Genette, who coined the word *paratext* as a combination of *peritext* (all the materials inside the book) and *epitext* (elements outside it such as interviews and reviews) (5). Genette distinguishes paratextual apparatuses from the literary work per se, which is constituted "entirely or essentially, of a text, defined (very minimally) as a more or less long sequence of verbal statements that are more or less endowed with significance" (1). Peritexts are the materials added in the publishing process that accompany the text in some way, including such elements as cover designs, the author's name, the dedication, titles, prefaces, introductions, chapter breaks, and endnotes. Paratextual materials—peritexts and epitexts—may appear to be "neutral" aspects of the presentation of a text, but Genette argues that they comprise a threshold that can dramatically affect its interpretation and reception by variously situated reading communities.

Extending Genette's study of paratexts to focus on the autobiographical, Gillian Whitlock considers how life writing circulates as a material object that takes up space on a shelf or in a display addressed to the public, whether or not individuals become its readers (*Soft Weapons* 56 ff). Think, for instance, of the importance of the book cover or jacket, which targets a potential market (often different in different nations or successive editions) and makes an appeal for the book to be read in certain ways. Whitlock suggests that marketing departments produce a "look" for a book, organizing it not only by its cover but by its epitextual surround, how it is displayed in stores or advertised online, as a commodity for consumption. Readers are solicited in an airport or during a casual Web browse by means of cover images and jacket blurbs. Whitlock focuses on the outpouring of "burka narratives" explicitly referencing veiled women after the New York World Trade Center attacks of September 11, 2001, as an example of how, in such stories, the "images, the titles, and the subtitles are designed to grab the Western eye with a glimpse of absolute difference, of the exotic" (59). She provocatively argues that such life writing offers Western readers the fantasy of explanatory stories about Islamic desires and rituals for their voyeuristic consumption (61–62). But the effects of paratextual apparatuses are indeterminate. Book jackets that invite Western readers to translate narratives across cultures may induce us to understand our own complicity in the circulation of cultural fantasies yoked to political realities of domination (67–68). And life writing may turn up in unanticipated venues where it is heterogeneously displayed, for instance, in supermarkets and discount department stores. As Whitlock emphasizes, paratexts concern not only who reads whom, when, and to what effect, but also the kind of audience solicited for a text at a given historical moment, and the kinds of audiences that may subsequently take it up for different occasions and purposes.

Let's think further about the peritextual process. Publishers, editors, compilers, ghostwriters, and translators often reframe a narrative through different kinds of mediations. Editorial choices involve conforming the story to publishing conventions and normalizing the plot by assigning titles, selecting typeface and page layout, organizing the chapters and rearranging their sequence, excising passages, correcting grammar and syntax, and regularizing idioms to make the narrative intelligible to a broad audience. Reframing might involve enhancing the truth claims of the narrative, as when James Frey's editor persuaded him to recast *A Million Little Pieces* as a memoir rather than a novel. Publishers and editors often add footnotes as verification and insert supplementary materials, such as the photographs already discussed, as documentation of people and events for general readers. Publishers incorporate prefaces that attest to the character of the author. Nineteenth-century slave narratives and twenty-first century witness narratives are often introduced and situated by an "expert" whose authority lends credibility to the veracity of the life narrative. These peritexts establish the bona fides of the person whose story is told, attaching authenticity to the tellers who may lack narrative authority at that moment and to their stories that contravene dominant narratives.

The peritextual packaging of autobiographical writing shapes and situates the narrative by constructing the audience and inviting a particular politics of reading. Compilers and editors sometimes produce collections that place conflicting life stories in dialogue or tension, as did the compilers of medieval saints' lives, called hagiographies. Similarly, in our times, there are contemporary collections of witness narratives by, for example, survivors of childhood sexual abuse or the "comfort women" who were forced into sexual servitude by the Japanese military during World War II. Packaging several heterogeneous stories as a collection can blur their differing contexts and truth claims, giving the misleading effect of a single, shared story.

Particularly in cyberspace, life writing is situated amid epitexts such as the publisher's advertising and reviews posted by customers on bookselling sites, indicating how it has been received and rated by readers (Whitlock, *Soft Weapons* 61–62). Inescapably, in the consumer culture of digital capitalism, our encounters with autobiographical narratives are multiply mediated, whether they occur in material spaces or in cyberspace. In their mediations, the paratext—peritexts and epitexts—helps determine how audiences cluster at a particular historical moment around particular kinds of narrative. Consider the power of Oprah Winfrey's talk show to shape reader responses to—and create massive sales for—the books she chose for Oprah's Book Club. Paratexts direct the habits of reading publics and may constellate new publics. By understanding that autobiographical narratives are situated in the paratextual materials and practices that surround them, and in the spaces they come to occupy in our daily lives over time, we can more carefully specify how readerly audiences are shaped and changed both historically and in this moment of global capital.

Conclusion

"The meanings of stories are never fixed," concludes Plummer, "but emerge out of a ceaselessly changing stream of interaction between producers and readers in shifting contexts. They may, of course, become habitualised and stable; but always and everywhere the meanings of stories shift and sway in the contexts to which they are linked" (21–22). This instability and periodic revision of meaning account for the ever-shifting effects of the autobiographical, and for the joint action of life narrator, coaxer, reader, and publishing industry in constructing the narrative.

Getting a life means getting a narrative, and vice versa. In his influential essay "Life as Narrative," Jerome Bruner powerfully articulates the complex interconnections between lives lived and the narratives of lives:

> Eventually the culturally shaped cognitive and linguistic processes that guide the self-telling of life narratives achieve the power to structure perceptual experience, to organize memory, to segment and purpose-build the very "events" of a life. In the end, we become the autobiographical narratives by which we "tell about" our lives. And given the cultural shaping to which I referred, we also become variants of the culture's canonical forms. (15)

It is in the contextual, provisional, and performative aspects of our autobiographical acts that we give shape to and remake ourselves through memory, experience, identity, location, embodiment, and agency. Understanding the profound complexities of these acts enables us to better understand what is at stake in life narrative, in the narrator-reader-publisher relationship, and in the international culture of the autobiographical prevalent in the early twenty-first century.

4

Life Narrative in Historical Perspective

I'm losing myself! An explosion of identity. Searching for oneself in death
to get to know birth! Beginning with the origins in order to understand the
end. Inventing a detail, patching it up and adjusting it to suit one's destiny.

Calixthe Beyala, *Your Name Shall Be Tanga*

Our goal in this chapter is to trace the production of autobiographical subjects over time. This history does not claim to trace a simple chronology
of successive notions of personhood. Competing versions of personhood
overlap and intersect at a given historical moment. Our focus is double, on
demarcating autobiographical subjects in their historical context and on
noting the emergence of various autobiographical genres through which
those subjects fashion themselves. Our aims in constructing this history
are both to identify exemplary autobiographical texts and to explore the
kinds of subjects those narratives inscribe.

We look beyond individual texts to the formation of the subject in
relation to larger collectivities of social classes, nation, religious community, ethnic group, and other defining identities. Understanding how individual representations of subjectivity are "disciplined" or formed enables
readers to explore how the personal story of a remembered past is always
in dialogue with emergent cultural formations. This brief anatomy, then,
examines autobiographical genres that are both formed by and formative
of specific kinds of autobiographical subjects.

We noted in chapter 1 the relatively recent coinage of the term *auto-*
biography in the West. The practice of writing autobiographically, however,
has a history extending back to, and perhaps before, the Greeks and Romans in antiquity and extending beyond Western culture. The oral performance of self-narrative has existed in many indigenous cultures prior to
literacy—in, for example, the naming songs of Native American cultures,
the oral narratives of genealogy and descent among Africans, the communal self-locating of the "song lines" of indigenous Australians, and others. In addition to the long-standing practices of oral tradition throughout

the world, there are modes of written self-inscription in China as early as two thousand years ago, in Japan as early as a thousand years ago, in Islamic-Arabic literature as early as the twelfth century,[1] in India during the medieval period (the *bhakti* poetry of devotional engagement with the sacred), and in North Africa in the fourteenth century (Ibn Khaldûn's *At-Ta'rîf*). This widespread use of self-representation in both preliterate and literate non-Western cultures contradicts the allegation of an earlier generation of literary critics that autobiography is a uniquely Western form and a specific achievement of Western culture at a moment of individuation in the wake of the Enlightenment.[2]

Given the current interest in the study of life narratives, we fully expect that scholars in the next decade will continue research into autobiographical traditions and their transcultural influence; and we anticipate that autobiography studies will become increasingly comparative and multicultural. For the purposes of this study, however, we have limited our focus to written life narrative as it has developed in the West.

Autobiographical Subjects in Antiquity and the Middle Ages

When we think of self-knowledge in classical antiquity, we are likely to think first of the figure of Socrates and his self-interrogatory understanding of the Delphic oracle's injunction "Know thyself": Socrates knows that he knows nothing. But although Socrates engaged others on the limits of their knowledge and revealed their blindness about themselves, even the "Apology" and the "Symposium" are, at best, obliquely self-referential. While the Platonic dialogues show the paradox of self-knowledge in the wise man's knowing admission of ignorance, they do not resemble autobiographical texts as we now understand them. Georg Misch, an eminent early-twentieth-century German scholar of autobiography, however, identified hundreds of texts and inscriptions in his multivolume history translated in part as *A History of Autobiography in Antiquity*.[3] Misch found evidence of an "I" commemorated in funerary inscriptions about feats of battle and in early texts such as funeral orations, familiar letters, and travel narratives that have both the autobiographical content and the structure of self-reference. Certainly the lyric poems of Sappho of Lesbos (c. 600 B.C.E.) present the voices of a woman candidly exploring her emotions and the somatic designs of love and physical desire, often with self-mocking wit, as feminist scholars have recently argued.

The "first" book-length autobiographical narrative in the West is generally acknowledged to be the *Confessions* of Saint Augustine, written around 397 C.E. Augustine's "I" retrospectively views his early life from the perspective of his conversion to Christianity. Saved, he looks back to assess the workings of grace in his wayward life and the steps to his spiritual salvation. The postconversion Augustine construes the first half of his life as a chronological narrative of errors and self-indulgence from his youth through his pursuit of education and erotic love. He narrates, in Book 8, the turning point of his life, the moment of conversion when he was called by a spiritual voice to seek dialogue with an unapproachable God, and to reflect on the centrality of memory to spiritual salvation.

Unlike Plutarch and other biographers of the Roman emperors who focus on the public careers of their subjects, Augustine writes extensively of his childhood, with its intimate desires; he writes as well about the psychology of virtue and vice that marked his troubled journey toward conversion and confesses a Christian sense of sin and shame. The identity that is the subject of Augustine's text is a paradoxical one. In this process of conversion, loss of self as it is commonly understood defines identity, and self-effacement becomes a means to a higher state, being subsumed in God. The mode of this autobiography as postconversion "confession" is directed simultaneously to Man and to God, in a narrative at once exemplary and highly personal.

In the next thousand years, most autobiographical writing was done by religious men and women as a form of devotion in the service of spiritual examination. Their narratives sought the signs of God's grace in the life of Christ and Christian saints and tried to erase the traces of sin by effacing the stubborn self. Medieval spiritual testimonies include such works as the *Shewings* of Dame Julian of Norwich and the meditations of mystics such as Hildegard of Bingen and Hadewijch in Germany, and Angela of Foligno in Italy. In the narrated visions through which they attempted to represent their relationship to the unrepresentable, female mystics, according to Laurie Finke, "claimed the power to shape the meaning and form of their experiences" even though they "did not claim to speak in [their] own voice[s]" (44).

In the fifteenth century in England Margery Kempe, a medieval mystic, told to a scribe a most remarkable story of one woman's life. Her *Book* sought to convince readers and Church authorities that she was a mystic, perhaps even a saint, who belonged in the genealogy of Christian saints.

As a married mother, Kempe had to remake herself as a public religious through a narrative of God's manifestations in her life and in her very body, a body whose testimony included weeping and wailing. Like other religious mystics, Kempe co-constructed the story of a subject in dialogue with a God who commanded her attention to the signs of his wonders. This version of life narrative offered a destiny and an itinerary for self-location and promised salvation through self-overcoming.

In fourteenth-century Italy, Francis Petrarch and Dante Alighieri introduced self-referentiality into traditional poetic genres to present the spiritual quests of their narrators and to define their relationship to a classical tradition. Petrarch's letter "The Ascent of Mount Ventoux," addressed to Saint Augustine, applies the terms of self-understanding in Augustine to his own arduous journey up the "mountain" of life. In his *Vita Nuova* (The New Life) Dante's young poet-narrator recasts his entire life in light of that transformative moment when he glimpsed Beatrice, a figure for, and a foreshadowing of, the encounter with the divine. And Dante the pilgrim, at the beginning of *The Divine Comedy,* represents himself as a straying wanderer who "woke to find myself in a dark wood" (*Inferno* 1:67), both a writer on a personal quest to resolve the dilemma of his identity and a figure of the struggling Christian soul.

Medieval Christian writers deployed a rhetoric of self-reference in their quests for salvation. It is important to note, however, that the challenges and complexities of self-reference and self-study in medieval mystics do not yet present the self-fashioning private individual of much early modern narrative. But as forays into autobiographical writing, these narratives, with their applications of sacred discourse to the profane private self, anticipate the terms of a dialogue about the private and public loci of self-conception that later humanist self-narrators will explore.

We know far less of everyday medieval uses of the autobiographical. The letters, journals, and chronicles of the secular world take place at the margins of records of official tasks, private communications, and household management. Chronicles recorded and celebrated the public actions of aristocrats and merchants. Letters and ledgers recorded the everyday workings of families, notably families whose members achieved prominence due to their social status and inherited identity. There is no one category of personhood to which we may assign these many modes of encoded self-presentation in medieval texts. In fact, much exploration of the forms of subjectivity in medieval texts remains to be done by scholars. But Meredith Anne Skura has recently suggested in a study of verse, hagiography, sermons, and husbandry manuals that readers may "listen" for the language and affective registers people in the sixteenth century used to talk about their lives and consider who talked about themselves and why. As scholars articulate news ways of reading these everyday texts, a more complex understanding of the autobiographical in early modern societies is emerging.

The Humanist Subject, Secular and Spiritual

As part of the transformations wrought in the early modern period of the fifteenth and sixteenth centuries, the problem of writing and imaging a secular and public self became increasingly pressing as people struggled with landscapes of interiority other than that of Christian spirituality and an exteriority other than that defined through the material signs of God's grace. In the poetic traditions of Italy, France, England, Germany, Spain, and the Netherlands, the sonnet sequence offered lyrical occasions for a narrator's extended introspective exploration of the range of emotions evoked by the beloved and the conflicting effects of love produced in the lover. Although highly conventionalized in form, meter, and rhyme, the sonnet sequences of writers such as William Shakespeare and Louise Labé conduct explorations of heightened states of feeling and evolve a vocabulary of interiority to delineate a nuanced subjectivity.

In his *Autobiography* Benvenuto Cellini, a sixteenth-century Florentine sculptor, narrated the story of his life, fulfilling what he considered the duty of all men "who have done anything of excellence" (7). Cellini mixes discussion of his everyday work as an artist with accounts of the manners and customs of his time, stressing his own importance as someone at the center of power and accomplishment. His text combines chronicle with a kind of early ethnography to construct a humanist subject who centers himself in the public world as both evaluator and actor. This humanist subject, epistemologically oriented in writers such as Desiderius Erasmus and Michel de Montaigne, engages with a material world that it can significantly act on and enter into dialogue with. As Stephen Greenblatt suggests, such "Renaissance self-fashioning" reoriented poets and thinkers toward a human measure and mode of the self.

Contemporaneous with Cellini, the mathematician Girolamo Cardano composed *The Book of My Life,* considered by some to be the first psychological life narrative. Cardano minutely inventories aspects of his life in chapters with such titles as "A Meditation on the Perpetuation of My

Name," "Those Things in Which I Take Pleasure," "My Manner of Walking and Thinking," and "Things in Which I Feel I Have Failed." His emphasis on self-evaluation remains open-ended, never coming to rest in the completed composition of his self-portrait. In *St. Ignatius' Own Story, As Told to Luis Gonzáles de Cámara* in three short sessions in 1555, Ignatius represents his history of inward growth and interior transformation differently. He presents himself as a contemplative in action by alluding to particulars of the world in which he studied, taught, and traveled. In such narratives the autobiographical subject objectifies himself as an actor in the world and records the externalization of his character, showing how the subject becomes a subject of history. Here the presentation of subjectivity is, as with the medieval mystics, in the service of an external source; that source is now not timeless and transcendent but embedded in the material conditions of history.

Teresa of Avila, working within a tradition of spiritual autobiography, engages the form to explore her visions and present herself to her confessors. In this process, she introduces a metaphorics drawn from everyday domestic experience that works against a discourse of transcendent spirituality, thereby creating a kind of personal, material subject and giving embodiment to interiority. In authorizing herself as a subject, Teresa challenges her confessors' suppression of religious women and articulates a mode of self-interrogation congenial to women mystics who also inhabit earthly realms of power. Similarly, Madame Guyon, trapped in a ruthless marriage, embraces in her narrative a mysticism that promises empowerment in its exaggeration of model femininity. By exploring their own private experience, then, some women writers find alternative access to self-knowledge in a church that forbade them formal learning. Here, autobiographical practice becomes an alternative form of education.

The first specific, sustained self-exploration in Renaissance prose occurs in the *Essays* of Montaigne, who for nearly thirty years used colloquial prose to test or "try" his reading of the writers of antiquity against the perspectives of his own times and his personal idiosyncrasies. In his extended self-portrait, Montaigne dramatizes his situation as both the subject and object of his own discourse. Asking himself, "Que sçay-je?" (What do I know?), he pursues an inquiry into how self-knowledge shapes the terms of subjectivity.

Montaigne's *Essays* are not a retrospective chronicle of his lived life; rather, they comprise a sustained investigation into the conditions of knowledge that enable his enunciation of an "I" in the terms of the self-portrait formed of ever-shifting perspectives. Montaigne's interlinear habit of writing commentary on his previous layers of text, however, adds reflexivity as his narrating "I" enters into ongoing dialogue with past narrating "I"s. Montaigne's "I" studies itself in a succession of moments refracted through the lenses of topics as exalted as "Of Experience" and as humble as "Of Thumbs." This mix of everyday topics, details of personal life, and classical learning makes a textual body that, in an act of secular incorporation, is recursively referential.

This practice of taking oneself as a subject of inquiry in time is engaged discursively by such dramatic figures as Hamlet and explored in the prose of John Donne's sermons, Robert Burton's *Anatomy of Melancholy,* and Thomas Browne's "Religio Medici," among others. Each of these writers, working within a received prose genre of the meditation, reshapes it as a forum for self-investigation by posing systems of knowledge against one another and locating his investigatory "I" at their nexus. With the philosophers Francis Bacon, John Locke, and David Hume, however, that inquiring "I" becomes embedded in new ontologies, the "I" a subject of a new system, as the interrogatory, experientially based stance of Montaigne is transformed in emergent systems of metaphysics.

The Migratory Subject of Early Modern Travel Narratives

The self-exploration of the early modern period both motivated and paralleled geographical exploration of the globe as travelers began to record the findings of their journeys in narratives that comprise another kind of autobiographical practice. These travel narratives posed an "I" in migration, encounter, conquest, and transformation.

The genre emerges in the West with *The Travels of Marco Polo* in 1271, which inaugurated, over the next four centuries, a plethora of narratives of voyages to exotic destinations. European adventurers and explorers returned home with tales of hardships and survival, of dangerous transit and wondrous encounters (Pratt, *Imperial Eyes* 20). Presenting themselves as heroic survivalists and their project as one of mapping new worlds, these writers used their self-referential narratives to articulate the subjectivity identified by Mary Louise Pratt as "a European global or planetary subject" (9). This global subject was "male, secular, and lettered" and viewed the world through the lens of a "planetary consciousness" (29–30).

Journeys to the New World provide a focus for these narratives of exploration, conquest, and empire, from the Portuguese through the French, Spanish, Dutch, German, and American explorers. Perhaps the best known of these is Columbus's log, a personal set of informational entries for the years of the Hispaniola visits, and the journals of Cortés, registering both the hardships of travel and the wonders of encounter. In letters such as those of Dominican friar Bartolomé de Las Casas to King Philip of Spain concerning the cruelties of Spanish conquest in the West Indies beginning in 1542 (translated into English in 1583), the critique of the predatory mentality and abusive practices of a "global or planetary subject" is fully achieved. Another kind of travel narrative was developed by Jean de Léry in the *History of a Voyage to the Land of Brazil, Otherwise Called America*, written in 1578. Speaking alternately as "I" and "we," Léry provides an eyewitness account that mixes encounters with "exotic" natives, tales of hardships at sea, religious controversy among the Huguenots, and personal reflections on contact with other worlds, a narrative project that gradually forms his own subjectivity. As in Montaigne's "Of Cannibals," which indicts colonizing Europeans as more barbaric than the "barbarians" of the New World, for Léry, contact with indigenous people calls "civilizing" practices into question and suggests that an "indigenous" collectivized subjectivity may be superior to that of the Western "new man."

Narratives of colonization, captivity, and contested hegemony continued to abound into the seventeenth century, wracked as it was by political conflict. While Captain John Smith's brash fabulations signaled one possibility of storytelling, captivity narratives in the New World reworked certain tropes of conversion narratives in the context of the radical dislocations created by contact in the New World. In the American colonies Mary Rowlandson's narrative of captivity, with all its ambivalences, became well known. As we noted in chapter 3, Rowlandson charts her shift from victim to flexible survivor among the Narragansetts, from the assumed superiority of an inerrant Puritanism to the less certain subjectivity and more complex worldview of transcultural encounter.

The Enlightenment Subject

Contemporaneously, in seventeenth-century Europe, Descartes situated the contemplative, epistemological self in a new house of philosophy. The solitary "I" of his *Discourse on the Method* subordinates body to mind, nature to intellect, and others to a sovereign philosophical self, the cogito. In isolating and individuating an identity, he transforms experience into metaphysical principles, stripped of everyday particulars. In the reflection of the cogito on its own mental processes, the Enlightenment subject is born and, with it, a new world of Cartesian dualism created from its desires and certainties.

In the wake of the cogito, forms of rational and scientific knowledge gained preeminence. Privileging sight and visual clarity, philosophers identified Enlightenment rationality with the intellectual standpoint of objectivity and understood the goal of man's intellectual labor as comprehending the totality of a problem. This claim to objectivity and universal knowledge enabled the postulation of a rational or objective subject able to transcend the perspectival sight of humanist writers and define his knowledge as outside that which he surveys. And the notion of an ideal knowledge, linking sight, knowing, rationality, and power, reordered conceptions of self-understanding, as the autobiographical investigations of such philosophers as Blaise Pascal and Thomas Hobbes suggest.

Motivated by this cultural belief in the thinker's objectivity, enlightened men set off on sustained journeys into interiors of continents, as scientific journeys superseded journeys of conquest. Enlightened men of science traversed the globe, collecting samples and information about flora and fauna, peoples and geographies. Bringing the entirety of the globe within sight and rationalizing it through the systematic classification of Linnaean taxonomy, these scientists exercised their enlightened subjectivity by naming the profligate chaos of the world and writing narratives of scientific inquiry through which they presented themselves as benign agents of reason and order (see Pratt, *Imperial Eyes* 14–37).

But the limitations of an overreaching rationalism and the social orthodoxies of emergent nation-states also provoked resistance and gave rise to the articulation of alternative subjectivities among dissenting marginal groups, including Protestant sects as well as some wives of the gentry.

The Dissenting Subject

After the sixteenth-century rise of dissenting sects in the Protestant Reformation, spiritual autobiography was increasingly employed to defend a community of believers. The Puritan revolution in England engendered John Bunyan's *Grace Abounding to the Chief of Sinners* and George Fox's

Journal. In his journal, Fox attempts to acquaint readers with his character and religious views. In Bunyan's project of self-biography, an ideal dissenting self assesses itself in terms of Puritan religious prescriptions. Eager to establish a place for both the dissenting self and the dissenting community in the body politic, Bunyan's narrator constantly attunes his salvation to what Felicity Nussbaum describes as "the promise and the threat of the loss of identity" (69). Often, she notes, his writing plays out a dialectics of subjection and agency for subjects of self-regulation: "The autobiographical subject may describe subjection to an authority's control while being bound to a belief that one is a free agent with an independent conscience and self-understanding" (77). The dissenting subject is an ethical subject located in the space of paradox. He or she is at once subservient and free: subservient to the extent of being free to choose the path to salvation; and free in the sense of choosing the path of subservience.

Men and women writing secular life narratives in the seventeenth century had few models clearly available to them, in part because many of the narratives written during the period remained unpublished for several hundred years. There were, however, two generalized conventions—the narrative of religious conversion, as we have seen, and the secular res gestae (the story of deeds done), tracing its roots back to classical antiquity. Some educated aristocratic women, finding means to write within the general constraints on women's writing, chronicled the deeds and achievements of their husbands, as did Lucy Hutchinson and Lady Ann Fanshawe. But others hesitantly asserted their own voices. For example, Lady Anne Halkett appended a narrative of her life to the biography she wrote of her husband. Margaret Cavendish wrote a personal account, one of the earliest secular life narratives written by a woman, but only after she had dutifully written a biography of her husband. In *The True Relation of My Birth, Breeding, and Life* she negotiated her ambivalent desires for public recognition and for proper femininity. In this struggle for meaningful autobiographical identity, Cavendish sustains two competing self-representations, the story of feminine self-effacement and that of masculine self-assertion.

The Bourgeois Subject

Perhaps the best-known life narrative of the English seventeenth century is Samuel Pepys's *Diary,* although it was not published until the early nineteenth century. In six large volumes, written over forty years (1660–1703),

Pepys recounts in minute detail London life, the great fire and the plague, as well as everyday life, trips to the country, and his weakness for women. Written as regular weekly entries throughout his life, the diary composes a secular world in which Pepys takes account of his daily life. His might be thought of as the accumulative subject, along the lines of Defoe's pseudoautobiographers Robinson Crusoe and Moll Flanders, all of whom are nascent bourgeois subjects accumulating the capital of experience. In some ways, too, this accounting resembles the self-survey of spiritual autobiographers. In both genres, the diurnal record and the narrative of spiritual progress, the life narrator becomes an eyewitness to events both great and daily, a kind of interested social historian.

Bourgeois subjects, like aristocrats before them, also set off on the road, traveling through Europe on what became known as the "grand tour" and writing about their travels as a *peregrinatio academica* (Leed 184–85; Chard 1–39). In their travel journals James Boswell, Charles Burney, and Thomas Nugent recorded their observations as educational journeys through successive cultures. Typically, grand tourists followed a prescribed curriculum and set of exercises codified in guidebooks written by their tutors, such as *The Compleat Gentleman; or, Directions for the Education of Youth as to Their Breeding at Home and Travelling Abroad,* written by Jean Gailhard. The bourgeois subject of both tour and journal imagined himself as the newly enlightened man of broad learning and experience preparing to assume "the responsibilities of the well-born male to family, class, and nation" (D. Porter 35).

At least one grand tourist discovered that the education she received through the grand tour made the return to family responsibilities impossible. Lady Mary Wortley Montagu, traveling with her husband, who was British ambassador to the Sultanate of Turkey, carefully composed and copied her letters to friends and family in England. In these "embassy letters," published after her death, Montagu turns an observant autobiographical eye/"I" into a detailed and revisionary ethnographic account of women's lives in the Turkish seraglio, refiguring the woman of the seraglio as a sign "of liberty and freedom" (Lowe, *Critical Terrains* 45) in comparison to the women of England.

In France the rise of the epistolary form enables other kinds of autobiographical presentation. Madame de Sévigné's renowned letters, many of which are addressed to a daughter unwilling to engage her in speech, reform for private disclosure the genre that Abelard and Héloïse had used centuries earlier for self-presentation as devout lovers. In a remarkable epistolary conversation with her daughter, Sévigné creates herself as a woman writing and, like Montaigne with the essay form before her, comments on the act of letter writing. The occasion of writing to her daughter provides Sévigné an occasion for dialogue in her absence; to herself, at least, she sustains her identity as "mother" to her daughter. Along with some novels of the century, such as Madame de Lafayette's *The Princess of Clèves*, Sévigné's writing signals a nascent bourgeois maternal subject characterized by nurturance and the appeal to filiality.

The Exceptional Subject of Modern Life Narrative

The eighteenth century comprises a vast and complex network of autobiographical discourses among the French encyclopedists, German Pietists, British diarists, American adventurers, and others. The figure of Augustine in the *Confessions* is revived for varied uses by philosophical autobiographers investigating issues in cognition and epistemology, how we know and how we know we know. In the *Autobiography of Giambattista Vico*, written between 1725 and 1731, Vico narrates his intellectual development as a philosophical historian and figure of all humanity. Vico's "true art of autobiography," in distinction to what he views as Descartes's false autobiography, is modeled on Augustine's mode of self-searching. In a fable written in the third person he presents himself as an autodidact engaged with the ancient problem of self-knowledge (Verene 71, 58, 48).

Another mode of autobiographical self-presentation occurs in *History of My Life*, the twelve-volume memoirs of Giacomo Casanova, who prided himself on being gifted as both a seducer and a memoirist. In contrast, Edward Gibbon, in the six versions of *Memoirs of My Life* written between 1788 and 1793, wavers between confidence and doubt about his mastery of the world and ability to shape his experience, as Roger Porter suggests.[4]

Jean-Jacques Rousseau employs another autobiographical strategy, reviving the genre of the confession before the French Revolution for very different ends. In his *Confessions* he turns the lens of his analysis on himself in all his licentious frailty, "confessing" not to some god in pursuit of conversion, but to a diverse "public" that rejects him and evokes his hostility. Rousseau's assertions about his project of self-representation are both well known and notorious: "I am commencing an undertaking, hitherto without precedent, and which will never find an imitator. . . . I am not made like any of those I have seen; I venture to believe that I am not made like any of those who are in existence. If I am not better, at least I am different" (3). His claim to being the exceptional subject, characteristic of much Romantic autobiography, is linked to his self-portrayal as natural man, in solitary quest of lost innocence in a corrupted society. Here confession becomes a method of self-justification and social indictment, as well as a medium for posing radical individuality.

If the *Confessions* celebrate a discourse of selfishness and egotism in pursuit of an ideal world, it also mirrors a self-reflexive imagination untiringly engaged in recording its own sensations, impressions, and motives. For some, Rousseau inaugurates modern autobiography, with his focus on childhood, his retrospective chronology, his radical individualism, and his antagonistic relationship to both his readers and posterity. For others, Rousseau's legacy in the *Confessions* is a radical individualism that privileges the white male citizen. For them, Rousseau inaugurates traditional autobiography, which, as we suggested in chapter 1, has become a suspect site of exclusionary practices. Rousseau's massive project of self-absorbed individualism continues to be an influential and controversial model of life narrative.[5]

New Subjects of Life Narrative in the Eighteenth Century

The eighteenth century saw an explosion in both the kinds and the sheer numbers of life narratives. New reading publics emerged with the rise in literacy, the expansion of print media, and the increased circulation of texts, goods, and people between Europe and the American colonies, and within both Europe and the colonies. In effect, there was a democratization of the institution of life writing. More and more people—merchants, criminals, middle-class women, ex-slaves—turned to life narratives as a means to know themselves and position themselves within the social world. We will consider two sites of such activity, in the American colonies and in England.

In retrospect, it has become clear that life narrative was one cultural location for negotiating the terms of the "New World" subject in the American colonies. In the context of settling the continent, life narrative took on added importance as people had to invent both their landscape and themselves. Outward exploration and inward exploration became coextensive, as Daniel Shea observes. This dual mapping of new terrains signaled "the flourishing of the Renaissance idea of the self as a microcosm in a period when the discovery and exploration of the macrocosm seemed to offer transformative possibilities directly to the person of the explorer" (Shea, "Prehistory of American Autobiography" 27).

Among the Puritans, Quakers, and other dissident religious communities in the New World, writers of spiritual autobiography found themselves in a dilemma: how could they validate narratives of conversion and salvation as authentic and irreversible when the self was "fallen"? Their autobiographical narratives indicate at once profound self-preoccupation and abject self-effacement. In these religious communities, too, the spiritual seeker was a profoundly public subject, commemorating the relationship of the introspective individual to the community of God's people. In different ways the mid–eighteenth century spiritual narratives of Elizabeth Ashbridge, Jonathan Edwards, and John Woolman read community and self through each other, in dialogue and dissent. The community's history and the individual's spiritual life narrative are interdependent, inextricable.

In the secular community self-writing became self-making, as can be seen in Franklin's foundational text of American republicanism. Franklin's self-examination, written in part in the same decades as Rousseau's, diverges sharply from that of the French philosopher in the social and prescriptive character of its self-examination. Aimed at molding the individual to the community, Franklin's autobiography represents the Rousseauian individualist as corrupt and unproductive in the new republic. It presents a flexible, pragmatic subject, adaptive to the needs and possibilities of the new republic and critical of the old world privileges of inherited status and legacy. Franklin secularizes the heritage of Puritan life narrative and emphasizes self-invention as an ethical rather than a spiritual project.

In Franklin's rhetorical drama, as Daniel Shea suggests, the "pose of casual self-invention" disarms readers with its provincial tone, its lack of interiority, and its notion of an endlessly revisable self, which enable "the cunning of its didactic design" to re-arm them (*Spiritual Autobiography* 38–39). Written over several decades and only published in the mid–nineteenth century, well after his death, Franklin's autobiography becomes a prototypical narrative for America's myth of the self-made man and the entrepreneurial republican subject, specifically marked as male, white, propertied, and socially and politically enfranchised.

In England, middle-class women who were sufficiently educated wrote letters (Mary Delany, Elizabeth Carter) and kept diaries (Hester Thrale,

Fanny Burney), seemingly the marginal forms of marginal subjects that since have been revalued as precise records of everyday life. Even as they wrote about themselves in what appeared to be a "free space of interiority beyond the boundaries of a gendered hierarchy in the unwomanly, the unspoken, and the undervalued," their writing of daily selves reproduced gendered ideologies that they both trouble and rescript. Other women, such as Charlotte Charke and Laetitia Pilkington, led more public lives and wrote "scandalous memoirs," encoding the sexual desire of an out-of-control female sensuality that escaped the control of the bourgeois family, at the cost of their own social status (Nussbaum 203, 179).

Other marginalized subjects struggled to find their own spaces of inscription. Take the case of slave narratives, which began to be recorded around 1750, in tandem with the intensification of the transatlantic slave trade. Many of the earliest slave narratives were by illiterate men, "as-told-to" recorders. A remarkable exception is *The Life of Olaudah Equiano, or Gustavus Vassa the African,* purported to be the life narrative of an Igbo West African captured as a child and enslaved on various merchant ships.[6] Equiano told a tale of escaping the repressive American colonies for the relative liberty of England, buying his freedom, and becoming a legislator active in repealing Britain's slave laws in 1806. Although this narrative traces a stirring journey to freedom, literacy, and masterful self-representation, its authenticity has been called into question as suspect (Carretta). If this allegation is substantiated, it will only suggest how important the discourse of the autobiographical had become as a means to imagine another life and identity and how salable autobiographical narratives had become in the marketplace of print culture.

The Romantic Subject of Lost Illusions

The struggle of marginal subjects for spaces of inscription becomes more prominent in the nineteenth century as, with the post-Revolutionary decline of aristocratic patronage, artists and writers move increasingly to the social margin. More dependent on selling their works in this less secure social position, writers began to rework the Romantic quest narrative to explore their own subjectivity outside the mainstream of national life (see Stelzig).

In the Romantic quest narrative, the autobiographical becomes an allegorical pursuit of an ideal or transcendent self desiring to merge with some "absolute" of nature, love, or intellect that is beyond the ego, that is sublime. The legacy of Rousseauian radical individualism was reshaped by Goethe in *The Sorrows of Young Werther*, an epistolary fictionalized life narrative of self-preoccupation to the point of suicide. *Werther* powerfully influenced the artistic self-portrayal of passionate obsession. Such Romantic writers in Europe as Novalis, Byron (in the pseudoautobiographical *Don Juan*), and Mary Robinson all in different ways engage this model of a self on a solitary quest. And Walt Whitman in *Specimen Days* and "Song of Myself" and Henry David Thoreau in *Walden* adapt the quest of the introspective seeker to the landscapes, both rural and urban, of the American Republic in crisis and transformation.

The most elaborate reflection on the growth of the poet's mind, cast as a retrospective autobiography of childhood, education, and external and internal voyaging, is William Wordsworth's extended poem *The Prelude*. The life of the artist is represented as that of a creative spirit, outside of and at odds with society, seeking to mirror his longing in the isolated grandeur of nature. (The legacy of this lyric autobiographical writing is seen in the early-twentieth-century works by such poets as T. S. Eliot, Ezra Pound, and Robert Frost.) Even life narrative treating the quest for the absolute ironically, as in Stendhal's diaries and *Life of Henry Brulard*, Thomas Carlyle's *Sartor Resartus*, or Thomas De Quincey's *Confessions of an English Opium Eater*, constructs what we might call a subject of lost illusions whose legacy can be discerned well into the twentieth century. Despite his critique of metaphysical selfhood, even Friedrich Nietzsche cannot fully extricate himself from this subjectivity, as *Ecce Homo* shows. Not all life narratives, of course, were as caught up in this dynamic of ideal, loss, and self-surrender, whether philosophical, political, or erotic. The narrator of Goethe's late and lengthy autobiography, *Truth and Poetry: From My Own Life*, looks back on Romantic idealism as a disease he overcame by immersion in the European classical tradition and relentless self-critique.

As the "modern" world exerted its conforming pressures on the Romantic subject, travel to "exotic" locales offered another avenue of escape. In narratives of exotic travel and erotic encounters, the traveler reimagined himself through exoticist tropes that had their genealogical roots in earlier travel narratives of biracial love, such as John Stedman's sentimental *Narrative of a Five Years' Expedition against the Revolted Negroes of Surinam*. But their most elaborate iterations emerged in the late nineteenth and early twentieth centuries. Through these tropes the traveler/narrator enacted his desire for the return of the repressed body, forced into routine conformity by the radical changes wrought by industrialization and urbanization (Bongie 12). In chronicling his experience of "going native," he enacted his surrender to the Other, and to the other in himself.

The subject of lost illusions is, however, conspicuously white and masculine in both its privilege to wander and its freedom from labor. Dorothy Wordsworth's *Journals* sketch a different set of daily preoccupations, as do the spiritual narratives of such African American "sisters of the spirit" (see Andrews) as Jarena Lee, Zilpha Elaw, and Julia Foote, or the letters and autobiographical fragments of such German writers as Rahel Varnhagen and Karoline von Günderrode. By midcentury George Sand (Aurore Dudevant Dupin) serializes a life narrative, *Story of My Life,* in a Parisian newspaper (1854–55) to raise money. Introducing the melodramatic structure of a popular novel into the telling of her life, and parodying the call to writing in Augustine's conversion in the *Confessions,* Sand's chatty text interpolates biographies of her parents, letters, sermons, stories of lovers and friends into the story of her early life and discovery of an inner voice. And throughout the last half of the century European and American women such as Harriet Martineau, Frances Trollope, Margaret Fuller, Nancy Prince, and Isabella Bird took to the roads and seas, bringing back home stories of adventures survived, accounts of knowledge gained, and/ or tales of "civilizing" colonized subjects. Often these narratives represented acts of female agency in the midst of continuing bourgeois constraints that coded travel as a male activity.

The Bildungsroman and the Bourgeois Subject

Perhaps the most influential genre of the nineteenth century was the bildungsroman, or novel of development. Writ large in such narratives as Goethe's *Wilhelm Meister's Apprenticeship,* Dickens's *David Copperfield,* Madame de Staël's *Corinne, or Italy,* and Charlotte Brontë's *Jane Eyre,* its structure of social formation unfolds through a narrative of apprenticeship, education in "life," renunciation, and civic integration into bourgeois society. The mode of the bildungsroman, as the pseudoautobiography of a fictional character distinct from the text's narrator, had some influence on forms of nineteenth-century life narrative and would be of growing significance in the twentieth. Its developmental model is evident, for example, in the autobiographies of John Stuart Mill, John Henry Newman, and Harriet Martineau, which in different ways use its paradigm of a self developed through education, self-directed "intellectual cultivation" through reading, and encounters with social institutions (Mill 45).

The bildungsroman narrates the formation of a young life as gendered, classed, and raced within a social network larger than the family or the religious community. But, as feminist scholars note, gendered norms differ for women, who historically have not chosen but been chosen (or not); who are not initiated into social life but retreat from participation; who awaken more to limitations than possibility (Fuderer 4–5). For women life narrators, then, the bildungsroman's model was inverted. This inverted structure of expectations disappointed by barriers of gender is implicit in such late-nineteenth-century works as the diaries of Alice James, for instance.

The structure of the bildungsroman is also implicit in many nineteenth-century slave narratives. Ex-slaves found a powerful rhetorical means of intervening in the repressive institution of slavery by telling or writing their narratives of enslavement, self-education, and quest for entry into the free society of American citizens. They at once testified to the circumstances of their degradation and the achievement of status as full human beings. The slave narrative became one of the most popular forms in the United States and Europe. In the nineteenth century hundreds of slave narratives began to be published, often by abolitionist societies of the northern United States. Unquestionably the most widely read of these now are *Narrative of the Life of Frederick Douglass* and *Incidents in the Life of a Slave Girl* by Harriet Jacobs.[7]

Douglass's *Narrative,* the first of three quite different and even contradictory accounts of his enslavement, fugitive days, and liberation, tells a story of conversion from an imposed mental enslavement to liberation as much through literacy and the creation of a community as through the struggle against and rejection of his slave status. Douglass writes as the subject of freedom, "a free man on free land," willing to indict the hypocrisy of Christian slavers. His narrative, important in the abolitionist cause before the Civil War, has been celebrated and taught in school curricula. Jacobs's narrative, by contrast, was long assumed to be the work of white abolitionist Lydia Maria Child, recording the story of pseudonymous Linda Brent. In the past three decades, with Jean Fagan Yellin's restoration and defense of Jacobs's text, has it gained recognition as a compelling narrative of the binds and brutality of the slave system for a young woman lacking a community of abolitionist sisters. But Jacobs's quest for liberation is at best ambivalently realized and troubled by the impossibility of either avoiding sexual encounters or achieving real economic and personal freedom. Douglass's subject of development and liberation is not realizable for Jacobs. Moreover, as William L. Andrews and Regina E. Mason show in their edition of the *Life of William Grimes, the Runaway Slave,* other long-ignored slave narratives fundamentally undermine the norms of social incorporation in the bildungsroman.[8]

American Subjects in the Nineteenth Century

Scholars in the past decade have begun to integrate nineteenth-century life narratives into the literary canon of the United States. For Lawrence Buell, rethinking American literary culture through the lens of autobiography studies involves paying serious attention to Douglass's *Narrative of the Life,* Emerson's *Journals,* Thoreau's *Walden,* and Whitman's *Specimen Days.* It means, as well, looking at generic inventions such as the carnivalesque of Franklinesque entrepreneurship in *The Autobiography of P. T. Barnum: Clerk, Merchant, Editor, and Showman, with His Rules for Business and Making a Fortune;* Lydia Sigourney's *Letters of Life,* the "first full-dress autobiography written by an American author of either sex whose primary vocation was creative writing" (Buell, "Autobiography in the American Renaissance" 60); and travel narratives such as John Neal's *Wandering Recollections of a Somewhat Busy Life: An Autobiography* (1869) and Francis Parkman's *The California and Oregon Trail: Being Sketches of Prairie and Rocky Mountain Life.* For Buell most of these autobiographers, particularly Whitman, are ambivalent about conventional, chronological narrative and adapt an "improvisational" and spontaneous style to resist its norm of linear plotting. While *Walden* pursues the symbolic "quest-into-nature-and-return story" of narratives of exploration and discovery, it also, Buell argues, portrays its "I" as untypical, its experience as mysterious, and its intricate autobiographical representation as inadequate to the complexity of the author ("Autobiography" 62, 64–65).

In the mid–nineteenth century American authors, then, employed multiple models of life narrative that introduce a tension between an "I"-centered model of the exceptional individual and one centered on events that either objectify or subordinate the "I" to communal discourses of identity, such as the narrative of conversion and the slave narrative (Buell,

"Autobiography" 64–65). If American myths of self-realization emerge powerfully in the life narratives of this century, most are also conflicted and unresolved.

After the Civil War autobiographical writing in the United States becomes more "self"-conscious, Susanna Egan argues, posing life writing not as memoir but as "history in the making," with the life narrator as a participant in that dialectical process ("'Self'-Conscious History"). In different ways Henry James, Henry Adams, Mark Twain, Booker T. Washington, and W. E. B. Du Bois locate themselves as subjects of American progress, if oftentimes with ambivalence.

The importance of affirming an American identity drives many life writings as, with westward expansion, people become increasingly mobile and migratory. Lucy Larcom nostalgically recalls her childhood in the mills of New England, from the "west" of an Illinois college in *A New England Girlhood*. Jane Addams in *Twenty Years at Hull-House* charts the significance of professional work to both her life and the immigrant community of Chicago as a means of making Americans and American history of its many immigrants at the century's turn.

The life narratives of Native Americans tell stories of mobility and migration from perspectives of loss and expropriation, often intermingled with other discourses of American subjectivity. Crucial to reading these narratives is the distinction Arnold Krupat makes about the production of life writings in these cultures that had not emphasized either the "auto" of the isolate individual or the "graph" or alphabetic writing of lives prior to contact. One kind, Krupat argues, is Indian autobiographies, which are "not actually self-written, but . . . of original, bicultural composite composition" and often composed by a white editor-amanuensis, a Native "subject" who orally presents a life, and a mixed-blood interpreter/translator in a process of unequal collaboration. The other kind is autobiographies by Indians, "individually composed texts . . . written by those whose lives they chronicle" (Krupat, "Introduction" 3). For example, in 1831, William Apess, in what is considered the "first" Native American life narrative in one's own words, "A Son of the Forest," mixes a narrative of exile from both his birth and adoptive families and a travel/adventure story with an account of his conversion to evangelical Christianity while negotiating his indigenous identity in an Anglo-American discourse that lacks a language for it. Zitkala-Ša in "Impressions of an Indian Childhood," however, contrasts her experience of growing up in an indigenous culture on a Sioux reservation and at a missionary school to show the brutal repressions of the latter conducted in the name of its civilizing and Christianizing missions. Her "sketches" at the turn of the twentieth century reflect on how an education intended to form her as a docile citizen in fact motivated her to reclaim the Indian culture being erased by assimilation and to narrate a personal history as a collective story of loss and a quest for dignity.

In the last half of the nineteenth century, too, in both the United States and England, the industrial revolution and the rise of the union movement led to the emergence of narratives by working-class people, as well as increased literacy among working classes and women. In the United States, narratives of immigrants begin to appear in the new century. Jacob Riis, in *The Making of an American,* writes and photographs his growing up as a Danish immigrant in the streets of New York from the perspective of an assimilated American, as does Dutch immigrant Edward William Bok in his Franklinesque *The Americanization of Edward Bok.* Mary Antin in *The Promised Land* and Sui Sin Far in such autobiographical sketches as "Sui Sin Far, the Half Chinese Writer, Tells of Her Career" and "Leaves from the Mental Portfolio of an Eurasian" show that making oneself an American, as both a personal and an exemplary figure, involves learning the value of the individual in a land of opportunity and promise. While this lesson was largely successful for most European immigrants (Bergland; Egan, "'Self'-Conscious History" 82), it was more ambiguous for indigenous peoples, immigrants from Asia and Africa, and Latinos and Latinas at the borders.

Recent scholarship has begun to focus increasingly on these other stories of Americanization among populations dominated and spoken for by the myth of the American melting pot. As Anne E. Goldman suggests, many early-twentieth-century Chicana women encoded the communal values of their heritage in everyday forms such as folkloric tales, cookbooks, and family narratives that can be read autobiographically as resistant to dominant cultural myths. Sau-Ling Cynthia Wong argues that immigration narratives among Chinese and Japanese Americans are by no means assimilationist, given the histories of racism both groups experienced in the United States, and points out that generational factors also reshape the story of Americanization ("Immigrant Autobiography").

For more politically radical autobiographers, such as Emma Goldman in *Living My Life* and Alexander Berkman in *Prison Memoirs of an Anarchist,* America is a corrupt land of greed and unequal privilege to be resuscitated by the international socialism propounded in the essays and manifestos of Rosa Luxemburg, Vladimir Lenin, and Leon Trotsky, and depicted by Maxim Gorky in the everyday miseries of life for the emergent urban subject in Russia. Although in the United States Mother Jones in her *Autobiography*, Charlotte Perkins Gilman in *The Living of Charlotte Perkins Gilman: An Autobiography*, Elizabeth Gurley Flynn in *I Speak My Own Piece: Autobiography of "The Rebel Girl*," and Dorothy Day in *The Long Loneliness: The Autobiography of Dorothy Day* link their autobiographical writing to social critique and a call for greater equity between the sexes and among classes, this representation of the autobiographical subject as interventionary social radical is, among Euro-American writers, male and female alike, less influential than is the presentation of immigrant Americans assimilated in the project of retrospectively writing their histories as new American subjects.

Conclusion

As this chapter's brief survey indicates, the history of autobiography in the West up to the latter half of the twentieth century cannot be read solely as literary history. Life writing in its multiple genres has been foundational to the formation of Western subjects, Western cultures, and Western concepts of nation, as well as to ongoing projects of exploration, colonization, imperialism, and now globalization. In the first decade of the twenty-first century, most prominently in the West, autobiographical discourse has become ubiquitous. As Jeff Bridges's character, Max Kline, says in the film *Fearless*, "Nobody apologizes anymore. They write a memoir."

Increasingly, people incorporate autobiographical genres, modes of address, and consciousness into their everyday lives. This contemporary fascination with confession and other modes of personal storytelling derives in part from the tenacious hold that the ideology of individualism has on Westerners. Americans in particular continue to be attracted to Horatio Alger–esque fantasies of the self-made individual overcoming adversity. In the contemporary culture of self-help, some people are also drawn to personal narratives of debasement and recovery as models for conversion, survival, and self-transformation. In many places, readers seek out life stories in which autobiographical subjects fracture monolithic categories that have culturally identified them, such as "woman" or "gay" or "black" or "disabled," and reassemble fragments of memory, experience, identity, embodiment, and agency into new modes of subjectivity. Others measure the impact of wars and cultural conflict in personal testimony—of child soldiers and displaced minorities, for instance. Around the world, readers confront contemporary investigations in subjectivity, such as those of Michel Leiris, Gloria Anzaldúa, Art Spiegelman, Bessie Head, Isabel Allende, Annie Ernaux, Günter Grass, J. M. Coetzee, and Orhan Pamuk, that mine the discontinuities, mobility, and transcultural hybridity of subjects-in-process.

In late capitalism, life stories, now the property of publishing houses and media conglomerates, circulate through local, national, and global markets as "hot commodities." With leisure time, disposable income, and heterogeneous desires for reading about other people's experiences, the audience for life stories expands in Western democratic nations and in pockets of modernity around the globe with increasingly literate populations. In the next chapter, we survey some contemporary genres of life storytelling in and beyond the West.

5

In the Wake of the Memoir Boom

Memoir is the Barbie of literary genres. It exaggerates the assets and invites the reader into an intimate alternative world, sometimes complete with a dream house. We hungrily buy and read memoir even as we express contempt for it. Memoirs are confessional and subversive; memoirs drop names. Memoirs print whispered secrets on their covers in 24-point type.

Susan Cheever

Whatever we call it—false consciousness, fantasy, or old-style ideology— there is, in each of our heads, a half-legible, half-secret text that makes sense of what we've done in life.

Orhan Pamuk, *Istanbul*

Over the past two decades, life writing has become a prized commodity in print and online venues. Publishers seek the next hot topic and market particular kinds of memoirs to niche audiences—for instance, coming-out stories to gay and lesbian readerships. Bookstores in airports and online companies such as Amazon.com bring these stories of other people's lives to customers whose responses may range from feel-good benevolence to titillation to compassion fatigue. To illustrate the range and variety of life stories, Appendix A, Genres of Life Narrative, provides brief definitions of modes, historical and contemporary, in writing and other media. While these categories overlap and their number is arbitrary (because narratives usually combine several genres, as in confession and apology), they project the capacious range of rhetorical acts, emplotments, and styles of self-presentation that mobilize autobiographical discourse to various effects.

Increasingly multifarious, life narrative includes forms that situate autobiographical subjectivity across diverse, discordant subject positions. Appendix A suggests that what is called "autobiography" is not at this historical moment (and, we would argue, never has been) a unified form, nor is it distinct from literary modes of either fiction or nonfiction. Most autobiographical narratives have addressed heterogeneous audiences, employed diverse kinds of storytelling, and presented disjunctive concepts of subjectivity and agency. Moreover, although new autobiographical media are emerging (see chapter 6 for a discussion of new visual, graphic, cinematic, and online forms), enduring forms, such as the diary and confession, persist. The coming-of-age narrative, although structured differently in premodern life writing from the post-Enlightenment bildungsroman, with its developmental ideology and integrative teleology, has been with us at least since ancient epitaphs. That is, even as the genres of life writing rework models of personal storytelling, they introduce innovations that adapt enduring templates.

In this chapter we survey some emergent forms that have recently gained prominence. These include the new-model national narrative; narratives of rights, testimony, incarceration, and reconciliation; embodiment stories of gender and sexuality, gastrography, and "conscious aging"; narratives of grief, mourning, and reparation; narratives of breakdown and breakthrough, illness, impairment, vulnerability, addiction, and recovery; autoethnography; ecobiography; and the celebrity self-advertisements of movie stars, sports heroes, and military leaders.[1]

Contemporary Bildungsroman

In autobiographical uses of the bildungsroman (or novel of development) we observe the persistence of the form and its adaptation to new kinds of stories. As noted in the previous chapter, this narrative of education, apprenticeship, and incorporation into society emerged in the late eighteenth and early nineteenth centuries, and remains a favorite way of narrating one's coming-of-age as a developmental story of forming consciousness. Some contemporary coming-of-age narratives in the West explore the psychic landscapes of a lost past (see Coe; Rooke) and of repressed childhood trauma, abuse, and patriarchal oppression. Contemporary postcolonial writers in particular are employing the bildungsroman form to cast their coming-of-age stories as encounters with powerful mentors at the cultural crossroads of metropole and (post)colony, where conflicting concepts of education and social value collide.

Theorists of narrative and modernity, recognizing the persistence of the bildungsroman, have explored its history and assessed its attraction and liabilities for contemporary writers in developing nations. Joseph

Slaughter, for instance, has elaborated the relationship of the bildungs-roman to the contemporary regime of human rights. Exploring the en-twined histories of the bildungsroman and human rights discourse in the West in the nineteenth century, Slaughter argues that the "realist" novel form of the bildungsroman not only projects and naturalizes its protago-nist as the self-determining individual with rights, but also incorporates its readers into the social sphere of the nation-state. "The *Bildungsroman* and human rights are cooperative technologies of incorporation," states Slaughter, "whose historic social work was to patriate the once politically marginal bourgeois subject as national citizen" (166). Contemporary post-colonial writers employing the form typically reshape the story of educa-tion as one of becoming alienated subjects of double legacies in ways that interrogate the form's ideology of development, self-determination, and incorporation of citizens into the new nation.

What Slaughter observes about the contemporary postcolonial novel usefully describes aspects of some postcolonial life writing using the bil-dungsroman. Bildungsroman—whether novel or life writing—written since the 1940s both within Europe and North America and in locations around the world undergoing uneven processes of decolonization and globaliza-tion participate in this process of projecting the subject as self-determining and incorporating contemporary readers into a global imaginary of uni-versal rights and responsibilities. As writers deploying the form test its limits, probe its ambiguities, reject its humanist norms, and intervene in the state violence it implicates, the postcolonial coming-of-age story be-comes a site of both reproduction of the individualist plot of development and the interruption of its troubling norms. In this way, contemporary uses of the bildungsroman form engage in disseminating claims to rights and registering conditions of rights violations; and the form itself "be-comes both a plot imposed by force and a potential space of refuge from and redress of state violence against the individual" (Slaughter 347).

Gayatri Spivak argues that for postcolonial women writers in particular autobiography has not been a congenial genre for women's self-reflexivity, given its traditional associations with universal individualism and posses-sive masculinity. And indeed, many postcolonial women writers elect the form of first-person fiction in writing personal stories. The deflection of confessional and self-exposing inquiry into imaginative forms of the novel in bildungsroman form takes experiential history as the ground but not the route of narration. This detour from life writing to novel renders post-colonial women writers less vulnerable to exoticization by metropolitan readers or to shaming within their own cultures.

Michelle Cliff's *Abeng* and *No Telephone to Heaven,* Maryse Condé's *I, Tituba, Black Witch of Salem,* Nawal El Saadawi's *Woman at Point Zero,* Mariama Bâ's *So Long A Letter,* Assia Djebar's *Women of Algiers in Their Apartment,* and Calixthe Beyala's *Your Name Shall Be Tanga* are examples of coming-of-age novels by postcolonial women writers who tactically use first- or third-person narrative to both displace and engage personal experience. Critics, notably Françoise Lionnet, have read these novels autobiographically, thereby acknowledging the permeable boundary of life writing and the novel. American Dave Eggers's writing of Valentino Achak Deng's autobiographical story as a Sudanese "lost boy" in the novel *What Is the What* also encodes layers of personal reference in ways that reference the bildungsroman and simultaneously deflect norms of traditional autobiography.

Nation, Citizenship, and Life Writing

Increasingly, life writing published since 2000 reflects the powerful transformations taking place in nations around the world and the realignment of national interests across regions of the globe. These narratives probe the relationship of modernity, the nation, and citizenship in the twenty-first century. Philip Holden has examined the "national autobiographies" written by political leaders who describe their struggles in anticolonial nationalist movements leading to the formation of independent nations of which they become "fathers." He asserts that the continuing production and popularity of these texts into the twenty-first century shows that the discourse of nationalist liberation movements remains an important one. Furthermore, he argues that not all life writing is postmodern, or transnational, or mistrustful of the Enlightenment legacy and processes of modernity that both shored up and were fostered by the modern nation-state.

The writings Holden discusses belong to a recognizable genre—the self-biography of the prenational leader—that, he rightly points out, often takes up the discourse of freedom developed in some slave narratives and other liberation struggles. But this mode is both complicated and ironized, we find, in such examples as Gandhi's *The Story of My Experiments with Truth* and *The Autobiography of Malcolm X.* And it is recontextualized in some instances by the history of alternative narratives. In her exploration of women's autobiographical writing in Turkey in the twentieth century, Hülya Adak suggests that the suppressed narratives of women activists such as Halidé Edib (Adivar) in *Memoirs of Halidé Edib,* the most prolific Ottoman Turkish woman writer of the early twentieth century, undercut certain claims of Mustafa Kemal Atatürk, the founder of the modern Turkish state who presents himself as Turkey's "author" in *Nutuk/The Speech,* his volumes of nationalist self-biography (see *A Speech Delivered*).

Increasingly, women from around the world are also producing narratives of their "rise" to public office. There are, of course, the official and unofficial biographies and the autobiographies of such famous figures as Hillary Clinton of the United States, Golda Meir of Israel, Angela Merkel of Germany (see Langguth), Helen Clark of New Zealand (see B. Edwards), and Ellen Johnson-Sirleaf of Liberia. But women in developing nations who have achieved high office are also writing versions of their rise to public prominence. From Pakistan, for example, have come several autobiographical narratives of political lives. The most widely read is Benazir Bhutto's *Benazir Bhutto: Daughter of the East*; others include Jahan Ara Shahnawaz's *Father and Daughter: A Political Autobiography,* Abida Sultaan's *Memoirs of a Rebel Princess,* and Salma Ahmed's *Cutting Free: The Extraordinary Memoir of a Pakistani Woman.* These are retrospective narratives that rehearse, through performative self-narrating, the progressive goal of women's advancement in the public sphere as viable candidates and effective politicians, despite the obstacles placed in their way. These subjects, too, claim their lives as embodiments of the modernizing nation.

In contrast, other narratives of nation by women use personal storytelling to reposition gendered citizenship. Given the U.S. "war on terror" and the rise of Islamic fundamentalism, it is not surprising that many narratives by women originate elsewhere but circulate in the West, where they are used in culture wars about the status of women in the Islamic states. Gillian Whitlock describes such autobiographical narratives as "soft weapons" in contemporary global politics. In the past decade, memoirs by Afghani and Iranian women have attained global prominence and have circulated, in several languages, throughout both literary and popular culture. In the next chapter we discuss the importance of Marjane Satrapi's *Persepolis* as an autographic story addressed to the West that offers both a critique of British and American imperialism and a revisionary history of the Iranian Revolution and the fundamentalism that maintains a dictatorial regime in Iran. Since 2000, several other memoirs by Iranian women have circulated internationally in English, among them the well-known *Reading Lolita in Tehran* by Azar Nafisi, *Lipstick Jihad: A Memoir of Growing Up Iranian in America and American in Iran* by Azadeh Moaveni, and *Iran Awakening* by Shirin Ebadi, who was awarded the Nobel Peace Prize in 2003 for her work on women's rights.

Nafisi, daughter of the mayor of Tehran before the revolution, was a professor of English literature at the University of Tehran who was expelled in 1981 for refusing to wear the veil and did not teach again until 1987. Her memoir chronicles how, in 1995, under surveillance by the authorities, she left the university and held regular secret meetings with seven of her female students at her home where they read and discussed great works of the Western tradition, such as Nabokov's *Lolita,* Flaubert's *Madame Bovary,* and the novels of Jane Austen, from a postrevolutionary Iranian perspective. In 1997, Nafisi emigrated to the United States, where she wrote the memoir (and became a university professor). "I left Iran, but Iran did not leave me," Nafisi notes, intertwining the pleasures of reading Western novels with nostalgia for a world and culture left behind. Some reviewers have noted the book's explicitly pro-Western stance and remarked on how it invites Western readers to reaffirm stereotypes of Iranian Islamicism, thereby providing a soft weapon in the "war on terror." (A second memoir, *Things I've Been Silent About: Memories,* appeared in 2009.)

Azadeh Moaveni's *Lipstick Jihad* takes another tack. A writer for *Time Magazine,* Moaveni becomes curious about an Iran she never knew (her family moved to California when she was a child) and relocated there for more than a year to write a memoir of discovering postrevolutionary Iran. Moaveni critiques the regime as a "culture of lies" but assesses the complex mixture of resistance and fundamentalist ideology informing a youth culture that is, beneath its surface proprieties, permeated by eroticization expressed in drugs, dancing, and sex. Her critique of the persistence of some gender-specific norms and the shattering of others with Iran's shift in national ideology and values suggests that no single story of the new nation is sufficient. (Moaveni's second memoir, *Honeymoon in Tehran: Two Years of Love and Danger in Iran,* continues this story.)

Another kind of response to shifts in concepts of gendered work and practices in the nation is articulated in *Iran Awakening: A Memoir of Revolution and Hope* by Nobel laureate Shirin Ebadi (with Azadeh Moaveni), which was published in sixteen languages but not in Farsi. As someone who had been, at age thirty-one, a leading judge before the revolution and critical of the United States–backed regime of the Shah, Ebadi remained in Iran, although she was gradually demoted and finally stripped of her position. At considerable danger to herself, she became a human rights lawyer protesting through the courts the premeditated killings of dissidents. In her memoir, she argues that Iran's legal system betrayed the revolution by diminishing women's rights but also narrates her ongoing challenges to the regime in the name of patriotism and morality. Although imprisoned in 2000 for videotaping the testimony of a key witness to the killing of a young activist during student riots in 1999–2000, Ebadi makes a case for social justice in the new nation and a progressive version of the Islamic Republic (see Boustany; Secor). Her complex negotiation of seemingly incompatible positions suggests how "double-voiced" and potentially dangerous to the writer such life writing of citizenship may be.

Rights Narratives and Allegations of Hoaxing

Life writing produced and circulated within contemporary human rights campaigns confronts readers with emotional, often overwhelming, accounts of dehumanization, brutal and violent physical harm, and exploitation. The speaker insists that the history of suffering and abuse he or she (or those for whom she or he speaks) experienced and remembered can no longer go untold. Often, witnesses understand and position themselves as members of a collectivity whose story must be recounted.[2]

Judith Butler suggests that the willingness to imagine oneself in the position of the other while remaining vulnerable before one's own opacity in giving an account of oneself importantly contributes to the human rights project of social justice and reconciliation after oppressive regimes and episodes of extensive violence *(Giving an Account of Oneself)*. Readers are asked to recognize the risks of witnessing, to validate suffering and survival, to confer a different status on those who have been disparaged by history, and to play a role in protecting the humanity and dignity of the other. Narratives of witness thus make an urgent, immediate, and direct bid for attention and call the reader/listener to an ethical response through their affective appeals for recognition. While there can be many unpredictable responses to the publication, circulation, and reception of personal narratives of suffering and loss, their scenes of witness entwine the narrator, the story, and the listener/reader in an ethical call to empathic identification and accountability, recognition, and oftentimes action (see Schaffer and Smith *Human Rights*).

Many kinds of testimonial life writing implicitly make the appeal for response on behalf of both single and multiple subjects. *Testimonios* emerging out of Latin American inscribe a collective "I" that voices stories of repression and calls for mobilizing resistance in ways that have influenced political struggle around the globe, as do Guatamalan Rigoberta Menchú's *I, Rigoberta Menchú* and Argentinian American Alicia Partnoy's *The Little School.* Partnoy's fictionalized "tales" powerfully combines the representation of incarceration as physical and mental torture with a testimonial call on behalf of a collectivity, many of whom did not survive. Other contexts of witnessing around the world encourage individual witnesses to join in collective action to bring a particular rights violation to public attention. This was the case of the former World War II sex prisoners whose witnessing and activism coalesced in the early 1990s when feminist activists in Korea and the Philippines sought out the women who had been brutally exploited by the Japanese military in its lands of occupation and supported their redefinition of that experience as one of violent rape and rights violation. Their stories have been collected in anthologies, and individual witnesses have spoken on college campuses in Australia and the United States. But as we noted earlier, anthologizing the stories of those witnessing a particular kind of suffering and harm can end in conforming individual narratives to a "master" script, thereby erasing differences among witnesses and stories (see Schaffer and Smith, *Human Rights* 123–52).

Contemporary narratives of witness often record the struggles of incarcerated subjects with dehumanizing systems and the forging or preserving of identity under duress. The focus of an increasing number of studies (see Barbara Harlow; Michael Hames-Garcia), prison memoirs critique state repression in particular national contexts. Such narratives include those that expose the contradictions of democratic nations such as the United States (Assata Shakur's *Assata: An Autobiography*; Eldridge Cleaver's *Soul on Ice*); the dangers of dissidence in new postcolonial nations (Ngũgĩ wa Thiong'o's *Detained: A Writer's Prison Diary*; Nawal El Saadawi's *Memoirs from a Women's Prison*); and the brutality of particular political regimes, such as South African apartheid (Ruth First's *117 Days: An Account of Confinement and Interrogation under the South African 90-Day Detention Law*; Breyten Breytenbach's *The True Confessions of an Albino Terrorist*; Nelson Mandela's *Long Walk to Freedom: The Autobiography of Nelson Mandela*);

and the military junta in Argentina (Jacobo Timerman's *Prisoner without a Name, Cell without a Number*). Stories of surviving incarceration project agency, resilience, and resistance and sometimes catapult the author/survivor to celebrity status. Readers in the West often interpret such stories as reinforcing the heroism of the single individual saying no to power and resisting the regime with integrity and purpose.

Another recent formation is the life writing of African child soldiers who tell shocking stories of coming of age as gun-toting, brutally violent young men captured and re-formed by campaigns of organized hyper-masculinization that turn them into perpetrators of violence. For example, in *A Long Way Gone*, Ishmael Beah tells of the coming of internecine war in Sierra Leone that destroyed his community and changed him and the boys with whom he escaped, first, into desperate wanderers and, upon capture, into drugged and brutalized trained killers. Beah's story of surviving his victimization and complicity and ultimately immigrating to the United States, where he was "rehumanized," was long a best-seller and made him a television celebrity. In 2007, however, Andrew Denton, an Australian interviewer, questioned the accuracy of dates and events in *A Long Way Gone*, suggesting it manifested troubling inconsistencies (Denton). The figure of the child soldier exploited by a brutal regime appeals to Western readers' fantasies of rescuing innocents under assault in civil wars whose complexity is not understood. As with the controversy about Menchú's narrative, child-soldier accounts may require readers to interrogate their own expectations about "evidence" and attend to differing conventions of storytelling.

Truth commissions in the aftermath of political repression and genocide have also prompted acts of witnessing. Over the past two decades, the majority of those bearing witness to profound degradation, vulnerability, and violence (psychic and physical) have been women. This was the case in the South African Truth and Reconciliation Commission (TRC) hearings, in which the witnesses at the victim hearings were preponderantly the mothers, wives, and daughters of those who had been tortured, murdered, or disappeared. Activists called attention to the fact that the terms of reference of the TRC failed to attend to gender-based violence, the harms suffered by women, including rape and social disintegration; in response, a series of women's hearings were held. But witnessing to rape publicly can revictimize women, who risk public shaming and ostracism (see Schaffer and Smith, *Human Rights* 68–69).

Nonetheless, the willingness to come forward to testify, however problematic in the context of human rights protocols and institutions, has produced critical interventions that bring to public attention the erasure of the kinds of violence suffered by women in contexts of radical harm. Marie Béatrice Umutesi's *Surviving the Slaughter: The Ordeal of a Rwandan Refugee in Zaire* is a case in point. Her narrative of genocide and survival combines the survivor's tale of violence, displacement, and vulnerability with the professional sociologist's vantage point of analytical objectivity. Umutesi's experience as a refugee of the Rwandan genocide displaced to a camp in Zaire motivates her journey through the recollected madness of unleashed violence and sanctioned human abandonment as she attempts to answer the question, "What led us to this extremity?" while her standpoint as a professional sociologist enables her to distance herself as she contemplates a time of horrific events.

In the South African context women have produced alternative witness stories that probe issues of perpetration as well as victimization. Antjie Krog, who covered the TRC as a journalist for the South African Broadcasting Company, reproduced witness testimonies in *Country of My Skull* in her own act of witness to the suffering and pain of the people who appeared before the TRC. A South African of Boer heritage, Krog weaves through the stories of the TRC her personal tale of incomprehension and disintegration, and her acknowledgment of her position as a beneficiary of apartheid, and makes a visionary call for a new future. In placing testimonies, analysis, and memoir side by side, Krog composes an autocritical collage in which political and personal discourses interrogate one another. Krog has been challenged for using the voices of black witnesses in her narrative and for including fictionalized scenes; but her effort to ponder the ambiguities and affective complexities of her identity as a South African of Boer ancestry offers one model for a transcultural ethics of care and citizenship (see Schaffer and Smith "Human Rights, Storytelling"). Another compelling narrative is that of Pumla Gobodo-Madikizela, a TRC commissioner and psychologist. Her book, *A Human Being Died That Night,* chronicles a series of meetings she had with Eugene De Kock, one of the most vilified of perpetrators witnessed throughout the TRC, after he was imprisoned for his crimes. In this portrait of a perpetrator, Gobodo-Madikizela entwines a quest narrative involving the discovery of the other in herself with a meditation on reconciliation.

Narratives attesting to human rights violations shape life writing to particular ends, raising complex questions about the invisibility and lack of power of those who suffer. They enter the dialogue about what constitutes a rights violation, as well as what contributes to suffering and trauma. They register the efficacy of witnessing, for witnesses and for organized networks of political activists, at this political moment. They expose how the United Nations and nation-based commissions operate by protocols and terms of reference, soliciting stories yet constraining the kinds of stories that can be told. They suggest that witnesses who find a sympathetic audience may also be subject to retraumatization and continuing violence. Moreover, audience reaction to stories of profound suffering and harm cannot be predicted. While some may respond to an ethical call to recognition, others may experience compassion fatigue. And, as recent allegations of hoaxing suggest, there are inevitably interested parties who seek to discredit the narrative told, as well as the witness. Thus the reception of narratives of witness troubles who can tell the story and speak for others, and what kinds of stories are likely to gain an audience and readership.

Admittedly, the rhetorical urgency that drives acts of testimonial witnessing in memoirs is vulnerable to exploitation by celebrity-seeking narrators eager to participate in international dialogues around the harm to victims (often women and/or children) who have been menaced by violent patriarchs upholding tradition (for example, under Islamic or Hindi law). The exaggerated or fabricated versions of events they tell may be readily accepted as truth by sensation-seeking or concerned readers who accord truth-value to stories that identify unproblematic victims and perpetrators. As gender stereotypes circulate through human rights discourse and activism, the possibility of exploitation grows, not least because the figure of the victim is often feminized as an oppressed subject of tradition or political oppression—passive, physically and sexually vulnerable, and emotionally overwhelmed by the act of remembering in public. Some Western responses to the condition and status of women in Islamic countries and cultures are an example of this dynamic. Consider *Forbidden Love* by Norma Khouri, which chronicles the illicit romance in Jordan she purportedly witnessed between her friend Dalia and a Christian boyfriend culminating in an honor-killing by Dalia's father and brothers. This apparent memoir of witness to gender-based honor-killing was enthusiastically received in Australia, until the *Sydney Morning Herald* exposed Khouri's "I-was-there" story as a fraud in summer 2004 (see Knox) and her publisher, Random House Australia, withdrew the book. Subsequent evidence suggests that Khouri's memoir was indeed a hoax (see Whitlock, *Soft Weapons* chapter 5). What such a case exposes is the economic and ideological investment in narratives of victimhood at a historical moment of tension between Islamic nations and the West, intensified by ideological polarization and increasing global consumption of some life writing composed as simplistic and sensationalist pastiche.

Narratives of Grief, Mourning, and Reparation

The success as a memoir and a Broadway play in New York of Joan Didion's *The Year of Magical Thinking* and in London of Richard McCann's *Just A Boy: The True Story of a Stolen Childhood* suggests that there is a growing audience for life writing focused on grief and mourning. Didion, to whose memoir we will return, recounts her inability to register her husband's sudden death; McCann narrates his memory of the wrenching loss of his mother in a murder. Such narratives of loss are by no means new. James Ellroy's *My Dark Places*, which details with clinical exactitude his boyhood memory of learning that his mother was violated and strangled in late-fifties Los Angeles and the ensuing police procedures that found no killer, is a cult classic. In several recent memoirs, however, narration acts ambivalently as memorialization of mourning and its melancholic refusal.

Nancy K. Miller has trenchantly suggested that "autobiography—identity through alterity—is also writing against death twice: the other's and one's own." For Miller, "every autobiography, we might say, is also an auto-thanatography," because the prospect of nonexistence looms inescapably ("Representing Others" 12). In making a textual record of a life, Susanna Egan asserts, autothanatography "focus[es] on illness, pain, and imminent death as crucial to the processes of that life" (Egan, *Mirror Talk* 224). When parents mourn the loss of a child, they probe the grief of outliving one's own progeny, of youth lost to war or accident or illness. In mourning, parents, siblings, extended family members, partners, and friends are also grieving about their own impending mortality and the menace of life-threatening illness.

In this age of pervasive communication and the online circulation of private emotions, new modes of memorialization and vulnerability to loss register transience and grief in more public forms than the family album traditionally did. Memoirs of grief are often passed from hand to hand as how-to guidebooks, serving as contemporary books of consolation. When the bereaved write memoirs of those lost to them as a form of grief work, they may seek repair or emotional compensation (see Nelson *Damaged Identities, Narrative Repair*). And the one who is dying may also seek the consolation of enduring in another medium, or recording his own transience, as does filmmaker Tom Joslin, whose *Silverlake Life* entwines excerpts from his films with footage of his condition.

Other aspects of narratives of grief and mourning address larger social, cultural, and political issues. Since the 1980s, what we might call the technologies of thanatography have been employed to express grief and outrage about those who succumbed to HIV/AIDS. In a life writer such as Paul Monette, a history of coming out as "always already" gay was linked to the romance of partnership, the story of struggle against social prejudice and economic disparity, and a diaristic chronicle of his lover's decline. Monette's memoirs (*Borrowed Time: An AIDS Memoir, Becoming a Man: Half a Life Story,* and *Last Watch of the Night: Essays Too Personal and Otherwise*), like many others, both confront and counter social intolerance of homosexuals and the linkage of gay sexuality to a culture of drug addiction and perversity. In such examples constructing memoir becomes an act of mourning not only personal loss but collective vulnerability and communal loss.

Memoirs using thanatography as a public form of mourning are finding new ways to tell stories of loss. Didion begins *The Year of Magical Thinking* with the sudden death, one night at dinner, of her husband of nearly forty years. Over several months, the narrator observes her own nonrational responses to the event, acts aimed at bringing him back or denying that his death really happened. This process is complicated by the sudden and ultimately fatal illness of their thirty-eight-year-old daughter, Quintana, who requires extensive hospitalization. Crafting a raw prose to evoke her feelings of pain and rage, Didion refuses conventional frames for understanding how this uncharted experience redefines being a "partner" and "mother." She interweaves citations from poets, psychologists, doctors, and etiquette advisers, as intertexts to her own sense of chaos that enable her to continue writing about loss. Refusing the comfort that writing such a story is supposed to bring—the healing of "scriptotherapy"—Didion insists on the fragmentary process of writing grief and articulates a vulnerability rendered in, but not contained or resolved by, life writing.

By contrast, the memoir by Haitian American author Edwidge Danticat, titled *Brother, I'm Dying,* is a generational narrative explicitly linking political and personal stories. Danticat was born in Haiti but left to join her immigrant parents in New York before the Tonton Macoutes, brutal soldiers of the Duvalier regime, ravaged the country, including the homes of her relatives remaining there. Although her father, Mira, a proud salesman, had to spend his American years driving a taxi, his brother Joseph experienced different forms of loss of home, position, and health in Haiti. As she focuses on their deaths within months of each other, the larger story of a family riven by inequities in two nations charges the diasporan stories of immigration. Connecting her extended family to centuries of national history, Danticat foregrounds the intersection of personal, communal, national, and transnational histories of colonial violence and relocation.

Although reviewers praised the "healing power" of this family story, Danticat is, like Didion, critical of the casual violence that narrating the brothers' deaths reveals. Her uncle, who had lost his voice to a radical laryngectomy, left Haiti at eighty-one and was detained by U.S. agents on arrival; he died a day later. Her father wasted away from pulmonary fibrosis. Both were buried in a remote New York cemetery, far from home. Concluding her memoir, "I wish I knew that they were offering enough comfort to one another to allow them both not to remember their distressing, even excruciating, last hours and days" (288), Danticat refuses the comfort that writing grief supposedly brings and underscores the vulnerability of refugees in the Americas.

Although the boundaries between narratives of witness and narratives of mourning are not easily drawn, some distinctions can be made. Narratives of witness are primarily directed at campaigns for human rights against state-generated or rebel-generated violence. The witness seeks to tell a story of radical injury and harm and to claim the stage for a narrative counter to the official story of the aftereffects of violence. Narratives of mourning, by contrast, are targeted at chronicling and contemplating the loss of a loved one, sometimes to achieve consolation, sometimes to acknowledge that consolation may never come. The distinction is, however, slippery because narratives of witness to the experience of violence and radical harm often mourn the loss of a beloved child or spouse or a younger self lost to the brutality of war, genocide, or upheaval, as in memoirs by former child soldiers.

Online sites of "collective" mourning that have emerged on the Web are also producing new formations of witnessing and mourning. Online communities now memorialize and grieve the death of celebrities or the victims of much-publicized events that resonate with the public. For example, a Web site is dedicated to the twenty-three young women murdered at the University of Montreal in 1989 (see McNeill "Death and the Maidens"). Similarly, sites of mourning were posted for those killed in the World Trade Center attacks and for the rescue workers who died in rescue efforts. Other large-scale public events—the train bombings in Madrid in 2003, Hurricane Katrina's drowned and dislocated victims in 2005—have become occasions for creating online communities that share their grief and loss by posting blogs, photographs, poems, and memorabilia. These sites establish new templates for expressing grief. Because they are interactive, they serve not just those close to the dead loved ones but a network of strangers whose affective relationships are sustained by participation in an extended community of mourners. Recent uses of mourning in and through life writing have prompted scholars to reconceptualize notions of trauma and its narration to account for a diversity of experiencs of violence and suffering. (In chapter 8 we briefly explore contemporary theorizing of trauma.)

Narratives of Breakdown and Breakthrough: Illness, Impairment, Vulnerability, and Addiction and Recovery

Illness Narratives

The body, in its senses and materiality, has long been a central site for remembering the past and envisioning a future. Writers positioned at the margins of discourse at various historical moments—women, slaves and colonized subjects, the dislocated and disabled—have narrated bodily experiences as a way to intervene in social arrangements while seeking to ameliorate their conditions. Increasingly, people are chronicling their journeys through illness, diagnosis, treatment, and survival as stories of self-reinvention, as Reynolds Price does in *A Whole New Life*, about his recovery from spinal cancer. In *Squint: My Journey with Leprosy*, social worker and activist José P. Ramirez Jr. chronicles the early struggle to find an adequate diagnosis for increasingly severe symptoms. The narrative reconstructs his teenage journey in a hearse to the United States' only leprosarium in Louisiana and his relocation in a much-misunderstood and shunned community. His memoir not only tells the story of survival and recovery; it also explores the cultural construction of the "leper" as a subject of God's punishment rather than a person living with Hanson's disease. Narrative acts of reclaiming a body that has been stigmatized or objectified by medical science often resist naming the body as abnormative and voice critiques of the damaged body as a social construction of Western medicine.

The burgeoning corpus of life writing about illness and disability, G. Thomas Couser suggests, often situates bodies as recovered and revalued, even if the impairment or illness persists. Narratives of illness and disability proffer stories of loss and recovery at the same time that they function as a call for increased funding for research, new modes of treatment, and more visibility for those who have been assigned the cultural status of the unwhole, the grotesque, the uncanny. In what Couser calls the "some body memoir" the narrator foregrounds the organs and desires of the literal body ("Introduction"). In HIV/AIDS memoirs, for example, memories of caring and loving are entwined with arguments for the destigmatization of the disease, thereby intervening in national and international debates about how to signify and respond to the pandemic. The narratives and performances of gay and transgendered activists often engage gendered and racialized bodies and the differential treatment given these bodies within both medical and larger cultural discourses in order to assert an increasingly vocal and complex community. Women living with cancer or other degenerative diseases such as multiple sclerosis may also address the cultural desexualization of the injured or modified female body, as do Audre Lorde in *The Cancer Journals* and *A Burst of Light,* Joyce Brabner and Harvey Pekar in *Our Cancer Year,* Jo Spence in *Putting Myself in the Picture,* Hannah Wilke in the installation project *Intra-Venus,* Nancy Mairs in her collections of personal essays describing the experiences of living with multiple sclerosis, and many other narratives.

Activist Disability Narratives

Social movements to address rights for the disabled have helped to produce memoirs written by those with disabilities and impairments. Initially, many life writers tended to portray themselves as victims and figure disability as a personal illness or tragedy to be overcome by extraordinary effort. But a recent shift in disability life writing repositions the body and, according to Susannah B. Mintz, refuses the familiar scripts of inspiration and triumph-over-adversity to address "the simultaneous fact of the flesh and scriptedness of subjectivity . . . crafting embodied selves through the revisionary properties of language" (212), a topic she explores more fully in *Unruly Bodies*. Rights activists argue that, if cultural conditions were changed, impaired individuals could be accommodated in society; and they insist that the social meaning of disability is stigmatizing and degrading to those with disabilities, because discourses of "disability" reproduce able-ist norms that encode the differences of those with various forms and degrees of impairments as abnormative (Gerschick 1264). Rosemarie Garland Thomson notes the analogical relationship of disability and gender as socially constituted axes of identity: "Disability, like femaleness, is not a natural state of corporeal inferiority, inadequacy, excess, or a stroke of misfortune. Rather, disability is a culturally fabricated narrative of the body, similar to what we understand as the fictions of race and gender. The disability/ability system produces subjects by differentiating and marking bodies" ("Integrating Disability" 5). Couser's critique of *autopathography*, a term coined by Anne Hunsaker Hawkins for patients' stories of illness or disability, has also spurred this reorientation. Couser now argues that *autosomatography*, a more formal term for the "some body memoir," is a more useful concept for designating life writing about illness and disability (Couser, private correspondence).

Some recent memoirs experiment with alternative genres of the autobiographical that are explicitly in dialogue with the social construction of their narrators' identities as differently abled and the social history of abnormative bodies. This "writing back" to conventional victim narratives of wounded suffering calls for social change. Especially in women's memoirs, the narratives enact or perform alternative subjectivities that claim the possibility of a sexualized body distinct from representations of disabled women as either desexualized or hypersexualized. In positioning themselves as disabled subjects who address the history of their own marginalization, disabled writers reframe their impairment by refusing the diagnosis of disability or stigmatized abnormality; but this self-presentation may come with the risk of making a spectacle of oneself.

Recent narratives expose some of the stakes of writing a disabled life in both its vulnerability and its materiality. In *Blind Rage: Letters to Helen Keller*, Georgina Kleege engages with the autobiography of the deaf and blind Keller, *The Story of My Life* (written in 1903 when Keller was twenty-three with the help of her teacher Anne Sullivan), as well as Keller's subsequent letters and later narratives. Kleege troubles Keller's portrayal of the helpless, trusting female child and contrasts it to her own experience of losing sight. Employing the concept of blind rage to signal her quarrel with the "plucky, chirpy self-reliance" expressed in Keller's narratives and letters, Kleege writes, "You set an impossible standard. You with your cheerfulness, your stiff upper lip, your valiant smile in the face of adversity" (190). In both critiquing Keller as "the first disability poster child" (192) and acknowledging that the trailblazer ironically cannot speak to her, Kleege stages an engagement with a disabled other that challenges the disability paradigm of silent, valiant, female suffering and suggests a mode of assertive rereading of bodies.

Similarly, Stephen Kuusisto in *Planet of the Blind* narrates his experience of passing as sighted throughout his childhood and indicts social practices that stigmatize and marginalize the "blind." And Anne Finger in *Elegy for a Disease: A Personal and Cultural History of Polio* takes issue with her own positioning as "paralyzed" to focus on a cultural condition that has made it difficult for her to negotiate her life. As Simi Linton asserts in *My Body Politic,* forming collectivities in disability studies at this time enables people to refuse being identified as pathological or abject. Acting collectively, they refuse a marginal location as outsiders and critique "how disability is represented in all kinds of texts—in literature, film, the annals of history."[3]

While Jean Dominique Bauby's posthumously published memoir *The Diving Bell and the Butterfly* did not become the sensation in the Anglophone world that it became in France, Julian Schnabel's 2007 film of the book brought it to an international public. Readers are first struck by the difficulty of its transcription. Bauby, a victim of "locked-in" syndrome after an auto accident that left only his left eye unparalyzed, blinked a code for the letters of each word of his story to an amanuensis. The narrative itself, however, presents a fierce effort not just to remember but to reinhabit moments of his past, each enclosed in a gemlike chapter and impelled by the metaphor of self in his title. As both narrative and testament, Bauby's memoir registers agency from a condition of seemingly impossible disability and joins the ranks of moving life narratives of dying, such as Harold Brodkey's *This Wild Darkness* and Anatole Broyard's *Thanatography: Intoxicated by My Illness.*

As with earlier wars, the American war in Iraq has generated a spate of narratives that encompass physical and psychological wounds. Alex Vernon notes that the conventions of the war memoir focus on "what war does to men as well as what men do in war" (165). Such memoirs often involve submission and the soldier's acknowledgment of powerlessness. But some war memoirists, such as Tim O'Brien, rework the form in an act of self-construction that changes its dynamic. Contemporary life writing about the Iraq War focuses on post-traumatic stress disorder (PTSD) as a diagnostic category and lived experience, the afterlife of wounding in devastated lives, and the struggle to adjust to prosthetics. The memoir by Bob and Lee Woodruff, *In an Instant: A Family's Journey of Love and Healing,* links the story of the severe head wound Bob Woodruff suffered while working as a foreign correspondent in Iraq and its aftermath to a critique of both medical intervention and American intervention in Iraq.

In the wake of the human genome project, a new kind of illness narrative focuses on the issue of life scripting. Such narratives will likely become a growth industry to explore lived experience in relation to the coding of the gene and genetic inheritance. Alice Wexler's *Mapping Fate: A Memoir of Family, Risk, and Genetic Research* was one of the first memoirs to link living with Huntington's chorea to questions of how to live when one's life is predetermined in a way beyond human agency.

Finally, we note the movement in medical schools across the country to develop the curriculum of what is now called narrative medicine (see Rita Charon's *Narrative Medicine: Honoring the Stories of Illness*). This movement attends to the kinds of exchanges that occur in doctor-patient relationships and seeks to equip professionals to listen to and for patients' stories. Emphasizing the role of the auditor in doctor-patient exchange, the field of narrative medicine asserts that empathic listening can facilitate a more informed and nuanced ethical response to the patient and the condition and situates individual stories within emerging bioethical concerns.

Breakdown and Breakthrough Lives

Although mind and body interact across a permeable border, it is important to distinguish narratives of mental breakdown or psychological vulnerability from those of physical impairment and illness because of different challenges in narrating the story as well as in the discourse around and treatment of such illnesses. The life narrator describing a breakdown from an asserted position of recovery is always suspect. How can memoirists authorize themselves as postbreakdown writers? "Given these instabilities [of diagnosis, treatment, and side effects], plus the stigma attached to mental illness," notes Timothy Dow Adams, "personal narratives in this subgenre are always filled with uncertainties on every level" ("Borderline Personality" 108). One suggestive critical approach is to read them as "narratives of catastrophe," as Miriam Fuchs has done in *The Text Is Myself.*

The paradoxes of telling a story of breakdown and breakthrough have been explored in Kay Redfield Jamison's *An Unquiet Mind* and William Styron's *Darkness Visible: A Memoir of Madness.* Lauren Slater's *Lying,* which tells of the physical and psychic effects of enduring bouts of epilepsy, deliberately blurs the boundary between what is viewed as physical disability and mental illness, but also foregrounds challenges to telling a credible story. In Susanna Kaysen's *Girl, Interrupted,* explored in chapter 2, the adult narrating "I" returns to the scene of her early institutionalization in the late 1960s, juxtaposing her narrated "I"'s version of a two-year stay in her late teens at McLean Hospital with the implicit narrative created by her interspersed succession of documents from the case file obtained by the older narrator. Thus the narrator uncannily exists in both worlds simultaneously. As the putatively recovered or "sane" narrating "I" and the institutionalized, "crazy," experiencing "I," she holds two socially constructed categories—normalcy and abnormalcy—in tension. Although Kaysen's narrating "I" works to establish a rapport with readers that will persuade us that her documented diagnosis is erroneous, at key points she shifts her narrative position to an edgy one at the border of sanity, enacting a move that figures borderline personality itself. Even as the narrator asks readers to accord her legitimacy as a fully confessing narrative subject, therefore, she both produces and undermines the truth effect of her narrative, marking the boundary between the fabulated and the documented as unstable.

A confusion of conditions may also characterize stories about eating disorders. In Marya Hornbacher's *Wasted,* and in anorexia blogs, the etiology of the disease transforms into mental pathology—a compulsive need to discipline the aberrant body. In narratives of anorexia the compulsions of the condition sometimes resonate in the compulsive quality of the narrating "I," undermining the reader's confidence in the healing and breakthrough narrated by the writer.

As shown in narratives of "talking back" to the authority of medical doctors, from Charlotte Perkins Gilman's *The Yellow Wallpaper* to Freud's patient the Wolf Man (Sergius Pankejeff) and his 1971 response to his pathologization, titled *The Wolf-Man,* there are powerful motives for writing narratives of mental breakdown and recovery.[4] Life writing may be used as a critique of the gendered and dehumanizing treatment accorded by institutions to vulnerable people, the way that case studies medicalize body and mind, and the orthodoxy of treatment regimes.

Addiction Narratives

Life writing chronicling addiction and recovery is hardly new, as De Quincey's *Confessions of an English Opium Eater* reminds us. But several changes in public life in the past three decades—the proliferation of self-help movements, the rise of psychopharmacology, the increase of drug and alcohol addiction in the middle class, and the shifting cultural status of addiction as less a moral than a medical condition—have altered the stories being told. In the United States, Elizabeth Wurtzel's *Prozac Nation* and Carolyn Knapp's *Drinking: A Love Story* were best-sellers in the 1990s that dramatized both addictive states and the process of "cure." Wurtzel's narrative privatizes addiction as an individualized fable of being lost and then found. Knapp renders alcoholism in a seductive and intoxicating prose that the book's second half, about finding support in an Alcoholics Anonymous (AA) group, cannot counterbalance. Other narratives, by contrast, have situated addiction within the context of structural inequalities of economic, social, political, and cultural disenfranchisement. Augusten Burrough's *Dry: A Memoir* mingles his story of alcoholism with a critique of AA and heterosexism from his position as a gay writer-editor. This larger cultural critique notably characterizes Native American memoir writing. Janet Campbell Hale's *Bloodlines,* for example, situates addiction in her family within a communal history of Native people experiencing centuries-long structural injustice that fosters addiction. For Hale, the addicted subject is located within the dysfunctional family, and the struggle with addiction is symptomatic of what has been denied or suppressed in oppressive conditions.

In many narratives of addiction, confessing to self-degradation and loss of control, then tracking its effects, become stages in the process of recovery. That template mirrors the steps of healing practiced by such self-help groups as AA. Diary writing or journaling serves as a form of testimony like that given at meetings, making such life writing a form of what Suzette Henke terms "scriptotherapy." Becoming able to write the addiction narrative thus becomes part of recovery. But the use of diary or journal writing as part of addiction therapy can also enforce a Foucauldian self-surveillance that conforms the writing subject to prescriptive norms.

Like narratives of suffering discussed earlier, addiction narratives have become commodified as conversion stories and are circulated broadly to readers eager for tales of abasement and recovery. In the increasingly depersonalized and dispersed communities of late capitalism, readers seek the intimacy of a one-on-one reading experience, imagining a personal connection with a narrator whose story of addiction resonates with their own struggles to find "wholeness" and "meaning." For young adults navigating the perils of the singles world, for parents and friends struggling to cope with addicted loved ones, such memoirs promise an intimate engagement with and potential knowledge about the addicted subject, as well as the hope that recovery is possible. As suggested by the scandal of James Frey's infamous addiction story *A Million Little Pieces,* published as a memoir, touted on *Oprah,* exposed as a hoax, then reissued as a novel, for some readers it may not matter if the story of addiction and recovery is in fact "true," as long as they can experience it as compelling and convincing.

New-Model Narratives of Embodiment: Gastrography; Conscious Aging; Sexualized Subjects

Gastrography

An interest in how life writing embodies materiality has also generated new kinds of memoirs and subjects that were formerly relegated to its margins. Consider the popularity of the food memoir as a way to tell stories of family and nation, ethnic heritage, and diasporan mixing. Although food has been a subject of narrative for as long as there have been cookbooks and eating diaries, the food memoir now enjoys a wide audience in many life writing venues and enables new reflections about the interplay of production and consumption. *Gastrography,* a term coined by Rosalia Baena, offers readers tasty pleasures and "food" for self-revision.

Some memoirs conjoin the story of preparing and eating food with the discovery of a vocation. Julia Child's *My Life in France* mingles travel memoir with the story of collaboratively writing the cookbook that brought her international fame. In *Tender at the Bone* and two subsequent memoirs, *Comfort Me with Apples* and *Garlic and Sapphires,* food critic Ruth Reichl chronicles how growing up in a dysfunctional home in the 1950s was mitigated by the pleasures of cooking, eating, and becoming an accomplished cook. Reichl supplements her story with recipes for gastric self-improvement such as the vegetarian casserole recipe from her Berkeley commune days. The food memoir incorporates food-laced memories that feed readers' desire to redefine themselves by both imagining pleasures and cooking them up, as a way of enacting the life chronicled.

Memoirs linking ethnicity and food also register difference and specify the coordinates of a writer's cultural identity, as in "soul food memoirs." Nikki Giovanni in *Quilting the Black-Eyed Pea,* for example, describes her grandmother's meatloaf as a metaphor for her family's story over generations. Austin Clarke in *Pig Tails 'n Breadfruit: A Culinary Memoir* incorporates ethnic food in a critique of how economic poverty and cultural richness were mixed during his childhood in Jamaica. Vertamae Smart-Grosvenor in *Vibration Cooking; or, The Travel Notes of a Geechee Girl* links recipes from the social context in which she made soul food dishes to stories of African Americans who passed through her life. And Esmeralda Santiago in *When I Was Puerto Rican* uses extended descriptions of Puerto Rican food, recipes, and instructions for eating a guava to reference the tangible sensuousness of her childhood that is unimaginable in the "apple" world of the United States.

More globally, in our age of internationalized cuisine, food can function as an evocation of the particularity of cultures and regions that life writers may imagine only in negative stereotypes. In *The Language of Baklava,* Diana Abu-Jaber interweaves the pleasures of smelling and eating the flavors of her father's Jordanian past with the family's negotiation of ethnicity in Los Angeles. The narrative gesture of including recipes offers a kind of gift to readers. Traditional foods become a part of the cultural folklore that gastrography revives and revalues in calling people to their communities of origin and educating the dominant community about histories and cultures occluded in urban life.

Life writing invoking food as both memory and metaphor may index a shift in subjectivity. A life narrator's invoking of a particular food may serve multiple purposes. It may reference everyday life and project cultural identity. Or it may transubstantiate an object, changing it into something else by interweaving the remembered pleasure of eating a food with the politics of hunger and scarcity as a sign of class or economic positioning. It may discuss particular diets as indicative of colonial regimes. Some gastrographies engage food to focus on self-sufficiency. In Barbara Kingsolver's *Animal, Vegetable, Miracle: A Year of Food Life,* a narrative of one year of eating only what was grown on her farm, food becomes a means to reorient herself to nature. Similarly, Wendell Berry's *The Art of the Commonplace: The Agrarian Essays of Wendell Berry* connects his life as an organic farmer to the seasonal cycle.

But gastrography can also be a dysphoric diagnosis of dysfunction. The autobiographical documentary film by Morgan Spurlock, *Super Size Me,* chronicles the internal damage done to the filmmaker's system by a diet exclusively of McDonald's fast food that he followed for six months. Life writing about anorexia, such as Hornbacher's *Wasted,* tracks a psychic struggle with self-starvation through binging and purging, in which food takes on metaphoric status as a kind of repulsive materiality, the abject. (Collective forms of self-disciplining in eating presented on anorexia and bulimia blogs are discussed in the next chapter.) The rise of gastrography may announce a radically personal form of memoir, in which "you are what you eat," with its provocative suggestion that the subjectivity of another can be "cooked up," reproduced, and tasted.

Narratives of Conscious Aging

Autobiographical narratives are often written in later life and construct a story line that extends from childhood to the present moment of narration. Narratives of self-made men, for instance, present the process of aging as teleological, climbing the rungs of the ladder to a pinnacle of success from where the rest of life may be contemplated in its afterglow. With the boomer generation beginning to retire, memoirs of aging—about desires to revamp the body, revive memory, and bewail the finitude of all things mortal—are likely to abound. Novelist Richard Ford in *The Lay of the Land* has already dubbed the sixties the "permanent period" of aging; and Philip Roth in *Exit Ghost* has meditated on the deteriorating aged male body. Similarly in memoir form, Nora Ephron in *I Feel Bad about My Neck* bemoans the recalcitrant neck's sagging betrayal. But not all memoir writers focused on the body, processes of aging, and the farther reaches of the life cycle have seen aging as unmitigated loss. Particularly in women's life writing about the life cycle, emphasis is placed on the benefits of some aspects of aging and the shift in family position from child to elder as well as the constraints experienced about cultural discourses of the aging female body.[5]

Aging for women is implicated in cultural fables of losing sexual attractiveness and becoming a "crone." Increasingly, with drugs and anti-aging technologies, however, women have intervened in the gendered narrative of a dignified decline into decrepitude. In *My Life So Far,* for example, Jane Fonda divides her life into three periods and names the last section, where she explores consciously living in the future, "Beginnings." Fonda reflects on her celebrity and her psychic struggle as the unloved daughter of a famous actor whose identity is repeatedly remade through liaisons with public figures and, finally, through religious conversion. Fonda thus replaces the narrative of decline and degeneration with one of agency through aging. Serial autobiographies or collections of essays may also track a sequence of lived conditions, as in Maya Angelou's six books of life writing over four decades and the volumes of journals about late life of May Sarton. Nancy K. Miller's *But Enough about Me* might also be read as a narrative of conscious professional aging, and growing into one's skin, history, and voice through life writing.

With longer lives, many writers shift from stories of coming of age to the crystallization of consciousness in maturity through aging. Much life writing has approached the individual's story as the fulfillment of previous generations' histories and aspirations. Edmund Gosse's *Father and Son: A Study of Two Temperaments* and Henry Adams's *The Education of Henry Adams* are stories of conscious aging that project selves outward and engage contexts larger than family and inherited class position. Increasingly, longevity may generate stories in the fullness of time. Harry Bernstein wrote *The Invisible Wall* at the age of ninety-six. "If I had not lived until I was 90," quipped Bernstein, "I would not have been able to write this book" (see M. Rich). With increased longevity, however, comes an increase in degenerative diseases such as Alzheimer's, and new narratives of the struggle of lovers and caretakers to come to terms with the changes in a beloved partner.

The contemporary outpouring of stories of conscious aging may have the transformative effect of focusing scholarly and professional attention on "age theory" itself. Both Kathleen Woodward and Margaret Morganroth Gullette have called for theorizing age as a means of reorienting cultural discourses of aging away from tropes of degeneration and decay. As Gullette suggests in *Declining to Decline,* "I am proposing an active concept of aging as self-narrated experience, the conscious, ongoing story of one's age identity. Once we can firmly distinguish between the culture's aging narrative and our own versions . . . we learn that its threats to being and becoming are resistible" (220). In this context, writing one's later life as a story of conscious aging prompts cultural rewriting of the life cycle.

Sexual Stories

Narratives of sexuality—sexual identifications, sexual transformations, and sexual violence—now constitute a distinct subgenre of the autobiographical. Coming-out and queer narratives make visible formerly invisible subjects. Gay, bisexual, lesbian, and transgendered subjects inscribe stories of the cost of passing as heteronormative and the liberatory possibilities of being validated in their chosen sexual identities.

The modern coming-out narrative emerged in the late 1960s with the circulation of post-Stonewall lesbian and gay histories, though earlier versions abound.[6] Now, stories of sexual awakening and self-transformation are shifting from an earlier narrative of victimization in solitude, secrecy, and difference as homosexual to stories of living in community and refusing a minoritized and stigmatized identity position. Moreover, new stories have become possible: about committed relationship, building a family, and wielding power and authority in social life. New models of gay and lesbian life writing are evident in Alison Bechdel's autographic *Fun Home*, which tracks the differences of being gay for her father's and her own generation; Augusten Burroughs's *Running with Scissors*, which explores his ambivalent relationship to family and his childhood performance of alternative sexual roles; Dan Savage's *The Kid*, which focuses on his and his partner's adoption of a baby boy, and *The Commitment: Love, Sex, Marriage, and My Family*, which uses his own experience of gay marriage and family life to comment on the issue of gay marriage. While feminist anthologies published by small presses such as *This Bridge Called My Back*, edited by Cherríe Moraga and Gloria Anzaldúa, and *Making Face, Making Soul = Haciendo Caras*, edited by Anzaldúa, have for decades served as an archive of lesbian writing, more recently the University of Wisconsin Press is publishing a series of gay memoirs, Living Out: Gay and Lesbian Autobiographies.[7]

Gay memoirs often unfold at an intersection of identies: Kenny Fries's *Body, Remember* negotiates his identifications as disabled, Jewish, and gay; Betty Berzon, in *Surviving Madness*, links her recovery from a mental breakdown and suicide attempts to coming out as a lesbian at forty and working as a gay therapist; Jaime Manrique tells his story of living as

a gay Latino artist through its intersections with the lives of three eminent Hispanic writers in *Eminent Maricones: Arenas, Lorca, Puig, and Me.*
Similarly, artistic and literary collaborations, such as that of Sandra Ortiz
Taylor and Sheila Ortiz Taylor in *Imaginary Parents* and the performance
art of Alina Troyano as Carmelita Tropicana, collected in *I, Carmelita
Tropicana: Performing between Cultures,* probe performative femininity as
a script imposed on diverse desires.

A decade of queer narratives has also challenged prevailing discursive configurations of the lesbian and the gay man, particularly as those
are conceptualized by Havelock Ellis, Sigmund Freud, and contemporary
Christian fundamentalists. Queer stories aim to complicate identifications
and the directions of desire by unfixing the alignment of body, desire, and
the performance of identity. Transgender life writing, also not a new form,
is important for queer theory. In Christine Jorgensen's *Christine Jorgensen: A Personal Biography,* the author reflected on early life experience as
a boy that led her to seek gender-reassignment surgery and change her
name. Deirdre McCloskey in *Crossing: A Memoir* narrates a similar story
of a mismatch between body and identity and the remaking of the body
to align with gendered identity and sexual desire. That paradigm is challenged by narratives that critique the politics of gendered identity such
as Kate Bornstein's *Gender Outlaw: On Men, Women, and the Rest of Us,*
which sees gender identity as radically performative. Similarly, Jay Prosser
in *Second Skins: The Body Narratives of Transsexuality* emphasizes the
physicality of embodiment. Discussing Leslie Feinberg's *Stone Butch Blues,*
Prosser observes, "the transgendered subject's role is that of a debunker";
in queer gender narratives "sex and gender appear not as distinctive and
substantial characters but as evanescent, nonreferential, and overlapping
codes" (485). That is, transgendered embodiment undermines the expectation of either being or becoming a fixed gender identity. Queer narratives, as illuminated through Prosser's transgender perspective, disrupt
and expose the linear narrative of consolidating a sexual identity, gay or
straight, that underlay an earlier generation of gay memoir.

Life writing centered on heterosexual experience is also taking intriguing turns. Jane Juska's *A Round-Heeled Woman: My Late-Life Adventures
in Sex and Romance* explores sexuality as an option in conscious aging.
Detailing sexual encounters she arranged long distance around the United
States, Juska reflects on how she was formed as a social subject in small-
town Illinois and developed a political consciousness by teaching reading

in schools and a prison. In her late sixties, she asserts fulfilling a lifelong goal of sexual encounter. By contrast, in the best-selling *The Sexual Life of Catherine M.*, French art dealer Catherine Millet invites readers to join her in "the quest for the sexual grail," detailing explicit encounters that attempt to demystify the erotic. A focus on embodied female sexual desire as formative of identity (or de-forming, for some) is crystallized in Toni Bentley's unabashed *The Surrender: An Erotic Memoir* of her discovery of submission as a route to "paradise."

Life writing about sexuality is not always celebratory; it has also explored the exploitation of women, men, and children. The women's movement created preconditions and provided discourse and motivation for women to tell stories of childhood sexual violence and incest. Although seventies consciousness-raising has passed, memoirs of violation continue to tell compelling stories. Alice Sebold's *Lucky: A Memoir* details her rape as a college freshman and her subsequent prosecution of her attacker; Kathy O'Beirne's *Don't Ever Tell: Kathy's Story: A True Tale of a Childhood Destroyed by Neglect and Fear* charts her extensive childhood abuse, rape, and incarceration in a laundry run by the Magdalens.[8] Michael Ryan's *Secret Life* interweaves a narrative of being sexually abused as a boy with the compulsion to be a sexual seducer that he developed as a young man. Thus, writers have shifted the terms of the story from victimization, humiliation, violent abuse, and a legacy of self-loathing and vulnerability to explorations of the erotics of encounter, the recoding of the body, and the agency that life writing may provide in the act of claiming a past. Since Kathryn Harrison in *The Kiss* (1997) broke new ground about the complexities of memory and desire in incest narratives, sexual stories can no longer be characterized simply as narratives of lost innocence or polarized tales of conquest and victimhood, as the conflicting pulls of desire and fantasy complicate the "authority" of experience.

New-Model Narratives of Displacement, Migration, and Exile: Family Stories and Postethnic Lives

Narratives of Family

Perhaps as a response to the cultural sense that "the family" as an institution is under assault in the West because of migratory societies, smaller families, greater mobility, and women's increasing participation in work and public life, there has been an outpouring of memoirs about family and filiation for an audience seeking cohesion. In this contemporary culture of confessional memoir, people are also attracted to the intimate domain of family life and relish exploring its secrets.

Narratives of family and filiation are often memoirs—usually of a father, less often a mother—by a son or daughter whose parent was remote, unavailable, abusive, or absent (see Couser "Genre Matters"). Paternal absence is part of the story Barack Obama tells in *Dreams from My Father* in which his African father abandons his American family to return to Africa when Barack is two years old. Maternal remoteness and absence due to mental illness are at the center of the story the Australian writer Drusilla Modjeska tells in *Poppy*. In his autobiographical series *A Child Called "It," The Lost Boy,* and *A Man Named Dave,* Dave Pelzer chronicles a childhood of abuse at the hands of his mother and his long years of recovery and learning to forgive that followed.

Sometimes the narrative of filiation is a story of detection in which the son or daughter conducts a journey to discover the story of the lost or abandoning parent. The process of detection explores the conditions of the parent's childhood and early adulthood and the contexts of abandonment. For example, in Mary Gordon's *The Shadow Man: A Daughter's Search for Her Father* the daughter discovers through archival research and dogged pursuit of her father's past that he was not the man the family myth figured him to be, that, in fact, he was an imposter and liar. And Paul Auster, in *The Invention of Solitude,* details his extended research into his father's "other life," supplementing in writing the father who was largely unavailable to him (see Timothy Dow Adams, *Light Writing and Life Writing* chap. 1).

Narratives of family may offer analyses of the dysfunctional family or trace complex genealogies linking one generation of the family to another.[9] Sometimes the motivation for and affect produced by the narrative are of imaginative reaffiliation, a desire to know and gain closeness to a parent who was unavailable in life. Sometimes the narrative is a struggle with grief and provides a consolation for loss. In narratives of adoption, sons and daughters seek reunion with a birth parent to recover disrupted filiation through conscious quest. As Jill R. Deans notes, the narrator takes a journey that tries to "restore the lost origins of the adoptee" (239) and "forge meaningful connections despite the indeterminacy of one's identity" (256).[10]

But there are also narratives of disaffiliation in which the motivation seems to be scandal, outing, and revenge on a parent for the failure of love, as Couser suggests. Annie Ernaux's many autobiographical narratives of her childhood and family, for example, disclose the complexity of relationships and the recollected unease and shame she experienced as a child around the violence of her family's intimate encounters. Ernaux's relational narratives negotiate both the "stain" of traumatic memories, as Nancy K. Miller has explored, and the remaking of a personal archive of documents and stories as an autoethnographic project to distance the narrator from the entanglements of her past. In other family memoirs, issues of autobiographical ethics come to the fore, as children reveal family secrets and tell stories that can disturb living parents or siblings. Alison Bechdel, for example, has alluded in interviews to the discomfort that her probing of her father's secret homosexual liaisons with boys and his putative suicide caused her mother and brothers. For readers and reviewers questions arise about the conflicting obligation memoirists have to the family and the privacy of family secrets versus the pull of exploring fraught lives.

The histories of oppressed and formerly colonized peoples also produce conditions in which family relations are violently sundered, as happened in Australia when official government policy separated indigenous children from their families and traditional communities and relocated them in orphanages or white homes. In response to human rights activism and the United National Decade of Indigenous Peoples, stories of a "lost generation" of such children, now adults, became a part of public life through the publication of life stories and commission hearings and reports. As noted in chapter 2, Sally Morgan's widely read hybrid narrative *My Place* constructs a story of detection that narrates her discovery that her mother and grandmother had passed as white, protecting the story of their aboriginal families and the grandmother's sexual exploitation by a white station owner. And the film of *Rabbit-Proof Fence* also brought to a worldwide audience the story of the escape and long trek of three young indigenous girls who struggle to return to their community in Western Australia after being forcibly taken away from family by the state. These family histories rewrite national narratives of settlement and colonization.

Postethnicity Narratives

Immigrant narratives and narratives of exile have long been sites through which formerly marginal or displaced ethnic and racialized subjects explore the terms of their cultural identities and their diasporic and transnational allegiances. They become a call, sometimes to revolution, to reform ethnic subjects through autobiographical acts.[11] But recently, new kinds of narratives have emerged that explore a postethnic identity that challenges earlier versions of ethnic identity as fixed in place, history, and culture.

Postethnicity narratives undermine the foundations on which identity is posited by shifting the ground of reference for identity. They unhinge the relationship of individual memory to any certain chronology of experience. They question notions of inherent belonging and posit communities that are multiracial. Some of these narratives, like Obama's, explore biracial heritages, parentages, and identities. For example, there are Gregory Howard Williams's *Life on the Color Line: The True Story of a White Boy Who Discovered He Was Black*; Faith Adiele's *Meeting Faith*; James McBride's *The Color of Water: A Black Man's Tribute to His White Mother*; Rebecca Walker's *Black, White, and Jewish: Autobiography of a Shifting Self*; and Natasha Trethewey's Pulitzer Prize–winning *Native Guard*, a book of poems that engages Trethewey's heritage as a biracial woman, growing up in Mississippi, whose mother was murdered by her stepfather when she was a child. Other postethnicity narratives explore the shifting meanings of whiteness in changing ethnic communities, as does Paul Clemens's *Made in Detroit*, in which the meanings of being white in Detroit undergo a radical shift after 1970 that requires Clemens to rethink his status as "minority."

Autoethnography

Autoethnography is a hybrid term that has gained increasing utility in autobiography studies for its focus on the *ethnos*, or social group that is the project of ethnography, rather than on the *bios* or individual life. Ethnographies and as-told-to narratives, the foundational texts of anthropology and folklore studies, were "authentic" documentation of the lives of "others." In classic ethnography, anthropologists did fieldwork on and wrote their observations of colonized cultures they were studying; without sufficient reflection on the subject position of the ethnographer as a culturally bound observer, they represented those studied as the others of Eurocentric discourses and cultural assumptions. In the 1980s, ethnography as professional discourse was challenged by James Clifford, Clifford Geertz, Michael M. F. K. Fischer, and other scholars who questioned its assumption of neutral objectivity, rethought the project of fieldwork, and proposed various models of participant observation. Now much qualitative research uses autoethnographic methods to incorporate the participant-observer's standpoint.[12]

In this vein within literary theory, Mary Louise Pratt asserts that the colonized subjects who were the objects of European explorers' observation are not passive; rather, they "undertake to represent themselves in ways that engage with the colonizer's own terms" (*Imperial Eyes* 7). In her model, autoethnography emphasizes "how subjects are constituted in and by their relations to each other" in "the contact zone" of cultural encounter (7), their identities interlocked despite histories of radically uneven power relations. Colonized subjects, as they engage with a dominant culture's discursive models, may "transculturate" them into indigenous idioms, to produce collectivized life stories in which a cultural "insider" simultaneously functions as a cultural observer. Françoise Lionnet's *Autobiographical Voices* makes a similar point about how colonial subjects engage with the language and practices of a dominant society through *métissage*, the practice of braiding cultural discourses and languages to convey hybridity and bring silenced histories into view.

While many postcolonial life writers reject the notion of autoethnography as implicated in the colonizing practices of anthropology, writers as diverse as Jamaica Kincaid, Wole Soyinka, Marjane Satrapi, and N. Scott Momaday use its tropes in counterethnographies that incorporate local knowledges into collective stories. In current usage, the practice of autoethnography is not restricted to postcolonial subjects. Many recent memoirs also incorporate extended study of regional culture, historical moment, and group practices, such as Paul Clemens's *Made in Detroit,* Kathleen Stewart's *The Space by the Side of the Road,* and Lorna Goodison's memoir *From Harvey River,* about her double location as a university professor in Michigan and a member of a community in Jamaica. Indeed, immigrant autobiography, from Mary Antin to Esmeralda Santiago and Michael Ondaatje, might productively be reread as autoethnographic struggles with "self-translation." Some life writers have situated the genre at the fiction-nonfiction border, as does Norma Cantú in characterizing *Canícula* as "fictional autobioethnography," "a collage of stories gleaned from photographs randomly picked . . . with our past and our present juxtaposed and bleeding, seeping back and forth . . . in a recursive dance" (xi–xii). Autoethnographic projects may also be a blend of scholarly critique and first-person testimony. In *Troubling the Angels: Women Living with HIV/AIDS,* Patti Lather and Chris Smithies incorporate multiple modes of knowing about HIV/AIDS, including oral histories, critical analysis, poetic engagement with metaphors of history, and factoids, to explore how telling one's story and hearing others' stories involve an ethic of knowing and caring in the time of the pandemic.

More broadly, collaborative life writing generally has an autoethnographic aspect. While collaboration may imply equal contribution, in practice that is often not the case. Mark Sanders suggests that an examination of co-constructed narratives in political arenas such as those of truth commissions challenges the terms of mutuality that often went unexamined in work about ethnographers and informants.[13] Particularly when the collaboration takes the form of an as-told-to project, its multiple levels and kinds of translation require analysis and theorizing. As Ruth Behar's *Translated Woman: Crossing the Border with Esperanza's Story* makes clear in its shuttling between discourses of critical ethnography and first-person witnessing, such projects can be richly problematic.

Collective autoethnographic testimony is also playing an increasing role in human rights projects. An important life writing project now reaching a larger international audience in translation is *Playing with Fire: Feminist Thought and Activism through Seven Lives in India.* The Sangtin Writers, a collective of Indian women assisted by a group leader and Richa Nagar, an Indian feminist scholar teaching in the United States, produced a collaborative life narrative, developed over three years, that was first published in Hindi in New Delhi, then translated for international distribution by an American university press. *Playing with Fire* narrates the group's "journey" *(yatra)* of understanding their lives through extensive memory work, writing, discussion-based revision, and theoretical analysis. By situating their personal life histories collectively, the nine women in Sitapur, Uttar Pradesh, India, attempted to address the forms of domination of an NGO that, in their view, spoke as the voice of Indian women in the region yet effaced their experience and in some cases the complexities of their caste positions. The experience-based collective action aimed to raise consciousness about Indian women's lives through a collective method that would not, as ethnographic projects typically did, leave them vulnerable to overwriting or appropriation as voiceless subalterns. Throughout, the group's personal journals and the postscript written by Nagar reflect on the problematics of who can produce knowledge in a postcolonial context and what methods enable this process.

Playing with Fire inverts the framework of ethnography in several ways.

It takes the self-study of women's lives as an originary point for a collective assessment of class position and the dynamics of power in a community. It maps multiple stages of the process by which individual reflection—"memory work"—and the writing or telling of personal narrative might not only contribute to individual transformation but also become a basis for collectivized self-understanding with potential for intervention in a repressive public sphere. It thinks about the project of life writing as sharable and a stage in the formation of group consciousness through incorporating and revising personal stories. Although the collaborative work in *Playing with Fire* cannot escape the effects of social inequalities and hierarchies—only two of the nine women wrote out the stories told by the seven others—the project is not an ethnography privileging more cosmopolitan members but a multiply relational and self-questioning autoethnographic narrative striving for a collectivized voice made of many perspectives. Although it initially received a critical and hostile reception within India, in its carefully conceptualized process of composing, analyzing, and revising a collective subject and its commitment to voicing and blending the life stories of indigenous "subaltern" women, *Playing with Fire* may provide a model for producing collaborative life narrative that seeks societal transformation in the developing world.

Ecobiography: Lives in Dialogue with Place

Ecobiography, more accurately, ecoautobiography, is not a new form. American naturalists John Muir and Edward Abbey in very different ways linked their life writing to stories of place. Thus, "autotopography," a concept usually linked to such visual modes as installation art, may be a useful way to think about acts of reading the "I" and its location through each other. Peter F. Perreten defines ecoautobiography as "a type of autobiographical text that enables nature or landscape writing to discover 'a new self in nature'" (1).[14] In such writing, internal terrain is mapped onto and illuminated by natural setting, as an intimate relationship between them is developed (Perreten 5). In the autobiographical essays of *Desert Solitaire* and *The Monkey Wrench Gang,* for instance, Abbey represents nature as at times a congenial site from which to critique "civilized society" as wasteful, routinized, and bereft of imagination. He explores how being in places like the Grand Canyon generates bonds of affinity that enable his "gang" to awaken to new political possibilities about themselves as agents protective of a natural world who share an interest in disrupting "civilized" living.

Other ecobiographical writers link immersion in nature to expanded human possibility and emotional growth. In *Refuge* Terry Tempest Williams suggests that the "wild" of natural place can reawaken the quiescent "wild" in humans. Like other Western life writers, Mary Clearman Blew in *All but the Waltz: Essays on a Montana Family* reads herself as "bone deep in landscape," linking her family history with the history of central Montana. For William Kittredge the place of self-definition is eastern Oregon; for N. Scott Momaday, the West of Arizona's Indian territory. Much life writing by indigenous Americans registers the deep connection of tribal identity to the land. In Australia and Canada as well, ecobiographers inhabit the space of the outback, marked with histories and permeated by indigenous imagination, as a surround that signifies and offers sustaining identifications. For indigenous Australia life writing the outback can be a source of cultural belonging offering an alternative history to the national story of assimilation produced by an official policy separating indigenous children from their communities and families. *Rabbit-Proof Fence,* for example, can be read as an ecobiography of children living off the land in their attempt to escape violent severance from their homeland.

Ecobiography can be a site of manifesto, a textual place from which to call for an ethic of care for the environment. Consider the recent bestseller (and documentary film) *An Inconvenient Truth* by former American Vice President Al Gore. His lonely crusade for the planet juxtaposes extensive data about changes in the earth's environment with autobiographical memories of his childhood on a Tennessee tobacco farm and his experience losing loved ones. For Gore the entire planet is a locus of identification and its degradation a call to arms to protect its fragile beauty.

Ecobiography is also taken up in life writing that narrates the adventures of subjects merged with or even lost in the wilderness. In *Into the Wild* Jon Krakauer imagines the interior life of Chris McCandless, a young adventurer in the Alaskan wilderness who kept a journal of his experiences, eventually dying from eating a poisonous plant. Werner Herzog's film *Grizzly Man,* which incorporates the autobiographical film of Timothy Treadwell, who was killed by bears, explores Treadwell's delusion about his power to unite with a nature he imagines as hospitable. A counterpoint to these masculinist narratives of adversarial triumph or death is the kind of subject that Annie Dillard creates in *An American Childhood* and *Pilgrim at Tinker Creek,* whose focus on the microparticulars of nature discovers patterns that link world and self, and awaken her sense of belonging to place, be it urban Pittsburgh or the rural landscape.

Life writing in dialogue with its location thus can occur in both wilderness and urban environments. The city as a space of history and memory that stirs life writing is celebrated in *Istanbul: Memories and the City* by Nobel Prize–winning Turkish writer Orhan Pamuk. Rescripting the shape of memoir through individual, historical, and photographic memories, Pamuk assembles an archive of the city drawn from its collective history during and after the Ottoman Empire, a familial memoir, and his story of coming of age as an artist. Capturing the shifting contours of the great city, he refracts the personal through the collective, the "I" through its spaces and locations, to make a dense, textured, urban surround, juxtaposing his prose to more than a hundred quarter-page black-and-white photographs embedded in the text. The subjectivity he ascribes to Istanbul is one of loss and melancholy *(hüzün)*, palpable in the decrepit mansions previously inhabited by the pashas and harems of the empire on the shores of the Bosporus. Although Pamuk includes his own moments of birth, youth, and coming to consciousness as a writer, his story is irreducibly in interplay with the sights, sounds, and history of the vast panorama of Istanbul. Haunted by both the city's mirroring and his sense of a doubled self, "another Orhan," Pamuk tracks how one recognizes oneself through a spatial other and asserts that what we think of as personal identity is already "the myths we tell about our first lives" (8). In *Istanbul* his multiply reflecting mirrors illumine his central paradox, that to tell one story is to tell many stories simultaneously. Subjective impressions and their "factual" counterparts are enmeshed, inseparable in this double vision, a relational world at the heart of the book's design: "I have described Istanbul when describing myself, and described myself when describing Istanbul" (295). This chiasmic structure of reflection encapsulates the dialogical relation that life writers trace as autogeographers living in the world.

Celebrity Lives: Self-Advertisements of Movie Stars, Sports Heroes, Military Leaders, and Other Public Figures

Annually, dozens of celebrity autobiographies are published, often with the aid of ghostwriters acknowledged and unacknowledged, by sports figures, musicians, movie stars, military heroes, and other public figures. In 2007, a veritable barrage of narratives by musicians whose fame was earned in the 1960s and 1970s hit the bookstores in time for holiday shoppers. Bob Dylan is one of the luminaries whose autobiographical stories have become best-sellers. In the contemporary commodification of culture, the growth industry in self-advertisement ensures that celebrities can cash in on the memoir boom. Some satisfy readerly desires for gossip and vicarious immersion in a fantasy world of drugs, sex, and rock and roll. Many are written only to capitalize on fleeting fame and possibly rejuvenate it. Others, especially in life writing by sports figures, seek to project positive role models for young people, particularly boys and girls of color.

A few involve the stories of people who are famous for being famous, with life and story a recursive formation, as in the case of Paris Hilton. Celebrity narratives can, however, be genuinely innovative life writing. Dylan's *Chronicles* resists telling a linear narrative of his rise to fame. Employing different voices in successive chapters and focusing on particulars—a friend's bookshelves in the East Village, surreal encounters during a motorcycle trip—he (possibly with a ghostwriter; the publisher refuses to comment) shapes a personal story as engagingly poetic and open-ended as his song lyrics and as shifting in personae as Todd Haynes's biopic about him, *I'm Not There.*

Celebrity sports memoirists often link their own experience in overcoming obstacles with reflections on sports culture, stardom, and finding a code of ethics for their subsequent careers. Although it has been mockingly referred to as "jockography," the sports memoir incorporates many autobiographical templates: the conversion narrative, the coming-of-age and overcoming-of-origins story, the physical limitations story, and the trajectory of early hope, achievement, disillusionment, and distilled wisdom. As a site employing multiple models of storytelling rather than a singular genre, sports memoir is a hybrid form of life writing. For example, *Life on the Run,* Bill Bradley's classic journal of twenty days in a basketball season, helped launch his political career. Phil Jackson's serial life writing, beginning with *Sacred Hoops: Spiritual Lessons of a Hardwood Warrior,* combines his story of coming of age in the rural West with observations on practicing Taoist meditation as a useful discipline for basketball. In *Days of Grace,* Arthur Ashe, with the help of biographer Arnold Rampersad, reflects on his career as a black tennis star, cut short by AIDS he contracted from blood transfusions for heart surgery, and links his reflections to a critique of political struggles ranging from gay rights to apartheid and American racism. Each of these narratives interweaves another genre of life writing: for Bradley, the diary; for Jackson, the spiritual autobiography; for Ashe, thanatography.

There are, however, many themes shared by sports memoirs. Michael W. Young and Noel Stanley observe that while sports biographies focus on inspirational narratives, sports memoirs are more likely to stress other characteristics: for many sports, the focus of the memoir is on "the team" as an important collectivity with a shared aspiration to transcend individual limits as a fundamental code that, depending on the sport, is linked to claims about conquest and prowess. As Young and Stanley point out, an emphasis on competitive achievement is a dominant theme of sports memoirs that "have tended to encapsulate, in a brutally simple way, the success/failure fulcrum of public lives" (839). For many prominent athletes, involvement in the cult of celebrity, linked in the narrative to an inability to live the "star" life, turns dream into nightmare. Memoirs by prominent male athletes, from Pélé in soccer to Michael Jordan and *Bad as I Wanna Be* antihero Dennis Rodman to Andre Agassi in *Open: An Autobiography,* have enhanced their influence and revenues even as they reflect ambivalence about stardom. To date, women athletes have been less sought after for memoirs, except in tennis, where Billie Jean King has published several collaborative memoirs since the 1970s, and other players such as Martina Navratilova and Steffi Graf are seen as potential role models. But the cachet and selling power of jockography suggest that their memoirs will also increase exponentially, particularly as stories for young women.

Celebrity life writing can be the literary equivalent of the handprints in the sidewalk of Grauman's Chinese Theatre in Los Angeles, a desire to leave a permanent trace of body and moment. It may seem the titillating fare of a culture enamored of larger-than-life, flamboyant bad boys and wild girls. But recent interest, at conferences and in essays, about the outpouring of celebrity lives around the world suggests that it is becoming a lens for cultural studies of personhood, everyday life, and public fantasy.

Conclusion

This survey of contemporary modes of memoir writing exposes how autobiographical acts take place at cultural sites where discourses intersect, conflict, and compete with one another, as narrators are pulled and tugged into complex and contradictory self-positionings through a performative dialogism. In these acts the terms of the narrator-audience relationship are renegotiated as writers and practitioners develop new rhetorics of identity and strategies of self-presentation for being heard as different subjects and subjects in difference. Indeed, contemporary life writing has become a storehouse, a remarkably flexible set of discourses and practices for adapting voices, claiming citizenship, traversing space and place, witnessing to violence, confronting grief, resituating embodiment and sexuality, chronicling addiction and recovery, feeding hungers, imagining nature, and negotiating celebrity. Although the memoir boom is complicated by allegations of hoaxes, its end is not in sight. Moreover, its generic modes have become increasingly multimodal, taking shape in plastic, photographic, comic, filmic, and virtual media, to which we turn in chapter 6.

6

The Visual-Verbal-Virtual Contexts of Life Narrative

*In feminism . . . truth [is] a fundamental project: but truth of what it is to
live, to struggle and to acknowledge our bondedness with others in webs
of affection, desire, and painful vulnerability, to care about others close to
us and suffering in ways removed from us, these truths require profound
artistic capacity to be brought before us, to see, and to know.*

Griselda Pollock

The self, we have it like an albatross around the neck.

Alice Neel

*Once underground cartoonists had unleashed their checkered demons
in the cheerfully vernacular medium of comics, [I] was able to focus on
the grammar of that vernacular and nail [my] own personal demons.
High Art and Low. Words and Pictures. Form and Content. It all might
sound dry and academic, but—Hell—for me then it was a matter of Life
and Death.*

Art Spiegelman

Open Diary
Read Life, Write Life.

Open Diary home page

Autographics. Installations. Performance art. Blogs. StoryCorps. Facebook.
MySpace. PostSecret. LiveJournal. YouTube. "This I Believe." SecondLife.
OpenSocial. Web cam documentaries. These are just some of the diverse
forms utilizing new media and locations for visual self-presentation and
self-narration. As the platforms, templates, and modes of communicative exchange increase and intersect hypertextually, they add to the forms
of visual life narrative produced during the twentieth century virtual
forms of social networking systems that link people around the world

instantaneously and interactively. What subjectivity becomes in the fluidity of digital environments is a topic that will occupy scholars in coming decades.

We cannot do justice to the burgeoning arenas of self-presentation in myriad visual and online forms that are transforming self-inscription through identity, relationality, agency, and embodiment. Taking up some examples, however, we survey some prominent sites that exhibit new formations of subjectivity and raise issues about the shifting limits and uses of autobiographical discourse. In approaching life storytelling in diverse visual and digital media, we need to expand our conceptualization of the media of life writing. A possible theoretical framework for doing so involves the concept of *automediality,* a term that Jörg Dünne, Christian Moser, and other European scholars of life writing developed to expand the definition of how subjectivity is constructed in writing, image, or new media.

Conjoining *autos* and media, the concept redresses a tendency in autobiography studies to consider media as "tools" for rendering a preexistent self. Theorists of automediality emphasize that the choice of medium is determined by self-expression; and the materiality of a medium is constitutive of the subjectivity rendered.[1] Thus media technologies do not simplify or undermine the interiority of the subject but, on the contrary, expand the field of self-representation beyond the literary to cultural and media practices. New media of the self revise notions of identity and the rhetoric and modalities of self-presentation, and they prompt new imaginings of virtual sociality enabled by concepts of community that do not depend on personal encounter.

Graphic Memoir

Graphic memoir, what Gillian Whitlock calls "autographics," is a rich site of self-representation reaching large audiences ("Autographics"). In Japan, France, Canada, the United States, South Africa, and elsewhere, the telling of autobiographical stories through cartoon books has produced multimodal stories with the potential to intervene directly in social and political debates, not least because they link the cartoon form of popular culture to the narrative practices and theoretical critique of contemporary life writing. Graphic memoirs have become a site for telling complex stories of gender, sexuality, trauma, and the nation that reach millions of readers and potentially circulate worldwide as they "open up new and troubled spaces" (976).[2]

Several features of autographics distinguish it from other media of self-representation. For one, graphic memoir is a hybrid, "cross-discursive form," as Hillary Chute and Marianne DeKoven emphasize, "composed of verbal and visual narratives that do not simply blend together, creating a unified whole, but rather remain distinct" (769). Mixing verbal and visual materials, autographics often present conflicting stories and oscillate between different planes of representation. Readers may observe stories in the visual plane that are not explicitly signaled by the verbal plane, and vice versa, thus engaging contesting stories and interpretations of autobiographical memory and meaning. Second, autographics present the reader with overlapping layers of self-presentation. There is the hand or aesthetic autograph of the author/artist that draws; the narrator/architect whose narrating voice runs above the frame; the autobiographical avatar, an "I" both imaged and voiced; the dialogue bubbles of the characters, including the narrated "I"; and the addressees within the comic and beyond. Third, with its syncopation of frames and gutters, the comic at once advances time and retards time, renders visual images and disrupts the visual plane. As a result, observes Jared Gardner, "all comics are necessarily collaborative texts between the imagination of the author/artist and the imagination of the reader who must complete the narrative" that the cartoon's segmented boxes and gutters both initiate and interrupt (Gardner, "Archives" 800). Finally, the distinctive character of graphic style, at once an effect of amplification and simplification, enhances what Whitlock notes is "its power to capture character, history and place in an economy of pictures and words" (*Soft Weapons* 198). "What charges life narrative in comics," she concludes, "is the particular tension and dissonance it generates by mixing codes from juvenilia into autobiographical narratives of history and trauma" (198).

As a powerful form/medium of autobiographical narration, graphic memoir gained wide recognition in the United States with the publication in 1986 of Art Spiegelman's *Maus I: A Survivor Tale: My Father Bleeds History* (though Spiegelman had been publishing pieces of *Maus* from 1973 in venues ranging from the avant-garde comic *Raw* to the *New Yorker*). Through *Maus,* Spiegelman joined the comic strip's codes of experimental and renegade juvenilia to a searing autobiographical engagement with his father's traumatic memory and his own postmemory of the Holocaust's effects on his family and community, troubling the notion of "survival." "Art" is not a fictional character but a figure embodying his creator's experience as a child of survivors growing up in the United States after World War II. In narrating and drawing a tale of his parents' Auschwitz experiences interwoven with a frame narrative involving his interviews with his father, Spiegelman constructs stories within stories entwined in multiple temporalities. The interviews seem to be located in the "I-now" present of the aged Vladek, often on his exercise bike, telling his story to the autobiographical persona, the resentful and guilt-ridden son. But Art, the coaxer in this autobiography embedded within family autoethnography, elicits from his father a heroic, partial story that fails to satisfy his own need to understand the horrors of victimization in the Holocaust. He yearns for his mother's alternative narrative—which could supplement the Holocaust memory he wants to create and challenge his father's—but that story remains inaccessible both because his father destroyed her postwar diaries and because she committed suicide in 1968 for reasons he feels guilty about but cannot untangle. Spiegelman's dilemma of postmemory, the dilemma of a child of survivors with insufficient access to that past, drives the conflicted urges of *Maus* in both its comic and tragic registers.

The experiential weight of a Holocaust at one remove situates Spiegelman within Paul Celan's question: how can there be "art" after such events? For its creator-character—ironically named both Art the artist, and Spiegelman the "mirror-man"—the quest for a memory-scape pushes the narrating "I" toward self-reflexivity. His role as coaxer of and editor-cartoonist to the testimony of Vladek inverts the usual father-son relationship. Art is both the angry, bereft son and, in *Maus II: A Survivor's Tale: And Here My Troubles Began* (published five years later), the increasingly celebrated, guilt-ridden author of a "comic book" about a horrific event. Such paradoxical narrative locations are foundational to the graphic memoir's recursivity.

This narrative boundary crossing is most evident in the half-page frame at the start of *Maus II*, chapter 2, "Auschwitz (Time Flies)," where the son's, the family's, and the Jewish collectivity's traumatic pasts seep into the narrating present. In this frame, Art the artist sits at his drawing table, a mouse mask visibly affixed to his human face instead of his mouse-persona, visually marking the performative narrating "I." He is perched precariously atop a heap of humanlike, emaciated dead mouse corpses. To the right is a curtained window through which the guard tower of Auschwitz (represented throughout *Maus*) is visible. Art is caught in a spotlight held by an invisible figure in the space off to the right, who declares that "we're ready to shoot" the movie. A dialogue bubble alludes to his predicament as a depressed, guilty son whose mother killed herself without leaving a note in 1968 and who is now a celebrity artist.

This moment of recursivity epitomizes the crossing and ultimate confounding of boundaries in visual-verbal narrative: Art is narrator, illustrator, and character, positioned both in the present drawing a cartoon panel like the one we see and temporally thrust back into the hallucinatory scene at Auschwitz of annihilation, corpses swarming with flies, that he as a postwar child cannot remember. And "Time Flies" insists on the irreverent punning practices of comics. He is addressed by the real-world media of the epitext and afterlife of *Maus I*—offers for movie rights and translations—and personally haunted by the memory of his mother's unexplained suicide that undermines his making of the art of Art that we are witnessing. In juxtaposing his "live" but masked, dejected body to those of exterminated mice-men, he makes each "reappear," in Chute's sense, through the other to graphically show the entanglements of postmemory as an act of "picture writing" the impossible simultaneity of memorializing history (Spiegelman quoted in Chute, "Texture" 108 n. 9).

Other recent autographics suggest the potential to address potent issues of gender, sexuality, and nation, and to circulate new multimodal stories about the personal and historical stakes of representation. Marjane Satrapi's two books of autographics about revolutionary Iran, *Persepolis* and *Persepolis 2* (published in French and made into a 2007 film), link the coming-of-age story of an only child in a Marxist-leaning, multigenerational bourgeois family reputedly descended from the kings of Persia to events in Iran between the late 1970s and the early 1990s. Through starkly abstracted black-and-white cartooning, Satrapi visualizes the psychic life of her childhood and early adulthood selves, the communal struggle of the family against and in the midst of the Iranian revolutionary masses, and the complexities of Iran's national struggle to forge an Islamic national imaginary at the site of its martyred opposition and war dead. The artist/narrator reconstructs "Marji," the protagonist, as a political witness to the Iranian revolution and its aftermath; from her position in exile, she narrates a journey of reparative memory, as Nancy K. Miller observes, a fraught journey through which she aligns the personal and political, singular and communal, across the generational lineage of women—her grandmother, her mother, and her younger self (Miller "Out of the Family"). Chute argues that *Persepolis*, "visually and verbally, is . . . the product and act of 'not forgetting'" the traumatic upheavals of the Iranian nation by conversing with "versions of [her] self" ("Texture" 97).

Satrapi's graphic narration sets up a transnational communicative circuit through which Western readers are invited to recalibrate their understanding of Iranian history and culture. Misperceptions—for example, that Iranians speak Arabic and that Iranian women "either have no place in our society or that they are hysterical black crows," in Satrapi's ironic phrase— are graphically revised in images that invite both identifying with its personal stories of family and becoming witnesses to scenes of mass public violence.[3] In using visualizations that "defamiliarize" scenes of trauma from a child's perspective, Satrapi, like Spiegelman, finds in autographics a new, multimodal way to gesture toward horrific historical acts (Chute, "Texture" 103; see also Tensuan).

Different autographic possibilities are mobilized in Alison Bechdel's *Fun Home: A Family Tragicomic*. A provocative exploration of sexuality, gendered relations in the American family, and modernist versions of what Bechdel calls "erotic truth," *Fun Home* is deeply invested in imaging and imagining memory and those intricate, intersubjective acts of storytelling that both bind and rend families. Specifically, the story concerns a family in 1960s rural Pennsylvania whose father is by profession a high school English teacher and funeral home director, by temperament an interior decorator and fanatic landscaper, and by desire a repressed homosexual who has liaisons with the family's babysitters and his students. That is, he practiced what heteronormative American society would then have called "perversion," which may have motivated him to commit suicide—unless his being run over by a truck was an accident, an irresolvable question. *Fun Home* is a memoir of both coming of age and coming out for "Alison," the avatar of Bechdel, an artist known for more than two decades for her biweekly comic strip *Dykes to Watch Out For*.

This autographic entwines the story of Alison's family's efforts to form her as feminine, despite her own transgressive desire, with the private trauma of her father's sexual double life and early death. It routes both his and her stories through references and images of several kinds of print texts: modernist literature, above all Proust's *Remembrance of Things Past* and Joyce's *Ulysses* and *Portrait of the Artist as a Young Man*; lesbian feminist manifestos, from Casey and Nancy Adair's *Word Is Out* to Jill Johnston's *Lesbian Nation*, and including Colette's *Earthly Paradise*; letters between her parents during their courtship and in her teenage years; newspaper pages that juxtapose personal events, such as her father's death, to the Watergate hearings occupying the nation during the 1970s under the Nixon presidency; and her own childhood diaries, which she began keeping at the age of ten. Graphic memoir here becomes a space of collage and counterpoint, nowhere more than in Bechdel's careful drawings of family photographs. In studying those images and inviting readers to see her and her family differently through the sexual tensions and reversals of gendered positions she uncovers in it, Bechdel creates an autographic family album as an act both of memorializing her dead father and charting shifts in the theory and practice of gendered relations in late-twentieth-century America. Moreover, in foregrounding her father's biography, Bechdel counters Second Wave feminism's injunction to women to think back through their mothers, by "queering" the narrative of genealogical recovery.[4]

Other graphic memoirists such as Julie Doucet, Phoebe Gloeckner, Harvey Pekar, and David B are producing autographics in which autobiographical subjectivity and readerly identification are shaped in innovative ways that combine the multiple kinds of images that now saturate our lives. The potential audience for autographics may soon exceed the robust audience for print memoirs. Indeed, as Whitlock has observed, the accessibility and adaptability of comics make graphic memoir a "global" mode of life narrative. As graphic memoirs become a dominant international form, ideas of autobiographical subjectivity may increasingly be shaped by the registering and archiving of embodied styles and practices that elicit the viewer's relational identification in co-constructing a narrative. Autographics, with their pages segmented into frames and marked by gutters, invite consideration of what is in and not in the frame, what has happened between frames. As the global reach of graphic memoirs expands as a popular form of witnessing to histories of trauma and marking the need to remember, new issues for scholars of life narrative arise: how autographics call us to know and see otherwise; how they produce us as different kinds of readers; how they witness and with what effects; and how they circulate and are taken up in larger projects of remembering.

Autobiographical Acts in Performance and Visual Arts

While the history of Western art includes a long tradition of self-portraiture, reaching back to Giotto in the thirteenth century, in the past decades artists have increasingly explored the self-presentational and memorial possibilities of various media. In the wake of the feminist art movement of the 1960s and 1970s, women artists especially have been engaged in changing the terms of self-representation. In 1999, for example, Tracey Emin, a young working-class British artist, was one of four finalists for the prestigious Turner Prize awarded by the Tate Gallery in London.[5] Emin submitted an archive of explicitly autobiographical memorabilia, including eight home videos, four miniature watercolor portraits, a wall of captioned drawings made during her adolescence, a quilt collage, and two assemblages of printed materials on her family's past. At the center was the installation *My Bed* (1998), a rumpled bed with stained, tossed sheets surrounded by overflowing ashtrays, used tissues and condoms, unwashed underwear, and medicine bottles—the detritus of her intimate life in Berlin in 1992–93, as the caption made clear. The photograph of the installation prominently displays a coiled rope hung from a gibbet-like hook in the background, which to some gave the scene a sadomasochistic, or even suicidal, feel.

Emin's assemblage enacts multiple autobiographical performances in both visual and verbal modes. The bed becomes a memory museum to a specific time and place in her past. The material artifacts seemingly attest to authentic citation of her past. Similarly, her labeled drawings evoke an adolescent's diaristic uncertainty about sexuality, with comments such as "I don't know what I want to do"; "What it looks like to be alone"; "I didn't say I wasn't scared. I said I'm not as scared as I used to be." With their misspellings and awkward phrasing, the doodles and childlike images create a sense of unedited and unpolished immediacy. Such immediacy underwrites the aura of "authenticity" in a presentation of her lived experience during moments of her past.

Emin's videos of summer vacations and high school days also catalog a young woman's self-representational possibilities as documents of self-chronicling. "MY C.V . . . (to 1995)," for instance, reminds her to "Plan the Tracey Emin Museum." This voice-over recitation of her résumé accompanies a visual walk-through of a "home" (with toilets, beds, a sitting room), which may be hers or her mother's. Collectively the videos seem to project a documentary assemblage that is not an "artful" reconstruction of the past but the "real" past reassembled in the present. As with the sketches and artifacts, these home movies, disarmingly unprocessed and unpolished, emit an aura of authenticity; and it is precisely this authenticity that has become commodified as cultural capital in this age of confession.

Deploying medium upon medium in chronicling these moments in her life, Emin insists on the autobiographical as her artistic origin, performative identity, and preferred mode. For some viewers, her work is narcissistically self-absorbed, referring line, color, form, and sound back to the emotions of her experiential history. For others, including the many young people who thronged her installation day after day, Emin's work introduces, through the interweaving of images and written text, an autobiographical voice not previously heard or witnessed with such raw intensity. In that sense, her daring self-making through self-chronicling is an avant-garde gesture performed publicly that expands the modes of self-representation at a shifting matrix of visuality and textuality. Moreover, through her extravagant performance of the autobiographical across media, Emin exploits and flaunts norms of gendered modesty about self-disclosure, testing the limits of decorum that women artists confront as they situate themselves and their work within and against the traditions of masculinist art historical practice.

Artists have also pursued photographic experiments to reconceptualize the very notion of self-portraiture in the past several decades. A photograph (or photographs) may accompany an autobiographical narrative, be alluded to but absent, or stand in the place of an absent but suggested narrative, as in the photographic series. In such series, that is, multiple self-portraits expose an autobiographical subject to view as they engage the illusory and unstable nature of the exposed subject. For the photograph presents the "I" in the photograph as at once a flesh-and-blood subject and a dematerialized phantom of an invisible photographer. The uncanny self-portraits of such self-photographers as Claude Cahun, Francesca Woodman, and Cindy Sherman interrogate self-identity, doubling "I"s, unfixing gender, and unmasking conventions of self-portraiture by their impersonation of popular or artistic images. Photographic self-representation, then, shares the troubled relationship of represented subject to the flesh-and-blood maker that we have observed in verbal autobiographical texts, and also engages viewers intersubjectively in acts of seeing differently.

In visual media, artists can palpably push the autobiographical to the very interior of the body, as Mona Hatoum does in her photographic renderings of the insides of her body and in her two-hour video performance titled *Pull* (1995). In this performance piece Hatoum placed herself in an area hidden from the visitor; only her long ponytail, hanging in a niche in the wall, was visible. Visitors confronted the "real" ponytail and above it a video of the artist who seemed to be hanging upside down. Invited to pull the ponytail by the very title of the piece, they could watch the effect of their pulling on the artist. While they assumed the video to be recorded, and thus the connection between pulling and facial expression nonexistent, they were in fact pulling the hair of the artist present behind the wall. In other words, the artist was there in person, connected to her hair, not merely represented on the video. Her hair, as Desa Philippi suggests, is materialized as fetish (369). Body and image, usually separated, are conjoined, compressed. As Guy Brett says of the piece, "at a certain moment the spectacle suddenly ceases to be a spectacle" (74) as visitors are confronted with their own role in causing pain to the artist whose art and body are conjoined.[6]

Hatoum's installations attach the processes of represented subjectivity to the very materiality of her body, forcing viewers to confront the conundrum of her presence in apparent absence. This absent presence is a central paradox of autobiographical acts and practices. In addition, her installations link presence to notions of female excess and women's embodied subjectivity. Hatoum's installations are, in a sense, like Emin's rumpled bed, synecdoches of subjectivity. Conjoining body and artistic medium, word and image, past and present moments, these artists insist on the coextensiveness of body, language, and art.

Contemporary artists also visualize the psychic interior of such drives as hunger and sexual desire, as Janine Antoni does. In her installation titled *Gnaw*, Antoni presents the viewer with two three-hundred-pound cubes, one made of chocolate, the other of lard, that the artist has eaten during off-hours in the gallery; out of the regurgitated gnawings she has fashioned new consumer products—lipsticks and chocolate hearts—identified with the social construction of heterosexual femininity. Here the autobiographical body, while absent, remains present in its traces: the teeth marks left on massive cubes of chocolate and lard, the chewings that re-form into lipstick and hearts. Through these traces of the body, Antoni puts autobiographical drives in the picture.

Hatoum and Antoni locate autobiographical inquiry in the materiality and drives of the body. Other artists turn to the ethnographic as another kind of contextualization that draws primarily on remembered scenes of collective memory in creating an image or performance that commemorates or revalues a past moment and links the personal, communal, and ethnic. This collective history resituates an autobiographical "I" within an ethnic "we" that is necessary to configuring her identity. That is, the "I"'s meaning is entwined with, read through, the "we" of collective memory and authorized by it. This interface is probed in a series of painted *recuerdos* by Carmen Lomas Garza. In paintings of what she calls "special events" and "unusual happenings," Lomas Garza captures the precise details of her childhood and young adulthood in images of collective everyday life in the Chicano community. "I felt I had to start with my earliest recollections of my life," she has stated, "and validate each event or incident by depicting it in a visual format" (*Pedacito* 13). Similarly, collage artist Aminah Robinson has produced more than twenty thousand works in her career, many of which combine her self-representation with the oral history of her African American family and community in Columbus, Ohio. Executed in painting, drawing, button-beading, fabric, stitching, and other media, these autoethnographic images connect past tradition and lore of midwestern African America to her own experiential history in a communal visual ethnography of a lost past (see Myers).

A dynamic relay between personal and communal memory reconfigures the relationship of forms of communal memory and aims to rework official memory in the nation. Working at this social-personal interface enables artists to foreground the experiential history of the identity statuses they bear, and bare. As they represent themselves in various media, they embody their experiential histories in culturally specific meanings. Particularly for postcolonial and multicultural artists who explore the relationship of a racialized identity to a national identity that has historically dominated and effaced it, visually recontextualizing received history generates new autobiographical stories by evoking the power of images to stir memory.

Other artists assemble and juxtapose documents of everyday life such as newspapers and official records to place the autobiographical subject in a sociocultural surround that makes visible the official, often stereotyped, histories through which they have conventionally been "framed" in order to reframe them. In Adrian Piper's *Cornered* (1988), mentioned in chapter 2, two birth certificates hang on the wall near a monitor that plays a videotape of Piper addressing the visitors seated before it. Next to the monitor is a table turned on its side. The two historical documents provide evidence of the fluidity of the social category of "race" and thus racial identity: one registers her father's identity as "octaroon"; the other registers his identity as "white." This doubled documentation reveals cultural confusion about reading "color" visibly off the body. In her accompanying monologue, Piper explores this cultural confusion about the readability of her own identity, a mixed identity "inherited" from her grandfather and played out in everyday life by her cultural position as an African American who is read as white. Piper's situating of birth certificates against her videotaped address deconstructs historical discourses of American racial difference and recontextualizes the conventional meanings of "whiteness" and "blackness" as arbitrary. Piper, as a contemporary racialized subject, acknowledges that she's "cornered" by a normative interpretation of bodily difference. But her juxtaposition of textual and visual media offers a new "angle" or possibility for understanding the instability of seemingly fixed categories of identity, one that "corners" the spectator. Using "authentic" historical documents and the public histories they invoke, Piper calls into question their truth status and our naive conviction that an autobiographical identity must stay in the corner to which racial politics have assigned it.[7]

Intensifying some of Piper's paradoxes about racial identification, African American artist Glenn Ligon in *Some Changes,* a 2007 traveling exhibition, assembles pieces from the past twenty years to situate his autobiographical narrative within multiply mediated discourses of racialization. In these works, he "question[s] the relations between self and shadow, master and slave—how he experiences them internally and with respect to others." Perhaps best known internationally of the American visual artists of racialized histories that continue to "corner" multiracial subjects is Kara Walker. Her large silhouettes in black and white of such acts as the lynching, hanging, and beating of African Americans by their white masters or racist groups are not individually autobiographical but refract her sense of a collective memory that was initially inscribed in popular forms such as lithographs, cartoons, and photographs. Although those visual forms are now repressed in the post–civil rights era, they continue to exercise a formative influence as cultural stereotypes that shape attitudes and values in American society. In South Africa William Kentridge also draws together a wide storehouse of popular media and official documents in which the values and ideology of apartheid were encoded. His brilliant cartoon sequences and films (and photographs), obliquely referencing his personal life, capture the racialized polarities that sustained the apartheid system and exerted formative influence on the shaping of personal identities. Whether explicitly or only implicitly self-referential, such documentations of practices of racialization reconfigure both the contours and performances of identity at this moment.

Artists around the world have intensified their engagement with multiple media installations, photographic sequences, and sculptural experiments in surfaces and depths in representing themselves within their communities. As they experiment with the limits and elasticities of subjectivity, identity, and embodiment, contemporary artists redefine the terms of legibility. They exploit the conjunction of narration and visuality and/ or narration and materiality to challenge cultural regimes of hypervisibility and invisibility. Their autobiographical performances interrogate cultural norms that have projected on them a subjectivity, an identity, and a life script—a biography of sorts—of a different order from their own experience of themselves. Confronting their "subordination in difference," they engage with codes of representation that have rendered them as objects of representation (Mouffe 382). As our examples only begin to suggest, these interfaces of media become complex sites of negotiation, appropriation, adaptation, resistance, and reformation of subjects-in-process struggling with the terms, limits, and paradoxes of visual self-representation.

Autobiographical Film and Video

The field of cinematic self-representation now encompasses a vast terrain. The formal issues that arise in autobiographical film and video are substantively different from those that arise in graphic memoir, and the media of visual self-representation invite analysis beyond our expertise. In what follows, we offer a brief survey of distinct kinds of autobiographical film and video productions from the past two decades and pose a few topics that readers might productively pursue.

The definition of what constitutes the autobiographical in film is not a simple one. Some might argue that the dense filmic signature of an auteur could be read as "autobiographical," calling attention to the distinctive qualities of a filmmaker's visual style and historical consciousness. Filmmakers from Frederico Fellini, François Truffaut, and Jean-Luc Godard to Werner Herzog, Spike Lee, and Jane Campion have inscribed subjectivity in their films in compelling ways, in the auteurist aesthetic. The auteur tradition is more frequently identified with filmmakers active in European cinema. In the United States, Hollywood production values and the sheer scope and complexity of the many hands required to make a film have previously made an auteurist notion of filmic autobiography too simple, though recent independent films are changing that paradigm.

The oeuvre of Werner Herzog could be read as a sustained act of auto-biographical filmmaking, as his *Grizzly Man* (2005) suggests.[8] In the film Herzog constructs a biographical portrait of bear activist Timothy Tread-well, who with his girlfriend, Amie Huguenard, was savagely killed by Alaskan grizzlies in 2003, after spending thirteen summers cultivating the bears and filming his interactions with and reveries about them. In more than a hundred hours of video footage shot during the last years of his life, Treadwell assembled a fascinating autoportrait of a young man, part maniacal narcissist, part nature-loving ecoactivist. Herzog embeds Treadwell's self-portrait within interviews of people involved with him during his lifetime, who offer conflicting views of his fanatical dedication as egomania and a seeming death wish. Herzog's voice-over reflections on the young man's pursuit of extremity, a familiar motif in his films, further frame the auto/biography as a self-reflexive story. Herzog inserts himself into the film as a witness at one remove when he mentions that he with-held the terrifying audio recording of the deadly bear attack recorded by Treadwell's video camera. In part a biopic, *Grizzly Man* incorporates what Paul John Eakin terms "the story of the story" *(How Our Lives)* by includ-ing Herzog's metanarrative on his own career and artistic choices.

Another mode of the autobiographical in film and video occurs in documentary projects that reference autobiographical evidence.[9] A well-known self-documenting film in the United States is Morgan Spurlock's *Super Size Me* (2004), which follows Spurlock as he endures thirty days of eating only McDonald's fast food for every meal, despite his vegan girl-friend's disapproval and the health issues he experiences—twenty-five pound weight gain, depression, and liver dysfunction. In effect, Spurlock turns himself into a social experiment and his body into a visual specimen for his audience to raise political consciousness about the American phe-nomenon of overeating and the elastic boundaries of the embodied self.

Composed on a Mac computer and self-distributed for a million dol-lars, Jonathan Caouette's *Tarnation* (2003) is a self-documenting film that employs home video differently in constructing an autobiographical por-trait of the filmmaker and his family. Caouette, who had filmed himself in video diaries with a Super-8 camera since the age of eleven, interweaves remnants of answering machine messages, family photographs, 1980s pop culture fragments, and scenes reenacted with family members and juxtaposes this barrage of images to his voice-over narration of his own coming-of-age and coming-out story. In constructing a narrative of a fam-ily life riddled with abuse, the mental illness of his mother, Renée, and his own experiments in transvestism, Caouette reinvents the documentary as a highly personal, fragmentary form of collage that interestingly parallels the tactics of such contemporaneous memoirs as Augusten Burroughs's *Running with Scissors.*

Autodocumentary filmmaking has an intriguing analogue in documentary of a group of lives that functions as filmic prosopography. For example, Michael Apted's *Up!* television series, which began in 1964 as a profile of fourteen seven-year-old children for the current affairs series *World in Action,* now revisits his subjects every seven years, with Apted directing. The series offers a decades-long snapshot of how ordinary lives unfold over time. Here the autodocumentary becomes a collective biography of subjects whom Apted understands as linked by living in a particular historical era, with their subject positions within the British class system marking their differing life trajectories. Guided by a different emphasis on a group of lives, some documentary life narratives about disability focus on the body, such as *Twitch and Shout,* directed by Laurel Chiten, which profiles about half a dozen people with Tourette syndrome who are seen as sharing a bodily commonality. Or there are Carol Jacobsen's video ethnographies of women who kill their abusive partners and who have been incarcerated and occasionally pardoned, speaking not to confess criminality but to articulate how they are entrapped in social structures of marriage, justice, and punishment. The videos intervene in this frame-up to enable the women individually and collectively to move from being victims of domestic violence and legal structures to becoming agents critiquing norms of justice, the penal system, and the institution of the family (see *Time Like Zeros*). In such projects, we can identify the conjunction of the autobiographical and biographical, the singular and the collective.

Cinematic self-narrative seems to guarantee the "truth" of the speaking subject. But Kathleen McHugh, among others, points to the problematic of "faux" autobiographical films—such as Rea Tajiri's *History and Memory,* Cheryl Dunye's *Watermelon Woman,* and *Crucero* directed by Ramiro Puerta and performed by Guillermo Verdecchia—that link auto- or biographical stories embedded in specific historical crises, such as the internment of Japanese Americans or the racializing of citizens of color, to impossible acts of memory or imaginary characters (McHugh "Lourdes Portillo"). Alexandra Juhasz and Jesse Lerner develop the important point that deploying technologies of the "real" in film can be used to show the impossibility of historical accuracy in the "life" being presented (155–78).

Many published life narratives are now being made into film, what we might term *autopics*. These translations from print to filmic version include *Angela's Ashes, Country of My Skull, Girl, Interrupted, Jarhead, Malcolm X, The Pianist, Rabbit-Proof Fence, Rescue Dawn,* and earlier films such as *Angel at My Table, The Miracle Worker* (about Helen Keller), *I Never Promised You a Rose Garden, My Left Foot, Out of Africa, Rosa Luxemburg,* and *Three Faces of Eve,* among many others. These translations of life writing into film offer opportunities for theorizing representational and storytelling choices in cinematic interpretation and rethinking what constitutes adapted filmic autobiography. And they raise the question of whether, in the act of translation through cinematic technology, the form shifts to an autobiographical hybrid or becomes a biopic.

Most memoirs, however, are rendered cinematically as versions of the biopic. For example, Reinaldo Arenas's memoir, translated from Spanish as *Before Night Falls,* was filmed by Julian Schnabel (2001) in sweeping panoramas that artistically embody the writer's vision. Javier Bardem sensitively portrays the dissident Cuban artist's life of artistic achievement, political struggle to smuggle out his writing, multifarious erotic encounters in the gay underworlds of Havana and New York, and grim death from AIDS. But the film remakes his narrative as a biopic interpreting Arenas's words and images rather than an autobiographical film that he participated in making. Similarly, although it tries to render the texture of a uniquely impaired and illuminated subjective perception, Schnabel's filmic version of Jean-Dominique Bauby's *The Diving Bell and the Butterfly* also must contextualize him as a biographical actor observed and interpreted by others within, and after, his life.

Nevertheless, counterexamples do exist of filmic autobiography, as in the ongoing series of films wittily and provocatively charting moments of his personal and political life by Italian director Nanni Moretti or the filmic version of *Les Nuits Fauves*. In 1989 French writer Cyril Collard published *Savage Nights,* an autofiction about the experiences of Jean, his persona, a Parisian in his early thirties who was diagnosed as HIV-positive in 1986. He continued to live an actively bisexual life with both a male lover, Samy, and a seventeen-year-old girl, Laura. In 1992, Collard (with his companion Corine Blue) wrote the screenplay, and Collard directed and starred in the film. Its controversial treatment of the linkage of desire and disease caused a sensation in France, precisely because of its autographic force. *Les Nuit Fauves* was awarded the French equivalent of the Oscar three days after Collard died of AIDS. In both scripting and impersonating himself and/as another, Collard enacts a kind of autocinema.

If recent independent filmmaking in the United States and Europe has brought diverse kinds of personal stories and innovative modes of visual self-representation to the fore, avant-garde film and video have had a much longer history, one too extensive for a full discussion here. The American avant-garde practice of autobiographical film is lengthy, from Maya Deren's *Meshes of the Afternoon* (1943), an experimental film oscillating between objective and subjective shots or points of view; to Jerome Hill's autobiographical collage of his life, *Film Portrait* (1972); to the experimental autobiographical films of Stan Brakhage. Idiosyncratic, visionary, and political, avant-garde film intensifies the record of an autobiographical consciousness behind the camera and at the editing table (see Sitney; McHugh; Lewis). Similar histories in France, Germany, Russia, Australia, Spain, India, and throughout Latin America and Africa provide rich sites for further investigation.

Online Lives

The burgeoning of online self-expression is shaping new projects of self-presentation.[10] Some, such as blogs, adapt written genres of self-writing. Other mixed-media forms such as social networking sites generate composite modes of digital life narrative. Yet others, such as massively multi-player online games, use avatars that allow users to reimagine themselves—with different gender, ethnicity, and/or bodily features. When such virtual self-recording is for unknown communities, how is self-presentation, and indeed self-experience, changed? In what ways is the previous reliance of life narrative on a stable self with recognizable features thrown into question? We are only at the beginning of the transition from analog writing to digital self-presentation, but such questions will increasingly occupy theorists. Consider how the following sampling of online sites are changing our concepts of what constitutes the digital self.

Journalistic Web logs, or blogs, are the most obvious link to written life narrative. On them users write extended personal narratives and update them regularly, airing deeply personal experiences and thoughts. Laurie McNeill observes that even as they project the newness of the digital revolution, online diaries reproduce traditional conventions of diaristic selves ("Diary 2.0?"). The majority of blogs, however, are unlike online diaries in that they are interactive sites for communities that allow users to comment by raising questions, offering the comfort of shared experience, and "being there" for others in the network of friends, most never met in the flesh. Such Web sites as Xanga.com provide a means of translating between languages, which facilitates international exchange and encourages diasporan users to communicate with others in their home countries.

The public site LiveJournal.com offers bloggers a method of both self-expression and self-help. While they may post photos, images, and music, it is driven by diary-like entries, grouped in forums that users join to engage in dialogue. On the Depression Forum, for example, members discuss a range of feelings, from teenage angst to struggles with mental illness and self-harming practices, such as cutting, that they may have engaged in. Although users attest to its therapeutic value and the comforts of having a responsive community, a skeptic might raise issues: to what extent are clichés of depression rehearsed by self-dramatizing writers adopting stereotypic personas? What of the voyeurism encouraged, especially among users who consume others' posts without participating? It is of course not possible to validate the authenticity of those posting, though regular users often claim someone is "posing"; but many seem unconcerned about accuracy if the "authenticity effect" is sufficient. And yet, interactive blogs encourage the sharing of self-experience and promote a view of the self as flexible, responsive, and dynamic. They enable users in remote or rural areas to discuss sensitive issues of sexuality, gender dysfunction, and isolation, which may promote greater education and foster resistance to repressive community norms. In an essay on the "digital queer," Julie Rak explores the ways in which queered writing circulates in blogs and on the Internet, engaging questions of desire, sexual confession, diasporic mobilities, and the intersection of sexuality and ethnicity (166–82).

Lest we assume that life narrative blogs are always liberatory, however, consider such sites as the so-called pro-ana and pro-mia blogs of anorexics and bulimics, which are popular among young women worldwide. These sites focus on how the community of users can achieve and maintain hyperthin bodies. They reject the notion that such practices constitute mental illness and encourage self-surveillance and discipline through confessing lapses and posting "thinspirational" songs and images of stick-thin models, which link the hyperthin body to fame and wealth. Concerned that such sites, typically only open to users, are contributing to illness and death, Microsoft shut down four of them in 2007 (see Catan). But does such censoring only drive true believers underground and strengthen their sense of persecuted dedication?

Among many kinds of online sites reshaping ideas of life writing, the following are particularly provocative:

- PostSecret (postsecret.blogspot.com) is a Web site created by Frank Warren to showcase postcards that people mail in anonymously. The option to confess dark secrets and participate in the voyeuristic pleasure of reading others' shocking, shameful, arrogant, plaintive, and often funny visual-verbal disclosures has made this site a favorite for the public performance of intimacy. The anonymity of submission may offer contributors an escape from the overorchestration of other social networking sites, such as match sites. But this online venue for confession raises questions about the ways in which the postcard format constrains the complexity of the secret to be confessed. In positioning readers as confessors, does it also produce a conformity in mass confession by publicizing secrets?

- YouTube.com, which emphasizes online performance, has a category called self-videos, where enterprising videomakers set up seemingly solo autobiographical presentations (although they require a crew or a Web cam). These videomakers often adopt personas and imitate other characters as they confide "private" feelings. Impersonation is everywhere on YouTube, and the line between disclosure and performance becomes a fluid, even illusory, boundary. YouTube was notoriously the site of the popular LonelyGirl15 videos, which in 2006 were revealed to be not the haunting disclosures of a teenager but the performance of a woman in her twenties stylizing moments of adolescent angst.[11] Will YouTube self-performance, with its instantaneous circulation and global audience, become an occasion for sustained and introspective self-narration or signal its impossibility? A century from now, people may record their life narratives in video capsules for posterity, producing extensive archives that fulfill the call to narrate the personal in ways as yet unimagined.

- Social networking sites such as Facebook and MySpace attract millions of friend-seeking users. On such sites, people navigate the anonymity of large institutions and the complexities of life away from family and friends. Such sites enable users to join collectives linked by their creation of a user profile and to gain numerous online "friends"; but their question protocols and limited formats restrict the possibilities of self-narration. Because business interests use social networking sites for advertising and gaining information on the consumption habits of users, do these sites work against a concept of the complex, interiorized self? Regarding users as social beings defined by consumer tastes and the size of their friend group may suggest a conformist sense of personhood. At the same time, social networking sites enable transnational exchange among those in the developed nations with the means and leisure time to do so, which may work against nation-specific self-concepts and enhance global community building, at least virtually.

- Avatar sites offer opportunities for enhanced self-referencing. While many online sites suggest that users are "authoring" themselves—as makers, filmers, expressers—virtual self-presentation can also occur on simulation sites that allow users to choose fantasy personas who may act out their desires as avatars, or alter egos, on user-created sites. Perhaps the best known of these is SecondLife.com, created by Linden Labs. It is defined as an unstructured virtual role-playing environment in which users can create new, dramatically different personas.[12] An avatar may be a creature with wings (as everyone can fly), horns, or bestial features, or a hybrid of several beings. The central activity of SecondLife is consumption through economic transactions, although it is increasingly being used for education and training and for political activism. While the site may hone entrepreneurial skills and reward a Franklinian notion of enterprise, the uses of SecondLife for encouraging autobiographical narration as yet seem limited. Its potential for autofictional reflection through visually projecting oneself and reflecting "otherwise" is, however, intriguing.[13]

- Tumblelogs (tumblr.com) present the online self as a reuse center in a virtual green economy. Such sites of self-making and visualizing combine found materials into a textual and visual mélange that is interspersed with a blog. One "expresses" oneself by reusing other people's materials—photographs, images, and icons from other users' sites are incorporated in new patterns. The imagined subject of the tumblelog is a green "bricoleur" with an interesting twist: collective materials, rather than self or identity or locality, are the content. That is, tumblelogs disperse the subject through heterogeneous others' relationality, rather than making claims to an isolated, unified, and centered self.

- An extreme example of online visualized life writing is LifeCasting, a kind of online neorealism that involves live video streaming from someone's home, 24/7. On some sites, the camera is limited to one room; in others, multiple cameras capture movement through home and life. Here the locale is a placeholder for the subject, in an "autobiography as a room," and assumes an identity as self-holder in everyday life. From one point of view, the real-time videocasting of the spaces of one's life functions to extend and apparently privatize state surveillance. As techniques of state and personal surveillance converge, we the viewers may become the eyes of the surveillance machine. Videocasting in real time may record the evacuation of subjectivity altogether as the subject registered becomes the serendipitous trace of movement across space.

- Finally, the phenomenon of Twitter (twitter.com) as a site for online narration enables the near-continuous communication of the user's location, activity, and moods. With 140 characters allowed for twittering information, the form forces condensation and fragmentation. It remains to be seen whether future users will produce online tweeted diaries as microrecords of everyday life.

As these examples suggest, the online possibilities for self-invention seem limitless. We can only speculate on how creating avatar lives in virtuality that explore, for instance, alternative gender roles—of feminine domination or masculine submissiveness in hybrid formations—will inflect the exercise of subjectivity in the daily domestic and political worlds of future women and men. And the range of "self"-soliciting performances we have not discussed, such as online dating sites and the oxymoronic genre of reality television, which emphasize marketing viable selves, suggests that autobiographical performance may increasingly mean getting a prefabricated life.

The Digital Archive of Life Narrative

Creating extensive archives drawn from the experience of everyday life is by no means new, as the British Mass Observation project begun in 1937 indicates. But digitalization of life narratives using the storage and communication capacities of the Web has led to the massive archiving of people's stories. Some archive projects are opportunistic, ephemeral, one-time events that briefly capture worldwide attention, such as the Six-Word Life project, begun in 2006 by the online storytelling magazine *Smith,* which invited readers around the world to compress their life stories into just six words.[14] Others are more targeted in their outreach and more focused in their agenda, organizing around a commonality of experience or identity or historical role. Many are directed to remembering the past, but some are forward looking, assembling stories that will be instructive to future generations. For example, mentoring sites offer young people information about how earlier generations have used a particular degree in their professional life. Some collections target microcommunities in an act of comparative prosopography, as does the Rutgers University History Department's Oral History Project, which collects the stories of alumni/alumnae who served "on the home front and overseas during World War II, the Korean War, the Vietnam War and the Cold War." Some take the nation as their scope. Some project a transnational collectivity, as does the Transnational Feminism archive of stories housed at the Institute for Research on Women and Gender at the University of Michigan.

Many prominent archiving projects are prompted by the desire to capture and preserve the life stories of "survivors," members of groups who have been the victims of organized violence. This desire intensifies as the generations of survivors age; ensuing generations worry that the stories will go untold and the history will be erased from collective memory. Two major projects in recording Holocaust survivor narratives, the collection at the Holocaust Museum in Washington, D.C., and the Fortunoff Video Archive of Holocaust Testimonies at Yale University, have amassed substantial archives and generated theoretical perspectives on modes and audiences of, and mediation in, oral testimony.[15] Several survivor archive projects in the American West, such as the Urban School of San Francisco's Oral History Archives Project, collect the oral histories of Japanese American men, women, and children detained in camps during World War II. Such projects of documenting survivors and commemorating the dead will likely be enhanced around the world as Internet technologies make them possible at the community level.

Another arena of life storytelling in the United States has been stimulated by National Public Radio. The recent collections of personal stories, such as StoryCorps, This I Believe, and Ira Glass's Chicago Project, are examples of ongoing projects through which National Public Radio serves as a repository for the stories of the nation. StoryCorps' mission is "to honor and celebrate one another's lives through listening" (StoryCorps .org). This collective oral history project, which claims to be the largest oral history archive of its kind, invites people across the country to visit traveling booths in cities to record a story.[16] "Since 2003," notes the Web site, "almost 30,000 everyday people have shared life stories with family and friends in our StoryBooths. Each conversation is recorded on a free CD to share, and is preserved at the Library of Congress. Millions listen to our broadcasts on public radio and the web." The StoryCorps Web site offers visitors an opportunity to hear stories, archived under rubrics or themes such as Friendship, Identity, or Hurricane Katrina. Many stories memorialize the dead, or celebrate love, or recall traumatic events from the past. There are also special initiatives to target populations: "In 2006, StoryCorps launched an initiative to reach out to people affected by memory loss. Our aim is to support and encourage people with memory loss to share their stories." A StoryCorps project called Griot explicitly calls for stories of African Americans. Such digitized oral history projects have democratic aspirations in their outreach to ordinary citizens and their effort to build community through projecting common values and shared listening.

With the ever-expanding storage capacity of the Web, collections of oral histories are easily accessed by the public. Life archives aim to be both educational and restorative or healing. They encourage community building and memorialization of the past through breaching differences and identifying shared values. The effort to build collective memory, one story at a time, strives for a participatory citizenship. Such projects of collective storytelling, whether published as books, film documents, recordings, or in digital media, situate the individual story in the larger metanarrative of a nation's social history, as "history from below," binding both tellers and listeners to the nation as an imagined community.

While digital forms for data collecting and streaming in video and audio formats enhance the opportunities to organize and search story collections, how are digital archives likely to affect the kinds of stories being told, the ways these stories will become available, and the kinds of "selves" they will encourage? Archivers and the institutions collecting stories have particular agendas. They assemble individual stories in frameworks by posing certain questions, not others; they group stories under thematic rubrics; they define communities based on ethnicity or particular historical experiences. Stories are scripted not only by the interests of interviewers but by the editing that may occur when they are translated for inclusion on a digital site. Which kinds of stories are likely to survive in digital form, and what versions of them are expected of the witnesses whose stories are collected?

In sum, how projects are organized will render certain stories intelligible, others unintelligible. And the politics of particular archives may determine whose story is retained in digital preservation projects. Archives may also be particularly vulnerable to degradation in storage memory and new technologies that render earlier data archives obsolete. Both the technologies of collecting and archiving life stories and the kinds of stories solicited and preserved are thus subject to pressures and changes that cannot always be known or avoided.

Conclusion

Visual and digital modes are projecting and circulating not just new subjects but new notions of subjectivity through the effects of automediality. Indeed, autographics, visual, sculptural, and performance art practices, and cinematic experiments in autodocumentary present subjects whose embodiment, visualization, and narration intersect, overlap, dissociate, and disperse as sound, light, touch, line, blank space, and box. Through heterogeneous media, the archive of the self in time, in space, and in relation expands and is fundamentally reorganized.

Furthermore, new digital subjects no longer rely on the written inscription that has dominated life writing thus far. As Brian Rotman argues, digitalization of code and network will radically transform our notions of the "self" itself, shifting us from the "alphabetic self" of written inscription with its technologies of disembodiedness, interiority, and authority of the singular to the self that is distributed, networked, and plural (see his *Becoming beside Ourselves*). He prompts us to consider whether the digitalization of code will bring the end of interiority and individuality as hallmarks of subjectivity and thus of life narrative; whether autobiographical discourse will reconstellate in this world of code, adapting older, recognizable tropes, topoi, and rhetorics of identity to new digital environments; or whether autobiographical discourse will disperse across virtual circuits as new selves and lives, not yet recognizable, take shape. In such an unmapped territory of the self, the archiving of selves and lives, made possible by the awesome storage capacity of computers and their myriad interfaces, may provide a comforting repository of our past selves and past lives in the midst of a future as yet unimaginable.

7

A History of Autobiography Criticism, Part I:
Theorizing Autobiography

As autobiography has been the dominant mode in literature of the twentieth century, so critical attention to the questions posed by the auto-biographical act has become the principal preoccupation of theorists across the entire critical spectrum.

James Olney, "Autobiography and the Cultural Moment"

No autobiography can take place except within the boundaries of a writing where concepts of subject, self, and author collapse into the act of producing a text.

Michael Sprinker, "Fictions of the Self: The End of Autobiography"

We are never really the cause of our life, but we can have the illusion of becoming its author by writing it, providing that we forget that we are no more the cause of the writing than of our life.

Philippe Lejeune, "The Autobiography of Those Who Do Not Write"

Scholarly books and articles about autobiographical narrative have appeared at an increasing rate in the past sixty years, particularly during the past three decades. The year 1980 saw the publication of two bibliographical essays that interpreted the history and shifting preoccupations of criticism up to that time: the essay appended to William C. Spengemann's *Forms of Autobiography: Episodes in the History of a Literary Genre* and "Autobiography and the Cultural Moment," the introductory essay to *Autobiography: Essays Theoretical and Critical,* edited by James Olney. Spengemann situated the first surge of critical interest in the practice of life narrative in the late nineteenth and early twentieth centuries, citing three contributing phenomena: the increasing number of life narratives reaching an interested public; the increasing number of critical essays focused on such narrative; and the influence of German historian Wilhelm Dilthey, who defined the genre of autobiography as "the highest and most instructive form in which the understanding of life comes before us" (*Pattern and Meaning* 85–86) and called for its use in the writing of history.

But earlier cultural influences forming notions of personhood also contributed to a surge of interest among critics and readers. These include:

- the eighteenth-century privileging of an Enlightenment or liberal-humanist subject understood as universal man and transcendent mind;
- the revolutionary movements of the late eighteenth century, with their pressures for greater democratization of society and the enfranchisement of women and some classes;
- the radical individualism celebrated by Romantic movements throughout Europe and the Americas in the early nineteenth century;
- Victorian Darwinism, most particularly social Darwinism, with its emphasis on the survival of the fittest and the primacy of evolutionary progress;
- the Industrial Revolution and its informing myth of the self-made man;
- the writing of history through the paradigm of the "great man";
- Freud's theory of the unconscious and the analytical methods used in psychoanalysis to organize self-reflection;
- the rise of literacy and the great outburst of literary activity that accompanied increasing democratization.

Social and philosophical transformations from the seventeenth through the early twentieth centuries contributed in new ways to the formation of the Western subject as an accomplished and exceptional individual, as Michael Mascuch has argued; the consolidation of that subject was a key means of legitimating the spread of imperialism around the globe. As we have suggested elsewhere (introduction to *De/Colonizing*), an important historical use—although by no means the only use—of "autobiography" has been as a master narrative of Western rationality, progress, and superiority. And the readings of generations of critics of life narrative shaped and authorized this understanding.

Historicizing the Origins and Cultural Contexts of Autobiography

Dilthey's student and son-in-law, German philologist Georg Misch, inaugurated the first wave of modern criticism of the field. In his vast, multivolume *A History of Autobiography in Antiquity,* Misch argued that the progressive unfolding of Western history can be read in the representative lives of the leaders who participated in this achievement of civilization; and he discovered particular types of Western man in the self-representational strategies of each generation of autobiographers.

Misch defines *autobiography* as "the description *(graphia)* of an individual human life *(bios)* by the individual himself *(autos)*" (5). Two introductory passages from Misch's *History* taken together suggest his critical orientation:

> Among the special relationships in life it is chiefly the self-assertion of the political will and the relation of the author to his work and to the public that show themselves to be normative in the history of autobiography. (14)

> Though essentially representations of individual personalities, autobiographies are bound always to be representative of their period, within a range that will vary with the intensity of the authors' participation in contemporary life and with the sphere in which they moved. (12)

For Misch, the normative generic characteristics of autobiography and the criteria for the success of any particular life narrator rest in the writer's relationship to the arena of public life and discourse. Public figures are the "representative" and appropriate subjects of what he designates as autobiography. Misch's emphasis on the autobiographer's role as a public presence is part of his scheme of a division between the "high culture" of achieved and elite civilizations and the "low culture" of popular and everyday forms. The autobiography of the great man, according to Misch, is a major achievement of high culture, entwined with the making of the modern nation-state. Dilthey and Misch were significant in inaugurating the last century's critical fascination with autobiography. They offered a working definition of the genre and its controlling trope—the life of the "great man." They situated that man and his actions in specific historical and cultural contexts and assessed how he and his deeds were "representative" of the times.

This German tradition of *Geistesgeschichte* (the spirit of the historical moment) excludes other kinds of life narrative practiced for much of human history—letters, diaries, journals, memoirs, and other autobiographical modes of everyday and private life. It also excludes other kinds of subjects. Unmentioned are the nonpublic figures such as women, slaves, and colonized peoples, whose assertion of human status and exercise of rights as social subjects were systematically restricted and often brutally repressed and whose acts of self-narrating either silenced, repressed, or ignored.

Misch's other prescriptive definition, the "representative" nature of autobiography, raises additional concerns about normative autobiographical subjects. His definition of the "supreme example" of human accomplishment is "the contemporary intellectual outlook revealed in the style of an eminent person who has himself played a part in the forming of the spirit of his time" (12–13). Just as historians have dismantled the notion of *Geistesgeschichte*, recent literary critics have dismantled this notion of the "representative life" that haunted earlier critical definitions of autobiography, asking such questions as the following: what is at stake when a life is described as "representative"? Whose lives can be considered representative of a culture or a historical moment? Who determines which lives are representative? As cultural critics have argued for several decades, such labeling of what is—or is not—representative is part of the cultural project of "naming, controlling, remembering, understanding" (Jardine 118–19) that sustains the patriarchal, and imperial, power to produce "knowledge" about the world and to authorize certain subjects to produce that knowledge. If only those people authorized as agents of existing institutions determine the economic value of lives, what are the consequences for our sense of which people can "get a life" and become cultural subjects?

We want to be clear here. We are not arguing that only "great" public men could and did write autobiographies in the past, or that others were always excluded from cultural production. Though their access was certainly constrained, many people, from diverse cultural locations, produced, wrote, and told their stories to confessors, amanuenses, and editors before the twentieth century. Our point is that the texts produced, some quite popular and influential in their own times, did not acquire the status of "representative autobiographies"; these life narratives were not seen as formative of "civilization" and thus not celebrated as the appropriate subject of study. In effect, then, Misch's notion of autobiography as the record of a representative life of the great man long served as a norm, a "master narrative" about the meaning and role of a particular model of life narrative in Western civilization.

Misch's work began to be invoked in scholarly definitions of *autobiography,* once interest in autobiography, which the New Critics had eschewed as an inferior literary mode, began to reawaken in a few corners of the academy in the late 1950s.[1] In Anglo-American literary scholarship generally, the New Critics crafted a concept of the literary text as aesthetic object and work of value, most fully achieved when irresolvably ambiguous. William K. Wimsatt Jr. and Cleanth Brooks trace a critical tradition since Plato in which the genre of autobiography and the practice of life narrative go unmentioned. Remarkably, the highly influential 1966 study *The Nature of Narrative* by Robert Scholes and Robert Kellogg also situates narrative only in the history of the novel, the epic, and the film, and nowhere alludes to life narrative. This striking omission is perhaps best understood as an enactment of Wimsatt's condemnation of "the intentional fallacy" as anathema to the work of verbal art, a romantic and positivist construing of verbal indeterminacy that privileges the author's psychology and reduces poetry to literary biography, "whether written by the author or a critic" ("Intentional Fallacy" 10). Wimsatt's concept of the autobiographical is implicit in his argument that self-referential narrative would be "external . . . private or idiosyncratic; not a part of the work as a linguistic fact; it consists of revelations (in journals, for example, or letters or reported conversations) about how or why the poet wrote the poem" (10). In effect, Wimsatt reads the self-referential reductively as "evidence of what the author intended" in his literary works; at best, he implies, the autobiographical is a form of marginalia about great works, not a kind of artful text in itself (11). For the dominant Anglo-American critical tradition, then, autobiographical writing was a suspect mode of "trivia" or "personal" writing, the site of writers' flawed notions about their artistic works, and therefore was to be bracketed out of the canon of poetic and narrative texts and critical theory that the implementation of New Criticism enabled in the academy. Thus the master narrative set in motion by Misch's landmark study has influenced subsequent studies of the genre— with significant effects in terms of the texts discussed and critical assessments of their cultural importance.

Similarly, critics reading through these assumptions rarely turned to forms of self-representation outside the West in the great biographical traditions of China, Japan, India, and Persia; and they omitted the North African ancestry of an immigrant such as Augustine. Nor did they recognize the significance of oral, nonalphabetic traditions of collective self-inscription in indigenous cultures throughout the world. If, by definition, Western Europe signified "civilization," then life narrative from elsewhere and nonwritten self-representation would be understood as properly the focus of disciplines outside literary studies, that is, of anthropology and folklore.

Canon Formation

Scholars contributing to the norms of autobiography criticism as a field of study focused their interpretations and built their theories around several key life narratives of "great men." How then was the canon of life narrative generated and how did it inform the criticism of autobiography?

A "canon" is a culturally valued set of texts that are agreed to represent the "best" that the culture has produced—the best novels or plays or poems, for instance, or the best life narratives, deemed autobiography.[2] Canons are determined by widely recognized sources of cultural authority, a person or group of people charged with establishing criteria of inclusion and exclusion that determine what fits and doesn't fit the criteria. But what criteria determine inclusion in the canon? Clearly, the criteria used vary with culture, the national language, and the historical period. Particular titles included in a canon will change over time. But the idea of a core of "the best" remains. Griselda Pollock notes that "the best" are assigned "transhistorical aesthetic value." They are read as "timeless." And that "timelessness," paradoxically, assures their value at a particular moment in time.

By the 1960s, scholars had established a set of texts that served to legitimate the field of autobiography studies. Some of the life narratives that emerged as "landmarks" in the critical study of self-exploration, confession, and self-discovery will be familiar, for example, Saint Augustine's *Confessions*, Cellini's *Life*, Rousseau's *Confessions*, Fox's *Journal*, Franklin's *Autobiography*, Goethe's *Truth and Poetry*, Mill's *Autobiography*, Cardinal Newman's *Apologia Pro Vita Sua*, and Thoreau's *Walden*. To midcentury, shifts in this canon meant moving beyond a Eurocentric focus and acknowledging significant life narrative in the Americas, especially by

Franklin, Thoreau, Whitman, and Adams. These core texts were the focus of interpretation in articles and book-length studies of autobiography; the accumulation of interpretations contributed to their maintaining canonical status.

Scholars brought a set of assumptions to their readings of these texts. They assumed the autobiographer to be an autonomous and enlightened "individual" who exercised free will and understood his relationship to others and the world as one of separateness. Focusing on the teleological pattern of development in narratives usually written late in life as retrospections on public and/or writing careers, they assumed a concluding point at which some kind of self-understanding through reflection on past achievement takes place. And, like Dilthey and Misch, they assumed the representative status of the narrator; that is, they assumed that even as the narrator speaks of his individual life, the patterns of behavior, achievements, intellectual preoccupations, and relationships with others he rehearses are the norm or—in the case of rebels such as Augustine, Rousseau, or Thoreau—the inspired choice of the culture. That these canonical texts can be (and are being) read very differently now suggests that the categories of freedom, individuality, coherent life design, and comprehensible, connected events of past life have been historical norms that have informed acts of critical reading.

A group of texts became canonical, common reference points for scholarly discussion and debate as the field emerged in the 1960s. These autobiographies were regarded as "high" culture, different from the life narratives of celebrities, military leaders, religious figures, and politicians that ordinary people sought out with pleasure during the century. Later we will consider how new "countercanons" have formed over the past forty years, as scholars recovered and reevaluated neglected and marginalized forms of life writing. With this countering of the canon (and the loosening of the hold of a concept of "representative lives"), scholars have brought a diversity of reading strategies to canonical autobiographies, offering innovative readings of, say, the "gay" Goethe or the "postcolonial" Augustine.

Theoretical Interventions I: Gusdorf, Hart, and Creative Self-Representation

James Olney ascribes the second surge of autobiography criticism to 1956 and the publication (in French) of Belgian critic Georges Gusdorf's article "Conditions and Limits of Autobiography." William Spengemann traces a new critical moment back to 1970 and the publication of Francis R. Hart's essay "Notes for an Anatomy of Modern Autobiography," arguing that much of the work done before 1970, including Gusdorf's seminal article, remained unknown in the English-speaking world. For both Olney and Spengemann, there are two significant turning points. The first has to do with the application of a rigorous critical analysis to autobiographical narration that parallels in intent and seriousness that addressed to the novel, poetry, and drama. The second has to do with the critical focus on self-narrating as the distinctive hallmark of autobiography.

First-wave critics, preoccupied with the *bios* of the autobiographer, understood autobiography as a subcategory of the biography of great lives and acted as moralists of sorts, evaluating the quality of the life lived and the narrator's telling of that truth. To treat autobiographical narration transparently this way is to assume, as James Olney astutely notes, that "there was nothing problematical about the *autos,* no agonizing questions of identity, self-definition, self-existence, or self-deception—at least none the reader need attend to—and therefore the fact that the individual was himself narrating the story of himself had no troubling philosophical, psychological, literary, or historical implications" ("Autobiography and the Cultural Moment" 20). In contrast, second-wave critics brought new understandings of the autobiographical subject, involving new understandings of the key concepts of self and truth. The Enlightenment or liberal-humanist notion of selfhood understood the "I" as the universal, transcendent marker of "man." Radical challenges to the notion of a unified selfhood in the early decades of the twentieth century eroded certainty in both a coherent "self" and the "truth" of self-narrating:

- The Marxist analysis of class-consciousness, linking individual consciousness determinatively to larger economic forces, defined the individual as subjected to economic structures and relationships rather than as autonomous agent. In this framing, humans lose agency; they are defined as perversely manipulated subjects who, in Louis Althusser's terms, will exhibit false consciousness and be "interpellated" by ideologies (see chapter 2).
- Freudian psychoanalysis destabilized the notion that the human being is a rational actor by reconfiguring "self" as a struggle of forces occurring outside conscious control. A subversive unconscious continuously threatens the individual's precarious illusion of conscious control over identity and experience.

- Freud also redefined the function of language in knowing oneself. Never neutral, language is always "interested." It speaks through the subject and is mysterious to its speaker because it encodes his desire. Indeed, in Lacan's reinterpretation of Freud, the unconscious is a language through which the subject spoken is always other to his own desire.

- Linguists such as Saussure and the Russian Formalists further problematized language by questioning the transparency of what was formerly conceptualized as a medium of self-expression. According to Saussure, language cannot and does not imitate reality or merely designate things through words. Language is a system of meaning produced through the relationship of signifier (*parole,* or word) and signified (*langue,* or referent). As a system, language operates outside the individual subject; and so, entering into language, the individual becomes more "spoken by" language than an agentic speaker of it. The individual is more a product of discursive regimes (culturally dominant knowledges) than the self-creator and explorer of any essence of self outside culturally coded systems of meaning. And the individual cannot know herself through language.

Critics shifted from the concept of a universal "self"—achieving self-discovery, self-creation, and self-knowledge—to a new concept of the "subject" riven by self-estrangement and self-fragmentation; and they explored the problematic relationship of the subject to language. As a result, the project of self-representation could no longer be read as providing direct access to the truth of the self. Truthfulness becomes a more complex phenomenon of narrators struggling to shape an "identity" out of an amorphous subjectivity.

The first phase of this shift called attention to the creative aspect of autobiographical representation. In "Conditions and Limits," Gusdorf argues that autobiography is a uniquely Western genre of life narrative, and more particularly a Christian form of self-writing, one that requires a historical rather than a cyclic notion of time and a concept of the individual as separate from the collectivity and as the highest achievement of civilization. Autobiography is, he says, an act of "reconstructing the unity of a life across time" (37). As such it functions for the writer as "a second reading of experience, and it is truer than the first because it adds to experience itself consciousness of it" (38). Thus, Gusdorf emphasizes the creative aspect of autobiographical writing. It is for him "art" rather than "history." As art the autobiographical act always fixes that which is in process, making it a cultural artifact. By definition, then, autobiography must fail to create the life of the writer, but it enshrines consciousness, the ability to reflect on oneself through the autobiographical process.

Olney extends this exploration of the "creative" nature of autobiographical acts by developing a theory that all writing, but most pointedly life narrative, creates "metaphors of self." For Olney, the autobiographical is a unique mode of writing because it has the potential to postulate self-reflection as a process rather than an essence, through the "doubling" of self-observation. But only certain writers, for instance, Montaigne and T. S. Eliot, realize this potential of autobiographical writing to create a structure of self-reflection in which the narrated "I" and the narrating "I" are interlocked.

Another aspect of this shift emphasized the forms of self-presentation. Conceding that "'unreliability' is an inescapable condition" (488–89), that is, that narrators cannot tell the truth disinterestedly, Hart redefines life narrative as a drama of intentions that "interact and shift" (491). Hart establishes three categories of autobiographical intention: the confession, the apology, and the memoir—each a modality of relationship to the addressee and reader. And he acknowledges "the continuous refocusing of expectation and intention as each autobiographer discovers his own fluctuating mixture of confession, apology, and memoir" (508).

Explorations of generic conventions fostered more nuanced readings of autobiographical texts by situating them within the parameters of literary production rather than the realm of history writing. But even as the Gusdorf and Hart essays directed readers to the creative complexities of life narratives, they continued to encode certain cultural models of selfhood. Gusdorf explicitly defines "autobiography" as "Western," only possible in a culture with a historical notion of time and a concept of the isolate individual. While a notion of individual, progressive time—as opposed to cyclical temporality—may underwrite certain narratives in the West, overemphasis on progressive time ignores the subjective time of memory and constrains recognition of autobiographical acts to a narrowly defined scope and limited possibilities. Similarly, Hart's anatomy was bound to the critical norms privileging individuality and separateness over relationality.

The staying power of Misch's and Dilthey's identification of autobiography with individuality and greatness, even in this second wave of critics, can thus be traced in these pivotal essays by Gusdorf and Hart, and in Karl Joachim Weintraub's *The Value of the Individual: Self and Circumstance in Autobiography.* Weintraub defines male and Western norms as human and universal norms and enshrines the sovereign self. Again we see how such a typology does not mark alternative racial origins or gendered identities.

Reconceiving self-referential narratives not as sites of the truth of a life but as creative self-engagements allowed the elevation of autobiography to the status of a literary genre. Critics were enabled to turn their attention to the history, forms, themes, and tropes of self-narrating but also tended to bracket out other kinds of life narratives, assigning them subliterary status. Wayne Shumaker, Margaret Bottrall, Paul Delany, Daniel B. Shea *(Spiritual Autobiography),* and other scholars of autobiography, for example, charted their versions of the genre's historical development. Roy Pascal and Jean Starobinski, like Hart, formulated concepts of generic conventions and poetics. William Spengemann and William L. Howarth defined its paradigmatic patterns. Others attempted to categorize life narrative's manifold expressions in a more expansive hierarchy of types, including memoir, confession, diary, journal, and chronicle.

The focus on self-referential narratives as narratives of autonomous individuality and representative lives narrowed the range of vision to the West. That focus also privileged "high" cultural forms, a focus that obscured the vast production of life narratives by ex-slaves, apprentices and tradespeople, adventurers, criminals and tricksters, saints and mystics, immigrants, and the representation of lives in such documents as wills and treaties. The gendering of the representative life as universal and therefore masculine meant that narratives by women were rarely examined; and on those rare occasions when their narratives were taken up, they were accorded a place in an afterword, a paragraph, a note—in marginal comments for what were seen as marginal lives. Or their achievements were defined through normatively feminine terms. But if we recall the diverse modes of life narrating by marginalized, minoritized, diasporic, nomadic, and postcolonial subjects throughout the history of life writing, the focus on liberal individuality as both the motive and achievement of autobiographical writing is insufficient as a determining force.

Theoretical Interventions II: Acts, Pacts, and Fictions

Poststructural and postmodern theorizing about the subject from the 1970s through the 1980s led to the reconceptualization of subjectivity and, therefore, of autobiographical acts. In telescoped fashion we might summarize these theoretical interventions, alluded to in chapters 2 and 3, as follows:

- The Lacanian revision of Freudian psychoanalysis challenged the notion of an autonomous self and proposed a split subject always constituted in language.
- The Derridean notion of *différance* captured the way in which "language, whose meanings are produced by differences . . . tries to set up distinctions necessary for there to be meaning." Meanings, always emergent in the system "as a whole," are never fixed, but rely on other signifiers that "lie in waiting, negatively supporting the signifier that has been uttered or written" (Pollock 30). Consequently, meaning is always in process, continuously put off, or deferred.
- Derridean and Lyotardian critiques of universalized or "master" narratives contributed to the deconstruction of "Truth" with a capital *T* and challenged generic boundaries between fact and fiction.
- Althusser argued that ideology constitutes not only socioeconomic relations but subjectivity itself. Social subjects are subjects of ideology, "interpellated" or "hailed" as a particular kind of subject by the very institutions through which those ideologies are reproduced.
- Foucault's emphasis on discourses of identity and his critique of power analyzed the multiple, dispersed, local technologies of selfhood through which subjects come to self-knowledge in historically specific regimes of truth.
- Bakhtin's concept of the dialogism of the word and the consequent heteroglossia of utterances replaced the unitary "I" with multiple dialogic voices spoken as the autobiographical "I" speaks in language that has "a multitude of concrete worlds, a multitude of bounded verbal-ideological and social belief-systems" (288).
- Anthropological research exposed critics and theorists to

ideologies of selfhood outside the West that challenge the universality and homogeneity of Western models. It also exposed the ways in which the framing of human thought and language is determined by culture.

- Feminist theories of representation problematized "experience" as a transparent category of meaning, examined the political dynamics of the "personal," focused on the body as a site of cultural inscription and practices of embodiment, and critiqued the notion of a universalized "woman" by exploring the differences among women.

- Frantz Fanon's critique of the specularity of the colonial gaze reconceptualized relations of domination and subordination in formerly colonized regions and linked the subjection of colonial peoples to international racism at a moment when national liberation movements were disrupting the interdependencies of identity in colonial relationships between the West and its Others.

- Postcolonial, ethnic, and feminist studies analyzed the effects of discourses of identity and cultural practices on minoritized and/or de/colonized subjects and proposed enabling models of margins and centers.

- Gay and, more recently, queer studies resituated subjectivity as performative and criticized binary models of the organization of gender and sexuality.

- Cultural studies, long-standing in Great Britain and taking hold in the United States, turned to popular, public, and everyday forms of textuality, including everyday practices of self-narrating in verbal, visual, and mixed modes.

- Alternative concepts of time challenged the primacy of notions of chronological and progressive time, relativizing external and internal temporalities of history and of memory.

- Interdisciplinary studies of memory and its encoding in the materiality of the brain offered new ways of understanding the processes of remembering and forgetting, and the effects of traumatic memories.

Taken together, these theoretical reframings suggest a paradigm shift in understandings of the subject. Derridean deconstruction, Barthesian semiotics, and Foucauldian analysis of the discursive regimes of power energized the dismantling of metaphysical conceptions of self-presence, authority, authenticity, and truth. As for Lacan, for Derrida the self is a fiction, an illusion constituted in discourse, a hypothetical place or space of storytelling. A true self can never be discovered, unmasked, or revealed because its core is a *mise en abîme,* an infinite regress. The origin and history of the self, then, are fictions, although the history of utterances of that fiction can be traced. Because the self is split and fragmented, it can no longer be conceptualized as unitary. At a given moment what calls itself the self is different from itself at any other given moment. As Virginia Woolf remarked, "'I' is only a convenient term for somebody who has no real being" (*A Room of One's Own* 4).

Some Influential Studies

Such challenges to the concept of a unified, sovereign subject and to belief in language's transparency have shattered the cultural authority of what Lyotard calls the "master narratives" of the West, including the institution of canonical autobiography. Although at this time the unitary self of liberal humanism remains a prevailing notion governing Western configurations and disciplines of selfhood, that universal self and the narratives through which it has claimed its authority are increasingly open to challenge. Around the globe, contesting versions of selfhood are posed in diverse kinds of life narratives that introduce collective, provisional, and mobile subjects. The conditions for this exploration were set up in a series of influential essays and books in the 1980s and 1990s that engaged the poetics and politics of the autobiographical, to which we now turn.

Elizabeth Bruss's 1976 *Autobiographical Acts: The Changing Situation of a Literary Genre* and her related essay on film argue for understanding autobiography neither mimetically, as a chronology of the representative life, nor expressively, as the writer's baring of experience, but as a performative act: "Autobiography is a personal performance, an action that exemplifies the character of the agent responsible for that action and how it is performed" (Bruss, "Eye for I" 300). While "act-value" is only one of three defining features of her theory—the others are truth-value and identity-value—and her orientation is toward the unitary makers of speech acts, her promising emphasis on autobiographical acts in various media anticipated a dominant trend of the 1990s toward theorizing autobiographical performativity.

If Bruss insists on the autobiographical occasion as an act, Philippe Lejeune insists on its function as a pact. In theorizing the autobiographical pact, Lejeune integrates a concept of both implied and actual (flesh-and-blood) readers into the meaning making of autobiographical writing. As he refines distinctions between autobiography and biography, on the one hand, and autobiography and fiction on the other, by considering linguistic modes of the "I," Lejeune takes the position of the reader as his starting point. According to Lejeune, the autobiographical text establishes a "pact" among narrator, reader, and publisher that "supposes that there is *identity of name* between the author (such as he figures, by his name, on the cover), the narrator of the story, and the character who is being talked about" ("Autobiographical Pact" 12). For Lejeune the "deep signature" of autobiography is the proper name: "What defines autobiography for the one who is reading is above all a contract of identity that is sealed by the proper name. And this is true also for the one who is writing the text" (19–20). Lejeune subsequently modified his schema in "The Autobiographical Pact (bis)" by acknowledging that "the real reader can adopt modes of reading different from the one that is suggested to him," and he acknowledged "especially that many published texts in no way include an explicit contract" ("bis" 126). While modifying the concept of the pact to account for the fictionality of the proper name, however, Lejeune reconfirms the necessity of an author-reader-publisher pact as central to autobiography.

In another version of the writer-reader contract, Janet Varner Gunn in 1982 situated a theory of autobiography in two moments of reading. The first moment of reading is that of "the autobiographer who, in effect, is 'reading' his or her life"; the second moment is that of "the reader of the autobiographical text," who is also, in the encounter with the text, re-reading his or her own life by association (8). For Gunn, the reader, like the narrator, is engaged in an autobiographical act.

Other theorists considered the vexed relationship of the autobiographer to his or her own past, his or her own status as an "I." Louis A. Renza's important 1977 essay "The Veto of the Imagination: A Theory of Autobiography" theorized autobiographical temporality and the relationship of the autobiographical subject to the only apparent "pastness" of the past. Renza argues that, in the act of writing, the life narrator "presentifies" that past; never simply recollected, it informs the present moment of writing. Furthermore, Renza argues, autobiography only appears to be an activity of imaginative cognition manifesting the writer's "screen [set up] between the truth of the narrated past and the present of the narrative situation"

(3). The writer engages imaginatively in what Renza terms the "'impersonating' effect of discourse" as a "diacritical retention of the 'I,'" a split intentionality (9). Renza's insistence on the self-referentiality of an "I" that both "presentifies" and reexperiences its past anticipates theories of the performativity of life writing.

Continental theorists challenged the very possibility of autobiography as an act and a genre. Paul de Man's influential essay "Autobiography as De-Facement" challenged autobiography as an inevitably self-deluded practice unable to represent the life or *bios* it took as its subject:

> We assume the life produces the autobiography as an act produces its consequences, but can we not suggest, with equal justice, that the autobiographical project may itself produce and determine the life and that whatever the writer does is in fact governed by the technical demands of self-portraiture and thus determined, in all its aspects, by the resources of its medium? (920)

For de Man autobiography as a genre is the exemplary case of prosopopoeia, or the representation of an imaginary or absent person as speaking and acting. While this strong challenge to the form's legitimacy may be qualified by de Man's own troubling lapses about his past collusion with occupying Nazi forces, his reading of prosopopoeia framed a question of autobiographical representation as an act of impersonation that remains a key issue.[3]

Roland Barthes, a germinal French critic who theorized the death of the author, the dispersal of the self into a fragmented subject, and the pleasures of the text, also wrote "autobiography" and autobiographically in many essays, experimenting with the media, the chronology, and the subjectivity of life writing. His putatively autobiographical *Roland Barthes by Roland Barthes* enacted at once an autobiographical and an antiautobiographical engagement with questions of the self, not least because Barthes urged readers, in his epigraph, to read it as a novel. Barthes routed this provocative intervention in conventions of self-representation through an assemblage of personal photographs and wrote it in quasi-alphabetical textual fragments that obscured his personal life by using first-, second-, and third-person pronouns. Candace Lang characterizes *Roland Barthes by Roland Barthes* as a text of fragments from Barthes's previous writings, combined with fragmentary comments on those fragments (*Irony/Humor*

165–72). Paul John Eakin notes that Barthes "explicitly disavows any connection between the 'I' of his text and any self anchored in an extratextual realm of biographical reference" (*How Our Lives Become Stories* 137), but he also insists that Barthes's seeming refusal of reference is anchored in an interpersonal discourse with his mother that "fosters the emergence of the extended self and its store of autobiographical memories" (139). Barthes's *Camera Lucida,* by contrast, combines his speculations on the effects of photography on the spectator with a meditation on his mother's death. It can be read in part as an elegiac portrait of the other, whose loss is felt through the effect of the *punctum,* the detail of the photograph that wounds and thereby creates a personal bond between the viewer and the lost loved one. Despite his personal reflection and interest in a new mode of writing, Barthes did not systematically organize a theory of the autobiographical; rather, he problematized its assumed transparency in ways that continue to be provocative for scholars (see Sheringham).

In the 1980s and early 1990s critics recast issues of referentiality, fictionality, and truth telling in life writing. Avrom Fleishman focused on figural representation in autobiography, for instance, and Alfred E. Stone, James Cox, and Robert F. Sayre rethought the rhetorics, texts, and tropes of American autobiography. In *Telling Lies in Modern American Autobiography,* Timothy Dow Adams examines limit cases in which autobiographers deliberately propounded lies, in some cases to exploit, in other cases to expand, the boundaries of autobiographical discourse. Moving to another limit, the interface of photography and life writing as modes of representing subjectivity for Americans over two centuries, Adams, in *Light Writing and Life Writing: Photography in Autobiography,* explores the "vexed history of referentiality" encountered in theorizing the ways in which photography and autobiography "represent" the world. Thinking about the two modes of referentiality together enables Adams to understand that "since reference is not secure in either, neither can compensate for lack of stability in the other" (xxi). In both studies Adams is preoccupied with the ways in which acts that expose and refer are also acts that conceal and blur.

In his 1985 *Fictions of Autobiography: Studies in the Art of Self-Invention,* Paul John Eakin argues that autobiographical writing is a form of self-invention that constitutes the self. In this sense, the self is the origin of "the reflexive center of human subjectivity" (198), although self as a concept is both historically demarcated and culturally specific. For Eakin the autobiographical act both reenacts and extends earlier phases of the entry into identity through language (226). While Eakin modifies this view of the textuality of the self in *Touching the World: Reference in Autobiography* by insisting on autobiography's referentiality to a historical and material world, his emphasis since has been on the processes by which lives are made into stories and on self-experience as "a kind of awareness in process" (*How Our Lives Become Stories* x). In *How Our Lives Become Stories: Making Selves,* Eakin probes interdisciplinary approaches to life narrative based on recent work in neurology, cognitive science, memory research, and developmental psychology and inquires into the implications of those approaches for contextualizing "the registers of self and self-experience" (xi). He has consistently been attentive to the ethics of narrating autobiographical stories, and, most recently, to "how we create identity in narrative" as part of a dynamic process of ongoing self-creation.

Throughout the 1980s and early 1990s, feminist critics and theorists turned their attention to the long tradition of women's life writing; such works by critics Patricia Ann Meyer Spacks, Mary G. Mason, and the essays gathered by Estelle Jelinek, Shari Benstock, Bella Brodzki and Celeste Schenck, and Julia Swindells made the new field of women's life writing the vibrant field it has become. Attentive to French feminisms, theorists Domna C. Stanton and Nancy K. Miller began the work of revising gender essentialism through theories of sexual difference. Miller's "Toward a Dialectics of Difference" calls for a new reading of the interplay of gender and genre. Stanton's "Autogynography: Is the Subject Different?" queries the erasure of women's life writing in the canon of Western autobiography and proposes the term *autogynography* to connote the difference of women's life writing practices and subjectivities. Other feminist theorists, such as Felicity Nussbaum, Susan Stanford Friedman, and Barbara Green have elaborated the history of women's life writing and theorized its differences. Sidonie Smith, in her 1987 *A Poetics of Women's Autobiography: Marginality and the Fictions of Self-Representation,* theorizes the linkage of gender and genre in exploring how women engage autobiographical discourse to renegotiate their cultural marginality and enter into literary history. As Smith's 1993 *Subjectivity, Identity, and the Body: Women's Autobiographical Practices in the Twentieth Century* makes clear, autobiographical subjectivity is enacted in cultural spaces between the personal "I" and the body politic. A life narrator's inscription of embodied textuality is thus an effect of discourses of embodiment. Linda H. Peterson develops a different line of argument in *Traditions of Victorian Women's Autobiography,* namely that women's negotiation of social and literary institutions made a space for the emergence of their extended autobiographical writings in Victorian England. In her 1989 *Autobiographical Voices: Race, Gender, Self-Portraiture,* Françoise Lionnet explores the intercultural zones of life writing by women of color, proposing the term *métissage* to designate the braided languages and discourses characterizing marginalized women's negotiations of identity and history. Lionnet's 1995 *Postcolonial Representations* situates women's encounters with the conditions of neocolonial asymmetry and violence across a wide range of cultures in the developing world. As scholarship and theorizing of women's life writing are too extensive to adequately encompass in this review, we refer readers to our introduction to *Women, Autobiography, Theory: A Reader,* which offers an overview of representative theories and work up to the late 1990s and to the 2005 *Encyclopedia of Women's Autobiography* (Boynton and Malin).

Conclusion

Engaging the challenges posed by postmodernism's deconstruction of any solid ground of selfhood and truth outside of discourse and by postcolonial theory's troubling of established hierarchies of authority, tradition, and influence, these theoretical approaches to life writing up to the late 1990s accomplished several things. They drew on and adapted aspects of postmodern and postcolonial theory, which are themselves heterogeneous rather than unified fields. They considered generic instability, regimes of truth telling, referentiality, relationality, and embodiment as issues that contest the assumptions of the earlier critical period's understanding of canonical autobiography. And they expanded the range of life writing and the kinds of stories critics may engage in rethinking the field of life narrative. In the next chapter we turn to exploring critical and theoretical approaches to autobiography studies during the past decade.

8

A History of Autobiography Criticism, Part II: Expanding Autobiography Studies

You've got your whole life to figure out your life story.

Garrison Keillor

I realize after being the Beatles that 99% of history is bunk.

George Harrison

One's real life is so often the life one does not lead.

Oscar Wilde

The very word biography strikes some academics as "elitist," as does its focus in the past on single remarkable or merely fashionably well-known people. Life writing has a different agenda and concentrates principally on people who belong to and represent categories or classes of people who have been victimised in the past. It offers retrospective justice.

Michael Holroyd

The previous chapter tracked the emergence of autobiography studies through critics and theorists who were influential in the development of the field during what we have described as the first and second waves of autobiography studies. In the past decade scholarly work in the field has so burgeoned that an overview of critical writing formative of a third wave of autobiography criticism since the 1990s will not capture its richness and complexity or the provocative terms of debate within literary and cultural studies.[1] Instead, we define a set of theoretical terms frequently invoked in recent explorations of life writing and examine a few organizing rubrics for critical and theoretical approaches to individual acts of life narration or to groups of texts, performances, and sites of life narrative.

Useful Theoretical Concepts

Chapter 2 set out theoretical concepts for understanding the complexity of autobiographical subjectivity in life writing: memory, experience, identity, space, embodiment, and agency. Three additional concepts, drawn from larger theoretical networks, now inform the field: performativity, positionality, and relationality. Focusing on these terms enables a more nuanced examination of how the rhetorics of identity, location, and address organize new forms of critical inquiry.

We adapt the concept of performativity from postmodern theory to define autobiographical occasions as dynamic sites for the performance of identities that become constitutive of subjectivity. In this view, identities are not fixed or essentialized attributes of autobiographical subjects; rather, they are enacted and reiterated through cultural norms and discourses, and thus remain provisional and unstable. Much contemporary discussion of life narrative as performative is informed by Judith Butler's deconstruction of a binary gender system and her assertion that gender is performative. For Butler, performativity "must be understood not as a singular or deliberate 'act,' but, rather, as the reiterative and citational practice by which discourse produces the effects that it names" (*Bodies That Matter* 20).

Critics of life narrative have found in theories of performativity a vocabulary for describing the complexities of how regulatory discourses of identity are related to material bodies, as well as autobiographical agency. Sidonie Smith reads autobiographical telling as performative because it enacts the "self" it claims has given rise to the "I." Responding to Butler's assertion that "the 'I' neither precedes nor follows the process of . . . gendering, but emerges only within and as the matrix of gender relations themselves," Smith explores how "the interiority or self that is said to be prior to the autobiographical expression or reflection is an *effect* of autobiographical storytelling" ("Performativity" 18).

Paul John Eakin locates the performativity of life narrative in what he terms a "shift from a documentary view of autobiography as a record of referential fact to a performative view of autobiography centered on the act of composition" (*Touching the World* 143). Eakin, however, argues that life writing is a process of constructing a "narratively constituted identity," not an instantiation of an autobiographical subject, in Barthes's terms, as "merely . . . an effect of language" (*How Our Lives* 139). As the significance of memory to autobiographical storytelling is increasingly explored, new understandings of memory will inflect theorizing of autobiographical performativity. Thus, in the conception of autobiographical subjectivity the locus and terms of performativity remain open to debate.

Positionality as a theoretical concept designates how speaking subjects take up, inhabit, and speak through certain discourses of identity that are culturally salient and available to them at a particular historical moment. These "subject positions"—for they are always multiple and often contradictory—are effects of social relations whose power is distributed unevenly and asymmetrically across difference. Subject positions thus form at the intersections of multiple discursive trajectories. Foucault's analysis of "technologies of the self" in confessional practices as imperatives for constituting the "disciplined" subject established a vocabulary for specifying subject positions ("Technologies"). Leigh Gilmore's nuanced reading of the "autobiographics" of a range of women's life writing attends to the subject positions that narrators negotiate within the constraints of discursive regimes as they engage with genres that prohibit that speaking (*Autobiographics*).

Issues of positionality and the geographics of identity are especially complex in autobiographical narratives of de/colonization, immigration, displacement, and exile. Critics and theorists such as Carole Boyce Davies, Caren Kaplan, Homi Bhabha, Françoise Lionnet, José David Saldívar, and Susan Stanford Friedman have found it necessary to define and deploy new terms for colonial and postcolonial subjects in process. A host of adjectival terms have marked the historical, sociocultural, and psychic traces left by the displacements and disidentifications characteristic of diverse histories of oppression, and theorized the subject as *hybrid, border, diasporic, mestiza, nomadic, migratory, minoritized*. These terms gloss the "in-between," the dynamic oscillations of subjects in motion and often uprooted.

Linked to performativity and positionality, relationality is a third theoretical term that has become increasingly important in explorations of life writing. Perhaps in response to the early theorizing of autobiography as a Western genre celebrating the autonomous individual, scholars of marginalized literatures and subjects in the late 1980s and early 1990s began to employ the concept of relationality to capture the "difference" of marginalized forms of writing and subjectivity. In discussions of women's life writing, feminist scholars adapted the sexual difference theory of psychologist Nancy Chodorow to argue that women's life writing, mimetic of women's lives, unfolded through what Susan Stanford Friedman

called fluid boundaries of relationality rather than by clear-cut ego differentiation. Feminists then incorporated this psychosocial approach in
analyzing life writing by women and men. The relationality/individuality
binary explored how sexual difference marked the thematics, formal aspects, and aesthetics of women's autobiographical practices. Scholars of
Native American autobiography in the 1990s brought this binary differentiation to readings of Native American narratives as a kind of relationality
born of communal social organization and a long history of kinship networks. They distinguished the thematics, aesthetics, and rhetorics of Native American writing from its Anglo-European/American counterpart,
which was more individualistic (see H. Wong 168). Eventually, there were
critiques of the binary theorization of difference (man/woman; indigenous/
European colonizer) as a rigid and inadequate account of the polyvocality
of autobiographical narration.

The concept of relationality, however, has been redefined and acquired
new theoretical force for subsequent theorists. In the mid-1990s both
Nancy K. Miller and Paul John Eakin retheorized the concept of relationality to argue that much autobiographical narrative is relational, that it is
often "the other's story" (*How Our Lives* 56). Both have pointed out that
the notion of autobiographical relationality, taken to characterize the difference of women's autobiography in early feminist scholarship, in fact
characterizes modes of relationship in much life writing by both men and
women. Miller, Eakin, and Susanna Egan in *Mirror Talk* approach autobiography as not a solitary but an interactive story. In Eakin's words, it can
offer not only "the autobiography of the self but the biography *and* the autobiography of the other" (*How Our Lives* 58; see also Miller "Representing
Others"). That is, the narrator's story is often refracted through the stories
of others, as in the autoethnographic constitution of the community of
identification, or in the confessional dramas of familiality and familiarity.
Eakin went on to analyze familial, community, and ethnic relational narratives, which he describes as autoethnographic in their extending of the
autos to a collectivity.

Relationality is narratively incorporated through what Bakhtin describes as heteroglossic dialogism, that is, the multiplicity of "tongues" or
the polyvocality through which subjectivity is enunciated (see the section
on voice in chap. 3). To reprise, the subject is always a subject of the other,
constituting and constituted by heterogeneous social discourses. The very
words through which the story is "spoken" or written are the language

of the other. Williams L. Andrews has effectively employed a Bakhtin-ian model to read how slave narratives enact the telling of "free" stories through dialogical shifts. Françoise Lionnet *(Autobiographical Voices)* turns to Edouard Glissant's concept of creolization to propose a theory of auto-biographical textuality as a *métissage* of disparate voices in subjects whose cultural origins and allegiances are multiple and conflicting. And Mae Gwendolyn Henderson takes inspiration from heteroglossia and glos-solalia, the practice of speaking in tongues of some African American churches, to account for the polyvocality of first-person narrative in African American women's writing. Further, relationality is rhetorical-ly implicated in the addressee(s) posited by the narrator, the narratee both within and the ideal reader to whom the narrative is directed and through whom it is imagined and circulated. Relationality, then, indi-cates how the subject is always in process and thus involved with oth-ers, not autonomous.

Relationality has also been invoked in explorations of how the eth-ics of self-narration relates to the vulnerability of the subject. As noted in the section on agency in chapter 2, Judith Butler develops a concept of the opacity of the self unto itself *(Giving an Account* 19). This opacity is an effect of several things: the self has only fitful access to the psychic life before and beyond self-consciousness; it is imbricated in the constant self–other interactions of social worlds; and it must employ storytelling modes, tropes, and self-positionings to tell about itself. In any personal act of giving an account, the "I" who "agrees" to tell its story has to enter, negotiate, and adapt to externalities that are "the recognizable norms of life narration." Thus experiential history and subjectivity are routed through cultural "modes of speech," producing defamiliarization (52). Such storytelling produces a disorienting instability into self-knowing and in-troduces difference, unease, and inscrutability. For Butler, recognizing the self's founding vulnerability is precisely what grounds the ethics of self-accounting (64). To the degree that the self eschews the fantasy of inter-pretive control and relinquishes its project of self-knowing, the lure of "egoic mastery," it opens itself to the opacity of the other as well as the other in itself (58). From this point of view, the relationality of subjects is neither disabling nor escapable. Rather, it is a founding condition of our psychic life, our narrative accounts, and our humanity.

In sum, these three enabling concepts of recent theory energize and redefine the terms of life narrative by calling formerly established critical norms into question. Theorizing performativity contests the notion that autobiography is a site where an authentic or prediscursive identity is recounted. Theorizing positionality, as informed by the location and discursive situatedness of the subject, contests the notion that there is a universal and transcendent autobiographical subject, autonomous and free of history. And theorizing relationality contests the notion that self-narration is the monologic utterance of a solitary, introspective subject that is knowable to itself. Critics have deployed these terms to decenter the concept of a unified, stable, autonomous individual prior to and outside connection to others that was previously assumed by readers to be the subject of life writing. Now we speak of a subject that is in process, a subject in context (historical, social, geographical), a subject whose self-knowing is always implicated, discursively and dialogically, in "the forms of ideological environment" (H. Wong 169). As we consider the complex ways in which new genres and new subjects may energize one another, these concepts enable more flexible reading practices and more inclusive approaches to the field of life writing.

Theorizing Emergent Genres of Life Narrative

The genres of life writing continue to preoccupy theorists of autobiographical practice. We have argued throughout *Reading Autobiography* that "autobiography" is an umbrella concept rather than a single genre, and that identifying the diversity of autobiographical acts, both at this contemporary moment and historically, is essential to a nuanced reading of texts. Appendix A offers a catalog of these genres, with brief definitions. Though the list is not exhaustive, it encompasses heterogeneous discourses of the self, names exemplary texts, and cites some of the many theorists whose work has mapped this capacious field. Here, we turn to a few areas so new and currently dominant that more discussion is necessary.

Vulnerable Lives: Trauma, Testimony, and Human Rights

In the past two decades many autobiography scholars, as well as historians and psychologists, have explored narratives of the vulnerable that tell stories of radical suffering and harm. While much of that testimony has been oral, taken by historians and archived in museums and databanks of interviews with survivors (as in the Holocaust archive at Yale University), much is also firsthand, or as-told-to, life writing. Narratives of trauma and survival range across many sites—genocides, abuse and incest, disability, and human rights crises. Such narratives can become potent weapons in political movements, rallying points for people who share a defining identity: for instance, women who have been victims of sexual and domestic abuse; those whose physical or mental impairment has located them socially as "disabled"; victims of race-based or ethnically motivated violence. These narratives of crisis have found ready publishers and ready audiences in a globalizing economy. Life stories of self-reinterpretation and testimony, focused on injury and loss, have proliferated in response to widespread pandemics and genocidal war. More broadly, survival narratives can be generated by profound changes in personal life and respond to the growing audience demand for personal accounts of survival that offer self-help. Scholars have begun to explore the ethics, aesthetics, and politics of these genres of witness that expand the field of life writing. For example, the outpouring of narratives by victims and survivors of the HIV crisis has produced a large and moving corpus of critical studies focused on the rhetoric of mourning and grief in these personal narratives, as in Ross Chambers's two books, *Facing It: AIDS Diaries and the Death of the Author* and *Untimely Interventions: AIDS Writing, Testimonial, and the Rhetoric of Haunting,* and Sarah Brophy's *Witnessing AIDS: Writing, Testimony, and the Work of Mourning.*

Similarly, the rich and growing field of disability studies has been fueled by the work of such scholars as G. Thomas Couser, Tobin Siebers, Brenda Brueggemann, and David D. Mitchell and Sharon Snyder. Surveying life writing related to deafness, breast cancer, HIV/AIDS, and paralysis, Couser, for example, considers how in such forms as memoirs, diaries, photo documentaries, and essays these narratives address the stigmatizing of disability and work to reclaim bodies from cultural marginalization, including that imposed by medical practice. Couser has mobilized the term *some body memoir,* to designate life writing that "is concerned with what it is like to live with a particular bodily configuration" *(Signifying Bodies).* Such narratives, along with erotic memoirs, Couser claims, attempt to "destigmatize various anomalous bodily conditions" as part of their effort to assert, against Cartesian valorization of the mind, our shared embodiment as human beings.

In a similar vein, Rosemarie Garland Thomson reflects on and destabilizes the cultural constitution of the differently abled as "freaks"

(Freakery). And Susanna Egan, focusing on genres of crisis in contemporary autobiography, observes how, in moments of crisis and decentering, the double voicing, or "mirror talk," of autobiographical acts "affects both the one who speaks and the one who listens" (*Mirror Talk* 25). As critics now turn to the place of disability in postcolonial life writing and the marking of disability, recovery, and embodiment in medieval and early modern life writing, including saints' lives, the field is becoming richly contextualized.

Trauma studies has consolidated itself as a field since the 1990s, as scholars across the humanistic disciplines work to theorize trauma and its aftereffects on survivors, including the succeeding generations who may be haunted by *postmemory,* in Marianne Hirsch's term. These works often focus on "the body in pain" (in the title of Elaine Scarry's influential book on torture) and the psychic residue of traumatic experience. They also theorize the possibilities and impasses of narrativizing and communicating histories of trauma. Indeed, many scholars of trauma, such as Cathy Caruth, Shoshana Felman and Dori Laub, Kelly Oliver, and Janice Haaken, consider modes of public confession as acts of witnessing in situations of both public and private crisis and theorize traumatic memory, the limits of memory, and false memory syndrome. There is at this time a reexamination of the trauma paradigm generated in early Holocaust studies that privileged the unspeakability of events and theorized that telling the story was inevitably a healing act. Autographic narratives such as *Maus, Fun Home,* and *Persepolis* prompt new conceptualizations of how, and to what end, trauma is narrated.

Increasingly, scholars are turning their attention to the ways in which life stories, and scenes of witness, are involved in campaigns for human rights, claims of citizenship, and disputes over property. Theorists of the regime of human rights have assayed its multivalent meanings: as an intricate formation of discourses, protocols, practices, and institutions for dealing with radical suffering; as a lingua franca for activism both nationally and transnationally; as a politicized regime, invoked and deployed in geopolitics; as a contested liberal regime identified with the West and its neoimperial politics; and as a contemporary global formation always in motion and transition.

Scholars in life writing studies have theorized the implications of human rights for life writing practices. They have situated narratives of witness at what Leigh Gilmore terms "alternative jurisdictions." They have critiqued the commodification of narratives of suffering in the production, circulation, and reception of witness narratives in global circuits of human rights movements. They have called attention to the constraints that institutional settings, protocols, and political contexts have on the terms of witnessing and the oppressive aspects of scenes of witnessing, as has Allen Feldman in his discussion of the South African Truth and Reconciliation Commission. They have noted the unpredictable and heterogeneous affective responses readers have to narratives of suffering. As Gayatri Chakravorty Spivak has noted, there is no assurance that the scene of witness can enlist the empathetic listener ("Three Women's Texts" 9); there can be a failure of the ethic of responsibility that would connect the witness and his audience across the divide of privilege and safety.

Many scholars are developing categories and reading strategies for the hybrid kinds of narratives that are being produced around the world.[2] Their studies are centrally concerned with questions of ethics. A different approach to the practice of ethical engagement in life writing has been mounted by several scholars recently. While G. Thomas Couser focuses on the vulnerability of the "some bodies," Paul John Eakin and others explore issues of exposure, betrayal, and authenticity. Richard Freadman links ethical issues to shifts in how the human will—in our terms, agency—is engaged in diverse texts of late modernity. Much of this discussion of autobiographical ethics has stayed at the level of the individual rather than engaging issues of collective citizenship in the nation-state. Yet questions of ethical representation are at the heart of autobiographical studies today, particularly for those working on the conjunction of personal narration and human rights, indigenous testimony, and global citizenship and the nation-state. Questions remain. For example, what is the relationship of the teller and the witness to the story? What are the problems in staging and participating in acts of witnessing to violence and suffering? Where are limits to a "Western" therapeutics of witnessing (a call for telling as the route to psychic healing)? How do we negotiate the tension between individualized cure and structural analysis of the causes of violence? Judith Butler's theorizing of loss and vulnerability to the other in her recent work has been particularly important in reframing central questions in trauma studies in the past half-decade; and the current state of the field can be seen in the two volumes of essays Kate Douglas and Gillian Whitlock edited for *Life Writing* in 2008. These essays, in their words, "relocated trauma studies" and integrated the field "into comparative perspectives that travel South and into various cultural frameworks and traditions" (3).

In an extreme case, life writing may be seen as a form of personal property that can be revoked by the state. A 2000 U.S. court decision in California is a fascinating case in point. In that decision, motel handyman Cary Stayner, a convicted murderer, was sentenced to life in prison without parole rather than the death penalty, with one provision: he must take his story of the crime to the grave to spare the victim's family any further media attention (see Hanley). That is, publication of his life story was treated as part of his personal rights, subject to being legally revoked in extreme circumstances. (Stayner, who later confessed to additional murders, was retried and sentenced to death in 2003.) Struggles over who has the right to use forms of life narratives, such as ex-slave narratives or women saints' chronicles, suggest that the ownership of one's story has historically been less an intrinsic right than a site of contestation, especially for those whose status as citizens was either denied or revoked under law. The complex relationship of rights and personal narrative is, increasingly, a topic in ethical, legal, and literary discussion.

Critical Geographies

As we explored in chapter 2, space, place, and location are central aspects of autobiographical situatedness. Theorists of life writing have explored the networks of subjectivity—psychic, social, and political, as well as locational. Critical geographies thus include both historical contexts and global locations. They examine how subjects are embedded in national imaginaries and in transnational and global circuits of exchange and identification. In retrospect, it is clear that movements to recover groups of noncanonical texts from obscurity contested the prevailing notion of autobiography as a single coherent genre and productively fractured the subject by specifying its diverse historical and geographic difference. In the United States, for example, scholars reclaimed diverse kinds of life writing by African Americans, including ex-slaves, Latinos/as and Chicanos/as, Asian Americans, and Native Americans. Elsewhere, scholars explored the terms of subjectivity across linguistic, cultural, and national divides in response to histories of exploration, conquest, settlement, and liberatory movements in colonial settings. Their reclamation and incorporation of a range of texts countered the prevailing canon, effectively introducing heterogeneous genres, including indigenous codices, life narratives of the religious, ex-slave narratives, and narratives of exploration and displacement.

Now, the cumulative effect of such interventions is evident in the articulation of fields of autobiography studies. For example, in African American life writing, scholars have traced the lines of a tradition from colonial through antebellum, Harlem Renaissance, and Black Power movements to contemporary explorations of racialization (Joanne Braxton, Barbara Rodriguez, Kenneth Mostern, Crispin Sartwell, Michael A. Chaney). For Latino/a and Chicano/a life writing, the connections among narratives of exploration, diverse kinds of folkloric writing, missionary journals, and contemporary narratives of coming of age as bi- or multicultural subjects have consolidated rich traditions of self-fashioning in relation to cross-border communities (Genaro Padilla, Sonia Saldívar-Hull, Ramón Saldívar, José David Saldívar, Chon Noriega, and the journal *Atzlan*). The complex field of Asian American life writing has been both formed and fractured by its diversity of geographic heritages and affiliations that access different histories and by new trends in transnational, oceanic, and archipelagic studies (Rey Chow, Lisa Lowe, Shirley Geok-lin Lim, Inderpal Grewal, Sara Suleri). The study of the indigenous and mestizo peoples of the Americas, initially the province of ethnographers in as-told-to narratives, has been reclaimed by a new generation of scholars who differently inflect these histories of encounter, resistance, assimilation, and sovereignty (Robert Warrior, Hertha Dawn Sweet Wong, Laura Beard, Sylvia Molloy).

Life writing around the world is no longer dominated by studies of the United States and England. In particular national locales, scholars are tracing, for example, the rise of a distinctive Canadian autobiographical writing of settlement, westward displacement, cultural conflict, bilingualism, and contemporary multiculturalism (Julia V. Emberley, Helen M. Buss, Susanna Egan, Shirley Neuman, Terrence L. Craig, Julie Rak). In Australia, critics have explored how autobiographical writing has reproduced central myths of Australian national identity such as the myth of mateship. They have also tracked how personal narrative became a venue for indigenous Australians to rewrite the history of encounter and state oppression as well as laying claim to alternative modes of collective identification (Kay Schaffer, Gillian Whitlock, Rosanne Kennedy, Mary Besemeres and Anna Wierzbicka, Joy Hooton, Rosamund Dalziell, Anne Brewster). Studies of life writing in China explore the intersection of autobiographical discourse and the discourses of modernization in the early part of the twentieth century, during the period of revolutionary consolidation, and now, with the radical transformations of a globalizing China (see Jing M. Wang, Lingzhen Wang, and Zhao Baisheng).

In Africa, scholars are attending to the relationship of oral narratives of identity and lineage to first-person life writing; examining the weave of indigenous and colonial languages and discourses in narration; linking testimonial stories of war and enslavement, such as child soldier narratives, to larger struggles for national liberation; and posing questions about Pan-African identity (see Judith Lütge Coullie, Françoise Lionnet, Sandra Pouchet Paquet). While life writing from the Middle East is as yet sporadically translated—and often only when it addresses the concerns of the West, as in the narratives of Nafisi, Satrapi, El Saadawi, and Edward Said—a rich historical heritage of autobiographical writing in Arabic and Farsi exists. As Western and Eastern European nations renegotiate their histories, borders, and increasingly multinational citizenships, the terms and focus of life writing are changing, not only for contemporary texts but also in how early national literatures are framed and investigated. As scholars define a new set of theoretical terms for investigating the geographical locations, itineraries, and trajectories of autobiographical texts, and engage in international conversations about these questions, the field is becoming global as never before.

It is notable that life narratives across dispersed geographical and geopolitical terrains have proved to be self-theorizing in ways productive for scholars. That is, autobiographical texts foreground differences in language, culture, tradition, and history. For example, Shirley Geok-lin Lim in *Among the White Moon Faces* contrasts growing up in Malaysia and coming of age as an academic in the eastern United States, and Eva Hoffman in *Lost in Translation* engages her multiple displacements across the Polish and English languages, locations, and remembering selves. In the wake of Said's influential *Culture and Imperialism,* studies in historical perspective on the formation and dissolution of empire have also turned to life writing as an important site of critical cultural inscription. Attentive to how autobiographical acts engage questions and practices of subjects in transition, critics employ Said's critique in examining the legacies of the past in the present for postcolonial subjects and the dispersal across the globe of diasporan subjects or subjects in exile. Comparative investigations of Anglophone autobiographical practices in the British Empire—in Africa, India, and around the world—and similar studies for other former colonial powers promise to contribute important insights about the dynamic relays between metropolitan center and colonial locations of writing and self-imagining.[3] Questions of translation, of "minor literatures," of citizenship and transnational belonging are resituating the story of life writing from national locations to sites marked by global flows and mobility.

New Contexts: Neuroscience, Cognitive Studies, and Genomics

Scholars of narrative generally, and life writing in particular, are engaging increasingly in conversation with work in neuroscience, cognitive studies, evolutionary biology, and genomics. Narratologists have turned to the work of cognitive psychologists for possible understandings of the origins of narrative competency and the evolutionary benefit of storytelling in the prehistoric mind.[4] Some have mined the diverse sciences of memory, including cell biology (the stuff of neuroscience) and computer modeling (the stuff of artificial intelligence), to project a notion of material "selfhood" that has implications for theorizing autobiographical narration. Other critics speculate about what it would mean to think of the self as quantum (holistic center of consciousness) or neural (networked at the synaptic level through which memories are distributed and reorganized) or connectionist (the notion of self adapted from computer modeling of distributed processing across the entire brain).

Both critics and life writers have also considered the makeup of a genomic self. With the culmination of the Genome Project and the circulation of discourses of genomics throughout the scientific and lay communities, new understandings of how memory and destiny infuse our bodies, as species and familial legacy, prompt the rethinking of discourse and materiality, representation, and embodiment. Braided in the material language of genomics, the self becomes a composite of genes and junk (as scientists so inelegantly call the material that is not genetic data but necessary to the binding of genes in the chromosome). While scientists early on thought of the genetic material as a "blueprint" for the future of each human being, they are now redefining genetic materials as a kind of "parts list" for the organism. As with the earlier metaphor of blueprint, the parts list functions as a set of future life scripts—material and narrative—encoded despite our ignorance of them. These are the histories that lie in material wait for us, as memoirs such as Alice Wexler's *Mapping Fate: A Memoir of Family, Risk, and Genetic Research* suggest and as G. Thomas

Couser probes in *Vulnerable Subjects* (189–95). Thus, the materiality of memory becomes a harbinger of the future as well as a legacy of past collective history. Our genetic coding could be seen not as a kind of intransigent embodied memory but as increasingly open to reconstruction and rearrangement, by surgical processes as well as by the telling of different stories.

If the materiality of our bodies makes it possible for us to tell stories about ourselves and to remake ourselves in the telling, those stories in turn become the lives that we live and reshape. Paul John Eakin has recently adapted work in neuroscience and cognitive and developmental science to consider how we become storied selves. Working with theories of cognition, memory, and embodiment enables him to think through the relationship between identity and stories, between healthy selves and healthy stories *(Living Autobiographically)*. In another arena, proponents of narrative therapy in medicine and bioethics argue that telling and healing are integrally linked, on the one hand as routes to survival, recovery, and transformation, and on the other, as a means to acceptance of one's vulnerable and dying body (see Charon; Hawkins). Coming to understand oneself and one's past through a different story, or a story given a different affective valence, may indeed affect a change in the neural networks that crisscross the brain, suggests neuroscientist Steven Rose, who describes the flow of memory across the brain in the metaphor of the wave. Rose argues against the sense that a memory is fixed in a particular location of the brain. Indeed, some critics argue that the term *life writing* is less appropriate than the concept of the *biotext* "to foreground the writer's efforts to articulate his or her self through the process of writing" (Saul 4). Their call to focus on the process of authoring a life rather than the finished product emphasizes how cognitive acts shape the emergent self. With a focus on "My DNA/Myself," in Kay Cook's words, life writing references other histories and expertise in areas radically different from what scholars were studying a mere generation ago.

Digitized Forms and Identities

Although, as surveyed in chapter 6, myriad online forms of life narrative are transforming the field, as yet no single generic term or large theoretical framework has emerged to describe how the practices of a digitized imaginary in cyberspace life writing and multimedia self-representation will differ from the analog writings of lines on the page. As Mark Poster presciently suggests, with these changes in the way writing enters the world, changes in the material structure of the trace are inevitable, as the trace becomes voice and image. Brian Rotman argues persuasively that digitality has replaced the alphabet, coding its Cartesian syntax in the hypertextual, though as yet we are haunted by alphabetic ghosts of the past paradigm of writing, dominant for two millennia. The changes to subjectivity that are being wrought by hypertextual, digitized "writing" and imaging shake up our notions of the figure of the author as a bounded subject creating, with copyright protection, an individual identity. Suggesting that the "author-function" will disappear in the heterotopic discourses of cyberspace, Poster argues for a new focus on links, associations, and dispersions of meaning through performances of subjectivity in the contexts of social networking *(Information Please)*.

In the future, critics of life writing will need to raise fundamental questions about what constitutes the autobiographical in cyberspace. Can self-inscription be anything but auto/phantasmographical when the referent, the "I" in the material world, is replaced by a virtual subject? Would the terms of an autobiographical pact have any binding force? As we have already observed, how users on MySpace and Facebook sites employ idealized photographs of their bodies (for instance, "thinphotos") and selectively, if at all, reference their histories and statistics, looking for traces of the human referent to authenticate "the real" may be a red herring. Rather, attending to the production of unstable self-images as porous fictions shifting in interaction with both other users and media imaginaries may prove a more productive inquiry, one that leads to fundamental redefinition of the autobiographical. As the referential terms of subjectivity are increasingly dislodged, while agency may be decentered or constrained, new formations of virtuality will engender a new rhetoric relating self, media, and interaction.

Theorizing Everyday Lives

In "The Autobiography of Those Who Do Not Write," Philippe Lejeune elaborates the many dimensions of everyday modes of narrative. He begins by questioning, in the as-told-to narrative, whether the life "belongs" to the one who lives it or the one who writes it. Problematizing the notion of authorship, Lejeune asserts that "a person's life can appear through someone else's narrative" in collaborations such as interview situations where questions are erased and the oral stories of those who do not write are recorded (190). A life, that is, "is always the product of a transaction between different postures" (197). This is particularly clear in working-class life writing, where the narrative records a struggle between the class consciousness of the worker and the form and patterns of the life story, which ideologically belong to the ruling class. While typically the lives of workers have been "studied from above," with the effect that the workers did not speak (199), the publication of everyday lives—by auto-didacts, or as manifestos, or orally, as in talk-show accounts—begins to redress a situation in which those living everyday lives could not write but only be written. Lejeune's extensive studies of the life narratives col-lected as ethnographies by social scientists, as interviews by historians, and as effaced interviews by journalists of those who do not write their own stories are some ways of negotiating an "ethnological gap" (211). And the long-standing tradition of British autobiography criticism fo-cused on working-class life writing importantly contextualizes the field in ways that American scholarship often overlooks.[5] As ordinary people increasingly interiorize their stories through the institutions of popular memory—primarily forms of media—theorists look to their reappropria-tion of life-knowledge and authority in ways that may be transformative of social relations. Unquestionably, many personal narratives with larger cul-tural and historical consequences remain to be "discovered," or compiled from the diaries of ancestors, as Suzanne Bunkers suggests, or interwoven with familial stories, as Jamaica Kinkaid, bell hooks, Michael Ondaatje, and many others have done.

Throughout the twentieth century the criticism of everyday lives has been conducted by scholars and researchers from many disciplines who investigate how individuals tell their life stories by borrowing from and in-venting with culturally available models of life writing. In Great Britain the Mass Observation project, founded in 1937 by sociologist Charles Madge, anthropologist Tom Harrisson, and documentary filmmaker Humphrey Jennings, made an extended—and still ongoing—study of the lives of or-dinary people. Cultural and social historians access its archive of life sto-ries in order to explore the multiple histories of twentieth-century Britain embedded in personal narratives (see Harrisson, Madge, and Jennings). And in *Getting a Life: Everyday Uses of Autobiography,* Sidonie Smith and Julia Watson present a collection of essays by cultural critics on sites and occasions for which people tell, indeed often are required to tell, stories of themselves couched within the disciplinary frameworks of the institutions of public and familial life: the health history at the doctor's office (Kay K. Cook), the academic curriculum vitae (Martin A. Danahay, "Professional Subjects"), the Alcoholics Anonymous meeting (Robyn R. Warhol and Helena Michie), the television talk show (Janice Peck), or places where they may strategically "forget" their identity, as in the police station (William Chaloupka).

Now as projects of collecting people's stories that were dominant in the first half of the twentieth century are revived with new recording technologies, as we suggest in chapter 6, a focus on the storytelling templates that narrators employ will link the collection of life stories, a folkloric framework, to the rich theorizing generated in the field of life writing.

Autocritical Practices

Although the boundary between critiquing and writing life narrative has been deliberately blurred in recent critical practice, it is hardly a new phenomenon. Montaigne's *Essays* repeatedly exploited this boundary in creating his self-portrait. In the 1920s and early 1930s, German aesthetic theorist Walter Benjamin wrote three autobiographical narratives that reformulate the modern autobiographical act by resituating the subject's relation to history. Gerhard Richter characterizes Benjamin's narratives as "archaeological montage" (47) and notes that they "offer an experience of singularity and transgression in which the history of the self is inseparable from the history of its culture" (33). Only recently, however, have we begun to think of the criticism of life narrative as centrally implicated in its practice. In the United States, for example, a few writers have consistently defined their writing practice as "autocritique."

In his essays, such as "Crows Written on the Poplars: Autocritical Autobiographies," Chippewa mixed-blood writer Gerald Vizenor composes a collage by interweaving citations from scholars of autobiography with his own critique of their limited understanding of hybridized identity and his extended narrative of growing up as that intersects with his memory of an act, the violent killing of a squirrel. Similarly, the narratives of Cherríe Moraga and Gloria Anzaldúa have often used autocritical writing as a practice of *mestiza* identity in which the polarity of critical and creative writing, like those of the English and Spanish languages, formal speech and dialect, Mexican and American identities, and hetero- and homosexuality, is fractured into hybrid writing (*Loving in the War Years* and *Borderlands/ La Frontera*). In many of her essays and her memoir, bell hooks has made autocritique an enabling form for illuminating observations about contemporary culture with examples drawn from her life. In *Bone Black: Memories of Girlhood*, critical concepts about the implicit norms of writing autobiography frame her coming-of-age narrative. Nancy K. Miller, as both critic and practitioner of life writing, incorporates a musing, reflective narrative voice into her essays on autobiography and interweaves a relational autobiographical narrative such as *Bequest and Betrayal* (on the deaths of her parents) with conceptual insights drawn from her study of the tropes and discourses of self-narration.[6] Taking a postcolonial turn on autocritique, Manthia Diawara, in his films and essays, interweaves critical discourse and life stories. Alternating analytical chapters on African American and African autobiographical writers such as Richard Wright with chapters framed as Sartrean "situations" and a travel narrative of his return to West Africa after several decades, he links his search for a childhood friend with the larger quest for a new Pan-African consciousness enriched by these multiple past iterations of African-centered experience (*In Search of Africa*).

Transgendered writers are also producing self-referencing books that join acts of self-narrating and self-performance to theoretical analysis of sexualized identities. Such narratives as Kate Bornstein's *Gender Outlaw: On Men, Women, and the Rest of Us*; Julia Serano's *Whipping Girl: A Transsexual Woman on Sexism and the Scapegoating of Femininity*; and the edited collection (from Joan Nestle et al.) *GenderQueer: Voices from beyond the Sexual Binary* capture the instabilities of gendered identities and register the lack of a "natural" alignment of bodies, sexualities, and gender assignments. Combining personal history with analysis that theorizes the dispersal of a fixed point of reference and identification around normative masculinities and femininities, their texts are simultaneously life stories, manifestos about the instability of gender identities, and invitations to readers to reimagine their own embodied identities as unfixed from gender norms.

The practice of autocritique has thus become more central to theorizing life writing, and for aficionados may be one of the pleasures of work in the field. Many critics now link their studies of filiation, for example, to a personal story about their own fathers, as do Richard Freadman, Roger Porter, and G. Thomas Couser, or a relative or grandparent, as do Sidonie Smith, Jay Prosser, and Elizabeth Hanscombe. Thus, the interweaving of personal and public stories continues to be a hallmark of theorizing life writing, which both the consciousness-raising practices of 1970s feminism and the workers' and everyday life stories of the earlier twentieth century used as forms of prosopography with political goals.

The Uses of Life Writing: How-To's and Pedagogy

While most of this book addresses critical frameworks for reading life writing, there is currently widespread interest in writing one's own family, ethnic, bodily, or generational story. The proliferation of workshops and seminars on "writing your memoir" and the recent flood of "how-to" books attest to the growing audience for advice on shaping the memoir one has been incubating throughout one's life.

Clearly, we read other people's narratives as spurs to self-understanding, self-improvement, and self-healing. Therapists often have their clients read a life narrative to induce self-reflection, such as Marie Cardinal's *The Words to Say It* or Hannah Green's *I Never Promised You a Rose Garden* or Barbara Gordon's *I'm Dancing As Fast As I Can.* Such narratives both model and elicit personal narratives from clients unused to putting fragments of their life experience into story form. Similarly, confessors have long urged the spiritually troubled to seek counsel by reading life narratives. Seekers who once turned to the struggles in the "dark night of the soul" of Teresa of Avila and Thomas Merton might now pick up Elizabeth Gilbert's *Eat, Pray, Love,* a quasi-religious quest narrative, or books on self-care by Thomas Moore or Eckhart Tolle. Such narratives, as guides to therapeutic self-reflection or as spiritual counsel, spur readers to find a voice and construct their stories of questing, questioning, discovery, and renewed interior life, through such practices as journaling, blogging, or writing about photographs of themselves.

Similarly, the how-to seminars easily found on the Web have become popular both for those trying to discern the shape and "passages" of their life stories and those hoping to cash in on the memoir boom. Guides to writing life narrative line the Biography shelves of bookstores as consumers in increasing numbers join groups or spend leisure time searching for their family and ethnic origins. How-to's offer instructions for stirring the creative juices, getting started, dealing with writer's block, identifying crisis moments and turning points, and using personal forms of evidence.

But what larger uses might how-to books have for teaching autobiography in the academy? While we have informally surveyed only a handful of books and Web sites, certain methods and themes emerge:

- The Franklinesque motive: studying and writing one's life is useful, practically and morally, as an exercise in democratic citizenship.
- The legacy motive: writing one's life is a gift of love and memory passed on to posterity, although it can also threaten family harmony because of the explosiveness of "secrets."
- The psychology-of-discovery motive: writing one's life is a self-authorizing and empowering "journey," "dance," or encounter.
- The indictment or revenge motive: writing one's life is payback to a troubling other, an assembling of evidence in an "alternative jurisdiction" (see Gilmore) that invites the near and dear to judge and condemn someone and vindicate the writer on the basis of formerly secret personal information.

Along with thematizing motivations for life writing, how-to guides catalog methods for producing the story. They encourage journaling, diary keeping, rereading past letters, consulting family albums, and interviewing family members and childhood friends. How-to's encourage linear chronologies or kinds of topical organization for sorting and grouping the past particulars of life experience. In *The Autobiography Box: A Step-by-Step Kit for Examining the Life Worth Living*, for example, Brian Bouldrey literally offers an owner's manual for assembling one's life narrative. The four sets of cards prompt specific ways of accomplishing the life narrator's tasks: to remember, discover, dramatize, and structure ordinary experience into an organized narrative. Typically, guides have paid little attention to audience, since they presume their readers are writing private memoirs. But the public status of the Internet and the wide availability of self-publishing will likely exert new constraints.

Increasingly, memoirs of ordinary citizens are being self-published or brought out by vanity presses (Lejeune, "Autobiography of Those Who Do Not Write" 220–23). Such publications are not necessarily trivial or inconsequential, as life writing from Franklin to many contemporary testimonies suggests. As online sites, with their ability to serve as multimedia archives of the personal, become a dominant mode of writing the personal memoir, the nature of life inscription itself is being radically altered.

How may the writing of everyday life stories be employed as pedagogical practice? Life writing is now a dominant form of teaching in composition courses, encouraging and authorizing student writers to explore alternative modes of critical investigation that link the personal and the analytical. Indeed, when life writing was introduced to rethink the norms of the critical essay and composition theory itself, composition courses underwent a pedagogical revolution, as Linda Brodkey has argued. In literature courses exercises in writing life narrative have encouraged students to become more sensitive, sophisticated, and patient readers of others' narratives. In such fields as ethnic studies and women's studies, studying personal narratives or constructing ethnographies of relatives serves a larger purpose of valorizing the lives of ordinary, often marginalized, subjects.

Recent theorists of autobiographical practices have reflected on the educational and political uses of autobiographical narrating, particularly in the university. Cynthia G. Franklin, for example, writes herself into her critiques of the "exclusionary logic and divisiveness of existing (identities)," to practice a personalized scholarship differentiated from personal criticism. Wendy S. Hesford argues that autobiographical practices are employed in college settings to legitimate students by "initiating critical reflexivity about self-positioning" (*Framing Identities* 95). And rhetorical theorists across a wide spectrum of disciplines, for a range of motives—from discouraging plagiarism to creating new collectivities in the classroom—link writing about one's life to reading the lives of others as a new pedagogy for engaging students directly.

Conclusion

The diverse fields being brought to bear on autobiographical criticism discussed here expand the boundaries and challenge the norms of life writing delineated by Misch and constructed in the second-wave work of Gusdorf, Hart, Weintraub, Olney, and others. Although this book aims at a comprehensive view of life narrative studies, it is useful to recall Spengemann's contention that the history of the field has not been a unilinear progression "from facticity, to psychology, to textuality" (16). Multiple, contesting approaches coexist in a productive ferment and generate new reading strategies, as critics and theorists continue to turn their attention to many kinds of life writing long excluded from the canon of autobiography as marginal. As the corpus of texts and media expands, the debates shift. Redefining the contexts of life narrative situates it as a rhetorical act embedded in the history of specific communities.

In place of a definitive conclusion, then, we offer a set of questions articulated by Stephan Meyer in a 2009 call for papers for the founding conference of the European chapter of the International Auto/Biography Association, which will resonate for the next decade: "What are promising theoretical paradigms for studying auto/biography as a form of world literature? What are the interconnections between auto/biography and globalization? To what extent can the notion of a world republic of letters be fruitfully applied to narrative identity practices across the globe?" As practices of narrative identity multiply and shift in the decade to come, scholars of life narrative will contribute to rich dialogues about their significance in understanding the intersections of self, community, and geopolitical transits.

9

A Tool Kit: Twenty-four Strategies for Reading Life Narratives

You pick up a memoir in your local bookstore that looks interesting and read the opening page. Or you're asked to read a well-known autobiography for a college course or exam. Or you come upon a personal narrative in an archive you're perusing for a history project. Or you find yourself a captive listener at a family gathering during which people regale one another with stories of the past.

Given the complexity of autobiographical acts that we have charted in chapters 2 and 3, what kind of questions might you ask as you become immersed in these autobiographical narratives? *How, exactly, might you read them?*

In this chapter we present you with a "tool kit" for approaching and engaging self-referential texts. The sets of questions in twenty-four categories in alphabetical order offer entering points and strategies for addressing the burgeoning array of life narratives available to us today. They might also generate points of departure for writing your own autobiographical narrative.

Agency

People tell stories of their lives through the cultural scripts available to them, and they are governed by cultural strictures about self-presentation in public. Given constraints, how do people change the narratives or write back to the cultural stories that have scripted them as particular kinds of subjects? How is this "writing back," this changing of the terms of one's representation, a strategy for *gaining agency*? How might they gain agency through the very choice of life writing practices, many of which have the potential to intervene in existing social and political formations? In what ways do they negotiate life writing to disrupt social arrangements and/or self-understandings? Is the narrator self-conscious about reproducing or interrupting cultural scripts?

Similarly, how do narrators negotiate strictures about telling certain kinds of stories? How, for instance, do particular women write around cultural strictures about female duty, virtue, and modesty when they are engaged in the act of telling their life stories for publication? How do post-colonial subjects write back to the empire that formerly colonized them as less than human, as childlike? That is, are there strategic means of writing through the narratives that have been used to fix colonial subjects toward a new or revised narrative of possibility? Do such narrators speak in multiple voices, employ diverse strategies, or alternate among several audiences as they negotiate their story of de/colonization? Is the political significance of language thematized in the text? What language(s) and strategies of translation does the narrator employ in telling her/his story?

Agency can also derive from acknowledging the limits of knowing ourselves. Where and how, then, does a narrator thematize his or her limits of self-knowing or ability to interpret his or her life, and perhaps recognize an obligation to an other?

Audience and Addressee

An autobiographical narrative may address *multiple audiences.* Is there a person to whom this text is explicitly addressed, perhaps in the dedication, or at a crucial moment in the narrative? Why might the narrator explicitly name and address a specific reader as narratee? Is there an implicit audience addressed? What kind of general reader does the text seem to be addressing? Another way of framing this question is to ask, what kind of reader or ideal audience does the text ask you to be? For instance, are you posited as a sympathetic and forgiving reader, a celebrity maker, a secret sharer, a confessor or therapist, a student? Where does the text instruct you to be that kind of reader? Are there instructions for reading encoded in a preface or embedded in the narrative?

Authority and Authenticity

We expect particular kinds of stories to be told by those who have a direct and personal knowledge of that experience. We also have notions about whose life is important, whose life might be of interest to a broader public, and what experiences "count" as significant. In these expectations we imply a set of questions about life narratives.

Does the narrator address the issue of *authority and authenticity,* that is, the "right" to speak this story, directly in the narrative? Does the narrator seem to be troubled by the act of telling the story? How does the narrator assert, or imply, or enact the authority to tell her story? And what about the transgressive aspects of public exposure? How does the narrator normalize or moderate them? Does she have recourse to an authority figure who introduces the text or is prominently cited in the text as a source of authorization? Does the narrator incorporate the biography of an authorizing figure into her text? At what points in the narrative must the narrating "I" reassert itself? How is it reasserted? By the end of the narrative, has the telling seemed to authorize the teller?

Authorship and the Historical Moment

What kinds of historical knowledge can be brought to bear when reading a life narrative?

First, there is the history of the cultural meaning of "authorship." What did it mean to be an "author" at *the historical moment* in which the narrative was *written, published, and circulated*? We know, for instance, that the notion of authorship changed radically when copyright became a legal requirement in the early nineteenth century. The legal concept of copyright implies that people hold a proprietary interest in their own stories. This new relationship to the personal story is radically different from earlier relationships. When a medieval mystic such as Margery Kempe dictated her narrative to an amanuensis, she didn't understand herself as an "author" with ownership rights in her story. She was, rather, a Christian supplicant before God and His earthly authorities.

Second, we might ask what cultural meanings a narrative acquired when it was written or published. Were there religious, juridical, political, and/or other cultural institutions invested in particular kinds of life narratives at this historical moment? Another way to think about these historical questions is to ask what kind of investments people have had in their own personal narratives and in other people's personal narratives. Why might it have been important to narrate to oneself a personal story, or to make it public? Who else might have had an investment in this particular story or in this kind of story?

Third, we might also ask how larger historical and cultural conjunctions and shifts bear upon the composing and publication of a particular narrative; that is, how did the narrative transform history? For instance, narratives by indigenous Australians of the so-called Stolen Generation have been crucial to the reconsideration of the history of state policies through which Aboriginal children were "stolen" from their families and communities in order to enforce assimilationist priorities.

Finally, we can historicize present practices by asking what kinds of narratives get published today. That is, who gets published and why? What political, social, cultural, linguistic, and economic forces affect publication and international circulation today?

The Autobiographical "I"

How may you distinguish among the historical, narrating, narrated, and ideological "I"s of the text? (See chapter 3.) What is the position of the *historical person writing the autobiography* within her cultural world? For instance, is she an outsider, a prominent figure, an immigrant or someone in exile, a child? If an outsider, what kind of outsider is she? What kinds of difference are significant to her identity in terms of gender, race or ethnicity, class, sexuality, occupation, legal status (for example, criminal, slave, captive)?

How would you describe the *narrating "I"*? What kind of tone comes through the narrative voice? Is it defensive, ironic, romantic, self-important, self-critical, transgressive? What kind of story does the narrator seek to tell about himself? How would you describe the gap between the narrating "I" (or narrator) and the narrated "I"? Is the *narrated "I"* in the text a less sophisticated figure than the narrator? What kind of attention does the narrator pay to the younger, or more naive or successful, persona or version of himself? Are there multiple narrated "I"s?

There are also important questions about the historical notion of personhood and the meaning of lives at the time of writing—that is, the *ideological notion of the "I"* affecting the self-narrator. How do changing notions of "I"-ness or personhood affect the self-narrative you are reading and interpreting? How is the life cycle understood? The relationship of an individual to the collectivity? The relationship of an individual to history and time? What kinds of public roles seem important and privileged?

Autographics

Consider how the medium of the comic book shapes the telling of the life story. What effects are produced by segmentation of the story into frames, panels, and gutters, as well as by the varying size and arrangement of frames—boxed or unboxed—on the page? What is the rhetorical and/ or affective impact of the juxtaposition of frames? Does the segmentation through gutters have a reinforcing or an ironic effect? What is the relationship of the voice-over narration above the frame to dialogue bubbles within it? Are there other kinds of verbal tags within the frame? How would you describe the style of drawing? Where does it reference or borrow from earlier comic book styles? What kinds of visual details are emphasized? Are other visual media—for instance, photographs, maps, print media, schematic drawings—reproduced in line drawing, and to what effect? Where do images and verbal text echo or support each other? Where does each supply information not shown in the other? Did the same person do both the graphics and the writing?

In addition to the narrating and narrated "I"s of life writing, what narrative levels are introduced through the graphics? How would you describe the intersection of levels of meaning and modes of self-representation? Are there places where the maker is explicitly self-referential, through showing his/her hand drawing the image (life-size or not), using a mirror or self-portrait, or incorporating references to her/his earlier comic or narrative work? Is a coherent or fragmented, multireferential subjectivity produced? Is the implied spectator or audience for the autographic represented within it, and to what effect? More broadly, what visual, cultural, and political knowledge does the autographic assume or require? How does it address the assumption that comics are subliterary?

Body and Embodiment

Several questions can be posed of a life narrative that bring *embodiment* into focus. Precisely when and where does the body become visible in the narrative? Which part, or functions, or feelings of the body? How does it become visible? What does that visibility mean? How are the narrator's body and its visibility tied to the community from which the narrator comes? In other words, how is the life of the real person outside the text affected by the visibility of his body?

What cultural meanings are attached to the narrator's body outside the text? Do particular bodily processes take on significance? Does the body, or parts of it, vanish from the narrative at some point? Are there bodies other than the narrator's that the narrator encounters, or labels, or acts on, or assigns meaning to in the course of the narrative? Is the body fetishized, that is, is it ritualized and eroticized? Is the body a locus of desire, or an impediment to the circulation of desire? What's the relationship between the material body of a narrating "I" and the body politic? How is the body represented as a site of sensuality and emotion? As a site of knowledge and knowledge production? As a site of labor, disease, disability? Does writing the life narrative seem to have a therapeutic function?

Coherence and Closure

Consider what claims the narrating "I" makes to a coherent story. Does the narrator explicitly assert the coherence of his or her story? Are there moments when that *impression of narrative coherence* breaks down in the text? Consider digressions, omissions, contradictions, gaps, and silences about certain things. How does noting this silence or gap affect your reading of the narrative of the historical person? How does a gap affect your understanding of the kind of "I" the narrator wants to project? Consider as well where multiple and conflicting voices emerge in the narrative (see the section on voice below). How do you account for a proliferation of voices at some points? What happens to them?

You might also look at the narrative's *closure.* In life narrative, the narrative by definition concludes prior to the death of the historical person; none of us can narrate beyond the end of our lives or know the shape of that end in advance. Does the ending seem to bring the narrative to a tidy closure and, if so, how? Does it seem to be a permanent closure? What alternative possibilities for closure might other threads of the narrative suggest?

Collaborative Autobiography

While readers cannot resolve either the psychodynamics or the politics of collaborative life writing, several questions arise about the *terms of collaboration.* Is the narrative a product of more than one person? What kind of collaborative involvement has there been? Is this an "as-told-to" or ghostwritten narrative? Has there been an editor, a transcriber, an amanuensis, or an interviewer involved in the project? What role has each person played in the making of the narrative, and what are your sources for knowing this? Who is presented as speaking in the narrative? To put it another way, who says "I," whose voice do you hear in the narrative? How has the editor or transcriber made her presence felt in the narrative, or, on the contrary, tried to efface her role in producing the narrative? Is there a preface, framing story, or notes that attend to the relationship between narrator/informant and editor/collaborator within the text? Does the plotting or presentational format of the narrative indicate problems or inequities in the collaborative relationship? What are the differences between the narrator and the editor or amanuensis? And what's at stake politically in those differences? Who has benefited socially or financially from the telling of the story?

Ethics

The ethical issues of writing life narrative are many; that is, real consequences upon the writer's or other people's lives may ensue from publishing a narrative and from reading it. Are there revelations in the narrative that might be hurtful or embarrassing to living people—the writer's family, friends, colleagues—or that might compromise other people's reputations? Where does the narrator signal that something he has divulged is potentially compromising or transgressive? What justifications does the narrator give for publicizing such intimate and potentially compromising details of personal life or the lives of others? What are the cultural conventions at the historical moment of writing that set established limits to self-revelation? What purposes or motives might the narrating "I" have in violating those norms?

There is also an ethics of readership. As readers, we may feel uneasy about reading narratives of radical suffering, difference, or self-disclosure. What is ethically involved for the reader in engaging, for example, a narrative of profound suffering? How is your own ethical sense differently addressed in such a life narrative from the way it would be in, say, a novel? What difference is there in the kind of story that is told? In your assessment of the narrator?

Evidence

How does the narrator win the reader's belief and seek to have the "truth" of the narrative validated? What *kinds of evidence* does the narrator incorporate into her text to persuade the reader of the narrative's claims to truth? How does the narrator authenticate certain truth claims or justify writing and publicizing a personal story? What kinds of authority does that evidence carry? That of personal memory? Dreams? Religious visitations? The testimony of others? What about "objective" evidence, such as photos and documents? References to historical events or places? The authority of other narratives? Note when particular kinds of evidence are introduced into the text. Why and with what effects might evidence from an authority be placed strategically at one point, and not another?

Try to be attentive to your responses to the narrating "I"'s bids for your attention. Is your trust in this story or the storyteller ever undermined? And how does that occur? Are there statements or ellipses in the text that conflict with other parts of the narrative, causing you to doubt it? What's at stake for the narrator in persuading you of the truth of his story? What's at stake historically (in the larger society) in having this text accepted as a "truthful" account of a life? What difference would it make to learn that the narrative is a fabrication?

Experience

How and when is an appeal to the authority of *experience* made in the text? Is that appeal to authority gendered? Is it made on the basis of sexual, or ethnic, or racial, or religious, or national identity claims? Are there any indications that the narrator doubts what claims can be made, based on the authority of experience?

Can you identify passages in the text where the narrator reflects on the very act of "reading" his own past? Or on the interpretive schema he brings to bear on that experience? Does the narrator critique his ability to understand the experiences of the past at any points in the text?

Do the different interpretations of an experience in narratives written at different times by the same person signal stages of, or changes in, the overall pattern and beliefs of the autobiographical story? Do the changes from one text to a "sequel" signal that the interpretation of experience is specific to a particular historical moment? Do such changes signal a shift in thinking about the narrator's belief system, or the nature of memory, or a cultural shift in the stories tellable at that historical moment?

The narrator is not the only one engaged in interpreting what constitutes experience. We as readers are also historically embedded, our understanding of what counts as experience historically situated. How does your historical situation as a reader affect the legibility or readability of experience in the text?

History of Reading Publics

The *reading public* is not a static entity but a collectivity with sharply differing competencies, interests, and needs. We may ask, who made up the reading public or consumers of the life narrative at the time it was written? Who might have heard the story recounted? Who would have been literate and what would the cultural meaning of literacy have been? Think of the reading public in expansive terms. Who would have purchased or borrowed the book? Who heard the story as it circulated by word of mouth? What roles might groups such as clubs, libraries, or talk shows have played in the circulation of the narrative? What evidence is available about the kinds of books people were reading at this time or what the author was reading while writing? Or, if there is little evidence about the text, are there other books or kinds of books you might hypothesize that the writer was reading? These can be difficult questions to answer because of the kind of research required, but they can yield fascinating discoveries.

Books with an extended printing history may suggest changing cultural responses to a narrative that materialize in different editions. The captivity narrative of Mary Rowlandson, for example, originally published in 1682, has a long history of editions, spanning more than three hundred years. Comparing several editions of a text such as the Rowlandson narrative may reveal changes in the text, illustrations, preface, and afterword. In looking at the history of publication, you might ask the following questions. What differences are noticeable in successive editions of the narrative—changes in book size, typeface, use of illustrations, design, quality of paper, cover page, exact title, and so on? Have there been changes in the content or the addition of introductions, prefaces, appendixes? How has the narrative been edited at the micro- or macrolevel? Who issued the various editions? Where were they published? What historical factors might account for these changes? What distinguishes the different historical moments of the multiple editions? Can you discern shifting audiences for, and cultural uses of, life narrative through the history of this book? Finally, how did this narrative come into your hands? Where might it go after leaving your hands?

Identity

What *models of identity* were culturally available to the narrator at her particular historical moment? What models of identity are used (recall the distinction between the person writing, the narrator, and the narrated "I") to represent the subject? What are the features or characteristics of the models of identity included in this self-representation? What qualities or experiences seem to have been excluded in conforming to particular models of identity? Are there several identities in succession or alternation within the narrative text?

How does the narrator negotiate fictions of identity and resistances to the constraints of a given identity in presenting her- or himself as a gendered subject, or a racialized subject, or an ethnic subject? Does one difference dominate or structure the narrative at all times? Or is there a multiplication of identities? Where do you find evidence of conflicting models of identity at work in the text? What's the significance of these contradictions and conflicts? Does the narrator seem to be aware of the conflicts? If identity is seen as conflictual, is this thematized in the narrative? If the narrator identifies himself as having multiply marked identities, what holds these differences in some kind of dynamic tension? How can we productively, rather than reductively, describe this multiplicity of identities?

Knowledge and Self-Knowledge

It is helpful to delineate processes or methods of *knowledge production.* Consider whether the narrative takes up a formal self-interrogation, for example, a formal "examination of conscience." Does the narrator have a method for interpreting dreams or particular experiences? Does the narrative give space to multiple kinds of knowledge—intuitive, irrational, supernatural, mystical, symbolic? How does the narrative interrogate cultural forms of knowledge valued at the historical moment of writing? What relationship does the narrating "I" make between knowledge of the world or of others and self-knowledge? Does the narrative itself generate alternative sources of knowledge? Does the act of narrating his life bring the autobiographical narrator to different ways of knowing that life? What kind of knowledge could the reading of the life narrative produce for readers?

Memory

Distinctions can be made about the kinds and *meanings of remembering.* What acts of remembering are emphasized? And what times of remembering? Childhood? Courting? "Firsts"? What triggers remembering in general, and particular memories? What feelings seem to permeate various kinds of memories in the text? Does the narrator always remember what he seeks to? Or does the narrator call attention to things forgotten, times irretrievable? Does the narrator make the very act of remembering a significant theme within the narrative? That is, how self-reflexive is the narrator about the problem of remembering?

What means of accessing memory are incorporated in the text? What are the sources of remembering? Are they personal (dreams, family albums, photos, objects, family stories, genealogy)? Are they public (documents, historical events, collective rituals)? Try to identify and distinguish sources of memory in the text. What is the relationship of personal to public forms of remembrance in the narrative? If one or the other predominates, how is it related to the life narrative's audiences and purposes?

Narrative Plotting and Modes

What *narrative plottings or patterns* are used to structure the self-narrative? Think about the pattern of action and ask yourself, is its generic pattern that of the bildungsroman, a story of development in the social world? A confessional self-examination? A coming to artistic self-consciousness? A story of conversion through fall and enlightenment? A story of individual self-making? A call to action? A narrative of the individual's realization that she is embedded in a larger collective? Are there multiple plottings in the text or does one pattern dominate? Where are the shifts in plotting? And what are the effects of those shifts? How does the narrative begin? How does it conclude?

What are the histories of the narrative plottings identified? That is, why are or were they available to the self-narrator? Where, culturally and historically, do the narratives employed come from? Which narratives come from the dominant culture and which from alternative or diverse cultural sources? Consider the social locations of these stories—schools, religious faiths, political beliefs and practices, family history, work or apprenticeship, cultural stereotypes. Does the life narrative resemble and become recognizable through other kinds of writing current at the time (novels, journalism, letters)?

Consider carefully the relationship between narrative plotting and models of identity. For example, a narrative of the self-made man requires a plotting that takes the narrative subject first through an apprenticeship and then through successive stages of public accomplishment and validation.

Think as well about ways in which the possibilities of life storytelling are drawn from and may incorporate a variety of fixed forms and media into the plotting. What forms, or organizing principles, are employed— for instance, lyric poem, fable, letter, essay, meditation, or testimony? Are visual images such as photographs and illustrations embedded in the narrative to tell the story and involve the reader? What are the effects of these images? What possibilities and constraints do each of these forms enable or disable? The fable, for instance, allows the individual "I" to be understood as an allegorical type of human aspiration. The meditation turns the attention away from what an "I" has done in the world and toward the meaning of a precise moment in a larger spiritual history of the individual. The photo at once gives flesh to the narrator, embodying her for the reader, and creates a phantom narrator, thereby dematerializing her.

Online Lives

The myriad online forms of self-narration include blogs, online journals, social networking sites, and multiplayer environments. These offer arenas to explore subjectivity in ways that raise provocative questions. How does the autobiographical avatar present her- or himself? Is there an emphasis on close correlation to the flesh-and-blood historical "I" or are liberties taken (for example, in SecondLife where all can fly and many choose animal or monster features)? Is the link between the historical personage and the assumed or impersonated online "I" important for the construction of an autobiographical "I," or is the online "I" a typical or exemplary "every-person"? What coordinates of identity formation—race, gender, sexuality, class, et cetera—are rendered legible or illegible within the site? What claims are made about the historical life of the narrator, and what media for verification of those claims are introduced—photographs, videos, statistics, documents, attestations by others? What kinds of experiences are referenced? Do they correspond to recognized autobiographical genres or discourse (for example, testimony to addiction and/or the conventions of recovery narrative)?

Online sites, templates, and protocols may also flatten and normatize subjects in the conventional and streamlined formats that typify online presentation of personal detail. Are there ways to introduce subjective details? What are the regulations of the site? How are they enforced, and can a user modify them in ways that allow heterogeneous autobiographical performances? That is, in the synthetic world of the site, what possibilities for counterimage can be mobilized? If the "I" is performing as an avatar online, does that performance stay within the hegemonic limits of the site's space, or can the autobiographical content disrupt assumed norms? Given the inevitability of enhanced online surveillance, are there ways in which digital subjectivity is linked to paranoic fantasy? How does the design of the site enable or disable the performative enactment of subjectivity for other users?

Online lives, unlike lives in print form, are vulnerable to technological obsolescence. They may disappear because they are overwritten or prove unreliable because they are not regularly updated; moreover, digital code itself breaks down. How is the archive of self modified by temporal shifts or the interactive possibilities of online sites? Given the options for multimedia archiving, how are the temporal and spatial layerings of "I"s reconfigured and their intersections made legible?

In sum, how do digitalization and virtuality complicate the notion of authenticity and truth? How do we understand the possibilities for self-fabrication or autobiographical hoaxing in digital worlds? What are the terms of an autobiographical pact online? How is the cultural machinery of confession rerouted through virtual worlds? In what ways do the options for others' responses to and editing or modifying of discourse in an intersubjective process make the subject inescapably collective and collaborative? Does the idiosyncratic, individual subject become a relic of print culture that is no longer viable online?

Paratexts

The term *paratext* encompasses *peritexts* (material inside the book) and *epitexts* (material contexts outside the book). These extranarrative components of books not only frame and contextualize the narrative but target certain reading publics and encourage certain kinds of audience responses and reading practices. What peritextual material is included in the book beyond the narrative—preface, foreword, notes, index, photographs or drawings, et cetera? How do the cover illustration and lettering present the life writing? Does the cover change with various editions? What epitexts have accompanied the marketing of the book, in stores, online, in newspapers and journals? Where has the book been reviewed and how have those reviews characterized the book? How has it been taken up by book clubs or activist groups? Is it in regular classroom use? Has it been translated and how is it presented for audiences elsewhere? Is there an audiobook, and how has it been vocally interpreted? Is there any history of recalling, renaming, or reclassifying the book, and to what effect?

For a discussion of paratext in online forms, see the section on online lives.

Relationality

What others inhabit the text? Is there a significant other posited in the text through whom, to whom, or about whom the life narrative is narrated? Who or what is that other—a family member, friend, mentor, lover, or even a divine force? To what extent is the knowledge of that relation made apparent to the reader? Do we hear the voices of this other (or these others) explicitly in the text, or implicitly? When do the voices of the other emerge? What kind of investment does the narrator seem to have in this someone or something and how does that investment affect the interpretation that the narrator makes of the life? What is the impact of this *relationality* on your understanding of the rhetorical "I" or the narrator's subjectivity?

Space and Place

Self-representation involves emplacements of multiple kinds. In what ways is the scene of writing spatialized? How do its coordinates position the narrator in social, geographic, and geopolitical locations? In ideological subject positions? What geographic spaces—for instance, urban, domestic, "foreign"—become legible in the narrative? Where does a myth of self attach to geographic location? This may occur, for example, in ecobiography, which joins the subject and a specific place (the American South or West, the Australian outback). How does the narrator negotiate boundaries—of rank, national, ethnic, religious, and gendered difference—that are both constructed and redefined in the acts of self-representation and in communicative exchange with the imagined addressee(s)?

What border zones of encounter between self and other (national, ethnic, gendered, etc.) are projected in the narrative? What psychic terrains of remembrance and reflection emerge as the narrator shuttles between social and private worlds or present-day locations and erased pasts? What histories are attached to the spaces of sociality in the text? What thematics of insider and outsider status inform the narrative? What thematic mobilities inform the narrative, for instance, mobilities of migration, diasporic transit, touristic travel, or exile?

Are there ways in which the chosen genre of life writing shapes the story, emplacing the narrator vis-á-vis others, his or her own past, and the meaning accorded the life? What stories—of possession, dispossession, invasion, displacement, erasure, forgetting—are told of geographic and cultural spaces? Is there a trope of spatiality that dominates the narrative? How do the material spaces of life writing—the printed page, the bookstore, the online catalog—situate the narrative? (See peritexts.)

Temporality

Can you identify the time of the telling, that is, the narrative moment? At what stage in his life does the narrator compose the text? Publish it? Does the narrator speak directly about the act of telling his story, that is, does he *situate the moment* of its telling? Does the narrator tell the story at one fixed moment, or are there two or more moments of telling? What characterizes these moments of telling? How are they different from or similar to one another? How do narrative tone and narrative intention shift with the shifts in historical moments or times in the narrator's life cycle? If the narrator has written or voiced a series of autobiographical texts, are the same events and life experiences narrated from successive, perhaps conflicting, perspectives? Or are successive stages of the life chronicled?

It may be helpful to contrast the time of writing with the time span of the narrative. Consider, for instance, how the times of past, present, and future are organized in the telling of the story. Does the narrative relate a continuous chronology from birth to adolescence to adulthood? Or does the narrative begin "in the middle" and use flashbacks and flash-forwards? How much concern is there for organizing the narrative through chronology? If the narrative is discontinuous or if it skips over long periods of time, what effects do these gaps have on the story produced? Why might the narrator have played with or manipulated chronological or historical time in these ways?

Trauma and Scriptotherapy

Does the narrative engage issues involved in *traumatic or obsessive memory* to find ways of telling about events and sufferings that defy language and understanding? Does the narrator struggle to find words to speak the unspeakable? Are those traumatic memories of a personal and/or political sort? Consider how the narrator deals with trauma and the resultant obsessional memory. Does it come to the fore fragmentarily, repeatedly, throughout the narrative? Does it seem to be, indeed, can it be, resolved in any way? What kind of understanding seems to be achieved?

Does the narrator discuss the therapeutic effects of writing in the text? Is the therapeutic value of writing itself a major theme? Does the process of writing seem to have changed the narrating "I" and the life story itself? Does the act of reading a narrative of trauma have therapeutic effects on the reader? Where and in what ways does the narrator offer the reader a possibility of community in identifying with the narrator? Where and in what ways does the narrator ask the reader to see his or her own identity differently?

Voice

While there is one narrator, the *voices of the narrator* may be many. Consider whether there seems to be one voice dominating the narrative or multiple and conflicting voices. That is, is the text monovocal or polyvocal? If one voice dominates throughout the narrative, where and how do other voices emerge? How does the narrating "I" contain or curtail them? If there are multiple voices, when do they emerge and when disappear?

Why? Is there a blending or an unresolved tension of voices in the narrative? Is a relationship posited between the individual narrator's voice and the collective voice of some larger political community? What values and discourses are identified with that larger collectivity? Is more than one group or collectivity invoked in the text, each with distinct values and languages? What form does that incorporation take? For instance, reported dialogue or explicit memories?

Consider also how voice itself is thematized. Does the narrator explicitly call attention to issues of voice in the text? Are speech and/or silence thematized? What happens at the end of the narrative to multiple voices? Is there a closure to these multiple voices?

Conclusion

This tool kit of questions may seem daunting. We have purposely multiplied the questions that you can ask of any life narrative. Probably few texts would sustain examination through all of these topics; and certainly, some questions are better suited to some texts or some readers. But if you habitually read in terms of, say, reader response, you may find it illuminating to take up the question of embodiment or of agency in narrative. In the multiple plottings, separate voices, divergent memories, and diverse audiences that even apparently uncomplicated life narratives invite, there is a world of identities and stories to engage.

Sixty Genres of Life Narrative

Life writers assign meaning to events, behaviors, and psychological processes that differ widely over time, place, belief system, and social position. As subjects of historically and culturally specific understandings of memory, experience, identity, space, embodiment, and agency, they both reproduce the various ways in which they have been culturally read and critique the limits of cultural modes of self-narrating. Through reading their lives within and against the terms of life writing, they shift its terms and invite different ways of being read. That is, autobiographical subjects register, consciously and unconsciously, their complicity with and resistance to the terms of cultural self-locating they inherit. In the contexts of those tensions they give shape to alternative modes of address, each with its own defining characteristics. Established generic templates mutate and new generic possibilities emerge.

While it is impossible to comprehensively survey the numerous autobiographical forms produced over centuries, this appendix offers a glossary of sixty genres of life writing, with brief definitions of their features. Many of these genres are discussed more extensively in the preceding chapters.

Academic life writing. Is academic life writing a separate subgenre, or a byproduct of academic infatuation with writing about memoir through writing memoir? Gillian Whitlock asserts that a case can be made for understanding the self distinctly in and through a disciplinary construct as a process of transformative transculturation ("Disciplining the Child" 47). Numerous examples of academic memoir have been produced in Great Britain, the United States, France, Australia, and elsewhere in recent decades. Historians who study their own histories as examples of the history of memory may alter their concept of historical objectivity to foreground personal experience, as Pierre Nora demonstrates in his collection of *Ego-Histoires* by French academics, arguing that the self can be used as a "device to claim more authentic and relevant styles of knowledge and scholarship" (cited in Whitlock, "Disciplining" 47). Jeremy Popkin's study of historians' life narratives observes the interplay between the context of public events and the texture of personal life. The serial memoirs of Nancy K. Miller, *Bequest and Betrayal: Memoirs of a Parent's Death* and *But Enough about Me,* interweave stories of her family's origins with reflections on memoir writing in probing how her past formed her. Laurel Richardson, in *Fields of Play: Constructing an Academic Life,* alternates traditional and experimental writing in connecting life to work and exploring the circumstances that shape the selves she, and we, become.

Among British academic memoirists, Terry Eagleton in *The Gatekeeper: A Memoir* and Lorna Sage in *Bad Blood* write themselves into their adult vocation of English studies by internalizing its norms. Carolyn Kay Steedman in *Landscape for a Good Woman* took her own family as a case history to refute the claims of social historians about the subordinate place of women and children in the rural class structure. Annette Kuhn in *Family Secrets: Acts of Memory and Imagination* and Gillian Rose in *Love's Work* interrogate the work of making a subject and expose how disciplinary ideologies can enforce conformity and traditional roles (Whitlock, "Disciplining" 51, 55).

Cynthia G. Franklin regards academic memoirs as a movement affording insights into how the academy functions. In her view, such memoirs explore challenges to the humanities, such as the corporatization of universities and the creation of a star system for a privileged few (*Academic* 1–4). She regards academic memoirs as potential sites for reinvigorating humanism and human rights struggles. Franklin thus expands the field of academic memoir to include many kinds of memoir writing that intersect with such theoretical fields as postcolonial and disability studies.

Addiction narrative. A kind of conversion narrative in which the reformed subject narrates his or her degeneration through addiction to something— alcohol, drugs, sex, food, the Internet. Some of the tropes and hallmarks of addiction narratives are the use of confessional discourse; a narrative structure of a fall into a state of craving often regarded as disease; a cry for help; first steps toward rehabilitation; and conversion to sobriety/recovery. Alcoholics Anonymous has helped to generate both the paradigm for and the popularity of many of these narratives such as Carolyn Knapp's *Drinking: A Love Story,* Augusten Burroughs's *Dry,* and James Frey's *A Million Little Pieces* (a hoax narrative). A new variation combines addiction with a narrative of filiation, as in the twin memoirs by David Sheff (the father),

Beautiful Boy: A Father's Journey through His Son's Addiction, and Nic Sheff (the son), *Tweak: Growing Up on Methamphetamines.* Addiction narratives are often best-sellers, tempting publishers to seek out and market to general and self-help audiences extravagant and sometimes exaggerated or fabricated stories of degradation and redemption, such as Frey's, which unwary readers responded to with intense empathy and identification. (See *self-help narrative.*)

Adoption life stories. Some critics argue that adoption memoir forms a distinct and coherent genre of life writing because personal identity is mediated by a primary rupture, separation from the biological family, whose "ghost-trace . . . lingers in the expression of the individual and resonates culturally because it challenges normative social patterns" (Hipchen and Deans 163). The scope of adoption memoir spans all members of the triad—birth parent(s), adoptive parent(s), and adoptee—but most narratives have focused on patterns of relinquishment and the narrating "I"'s efforts either to reconstruct the family of origin or to dispute its claims. The contemporary adoption story is typically narrated as a quest that tries to "restore the lost origins of the adoptee" (Deans 239) and "forge meaningful connections despite the indeterminacy of one's identity" (256). In its focus on "ghost remnants, a road not taken, shadowy traces of memory mixed with desire," such adoption memoir valorizes origins and troubles the primacy of social construction (Hipchen and Deans 167). Birth mothers, however, may also generate adoption narratives, as does Janet Mason Ellerby in *Following the Tambourine Man.* Her story situates the act of giving up her baby at sixteen and the decades of loss that ensued within the shift in values about adoption culture in mid–twentieth-century America.

Yet in life writing all identities are constructed, and such acts as transracial adoption highlight the negotiation of racialized boundaries by foregrounding "the literal social construction of families" (Patton 274). Whether adoption life story is more than an enhancement of the filiation narrative that inevitably emphasizes the estrangement of child and parent—on either side—and the desire to recover always already lost origins by reconstructing identity within the family remains a subject for debate.

Apology. A form of self-presentation as self-defense against the allegations or attacks of others, an apology justifies one's own deeds, beliefs, and way of life. Typically, the formal genre of the apology admits wrongdoing or expresses regret primarily to excuse its speaker. The mode is famously employed by Socrates in Plato's *Apology* and by Montaigne in the "Apology for Raimond Sebond." Apology is both a genre in itself and, as Francis Hart notes, a major stance of self-presentation in personal narratives, often in the autobiographical writings of statesmen. Former Secretary of Defense Robert S. McNamara, for instance, wrote a justification of his positions and role during the Vietnam War in his 1995 *In Retrospect: The Tragedy and Lessons of Vietnam.* Women writing in the mode of apology may mount a defense of women's intellectual and moral equality, as did Mary Wollstonecraft in *A Vindication of the Rights of Women* and Sor Juana Inés de la Cruz in *The Response.*

Autie-biography. G. Thomas Couser uses this term to signal a first-person life story written by a person with autism, as opposed to earlier narratives that were written by a relative or clinician (*Signifying Bodies* 5). Examples include Donna Williams's *Nobody Nowhere: The Extraordinary Autobiography of an Autistic* and *Somebody Somewhere: Breaking Free from the World of Autism* and Temple Grandin's *The Way I See It: A Personal Look at Autism and Asperger's* (see Sidonie Smith's "Taking It to the Limit"). Autism rights activist Amanda Baggs uses YouTube to critique notions of the autistic as incommunicative in "In My Language." She explores the available "shapes of personhood" and critiques the language of self-described "normals."

Auto/biography, or a/b. This term signals the interrelatedness of autobiographical narrative and biography. Although the slash marks their fluid boundary, they are in several senses different, even opposed, forms (see chapter 1). The term also designates a mode of the autobiographical that inserts biography/ies within an autobiography, or the converse, a personal narrative within a biography. Older instances of this form include Margaret Cavendish's biography of her husband to which she appended her own brief autobiographical narrative. More recent instances include John Edgar Wideman's *Brothers and Keepers,* in which Wideman's biographical narrative of his imprisoned brother is entwined with his own memory of growing up in the harsh urban environment of Pittsburgh. While earlier forms tended to distinguish biography from autobiography, contemporary writers often intermix biographical and autobiographical narrating into a "relational" story. (See *relational autobiography.*)

Autobiography in the second person. In this style of address the narrating "I" replaces the narrated "I" with the second-person "you" and conflates or confounds that "you" with the reader, though it is also understood as the subject talking to her- or himself. For example, in *Patterns of Childhood,* Christa Wolf often uses the second person to address both her childhood memories and those of Germans during the Hitler years. In *Wasted,* Marya Hornbacher shifts into "you" to insist on her reader's identification with her descent into the dark night of the anorexic's self-erasure, personalizing the generalized pattern of the anorexic's struggle with her diminishing body and absorbing hungers.

Autobiography in the third person. In this case the narrating "I" refers to the narrated "I" in the third person, as "he" or "she." Philippe Lejeune characterizes this as a situation in which one narrator pretends to be two ("Autobiography in the Third Person"). Another way to describe this style is to understand the "I" as an implied narrator speaking as a ventriloquist through "he," or "she," or "they." But why have recourse to autobiography in the third person? Jean Starobinski suggests that "though seemingly a modest form, autobiographical narrative in the third person accumulates and makes compatible events glorifying the hero who refuses to speak in his own name" (77). In this style, the narrator seems to take on "the impersonal role of historian" (77), presenting the protagonist in the third person. But the covert identification of the author and third-person pronoun belies this apparent objectivity. And as the third-person self-presentation of Henry Adams in *The Education of Henry Adams* suggests, the role of an apparent self-historian may be ironic and self-deprecating rather than heroic. Aleister Crowley, whose *The Confessions of Aleister Crowley: An Autohagiography* is written in third and then first person, ironically, in his "saintly" send-up of the genre, comments on the impact of writing in the third person:

> Previous to the death of Edward Crowley [Aleister's father], the recollections of his son, however vivid or detailed, appeared to him strangely impersonal. In throwing back his mind to that period, he feels, although attention constantly elicits new facts, that he is investigating the behavior of somebody else. It is only from this point that he begins to think of himself in the first person. From this point, however, he does so and is able to continue this autohagiography in a more conventional style by speaking of himself as "I."

(See also *autohagiography.*)

Autobiography, variants. Many critics have taken pleasure in punning on the etymologies and referential possibilities of the three Greek words that compose *autobiography (autos, bios, graphe).* Some feminist critics have varied or removed the "life" that was understood to be a masculinist universal: Domna Stanton theorized *autogynography*; Jeanne Perrault writes of women's *autography*; Leigh Gilmore finds the difference of women's life writing in acts of *autobiographics*; Jana Evans Braziel emphasizes the different positioning of diasporan women life writers in their *alter-biographies.* Memoirists and novelists have also troped on the term. J. M. Coetzee has used the term *autrebiography* and practices it in his *Diary of a Bad Year,* a work of autobiographical fiction interweaving three narrative voices for its personas—Señor C, JC, and Anya—in "a kind of metaphysics of the self" among analytical reason, emotional need, and the body. Coetzee observes, "Writing is dialogic, a matter of awakening the countervoices in oneself and embarking on speech with them" (quoted by William Deresiewicz 32). Frank Kermode has termed Coetzee's 2009 *Summertime* "fictioneering" to capture the sense of its experimentation with boundary dissolution. Derrida famously used the term *otography* to suggest that autobiography happens "in the ear of the other." Exploring "the difference in the ear," Derrida transforms *auto* into *oto,* asserting that "the ear of the other says me to me and constitutes the autos of my autobiography." That is, the autobiographical signature (the proper name) in a sense is activated on the addressee's side, in its hearing and apprehension (50–51). Cartoonist Lynda Barry uses the term *autobifictionalography* to characterize *One Hundred Demons,* a graphic narrative based on her experience but with some fictionalizing "to make myself look as cool as possible" ("Interview"). While some would argue that all life writing is inescapably a Franklinesque *erratography* (a cataloguing of one's mistakes and moral lapses) or, conversely, a morally driven *oughtabiography,* in Chon Noriega's phrase (a narrative of regret about all the things one should have done), critics continue to encapsulate theoretical positions in witty phrases about the complexities of self-writing.

Autoethnography. This is collectivized and situated life writing in which the *bios* of autobiography is replaced by *ethnos* or social group. This term emerged in the wake of wide-ranging critiques during the 1980s of the investigator-informant model of ethnography as a practice that sustains asymmetrical relations of colonialism. Critics such as Mary Louise Pratt, Françoise Lionnet, Anne E. Goldman, and Julia Watson have argued that the terms of transculturation in contact zones of encounter between indigenous and metropolitan subjects need to be redefined. Pratt, for instance, explores how indigenous or oppressed subjects in taking up writing may both collaborate with and appropriate a colonizer's (or dominant culture's) discursive models, thereby transculturating them into indigenous idioms and producing hybrid forms of collectivized life narrative. Whether tracing autobiographical inscription in such collective forms as the cookbook and the labor-organizing narrative, as Goldman does; or in the simultaneous practice and parody of ethnographic discourse within Latin American *testimonio,* as Pratt does; or in the life narratives of emergent African women writers, as Watson does, these critics frame autoethnography less as a genre than as a situated practice of self-narration contesting the traditional Western limits of individuality and normative discourses. Examples of autoethnography include Quiché Indian Rigoberta Menchú's *I, Rigoberta Menchú* and more recently Jamaican poet Lorna Goodison's *From Harvey River: A Memoir of My Mother and Her Island.*

The critique of ethnography as an epistemological project has produced variant terms, particularly in the social sciences, to describe forms of qualitative ethnography in which the writer-observer is self-reflexive and critical of the discursive practices and history of the field. Marilyn Strathern uses *auto-anthropology* for "anthropology carried out in the social context which produced it" (13); David Hayano discusses *self ethnographic texts*; and Deborah Reed-Danahay, in surveying the field from an anthropologist's point of view, distinguishes between *native ethnography* as the study of one's own group and *ethnographic autobiography* as a life narrative of ethnographic interest (1–9). The scholar of life writing may find the emphasis on the observer-critic in these approaches different from the concept of the narrator who grows up in a particular culture but has become, by education, linguistic skill, and reflexivity, able to reflect on the *ethnos* as both insider and outsider.

Autofiction. A term used often in France for autobiographical fiction, or fictional narrative in the first-person mode. Ultimately, the attempt to distinguish "autobiography" from "autobiographical fiction" may, as Paul Jay argues, be "pointless" (16), "for if by 'fictional' we mean 'made up,' 'created,' or 'imagined'—something, that is, which is literary and not 'real'—then we have merely defined the ontological status of any text, autobiographical or not" (16). Despite the difficulty of fixing the boundary between fiction and autobiography, the reader comes to an autobiographical text with the expectation that the protagonist is a person living in the experiential world, not a fictional character, and that the narrative will be a transparent, truthful view of that world. But as the autofiction of *Roland Barthes by Roland Barthes* and others in France in the 1970s suggests, no definitive truth about the past self may be available. The referential "real" assumed to be "outside" a text cannot be written; the subject is inescapably an unstable fiction; but the autobiography-fiction boundary is marked. While autobiographical storytelling employs fictional tactics and genres, however, autofiction uses textual markers that signal a deliberate, often ironic, interplay between the two modes. Raymond Federman's notion of *surfiction* may capture this borderland in its mining of how his writing generated his life: "I do not think my life and history are the sources of my fiction, but that in fact my fiction is what invents my life and history. . . . In other words, the stories I write are my life" (quoted in M. Fox). Conversely, some writers insist on the factual truth of their memoirs that have been "fictionalizing" or outright lying about their experience (see *Forbidden Lies*).

Autographics. Gillian Whitlock proposed this term for graphic memoir to highlight "the specific conjunctions of visual and verbal text . . . and the subject positions that narrators negotiate in and through comics" ("Autographics" 966). Drawing on Marianne Hirsch's notion of "biocularity" to emphasize the distinctiveness of the verbal-visual conjunction that occurs in comics ("Editor's Column" 1213), Whitlock stresses its potential for a unique response to the historical moment by mediating across cultures and prompting new imaginings (973). As a medium, autographics segment narrative spatially and require the reader to make an act of interpretive closure. Thus the "I" is complicated both verbally and graphically. Such contemporary autographics as Art Spiegelman's *Maus,* Marjane Satrapi's *Persepolis,* Harvey Pekar's *The Quitter,* Alison Bechdel's *Fun Home,* and David B's *Epileptic* have made complex literary narratives interweaving autobiographical and biographical stories.

Autohagiography
Hagiography is biographical writing praising the life as exemplary, making the person a "saint." Autohagiography can be used playfully for life writing in which the subject celebrates him- or herself as "saintly," often ironically, as in Aleister Crowley's *The Confessions of Aleister Crowley: An Autohagiography.*

Autosomatography/autopathography. This second term has been used to characterize personal narratives about illness or disability that contest cultural discourses stigmatizing the writer as abnormal, aberrant, or in some sense pathological. But G. Thomas Couser has suggested that such narratives be seen instead as "antipathological" because "in my experience the impulse to write a first-person illness narrative is often the impulse to depathologize one's condition" (personal correspondence). Couser proposes the term *autosomatography* to distinguish first-person illness narratives from those told by another, in the third person. Such narratives critique social constructions of the disabled body and incorporate a counternarrative of survival and empowerment that reclaims the individual's or a loved one's body from the social stigmatization and the impersonalization of medical discourse. (See also Anne Hunsaker Hawkins on pathography.) Couser observes that a few conditions of disease or disability have generated extensive life writing narratives. His *Recovering Bodies* identifies these as breast cancer, HIV/AIDS, deafness, and paralysis. More recently, he points out that blindness, depression, autism, and arguably addiction, if considered as an illness or disability, could be added. He notes that other conditions have produced only small numbers of life narratives, including some that would seem resistant to verbal representation, such as early-stage Alzheimer's.

Autothanatography. This term has been applied to autobiographical texts that confront illness and death by performing a life at a limit of its own, or another's, undoing. Nancy K. Miller suggests that "autobiography— identity through alterity—is also writing against death twice: the other's and one's own." For Miller, in a sense "every autobiography, we might say, is also an autothanatography," since the prospect of nonexistence looms inescapably ("Representing Others" 12). Susanna Egan, in an extended treatment of autothanatography, focuses on how the attention of recent life narrators to issues of terminal illness "intensifies the rendition of lived experience, the immediacy of crisis, and the revealing processes of self-understanding" in the process of dying (*Mirror Talk* 200). AIDS-related autothanatography, Egan notes, confronts death head on: "Death writing becomes preeminently life writing, and a bid to take charge of how that life writing is read" (207). It is "part of a complex claiming of agency" that attempts to connect the organic to the symbolic (208). At the zero-degree of both life and autobiography, with the death of the writing, or visual, or filmic life narrator, "the subject becomes an object entirely exposed to being read, entirely dependent on its reader for constructions of meaning" (212). A case in point is Harold Brodkey's *This Wild Darkness*. Indeed, the narrative may be completed by another after the subject's death, as was Tom Joslin's film *Silverlake Life: The View from Here* (214). Egan suggests that even in monologic autothanatographies, such as Audre Lorde's *The Cancer Journals* and *A Burst of Light*, the text is dialogic, the voice polyphonic, in integrating the anticipation of death into living (215). Making a record of living in a text that outlives the life, autothanatographies intensively "focus on illness, pain, and imminent death as crucial to the processes of that life" (224).

Autotopography. This term was coined by Jennifer A. González to define how a person's integral objects become, over time, so imprinted with the "psychic body" that they serve as autobiographical objects. The personal objects may be serviceable, such as clothing or furniture. But they may also be physical extensions of the mind—photographs, heirlooms, souvenirs, icons, and so forth: "These personal objects can be seen to form a syntagmatic array of physical signs in a spatial representation of identity" (133). Organized into collections, such material memory landscapes might be as elaborate as a home altar or as informal as a display of memorabilia. Autotopographies are invested with multiple and shifting associative meanings; they are idiosyncratic and flexible, although their materiality prevents free-floating signification (144). The autotopography may act either as a revelation or as a kind of screen memory to aid the forgetting of a traumatic moment. An autotopography can also be a space of utopian identification and mythic history, idealizing the subjectivity that is re-created through the material evidence of artifacts (145). Finally, an autotopography may be thought of as a "countersite" to both resist and converse with mass-media images. It draws from life events and cultural identity to build a self-representation as a material and tactical act of personal reflection (147). Mieke Bal has characterized Louise Bourgeois's "Spider" sculpture as autotopography.

Bildungsroman. Traditionally, the bildungsroman has been regarded as the novel of development and social formation of a young man, as in Dickens's *Great Expectations*. This "apprenticeship novel," argues C. Hugh Holman, "recounts the youth and young manhood of a sensitive protagonist who is attempting to learn the nature of the world, discover its meaning and pattern, and acquire a philosophy of life and 'the art of living'" (31). The plot of development may involve escape from a repressive family, schooling, and a journey into the wide world of urban life where encounters with a series of mentors, romantic involvements, and entrepreneurial ventures lead the protagonist to reevaluate assumptions. The bildungsroman culminates in the acceptance of one's constrained social role in the bourgeois social order, usually requiring the renunciation of some ideal or passion and the embrace of heteronormative social arrangements.

And yet the form of the bildungsroman has been taken up more recently by women and other disenfranchised persons to consolidate a sense of emerging identity and an increased role in public life, as in Esmeralda Santiago's *When I Was Puerto Rican.* The bildungsroman can also be used negatively as a norm of assimilation into the dominant culture that is unattainable and must be relinquished or that produces alienation from the home community, as in Richard Rodriguez's *Hunger of Memory.* In much women's writing, its plot of development culminates not in integration but in an awakening to gender-based limitations (see Fuderer 1–6), as in Ken Bugul's *The Abandoned Baobab: The Autobiography of a Senegalese Woman.*

Biomythography. This term was coined by Audre Lorde to signal how the re-creation of meaning in one's life is invested in writing that renegotiates cultural invisibility. Lorde redefines life writing as a biography of the mythic self (see Raynaud, "'A Nutmeg Nestled'"), a self she discovers in imaginatively affiliating with a mythic community of other lesbian women. In *Zami: A New Spelling of My Name,* Lorde uses the term to refer to an affiliation with her mother's place of origin and a sisterhood of lesbian friends. In *The Cancer Journals,* she exemplifies it by combining journal entries and analytical essays to reconstitute herself as an empowered Amazon, a one-breasted warrior/survivor of cancer.

Captivity narrative. An overarching term for any narrative told by someone who is, or has been, held captive by some capturing group. This category includes Indian captivity narratives, slave narratives, spiritual autobiographies, UFO stories, convent captivity stories, and narratives of seduction. Indian captivity narratives, the stories of non-Indians captured by indigenous people such as Mary Jemison's as-told-to *A Narrative of the Life of Mary Jemison,* have since the sixteenth century numbered in the thousands, many written by or about women. They were produced predominantly in what is now the United States, though some were produced in Canada, Australia, and by Africans escaped from slaveholders, and some published in languages other than English. According to Kathryn Zabelle Derounian-Stodola, "the Indian captivity narrative concerns the capture of an individual or several family members . . . and its plot is most commonly resolved with the captive's escape, ransom, transculturation, or death" (xi). Archival and interpretive work in the paradoxes of identification and reconversion in captivity narrative as a genre of public testimony is likely to rewrite the field of autobiography studies in many modern languages as literary scholars and historians jointly recover more of these narratives.

Case study. This term designates a life narrative that is gathered into a dossier in order to make a diagnosis and identification of a disease or disorder. Susan Wells, tracking the history of the case report, which "was written retrospectively, usually included references to the literature, and articulated the specific case within the context of the ongoing conversation among professionals about issues of diagnosis and treatment," points to the exigent nature of the case report and its hybridity as an amalgam of "adjacent genres" such as social science discourse, the medical case study, and fiction (355). This mode of life reporting is often associated with Freud's extended analyses of the cases of various patients with symptoms such as hysteria and gender-identity disorder. The treatment begins with the patient's producing of a story of unhappiness and illness. The unsatisfactory nature of this first narrative usually lets the analyst "see his way about the case" (Freud 66) in gaps, hesitations, inconclusiveness, and changes in dates, times, and places. That is, the narrator/patient presents clues to another story she is unable to tell. Freud's emphasis is on making, with the patient, a new and coherent narrative that, in giving the patient possession of a past life, enables her to own her story. Another sense of the case study is discussed in *Landscape for a Good Woman* by Carolyn Kay Steedman, who critiques its ability to embed gendered social history in the story of rural working-class British mothers (130–31).

Collaborative life writing. A term that indicates the production of an autobiographical text by more than one person through one of the following processes: the as-told-to narrative in which an informant tells an interviewer the story of his or her life, as in *Black Elk Speaks*; the ghostwritten narrative recorded, edited, and perhaps expanded by an interviewer, as in many political and celebrity autobiographies; a coproduced or collectively produced narrative in which individual speakers are not specified or in which one speaker is identified as representative of the group. Collaborative narratives are multiply mediated by the interviewer and editor, and often two or more parties are included in the production of the published story, particularly when translation is required. In collaborations, despite assurances of coproduction, power relations between the teller and recorder/editor are often asymmetrical, with the literarily skilled editor controlling the disposition of the informant's narrative material. (Also see *heterobiography*.)

Confession. An oral or written narrative, the confession is addressed to an interlocutor who listens, judges, and has the power to absolve. Confession was originally doubly addressed, to God and to a confessor. Since Augustine's narrative, the double address of the confession has been directed to God and the human reader who needs a narrative explanation of sinfulness and redemption. As Stephen Spender argues in "Confessions and Autobiography," the penitent's "purpose is to tell the exact truth about the person whom he knows most intimately . . . himself. His only criterion is naked truth: and usually his truth is naked without being altogether true" (118). Further, he adds, "all confessions are from subject to object, from the individual to the community or creed. Even the most shamelessly revealed inner life pleads its cause before the moral system of an outer, objective life" (120). Confessional life narrative may be a record of some kind of error transformed; it may also be the narrator's attempt to reaffirm communal values or justify their absence (121).

Daniel B. Shea's *Spiritual Autobiography in Early America* explores the uses of confession in Puritan narrative, particularly the conversion experience, and suggests how it is a foundational discourse of American public culture. Rita Felski, in a chapter titled "On Confession" in her book *Beyond Feminist Aesthetics: Feminist Literature and Social Change,* understands feminist confession as a public mode of self-presentation that constitutes feminist community and a counterknowledge founded on the authority of experience. Foucault has written extensively on how confession in the West has served to discipline subjects by managing illegitimate desire and producing knowledge about sexuality (*History of Sexuality* 58). His analysis has been productively applied to contemporary modes of the confessional such as talk shows, where people's obsessive confessing ritually enacts disorderly desires and behaviors, as well as their containment by the format of the talk show itself (see Peck). And in the past several years scholars from a variety of disciplines, including communications, media studies, cultural studies, as well as literary studies, have focused on social networking sites and blogs as new forms of digitized confession and the Internet more broadly as a global confessing machine.

Conversion narrative. This narrative mode is structured around a radical transformation from a faulty "before" self to an enlightened "after" self. The typical pattern involves a fall into a troubled and sensorily confused "dark night of the soul," followed by a "call for help," a process of transformation, and a journey to a "new Jerusalem" or place of membership in an enlightened community of like believers. Conversion experiences as varied as those recounted in Frederick Douglass's *Narrative,* Malcolm X's *Autobiography,* John Bunyan's *Grace Abounding,* e. e. cummings's *The Enormous Room,* Elizabeth Gilbert's *Eat, Pray, Love* (which she calls "a religious *conversation*" [16]), and Alcoholics Anonymous narratives share these paradigmatic features. Conversion may be neither definitive nor final, as suggested in Malcolm X's chronicling of his multiple conversions.

Diary. A form of periodic life writing, the diary records dailiness in accounts and observations of emotional responses. While diaries may seem incoherent or haphazard in their preoccupations, they "gather force by accretion of experience, always chronological" (Roorbach 163). And through the force of that accretion, the diarist's voice takes on a recognizable narrative persona (Culley, *A Day at a Time* 12), from Samuel Pepys to Virginia Woolf, to Salam Pax in *The Clandestine Diary of an Ordinary Iraqi,* taken from his blogs, and Phoebe Gloeckner in *The Diary of a Teenage Girl: An Account in Words and Pictures.* Margot Culley also notes that a diary is fragmented, revisionary, in process, although its self-constructions in the pages of a written diary are available to the diarist for later viewing, and for comment or emendation (20). The immediacy of the genre derives from the diarist's lack of foreknowledge about outcomes of the plot of his life, which creates a "series of surprises to writer and reader alike" (21). Some critics distinguish the diary form from the journal by noting that the journal tends to be more a public record and thus less intimate than the diary.

Philippe Lejeune, who does not make a distinction between the diary and the journal, regards diary writing as fundamentally different from autobiography in its orientation toward futurity and the moment. It is "an immense field, as yet largely unexplored" and "a social outcast, of no fixed theoretical address" ("Practice of the Private Journal" 202). Lejeune asserts that his many books and essays on the diary in the past decade—the French diaries of ordinary people, of girls in the nineteenth century, and of Anne Frank—have, in his eyes, "erased the dichotomy between journal and autobiography" (201). Lejeune observes that "the private diary is a practice . . . a way of life, whose result is often obscure and does not reflect the life as an autobiographical narrative would do" (187). A diary has a wide range of functions and forms and may incorporate many kinds of writings, drawings, documents, and objects (191). Perhaps never truly "sincere" or secret, the diary is "motivated by a search for communication, by a will to persuasion" (192). Lejeune suggests several directions for future research: on who keeps diaries and attitudes about them; how one reads another's and one's own journal; and the rights and duties of the diarist (198–200). The recent translation of several of his essays in *On Diary* will facilitate these projects.

Liz Stanley and Helen Dampier propose the term *simulacrum diary* to characterize a life narrative that appears in various forms, for example, letters, a journal, and a published memoir, in which "the moment of writing" is not synonymous with "the scene of what is written about" (25A). They invoke the term *simulacrum,* developed by Jean Baudrillard, to signal a text that "disputes notions of the real," being neither un/real nor a mis/representation but "a replication of the thing itself," disrupting the polarities of original/copy and real/fake (40). Using the example of Johanna Brandt-Van Warmelo's diary, they trace how "something" that she had written as a case worker in a concentration camp during the South African war in 1901 was later published as a diary of her war experience that effectively "mimics . . . the 'present-ness' and temporal immediacy of diaries written at the time of the events they describe" (41) despite its belated writing. Stanley and Dampier argue that this doubling of diaristic writing makes it difficult to discern the "real" (a private manuscript) from the "copy" (a public book), thus confusing categories of the authentic and inauthentic, the true and the fictive. It remains to be seen how useful this term will be, as relatively few texts have multiple forms and circumstances of production.

As is evident, the diary, once seen as a transparent site of diurnal recording, is now theorized as a complex practice of life writing, by, in addition to Lejeune, Rebecca Hogan, Suzanne Bunkers, Cynthia Huff, Helen M.

Buss, and others. They argue that recovering and reading these often un-published life writings requires sophisticated interpretive strategies that explore the contexts of its composition and circulation. Online diaries, both visual and written, are likely to radically change both the concept of the diary form and its theorizing.

Digital life stories. Some life writing critics argue that digital life stories are different in kind from their written counterparts. Michael Hardey defines them as life narratives that are "created and consumed within a . . . [medium] framed by digital data" (185). He argues that in digital space the boundary between writer and reader may blur in their interactive co-constructing of a life story. While personal home pages and blogs adopt a diary approach that permits the regular addition of new material and emphasizes chronology, they store archival materials by way of hyperlinks that radically alter the diurnal character of the diary. Hardey also points out that digital life stories "lack a defined audience" because anyone may visit them at any time (189). In their focus on dailiness, digital life stories comprise a kind of backyard ethnography. To date, Hardey asserts, they have typically focused on family life stories, narratives countering the re-ports of experts, or conversion stories (191–93). And they may thematize issues of authenticity and detachment from off-line identities whose authority was assured by the interview situation in fixed forms of writing. A central tension of digital life stories is the play between fluidity of context and intensified surveillance in online media.

Ecobiography. Life writing that interweaves the story of a protagonist with the story of the fortunes, conditions, geography, and ecology of a region and reflects on their connection (sometimes failed) as a significant feature of the writing. *Eco-autobiography,* as Peter F. Perreten terms it, is less a genre than "a class of landscape/life writing where the two elements work together to form a richly textured, nuanced text," as in narratives by Annie Dillard and N. Scott Momaday (21 n. 3). Ecobiography charts human en-counters with the regional specificity of a place, as in Utahan Terry Tem-pest Williams's *Refuge.* It may interweave biography and autobiographical documents, as does Jon Krakauer's *Into the Wild,* the story of young ad-venturer Chris McCandless's attempt to live in the Alaskan wilderness, where he eventually died from eating a poisonous plant.

Ecobiography is related to travel writing in Rory Stewart's *The Places in*

Between, about his experience of walking through a war-ravaged Afghanistan, where ecodestruction makes survival challenging. Ecobiography may also focus on sustainability, as in Barbara Kingsolver's chronicle of her family's effort to live off the food produced on its and neighbor farms for a year in *Animal, Vegetable, Miracle.* (For fuller explorations of ecology and narrative, see Dana Phillips on "ecocriticism, literary theory, and the truth of ecology," Lawrence Buell on "the environmental imagination," and *The Ecocriticism Reader: Landmarks in Literary Ecology,* edited by Cheryll Glotfelty and Harold Fromm.)

Ethnic life narrative. A mode of autobiographical narrative, emergent in ethnic communities within or across nations, that negotiates ethnic identification around multiple pasts and "multiple, provisional axes of organization" (S. Wong, "Immigrant Autobiography" 160). Within this larger category critics have differentiated immigrant from exile narratives. William Boelhower, following Werner Sollors, presents a transethnic schema of descent and consent through which to read immigrant narratives ("Making of Ethnic Autobiography"). Sau-Ling Cynthia Wong, critiquing Boelhower's universal ascription of these patterns across ethnic and generational lines, suggests that such a scheme telescopes the experience of different generations into one universal pattern of transindividual ethnic subjectivity and fails to account for generational differences in the mediations of memory and "the historical particularities of various ethnic groups" (160). Narratives of exile inscribe a nomadic subject, set in motion for a variety of reasons and now inhabiting cultural borderlands, who may or may not return "home" but who necessarily negotiates cultural spaces of the in-between where "hybrid, unstable identities" are rendered palpable through the negotiation "between conflicting traditions—linguistic, social, ideological" (Woodhull 100).

Ethnocriticism. A term proposed by Arnold Krupat for studying Native American and other indigenous cultural productions, particularly life narratives, that methodologically fuse a mixture of anthropology, history, and critical theory. Its focus, Krupat argues, is properly on the frontier, understood as a "shifting space in which two cultures encounter one another," a kind of unmappable social setting in which peoples of different identities meet, though relations in this hemisphere are inevitably within a context of dominant imperialism (*Ethnocriticism* 4–5). Ethnocriticism "seeks to traverse rather than occupy a great variety of 'middle grounds'" in critical positions (25). Its focus on borders and boundary crossings, the "in-betweenness" of transcultural processes, is expressed in the rhetorical figure of the oxymoron as a process of meaning making through apparent contradiction (28). Krupat argues that ethnocriticism is situated as a relativist mode of analytic discourse positioned at multiple "frontiers" of historical and cultural encounter. Unlike postmodernist theory, it pursues a form of strategic essentialism (6–8).

In a somewhat similar vein, Georges E. Sioui has proposed the term *Amerindian autohistory* as a method for enabling a process of what he terms "reverse assimilation." Scholars should study the correspondences of Amerindian and non-Amerindian sources to identify what is original in Native American culture and make Euro-American immigrants aware of their potential "Americity" if they attend to the model offered by Native people (xxiii).

Filiation narrative. Much life writing seeks to memorialize the relationship to a parent, sibling, or child, someone with whom one has had a longstanding affiliation. According to Couser, the vast majority of narratives of affiliation, from Edmund Gosse's *Father and Son* to Paul Auster's *The Invention of Solitude,* are written by sons and daughters about their fathers— imposing, absent, tyrannical, indifferent, duplicitous. There are of course memoirs by daughters and sons that seek to recover a relationship with a lost mother, as in Mary Gordon's *Circling My Mother* or that critique and disavow mothers, such as Ruth Reichl's *Not Becoming My Mother: And Other Things She Taught Me along the Way,* Rebecca Walker's *Black, White, and Jewish: Autobiography of a Shifting Self,* Kim Chernin's *In My Mother's House,* and Roy Kiyooka's *Mothertalk.* Narratives of filiation are sometimes co-constructed, as in Sheila Ortiz Taylor and Sandra Ortiz Taylor's memoir of family, *Imaginary Parents.* A new genre to emerge in the past decade has been labeled the Motherhood Memoir, as in Anne Roiphe's *Fruitful: Living with Contradictions: A Memoir of Modern Motherhood,* in which women write about how becoming mothers affects their working lives, sexuality, and writing lives. Some fathers, particularly in gay couples, write about parenting adopted children, such as Dan Savage in *The Kid: What Happened after My Boyfriend and I Decided to Go Get Pregnant.* David Parker observes that, in intergenerational autobiography, there is an interplay between autonomy and relationality that marks it as a subgenre. He notes "a complex sense of moral obligation" about recasting the dominant family narrative as an ethical imperative (both "self-constituting" and "other-regarding") that drives such storytelling.

Adoption narratives are a special case of filiation stories (see *adoption life stories*).

Gastrography. Rosalia Baena proposed this term to designate life writing in which the story of the self is closely linked to the production, preparation, and/or consumption of food. Austin Clarke's *Pig Tails 'n Breadfruit*, for instance, explores the colonization of Jamaica and resistance practices through food. Ruth Reichl's *Tender at the Bone* and its sequels tie her coming-of-age narrative to learning to prepare gourmet meals and write restaurants reviews. In a different vein, Diana Abu-Jaber links her family's immigration to Los Angeles with preserving cultural traditions in *The Language of Baklava*. Barbara Kingsolver's narrative of her family's effort to produce their own food for a year chronicles the sustainability of local farming and the relational story of family. Hunger, satiety, and illness produced by junk food are the themes of Morgan Spurlock's *Super Size Me*.

Genealogical stories. A method for charting family history, genealogy locates, charts, and authenticates identity by constructing a family tree of descent. Its key concept is the "pedigree" of ancestral evidence based on documents and generational history and verified through fixed protocols, such as trees and charts. Genealogical projects recover the recorded past, which they can verify as official. They are interested in the objective documentation of relationship, not in the subjective stories people remember (see J. Watson "Ordering the Family"). Life writing can also engage in a critique, implicit or explicit, of genealogy. Shirlee Taylor Haizlip includes a genealogical chart in her family memoir *The Sweeter the Juice* but also speculates on those who disaffiliated themselves from African origins by passing as white. A narrative like Sally Morgan's *My Place* exposes the limits of genealogical storytelling. While she reconstructs the narrative of her mixed-race mother and her indigenous grandmother, the identification of the grandfather and father remains hidden from history, even though implications of a white father and grandfather haunt the narrative. And Bliss Broyard, who was raised as white, explores the secret her father, Anatole Broyard, kept from his family about his Haitian maternal ancestors as he constructed a professional life as a white writer and "hipster" critic, at the cost of abandoning his black relatives, in *One Drop: My Father's Hidden Life—A Story of Race and Family Secrets*. Raising the question "What am I?" after her father's death, Bliss Broyard addresses her own ingrained assumptions about the racial inferiority of African Americans, detailing her quest for her now-scattered black relatives from New Orleans and her discovery of the cultural meanings of being Creole in the United States.

Heterobiography. A term coined by Philippe Lejeune to describe collaborative or as-told-to life narratives as the inverse of what occurs in autobiography in the third person. In third-person narrative there is a narrator who pretends to be another; in heterobiography there are "two who pretend to be only one" ("Autobiography of Those Who Do Not Write" 264 n. 10). Lejeune also explores the concepts of "autoethnology" and the "ethnobiographer" in considering how they redirect the practice of life narrative away from the control of the ethnographer to informants, "those who do not write."

Jockography. Term for sports memoir used by Bryan Curtis, who describes its formula: a jockography begins with an account of the athlete's most memorable play, chronicles how sports got him or her through an unhappy childhood, and tracks the rise to major league stardom. Although most sports memoirs are ghostwritten by sportswriters, Curtis praises a few as memorable: pitcher Jim Bouton's *Ball Four,* an iconoclastic report from the Yankee dugout on Mickey Mantle and more; Dave Meggyesy's *Out of Their League* on football as "one of the most dehumanizing experiences," characterized by systematic humiliation and racism (36); and, more recently, José Canseco's *Juiced: Wild Times, Rampant 'Roids, Smash Hits, and How Baseball Got Big,* an unsparing testimonial to injecting steroids for better play and sex that precipitated a congressional investigation. Although he calls most sports memoirs "ludicrous performance art," Curtis maintains that some, like John Amaechi's *Man in the Middle,* intervene in larger contemporary discussions. (The NBA player details the trials of being gay in the homophobic Utah Jazz locker room.) For Curtis, athlete memoirs overall reveal that "pro athletes have brutally repetitious, uninteresting lives. . . . Sports memoirs may be intended as post-retirement victory laps, but many of them read like a cry for help" (36).

Journal. A form of life writing that records events and occurrences, as in Daniel Defoe's *A Journal of the Plague Year.* Some critics distinguish diary from journal by characterizing the journal as a chronicle of public record that is less intimate than the diary. Philippe Lejeune, however, does not distinguish between them but uses the terms interchangeably. (See *diary,* and Lejeune "Practice of the Private Journal.") Journaling is the practice of regular, free life writing, emphasized in the journal-writing workshops that Ira Progoff has organized and written about.

Letters. A mode of directed, and dated, correspondence with a specific addressee and signatory, letters seem to be private writings, but in the late eighteenth century they began to be understood as both private correspondence expressing the inner feelings of the writing subject and as public documents to be shared within a literary circle. Bernhard Siegert argues that at that moment "every self thus became the subject of its own discourse a priori," and the subject was presumed to precede its representation, circulating as its property in the mail. Letters become vehicles through which information is circulated, social roles enacted, relationships secured, often in a paradoxical mix of intimacy and formality. And they are highly stylized in terms of conventions of politeness and modes of conveying information that are implicated in ideologies of gender, ethnicity, class, and nationality. Often letters remain unpublished. But some famous correspondences, such as those of Abelard and Héloïse, Lady Mary Wortley Montagu to friends, and Hester Lynch Piozzi (Thrale) and Samuel Johnson, have been published and critically studied for their interactional modes of self-presentation. In *Love and Struggle: Letters in Contemporary Feminism,* Margaretta Jolly links women's contemporary use of epistolary forms to foreground both politics and intimacy. Liz Stanley has theorized the formal properties of letters and proposed the concept of the *epistolarium* as, in different ways, an epistolary record, a collection of surviving correspondence, and the "ur-letters" created in work on actual letters ("Epistolarium" 218).

Life narrative and life writing. See chapter 1 for a discussion of the distinction between these terms.

Meditation. A prominent form of self-reflexive writing during the Protestant Reformation of the sixteenth and seventeenth centuries. According to Louis Lohr Martz, the "meditation" is a rigorous exercise in self-contemplation whose aim "is the state of devotion" (15). When the meditation is put into literary form, its emphasis is on "a process of the mind rather than a particular subject-matter" (324) as the narrator seeks "the work of special grace" (16). The history of self-reflexive meditation in nonfictional prose can be traced through Montaigne's *Essays,* Donne's sermons, Browne's "Religio Medici," Pascal's *Pensées,* Francis de Sales's *An Introduction to a Devout Life,* Teresa of Avila's *Interior Castle,* and, more recently, Thoreau's *Walden* and Yeats's *A Vision.* Poetry as well offers occasions for meditation, as in the poetry of Gerard Manley Hopkins, Emily Dickinson, Paul Valéry, Rainer Maria Rilke, Wallace Stevens, and T. S. Eliot. The meditative poem, writes Martz, "is a work that creates an interior drama of the mind; this dramatic action is usually (though not always) created by some form of self-address, in which the mind grasps firmly a problem or situation deliberately evoked by the memory, brings it forward toward the full light of consciousness, and concludes with a moment of illumination, where the speaker's self has, for a time, found an answer to its conflicts" (330). Meditative discourse is interwoven in many life narratives and is prominent in such texts as Thomas Merton's *The Seven-Storey Mountain,* Dorothy Day's *The Long Loneliness,* and Elizabeth Gilbert's *Eat, Pray, Love.*

Memoir. Historically, a mode of life narrative that situated the subject in a social environment, as either observer or participant, the memoir directs attention more toward the lives and actions of others than to the narrator. Secular memoirs, written by public figures such as diplomats and soldiers, emphasized life in the public sphere, chronicling professional careers and activities of historical import. In contemporary parlance *autobiography* and *memoir* are used interchangeably. But distinctions are relevant. As Lee Quinby notes, "whereas autobiography promotes an 'I' that shares with confessional discourse an assumed interiority and an ethical mandate to examine that interiority, memoirs promote an 'I' that is explicitly constituted in the reports of the utterances and proceedings of others. The 'I' or subjectivity produced in memoirs is externalized and . . . dialogical" (299).

Currently, the term refers generally to life writing that takes a segment of a life, not its entirety, and focusing on interconnected experiences. Memoirs have been published in many contexts. Domestic memoirs, written as private narratives, focus on accounts of family life, as in Jonathan Franzen's memoir of his father's descent into Alzheimer's "My Father's Brain."

Tracing the treatment of the memoir form in the history of autobiography criticism, Julie Rak notes that memoir, in Derridean terms, has been positioned as a *supplement* to autobiography: "Very much like the relationship of 'writing' to plenitude in spoken language . . , in autobiography criticism memoir presents itself as a threat to autobiography because it points out that there is lack in the genre in the first place. Then, like writing, memoir offers itself as a substitute, or sublimation to what should be complete without it" ("Are Memoirs Autobiography?" 317). Efforts to position memoir in a degraded status vis-á-vis its more august sibling autobiography have failed; and its contemporary popularity and attraction to "ordinary readers," according to Rak, suggest that the social practice of writing and reading memoirs "could contribute to understanding the changing relationship between ideas of selfhood and the role of public and privates spheres in late capitalism" (324). For Nancy K. Miller "memoir is fashionably postmodern, since it hesitates to define the boundaries between private and public, subject and object." Central for Miller is the etymological root of the word in the double act of recalling and recording: "To record means literally to call to mind, to call up from the heart. At the same time, record means to set down in writing, to make official. What resides in the province of the heart is also what is exhibited in the public space of the world" (*Bequest and Betrayal* 43).

Nobody memoir. The term *nobody memoir* was first used in a review essay "Almost Famous: The Rise of the 'Nobody Memoir'" by Lorraine Adams in the *Washington Post*. It was then introduced in life writing circles by Couser, among others *(Signifying Bodies)*. As he points out, the classification of a memoir depends on whether its author was known before its publication, like Hillary Clinton, or becomes known through its publication, like Lucy Grealy. Adams's taxonomy of the "nobody" memoir includes childhood memoirs of growing up marked by some kind of disadvantage, trauma, or addiction; memoirs of catastrophic physical circumstance; and memoirs of mentally extreme states. Couser extends Adams's distinction by discussing the "some body memoir," that is, the narrative that explores the limits of and circumstances particular to one's embodiment.

Oral history. A set of techniques for gathering a story in which an interviewer listens to, records, shapes, and edits the life story of another. In oral history the one who speaks is not the one who writes, and the one who writes is often an absent presence in the text who nonetheless controls its narrative. Oral history is, then, a mediated form of personal narrative that depends on an interviewer who intervenes to collect and assemble a version of stories that are situated and changing. Sherna Berger Gluck and Daphne Patai, in addition to publishing oral histories, have given suggestions on how to conduct them. In its focus on the gatherer and the gathering of the story, oral history is distinct from collaborative autobiography.

Otobiography. In *The Ear of the Other* Jacques Derrida, in discussing Nietzsche and the politics of the proper name, proposed this term to deconstruct the "problematic of the biographical within philosophy" by recuperating the signature in the discourse of Hegel, where it is apparently subordinated, and by asserting its deferral in Nietzsche, where it seems writ large (56–57). Derrida notes, of Nietzsche, "When he writes himself to himself, he writes himself to the other who is infinitely far away and who is supposed to send his signature back to him." His self-relation is inescapably deferred by "the necessity of this detour through the other in the form of the eternal return" (88). Finally, the autobiographical is the *fort-da* of self-relation, "the effect of a process of ex-appropriation which produces only perspectives, readings without truth, differences, intersections of affect, a whole 'history' whose very possibility has to be disinscribed and reinscribed" (74).

Periautography. This term is used by James Olney to mean "writing about or around the self" as one mode of life writing he takes up in *Memory and Narrative*. He notes that the term was first used in the seventeenth century by Count Gian Artico di Porcia, who proposed that Italian scholars write their memoirs to benefit the young, a call to which Vico responded with a new mode of autobiography. Olney states, "What I like about the term 'periautography' . . . is precisely its indefinition and lack of generic rigor, its comfortably loose fit and generous adaptability" (xv).

Personal essay. A mode of writing that is literally a self-trying-out, the personal essay is a testing ("assay") of one's own intellectual, emotional, and physiological responses to a given topic. Since its development by Montaigne as a form of self-exploration engaging with received wisdom, the essay has been a site of self-creation through giving one's perspective on the thoughts of others. The personal essay can be strongly self-referential, as in several essay collections by Nancy Mairs.

Poetic autobiography. A mode of the lyric distinguished, according to James Olney, not by content but by "the formal device of recapitulation and recall" ("Some Versions of Memory" 252). It may appear that all lyric poetry is life writing in that the speaker of the lyric inscribes a subjective self as he or she explores emotions, vision, and intellectual states. We need, however, to distinguish certain kinds of lyrics that announce themselves as "auto-biography" from *lyric* as an umbrella term for many forms of poetic self-inscription. Exploring texts he calls *poetic autobiographies,* such as T. S. Eliot's *Four Quartets* and Paul Valéry's *The Young Fate,* Olney argues that what characterizes the lyric as autobiography includes extended engage-ment with the uses of memory, "the web of reverie," and internal states of consciousness. Since the early nineteenth century, he notes, autobiography in poetry has centered on a sustained exploration of "the consciousness of consciousness" and "the growth of a poet's mind," as in Wordsworth's subtitle *The Prelude; or, Growth of a Poet's Mind.* The broader question of lyrical life narrative needs further study but is suggested in works such as Robert Lowell's *Life Studies,* Adrienne Rich's *Diving into the Wreck,* A. R. Ammons's *Tape for the Turn of the Year,* John Ashbery's *Self-Portrait in a Convex Mirror,* Anne Sexton's *Live or Die,* and Natasha Trethewey's Pulit-zer Prize–winning *Native Guard.*

Prison narratives. A mode of captivity narrative written during or after in-carceration, writings from prison often become occasions for prisoners to inscribe themselves as fully human in the midst of a system designed to dehumanize them and to render them anonymous and passive. Addi-tionally, H. Bruce Franklin suggests, "most current autobiographical writ-ing from prison intends to show the readers that the author's individual experience is not unique or even extraordinary" (250). Barbara Harlow distinguishes two categories of prisoners—common law and political detainees—but insists that they cannot be sharply distinguished ("From a Women's Prison"). She also suggests that these narratives emerge from political and social repression in the contemporary Third World. In the case of prisoners identifying themselves as detainees, she notes, "their per-sonal itineraries, which have taken them through struggle, interrogation, incarceration, and, in many cases, physical torture, are attested to in their own narratives as part of a historical agenda, a collective enterprise" (455). (See also Harlow's *Barred.*) Such life narratives as Ruth First's *117 Days,* Jacobo Timerman's *Prisoner without a Name, Cell without a Number,* Steve Biko's *I Write What I Like,* and Breyten Breytenbach's *The True Confessions of an Albino Terrorist* are centrally concerned with narrating the shifts in consciousness occasioned by imprisonment.

Prosopography. A practice of making a collective study of the characteristics shared by a group whose members' biographies often cannot be referenced, in order to discover relationships and patterns among their lives at a particular historical moment. While Quintilian, in classical rhetoric, related it to prosopopoeia, the figurative evocation of an absent or imagined person, prosopography has become an important form for analyzing the structure and changing roles of groups for historians using data of various kinds. Social historian Lawrence Stone in an essay on the topic emphasizes that prosopography is a method for discovering connections and assessing the mobility of social actors. It requires amassing data (now often electronically) in order to perceive and analyze relationships among a group of lives. The populations explored may be quite large, as in the case of Emmanuel LeRoy Ladurie's *Montaillou: The Promised Land of Error* or Stone's own work on marriage and the family. It is not, however, just a collection of biographies, because the lives studied must have enough commonalities to establish connections. Nor is it identical with genealogy, because prosopography aims at a wider study than reconstructing family history. G. Thomas Couser (personal correspondence) points out that prosopography is used in representing lives in contemporary media. Michael Apted's *Up!* television shows for the British current affairs series World In Action began profiling fourteen children who were seven years old in 1964 and have revisited them every seven years since to chart their profile as a group.

Relational life writing. This term was proposed by Susan Stanford Friedman in 1985 to characterize the model of selfhood in women's autobiographical writing, against the autonomous individual posited by Georges Gusdorf, as interdependent and identified with a community. Drawing on Sheila Rowbotham's historical model (in *Woman's Consciousness, Man's World*) and Carol Gilligan's psychoanalytic model (in *In a Different Voice*), Friedman argues that women's narratives assert a "sense of shared identity with other women, an aspect of identification that exists in tension with a sense of their own uniqueness" ("Women's Autobiographical Self" 44). And they do so across "fluid boundaries" between self and an Other or others. More recently, both Nancy K. Miller ("Representing Others") and Paul John Eakin ("Relational Selves") have challenged the notion that only women's life narratives are relational, by turning to Jessica Benjamin's theory that in childhood development both relational and autonomous tendencies occur and are intertwined in processes of individuation. For example, Eakin argues that "because the assertion of autonomy is dependent on this dynamic of recognition [of the intersubjectivity of identity], identity is necessarily relational" (*How Our Lives* 52). In our view, relationality characterizes all autobiographical writing. See chapters 3 and 8 for a fuller discussion of relationality and autobiographical acts.

Scriptotherapy. A term proposed by Suzette Henke to signal the ways in which autobiographical writing functions as a mode of self-healing, scriptotherapy includes the processes of both "writing out and writing through traumatic experience in the mode of therapeutic reenactment" (xii). Henke attends to several twentieth-century women's life narratives that focus on such childhood trauma as incest and abuse, which adult narrators—for example, Anaïs Nin and Sylvia Fraser—record in order to both heal themselves and reconfigure selves deformed by earlier abuse. Some theorists, however, dispute that writing is always a form of healing from abuse or loss.

Self-help narrative. This genre of everyday narrative requires people to publicly tell stories of some form of addiction or dependency from which they are seeking recovery. The formulaic pattern of the self-help narrative involves a fall into dissolution and self-indulgence, alienation from a community, hitting bottom, recognition of the need for help, renunciation of the substance or behavior, and, with trust in a higher power, recovery of a truer postaddiction self. Charlotte Linde describes how this formula reflects a "coherence system" involving "systems of assumptions about the world that speakers use to make events and evaluations coherent" (11). For instance, in Alcoholics Anonymous narratives, as Robyn R. Warhol and Helena Michie argue, "a powerful master narrative shapes the life story of each recovering alcoholic, an autobiography-in-common that comes to constitute a collective identity for sober persons" (328).

Self-portrait (in French, *autoportrait*). Primarily this term is used for an artist's painted, photographed, drawn, or printed portrait of him- or herself. But in literary studies, *self-portrait* has been used to distinguish the present-oriented from the retrospectively oriented autobiographical narrative. William L. Howarth argued that "an autobiography is a self-portrait" (85) and explored analogies between Renaissance self-portraits and autobiographies throughout Western history. But later theorists, such as Michel Beaujour, challenge this analogy between visual and written self-portraiture. Beaujour distinguishes the literary self-portrait from the autobiography as a "polymorphous formation, a much more heterogeneous and complex literary type than is autobiographical narration" (25). Self-portraiture is not self-description but "the mirror whose reflecting function is mimicked in the symmetrical statement: me by me" (31). Insisting that the literary self-portrait as an act of "painting" oneself is inescapably metaphorical not literal, Beaujour defines verbal self-portraiture as "focused on the present of writing rather than the remembrance of the past and referring all things to the speaking subject and his perceptions" (340). In the self-portrait, according to Beaujour, the intent is not as much to reconstitute the subject of history in a remembered past as to meditate on the processes of self-writing itself. Here the narrating "I" as agent of discourse is concentrated in a present in which the self can never be fixed. In contemporary French studies, Candace Lang has argued that the literary self-portrait is not a memoir but a genre of postmodern autobiography, with Roland Barthes its best-known practitioner ("Autobiography").

The artist Joanne Leonard of the University of Michigan has recently noted that one of her students deftly referred to a photo essay with herself as the main character as an *autoimaginography.*

In modernity and postmodernity, autobiographical inscription inheres in a variety of media, including performance, installation, visual/verbal diary, collage, quilting, sculpture, and so forth. See our introduction in *Interfaces* for a fuller account of self-portraiture.

Serial autobiography. A term that designates an autobiographical work often published in multiple volumes (or films, videos, artworks). Although some writers may consider these as "chapters" in an ongoing life story, many writers significantly revise their narratives from the perspectives of different times of writing. In Mary McCarthy and Frederick Douglass, for example, the emphasis falls on dramatically different moments and interpretations of their significance as they publish books of life writing during youth and middle age. Seriality in relation to memory and the terms of various autobiographical genres calls for more sustained study.

Slave narrative. A mode of life narrative written by a fugitive or freed exslave about captivity, oppression—physical, economic, and emotional—and escape from bondage into some form of freedom. In the United States slave narratives were usually antebellum (published before the Civil War), though the dates of enslavement differ in different nations, and some narratives are published well into the twentieth century. For example, *The Autobiography of a Runaway Slave,* the life narrative of Esteban Montéjo, enslaved in Cuba, as told to Miguel Barnet, was first published in Spanish in 1966. Frances Smith Foster notes that U.S. slave narratives were a popular form; hundreds were published, and some went through many editions and sold thousands of copies. The form has also generated a rich critical literature and been influential for the development of later African American narrative forms, as Robert B. Stepto notes in describing four modes of slave narratives—eclectic, integrated, generic, and authenticating.

Olney describes ten conventions characteristic of slave narratives, including, among others, the narrative's engraved, signed portrait; a title page asserting that the narrative was written by the ex-slave; testimonials and prefatory material by white abolitionists; a beginning of "I was born"; accounts of whippings by cruel masters and mistresses and a slave's resistance to them; an account of the slave's difficulties in learning to read and write; denunciations of Christian slaveholders as the cruelest; accounts of successful effort(s) to escape; and the choice of a new last name (Olney, "'I Was Born'" 152–53). Because the ability of ex-slaves to become literate was often contested, several narratives were denounced as inauthentic, for example, Harriet Jacobs's *Incidents in the Life of a Slave Girl* (later shown by Jean Fagan Yellin to have been authored by Jacobs under the pseudonym Linda Brent). The narratives of ex-slaves importantly challenge myths of the slave system promulgated in the plantation culture of Southern literature and history and, according to William L. Andrews, "culminate in texts that weave together multiple autobiographical traditions and voices to produce a sense of collectivized black identity" ("African-American Autobiography" 206–207). Samira Kawash calls for rethinking concepts of the slave narrative because the "freedom" promised in emancipation from slavery as a negation of the slave as property is interrogated in many of these narratives as incomplete, since ex-slaves were unable to claim the property rights of liberal citizen subjects (50).

Spiritual life narrative. This mode of writing traces the narrator's emerging consciousness back to "the acquisition of some sort of saving knowledge and to an awakening of an awareness within" regarding a transcendental power (Andrews, *Sisters of the Spirit* 1). Spiritual life narrative typically unfolds as a journey through sin and damnation to a sense of spiritual ful-fillment and arrival in a place of sustaining belief. Sometimes the journey motivates rededication, intensification, or clarification of spiritual beliefs and values (see Barbour; Ibsen). The pattern of conversion and its after-math is a traditional feature of spiritual life narratives. (See *Conversion narrative.*)

Sports memoir. See *jockography.*

Survivor narrative. This term designates narratives by survivors of trau-matic, abusive, or genocidal experience. Linda Martín Alcoff and Laura Gray-Rosendale propose this term to distinguish the political utility of self-referential discourse from the more limited discourse of confession. They note that while "survivor discourse and the tactic of speaking out may often involve a confessional mode of speech, including personal dis-closure, autobiographical narrative, and the expression of feelings and emotions," effective voicing of certain kinds of trauma must go beyond the confessional to acts of witnessing (213). The confessional mode, they suggest, focuses attention on a victim's psychological state rather than the perpetrator's act and invests power in a confessor as interpreter and judge, stripping the survivor of authority and agency (213). Victims must be remade as survivors through acts of speaking out, telling their stories in ways that move beyond a concentration on personal feelings to testimony that critiques larger cultural forces. "What we need is not to confess, but to witness," they argue (220).

Testimonio. The term in Spanish literally means "testimony" and connotes an act of testifying or bearing witness legally or religiously. John Beverley defines Latin American *testimonio* as "a novel or novella-length narrative in book or pamphlet . . . form, told in the first person by a narrator who is also the real protagonist or witness of the events he or she recounts, and whose unit of narration is usually a 'life' or a significant life experience" ("Margin at the Center" 92–93). In *testimonio,* the narrator intends to communicate the situation of a group's oppression, struggle, or imprison-ment, to claim some agency in the act of narrating, and to call on readers to respond actively in judging the crisis. Its primary concern is sincerity of intention, not the text's literariness (94). And its ideological thrust is the "affirmation of the individual self in a collective mode" (97), as in Nobel Peace Prize–winner Rigoberta Menchú's *I, Rigoberta Menchú.*

Trauma narrative. Trauma, derived from the Greek word for "wound," describes an experience of extreme horror or shock that cannot be incorporated unproblematically within memory. Leigh Gilmore notes that "the subject of trauma refers to both a person struggling to make sense of an overwhelming experience in a particular context and the unspeakability of trauma itself, its resistance to representation" (*Limits of Autobiography* 46). She stresses in the experience of trauma its self-altering or self-shattering character and the difficulties in attempting to articulate it (6). Psychoanalytical theorists of trauma, among them Cathy Caruth, Shoshana Felman, and Dori Laub, argue that speaking the unspeakable involves the narrator in a struggle with memory and its belatedness; for, as Caruth argues, "the experience of trauma . . . would thus seem to consist . . . in an inherent latency within the experience itself" (7–8). This latency of traumatic memory, and the way in which "to be traumatized is precisely to be possessed by an image or event," manifests itself in the psychic delay of memory's temporality and the crisis of its truth (4–5). Caruth asserts that "the fundamental dislocation implied by all traumatic experience" lies in "both its testimony to the event and to the impossibility of its direct access" (9).

Stories of traumatic experience focus on the narrator's reliving of a past event and emphasize a gap that cannot be closed between the narrative present and the narrated past. Thus, while the act of remembering recalls the originary trauma, it does not heal but rather exposes the wound. Gilmore points out the central conundrum of such narratives: "Although trauma must be spoken in order to heal the survivor and the community, language is inadequate to do this" ("Trauma" 885). Trauma, with its troubled relationship to processes of memory, is thus not only located in the past event but may be reexperienced in the narrative present of storytelling. Nancy K. Miller characterizes the effects of trauma as memory stains, "indelible stains in the brain" that writing seeks both to expunge and to preserve ("Memory Stains" 41). Life writing on trauma can elicit an experience of disorder in the reader, as Bella Brodzki observes, by choosing not to represent an experience of horror or trauma explicitly but to figure it through a text's structure or the use of flashback and repetition ("Trauma" 128-30).

Trauma narratives have become widespread and pervasive in contemporary life, as stories of personal experience circulate internationally in ways that reshape the relationship of public and private discursive spheres, producing a counterdiscourse aimed at the erasure of individual suffering in official historical memory (Gilmore, "Trauma" 885). The many forms of life writing that transmit traumatic memory are shaped by particular cultural and linguistic contexts, as well as the limits of genre. With the intensified recording, archiving, and analysis of traumatic experience during the past two decades, trauma stories of many kinds have come to the fore: of personal experience of violation or abuse; of experience in the Holocaust and other genocidal wars, some told at truth commission hearings or in the memoirs of child soldiers; of dislocation for the children of the "stolen generations" in Australia and Native people in Alaska and throughout the Americas; and in the testimonies to atrocity of antiwar activists around the world.

While in the nineties scholars tended to assert that trauma may facilitate self-help and healing (see Henke on *scriptotherapy*), in the past half-decade witnessing has been retheorized. Scholars exploring the effects and impact of the Truth and Reconciliation Commission hearings in South Africa, for instance, have noted that organized scenes of witness to the traumatic past may restage the violence of the perpetrator-victim relationship (see Feldman), affecting retraumatization rather than healing or recovery. In non-Western contexts the critique of a psychoanalytically based talk therapy model of witnessing to trauma is especially pertinent. Some scholars point to alternative strategies for surviving and healing from violence and harm that may draw on collective healing practices, as in the project of telling, listening, and collaborating undertaken by the Sangtin Writers in *Playing with Fire: Feminist Thought and Activism through Seven Lives in India*. Others note that the notion of trauma needs to be unhinged from psychoanalytic discourses in order to engage "concepts of social suffering that address the communal without assuming a uniformity of trauma across a social spectrum" (Kennedy and Whitlock). (See also *witnessing, acts of.*)

Travel narrative. This broad term encompasses multiple forms: travelogue, travel journal, (pseudo)ethnography, adventure narrative, quest, letter home, narrative of exotic escape. Travel narratives have a long history, extending in the West back to the Greeks and Romans and employed by travelers in Arabic and Chinese lands long before the printing press. Travel narratives are usually written in the first person and focus, in progress or retrospectively, on a journey. Subordinating other aspects of the writer's life, they typically chronicle or reconstruct the narrator's experience of displacement, encounter, and travail and his or her observations of the unknown, the foreign, the uncanny. In this way they become occasions for both the reimagining and the misrecognizing of identity (Bartkowski xix), and for resituating the mobile subject in relation to home and its ideological norms.

War memoirs. What should comprise the parameters of war memoirs or military life writing as a subgenre is under discussion, given the different terms of the memoir of a child soldier in Africa and that of a participant in an organized national army. Alex Vernon notes that the conventions of the war memoir focus on "what war does to men as well as what men do in war" (165). Such memoirs often involve the soldier's submission to and acknowledgment of powerlessness, as does Anthony Swofford's *Jarhead,* with its wry humor. But some war memoirists, such as Tim O'Brien in *The Things They Carried,* rework the form of the war memoir in acts of self-construction that change its dynamic. At a time when nations are increasingly incorporating women in combat positions in their militaries, writers and scholars of gender difference are also revising some previously held assumptions about the form of the war memoir, as is the extensive use of digital technologies in combat. Whether historians will continue to find war memoirs reliable evidence for the everyday experience of military life may consequently also be in question. But literary scholars of war memoir are assembling canons of war life writing and probing problems of definition, among them Alex Vernon, Craig Howes on oral histories of veterans, and Jon Alexander on POW memoir.

Witnessing, acts of. As an act of being present to observe or to give testimony on something, witnessing is indicative of how subjects respond to trauma. The witness can be identified as an "eyewitness," a firsthand observer whose narrative has multiple functions—chronicle, testimony, consciousness raising; or a secondhand witness, someone who responds to the witness of others. Kelly Oliver notes, "Witnessing has the double sense of testifying to something that you have seen with your own eyes and bearing witness to something that you cannot see" (18). Thus an eyewitness is judged by the accuracy of her testimony based on firsthand knowledge, while bearing witness implies a stance toward "something beyond recognition that can't be seen" (16). Oliver emphasizes that witnessing is an act addressed to an other, real or imagined, with the possibility of response.

The two senses of witnessing are inevitably in a tension that Oliver argues may be productive for getting beyond the repetition of trauma to a more humane, ethically informed future (17–18).

For traumatic testimony to be heard, a sympathetic listener is required to serve as a witness and help redress the psychic isolation that traumatic experience produces. Communities that form to testify against violence focus on both the site of trauma and perceptions of the traumatic event. The circulation of acts of witnesses may raise issues of "secondary witnessing" if exposure to a narrative of violence evokes a traumatic experience for the hearer (Douglas and Whitlock 139). Although becoming aware of "the strange and estranging legacy of trauma" is difficult, people often feel an ethical imperative to read and circulate such stories (Brodzki, "Trauma" 129).

Acts of witnessing propel a variety of life narratives. Some embed witness in historical or political events, such as Vladek's testimony in Spiegelman's *Maus* (on the Holocaust), the testimonies Antjie Krog incorporates in *Country of My Skull* (on the Truth and Reconciliation Commission hearings in South Africa), Ishmael Beah's *A Long Way Gone* (as a child soldier in Sierra Leone), Maria Rosa Henson's *Comfort Woman: A Filipina's Story of Prostitution and Slavery under the Japanese Military* (testifying to World War II sex slavery), and Doris Pilkington's *Rabbit-Proof Fence* (on the forced separation of Aboriginal children from their families in Australia). Witnessing to trauma as a performative act in personal contexts occurs in such narratives as Alice Sebold's *Lucky*, Kathryn Harrison's *The Kiss*, Dave Pelzer's *A Child Called "It,"* and Bettina Aptheker's *Intimate Politics.*

The fast pace of technological change and the move of witnessing to digital media raise new questions about acts of witnessing in the digital age. How do technical media change our understanding of testimony? Will ubiquitous video cameras supersede eyewitnesses? Does live transmission on television make us witnesses of events? (See also *trauma narrative.*)

Group and Classroom Projects

We offer here suggestions for classroom projects, organized in no particular way. See also the Miriam Fuchs and Craig Howes collection Teaching Life Writing Texts, *for many excellent suggestions on how to teach particular genres, issues, and texts.*

Do a collective investigation of Web sites about identity and generate a list of their characteristics. Note the proportion of visual to written text in them and the extent of hypertext organization, with an eye to generational and other differences.

Compile a Web site on life narratives in an area that interests you, such as a particular sport, a kind of self-help, or set of ethnic or national stories.

Visit a real-time Web site for one week and report back on the autobiographical acts that it performs. How do you distinguish such a real-time site from someone simply living his or her daily life?

Visit some visual diaries on YouTube. Describe the presentational styles of the diaries. How does the spoken narrative match or conflict with the video track (or images)? Is the speaker impersonating someone or telling his or her "authentic" life? Who is involved in the production crew? What does observing these details tell you about the complexity of autobiographical self-presentation on video?

Analyze a scrapbook project. What stories about the maker or family are being told? What kinds of events are emphasized or omitted? Is there a single coherent narrative or conflicting ones? What are the effects of the juxtapositions of materials, such as photos, material objects, and text?

Select a particular kind of blog site—for depression, anorexia/bulimia, suicide, muscle building, for instance. Is this a single person or multiperson site? What kind of interactivity or collaborative storytelling do you observe there? Do certain stories get told over and over? How do the entries of responders rewrite or reshape the original issue posed? If the entries seem formulaic, describe the features of the formula. Do you feel some writers are "posing" in their entries? What media in addition to written text are included in the site?

Read a week of postcards published on PostSecret. What do they tell you about confession—the kinds of secrets people reveal and the ways those are imaged? How are you positioned as an onlooker or eavesdropper on the site, and what does this suggest about issues of public intimacy?

Compose an event in your life as a comics page. Then write an essay exploring issues in designing the page—frames, dialog bubbles, narrator's voice-over, gutter size, visual style.

If you have participated in a virtual world such as Second Life, describe the avatar you designed, the spaces you purchased, the roles you adopted, and the encounters you had. What did you discover about the possibilities and constraints of having an avatar? What did you observe about the avatars of others?

Find a book that compiles multiple testimonies about a particular life experience into a prosopography, such as Studs Terkel's *Working* or Victoria Morris Byerly's *Hard Times Cotton Mill Girls* or collections of sexual-abuse narratives, AIDS narratives, oral interviews, or testimonies on giving birth. What narrative strategies are employed in writing about this particular experience? What collective patterns emerge? What positioning do these people share that makes them a collective? What cultural work does the volume do? Is there any evidence within the narratives about how the narrators/speakers would like their narratives to be used? Can you find any information about how their narratives have been used? What role has the oral interviewer or collector played, and how do you evaluate its significance?

In a small group or a pair, go to a particular place to observe how people tell stories about themselves. Examples of such sites include a recovery group, a senior citizens' group, a genealogy project. Who are the coaxers and what kinds of stories do they prompt people to tell? How do particular people narrate their stories? What group rituals organize the telling of the stories (before, during, and after)? Use the material provided by one of these sites to analyze the kinds of coaxer-teller relationships they construct and their long-term aims.

Target a particular talk show. Watch and take notes on it for a period of time. Do an analysis of the way the talk show format structures people's telling of personal stories and the kinds of stories that are elicited and rewarded.

Gather several kinds of data forms that request autobiographical information and analyze the life narratives they call forth. Here are some examples: medical history forms, social service client forms, applications to graduate school, résumé guidelines, job applications.

Collect and analyze the life writing published by political candidates, or incorporated in their speeches, or posted on their Web sites. Write a study or make a video that shows their use of autobiographical narratives. To what uses do candidates running for office put their life stories?

Write a personal narrative of a particular part of your body as both seen from the outside and felt from the inside. Imagine yourself as that body part and speak in its voice.

Read a life narrative of both a male sports figure and a female sports figure. Compare and contrast the kinds of stories they tell about some of the following: experiences growing up, role models, training methods, view of physical and emotional conflict, relation to other team members, long-term goals, sense of their own bodies. Consider also to what extent gendered differences intersect differences of ethnicity, race, sexuality, or cultural location.

Watch a particular music group on a network such as MTV or Black Entertainment Network. Analyze the ways in which the group's performance and lyrics inflect its enactment of a "life" narrative.

Compile an anthology of writing about war, as Jon Alexander had his undergraduate students do as *American POW Memoirs from the Revolutionary*

War through the Vietnam War. Such a project may be a productive way to engage students in memoir research.

In a discussion group, develop a set of questions to be asked in oral interviews around a particular aspect of life experience. Examples might include the following: becoming an American, being a young girl in different decades, the rewards and conflicts of professional identity, familial versus regional versus national identities, being a medical patient, attitudes toward the body. Interview one or more people about this topic, then write up the oral interview. Attach to it a critique that explores the process of doing the interview and developing the essay. Try to reflect on what issues are involved in one person soliciting and editing another person's life narrative.

Write a narrative of your own childhood, then research the history of childhood at the time of your childhood. Rework your autobiographical narrative to reflect and/or critically evaluate the historical moment of its place and time.

Take a family album and find a selection of six to eight photos that seem particularly revealing of what characterizes your family. Write the narrative that the photos seem to tell. Contrast that story with your memory of particular events that were photographed. You may also want to interview one or more family members about their memories of the events—but be sure to record your own story first.

Go to a shopping mall and watch people go by for a few hours. Observe what you would call the "identity markers" that people use to communicate a story about themselves. Identity markers might include clothing, objects, hairstyles and jewelry, body markings, and body language. Observe as well identity markers of groups and whether they support or conflict with those of the individual.

Similarly, go to a shopping mall and try to listen to the stories people are telling one another as they walk by you. What kinds of stories do you hear and how would you complete one or two particular stories? Write up a narrative based on these fragments of others' stories that extends or speculates on their identities.

Using the personals ad section of your local alternative newspaper, pick out and contrast the self-presentation in several ads. Identify the autobiographical markers of each ad as aspects of an ideal person that each narrator is trying to construct. How well does each succeed in making a coherent portrait of a prospective date?

Write three forms of self-advertisement: your own personal ad; your job letter after graduation; and your obituary. Contrast the self-presentations in all three and discuss how their intended audiences shaped what you put in or left out.

Assemble a collective work history of your family. Or its collective educational history. Or a narrative of your family origins over three generations. What narratives about larger sociocultural forces and events does this collective history point to?

In a group, brainstorm why someone would write a life narrative. What are some occasions, passages, transitions, losses, realizations, rationales, conditions that might motivate someone to write a story of her or his life?

Make a list of life narratives you've read. What famous people do you know about through their autobiographical writing? Make a list of people whose life stories you'd like to read. In what ways does life writing introduce you to people you've never met?

Pick a historical figure who has written his or her life story and about whom one or more biographies have been written. Read the life narratives and biographies against one another and explore the different kinds of subjects represented in the two modes of life writing.

Is there a storyteller in your family on whom people rely to tell and to keep the family stories together? What are the characteristics of that person's stories? How do particular family members respond to the storyteller and to the stories told?

What memorable stories are preserved within your family? Within your community? Within your region/nation? Who is expected to tell their stories within the family, within the community, within the region/nation?

If you have seen any painted or photographed self-portraits, what makes a visual self-portrait seem different from the image made of that person by some other artist or photographer?

Write a brief food narrative or keep a food diary and incorporate in it a discussion of food, culture, and the gendered body. Topics might include eating disorders and the politics of fat; genetic modification of food and its impact on children; famine and scarcity in the developing world; and the gendered division, in the home and professionally, of food labor.

Look at the beginnings of three or four life narratives. Describe when and how the narrators begin their stories. Do they begin at the beginning, middle, or end of their lives? If you were to start your autobiography in some way other than "I was born," what are two or three possible points of departure?

Write an autobiographical paragraph about yourself in the third person. Then after a few hours rewrite it in the first person. Note the kinds of changes you made in it.

Take your autobiographical paragraph and recast it for three audiences: the audience of a personals ad, readers of a college application essay, and the audience for an election speech.

Imagine for a moment what kind of story you would tell about yourself in another ten years. Write a set of notes about it. Then, at a later date, consider how it contrasts with how you now see yourself.

What books or kinds of books that you've read might provide you with models for or ways to tell a story of your life? Name and describe a few of these texts.

When you read a narrative of someone else's life or listen to someone's self-narrative, what interests you most about it? What kinds of questions do you begin to ask about the story? About the teller?

Gather three of four editions of a life narrative republished at separate historical moments. Some examples of often-published autobiographical narratives include those of Franklin, Rowlandson, Jemison, Douglass, and Twain. Analyze the way the story is "framed" and introduced in each of the republications. What physical differences are visible in the presentations? What might account for these differences?

Journals and Internet Resources

An invaluable resource for scholars and students of life writing studies is the listserv run by the International Auto/Biography Association (IABA), moderated by Craig Howes, editor of *Biography*, and housed at the University of Hawai'i. The IABA Web site provides an extensive list of life writing centers and institutes in biography, oral history, autobiography, diary, and life story archives around the world. Its biannual conference call for papers is regularly posted as well as calls for papers for all conferences, edited collections, and special issues worldwide. Material for submission to the list should be sent to Craig Howes. To join the IABA listserv, e-mail listserv@hawaii.edu. http://www.iaba.org.cn/

a/b: Auto/Biography Studies. Published biannually. Autobiography Society and University of North Carolina, Chapel Hill. Editors: Rebecca Hogan, Joseph Hogan, and Emily Hipchen. Contents of back issues can be accessed through the journal's home page. http://facstaff.uww.edu/hoganj/ab.htm

Auto/Biography Yearbook. (Previously *A/b: Auto/Biography Studies* until 2006.) Russell Press. Editor: Andrew C. Sparkes. British Sociological Association Study Group on Auto/Biography, School of Education, University of Exeter, Exeter, United Kingdom. http://www.britsoc.co.uk/specialisms/autobiography.htm

Biography: An Interdisciplinary Quarterly. Published quarterly. Center for Biographical Research, University of Hawai'i, Honolulu, Hawai'i. Editors: Miriam Fuchs, Cynthia Franklin, and Craig Howes. Index is available on the journal's homepage, and essays may be accessed through Project Muse online. http://www.hawaii.edu/uhpress/journals/biography

Life Writing. Published biannually. Taylor & Francis Group, Routledge. Editors: Mary Besemeres and Maureen Perkins. Division of Humanities, Curtin University of Technology, Perth, Australia. http://www.tandf.co.uk/journals/titles/14484528.asp

Lifewriting Annual. Published annually. AMS Press. Editor: Thomas Smith. Department of English, Penn State, Abington. http://www.personal.psu.edu/users/t/r/trs8/Lifewriting%20Annual%20Information.htm

Other journals that regularly review studies of life narrative and publish essays in the field include *Melus, Prose Studies, Narrative,* and *Mosaic. Fourth Genre* is a creative nonfiction journal published at Michigan State University. Recently launched, memoirs.com is a comprehensive listing of memoirs, with synopses and reviews. http:///www.memoirs.com

Notes

1. Life Narrative

1. See Olney, "Some Versions of Memory/Some Versions of Bios," for a parsing of the Greek etymology.

2. See Folkenflik for a translation of this passage from Lejeune's *L'Autobiographie en France*, 13–14 n. 42, 241.

3. Although Ann Yearsley's preface to the fourth edition of her *Poems, On Several Occasions,* published in 1786, is an extended autobiographical refutation of the charge of ingratitude to her patron, Hannah More, the *autobiographical* does not appear in its title ("Mrs. Yearsley's Narrative"), as we incorrectly claimed in the first edition, citing Robert Folkenflik. He has since noted this error (private correspondence, 22 December 2009).

4. James Olney has similarly opted, in *Memory and Narrative: The Weave of Life-Writing,* for a term more inclusionary than *autobiography* in discussing the writings of Augustine, Rousseau, and Beckett. Interested now in exploring the autobiographical rather than fixing its rules and conventions, Olney employs the term *life-writing* to embrace diverse modes of the autobiographical: "Although I have in the past written frequently about autobiography as a literary genre, I have never been very comfortable doing it. . . . I have never met a definition of autobiography that I could really like. . . . It strikes me that there has been a gradual alteration—an evolution or devolution as one may prefer—in the nature of life-writing or autobiography over the past sixteen centuries, moving from a focus on 'bios,' or the course of a lifetime, to focus on 'autos,' the self writing and being written; and this shift . . . has introduced a number of narrative dilemmas requiring quite different strategies on the writers' part" (xv).

5. We are grateful to G. Thomas Couser for pointing out the usefulness of this distinction and tracking the somewhat inconsistent shift between the two terms in the first edition of this book.

6. For expanded analyses of the genre of biography and its relationship to other forms of life writing, see Nadel; and Backscheider.

7. "The new biography" is a historically recurrent term. It was used by James Boswell in his *Life of Samuel Johnson* and by Lytton Strachey in *Eminent Victorians.* It

was deployed by several literary biographers at the American Studies Association conference in 2006.

8. Saldívar acknowledges that his "biography" is an autoethnographic work that incorporates aspects of his own experience as a young Chicano man growing up in the Southwest and that Paredes was an intellectual mentor.

9. As Morris told the audience for the audio version of *Dutch,* "When the biographer sits talking with the still living subject, as I did so often with President Reagan . . . the story of his journey becomes, in effect, an autobiography that interrelates with the biography he's writing. In other words, this is the true story of a real person told by an imaginary narrator who eventually mutates into myself."

10. See the special issue on the biopic in the winter 2000 issue of *Biography* for an overview of the genre and several suggestive essays on its norms and practices in film, television, video, and other media formats.

11. See ibid.

12. Though he uses the term *autobiography* in his many studies of life narrative, Lejeune expanded the scope of autobiographical texts beyond traditional works of bourgeois subjects in the nineteenth and twentieth centuries to include narratives by those who self-publish their life histories in France and those whose personal stories are dictated because they are not authors. See "The Autobiography of Those Who Do Not Write" and "Practice of the Private Journal."

13. Popkin also notes how history, in reconstructing the "big picture" of the past, is modified in the genre he identifies as historians' autobiographies, the life narratives of scholars becoming historians.

14. At the American Studies Association conference session on biography in 2005, participants used the term *new biography* to describe a series of practices that their own work was incorporating: the relaxing of constraints of evidence, greater use of such storytelling forms as dialogue and setting, and the introduction of uncertainty or speculation.

15. The Cretan Liar paradox is: all Cretans are liars, says Epimenides of Crete. See Rosalie L. Colie for a history of self-referential discourse as paradox.

16. We thank Julie Rak for raising questions about our concept of genre and directing us to Miller's work.

17. We would qualify Miller's distinction of private and public as separable realms by suggesting that both realms are mutually constituted, but adopt nonetheless her argument that genre is social action.

2. Autobiographical Subjects

1. For a genealogy of critical scholarship on memory as a key concept of new historicism, see Kerwin Lee Kline's provocative study.

2. For a discussion of postmemory, the memory of the child of survivors, see

Hirsch, who notes that postmemory is distinguished from memory by generational distance and from history by deep personal connection (*Family Frames* 22).

3. *New York Times,* 14 October 1999, A–19.

4. The hoax alleged by David Stoll in the case of *I, Rigoberta Menchú* is a more complex case of claims and counterclaims about collective testimonio of the Quiché. For a thorough discussion of issues in this ongoing debate, see Pratt, "Mad about Menchú"; and Canby.

5. Kelly Oliver distinguishes between subjectivity and subject position: "Subject positions, although mobile, are constituted in our social interactions and our positions within our culture and context. They are determined by history and circumstance. . . . Subjectivity, on the other hand, is experienced as the sense of agency and response-ability that are constituted in the infinite encounter with otherness, which is fundamentally ethical" (17). Thus, while historical situatedness underlies subject positioning, subjectivity is psychoanalytically driven in familial relations by the subject's original separation and alienation, which some view as traumatic (65). Our experience of subjectivity, however, resides in the tension between subject position and the subjectivity that, although prior to position, is interconnected with it. For Oliver that tension is fundamental to the concept of witnessing (17).

6. In *Mappings* Susan Stanford Friedman asserts, "a locational approach to feminism incorporates diverse formations because its positional analysis requires a kind of geopolitical literacy built out of a recognition of how different times and places produce different and changing gender systems as these intersect with other different and changing societal stratifications and movements for social justice" (5). Friedman elsewhere productively emphasizes "a compensatory emphasis on space" interacting with time in the production of narrative, a return to Bakhtin's notion of the chronotope as "time space" ("Spatial Poetics" 194).

7. See the transcription of Piper's performance in *Voicing Today's Visions: Writings by Contemporary Women Artists* (Witzling 302–305).

8. Montaigne (n. 49, 241). The sentence is worth citing: "Il se faut reserver une arriereboutique toute nostre, toute franche, en laquelle nous éstablissons nostre vraye liberté et principale retraicte et solitude" (241), translated as "We must reserve a back shop all our own, entirely free, in which to establish our real liberty and our principal retreat and solitude," in *Complete Essays* (177 n. 50).

3. Autobiographical Acts

1. This catalog of everyday situations is excerpted with permission of the University of Minnesota Press from our introduction to *Getting a Life* (2–3).

2. In *Angela's Ashes,* Phelan argues, the implied author is distinct from the child's voice narrating his "miserable" youth in Limerick, Ireland, although only the first

page of the memoir signals his role explicitly; but the many tongue-in-cheek, counter-to-fact assertions the "I" makes are set up as the misapprehensions of an uneducated youth by the implied author. In adult autobiographies of childhood experience such as *Angela's Ashes,* Phelan asserts, the narrating "I," speaking as a child close in age to the experiencing "I," often misreads events, people, and moral issues that the adult narrator has learned from and now can evaluate differently, with ethical insight. The reader is solicited, through a voice implicit in the arrangement of the narrative and often explicit in its frame story and interpolations, to mistrust—and learn from—the erroneous judgment of the narrating child "I." As readers, we understand the difference between what the narrator espouses and what we readers have been led to discover. We do so because we make inferences about an implied author, though that implied author is not available to us.

3. The ethnography of speaking and the incorporation of orality in life writing have received critical attention from folklorists such as John Laudun (see the *Encyclopedia of Life Writing* on "orality") and theorists of social action such as Erving Goffman (*Gender Advertisements* and *Presentation of Self*).

4. Twentieth-century modernism is the high point for the association of voice with interiority in such innovations as the interior monologue and stream-of-consciousness techniques identified with Marcel Proust, James Joyce, Virginia Woolf, and F. Scott Fitzgerald, among others. In this central innovation of the modernist novel, voice is rendered not in dialogue but through indirect discourse as textured subjectivity. The reader is invited into an interiority that involves an intimate exchange with a fictional presence.

5. See Phelan's discussion of Frank McCourt's *Angela's Ashes* for a nuanced reading of how the difference between the narrating and narrated "I"s affects the reader's sense of McCourt's ethical stance in the first book and, by contrast, in his sequel *'Tis (Living to Tell about It).*

6. Susanna Egan observes that a text may generate the "polyphonic harmony" of a community of voices, either between dual narrators or the narrator and the reader. See *Mirror Talk.*

7. See our more extended discussion in *Women, Autobiography, Theory* (30–31).

8. We thank Catriona niDhoull for recommending this narrative to us as an example of voice in life narrative.

9. Friedman is interested in the geographics of identity as a contemporary cultural practice in this time of global capitalism: "Rhetorically speaking, geographics involves a shift from the discourses of romanticism to those of post-modernity" (*Mappings* 19).

4. Life Narrative in Historical Perspective

1. See, for example, Richard Bowring on Heian Japan; Georg Misch's discussion of Islamic scholars' autobiographies in *A History of Autobiography* (962–1006);

Tetz Rooke's and Farzaneh Milani's studies of Arab autobiography; and Erwin Panofsky's interesting discussion of tombstone epigraphs in ancient Greece.

2. Georges Gusdorf makes this assertion explicit when he states, "Autobiography becomes possible only under certain metaphysical preconditions. . . . The curiosity of the individual about himself, the wonder that he feels before the mystery of his own destiny is thus tied to the Copernican Revolution. . . . It asserts itself only in recent centuries and only on a small part of the map of the world. . . . The conscious awareness of the singularity of each individual life is the late product of a specific civilization" (29–31). But the assumption that writing autobiography is the mark of attaining individuality and the highest achievement of Western civilization is evident in the work of such critics as Karl Joachim Weintraub and Roy Pascal as well.

3. Only part of Misch's work on autobiography in antiquity has been translated; none of the later books on the Middle Ages and the Renaissance, which were finished by his students from his notes, has been. Although there are three "volumes," each has two parts, comprising six books.

4. See Porter's discussion of "Gibbon's Autobiography: Filling Up the Silent Vacancy" in his *Self-Same Songs: Autobiographical Reflections and Performances.*

5. Verene notes that most critics consider Rousseau the "father" of modern autobiography, though both he and Michael Sprinker argue for Vico's importance (59). Mary G. Mason finds the "egoistic secular archetype" of Rousseau's *Confessions* inappropriate as a model for women's autobiography (210).

6. Vincent Carretta, the editor of a recent edition of Equiano's narrative, claims that, based on new biographical findings, Equiano may have been born in South Carolina rather than West Africa and that the chronology he gives of his early years is contradicted by factual evidence. Carretta asks whether Olaudah Equiano was "an identity revealed, as the title of the autobiography implies, or an identity assumed by Gustavus Vassa in 1789 for rhetorical (and financial) ends?" (96). And he asserts, "There can be no doubt that Vassa manipulated some of the facts in his autobiography" (103).

7. See William L. Andrews, in *To Tell a Free Story,* for an overview of the origins and development of the genre. His "African-American Autobiography Criticism: Retrospect and Prospect" surveys the development of criticism of the slave narrative. James Olney's essay "'I Was Born': Slave Narratives, Their Status as Autobiography and as Literature" discusses conventions of the genre. Samira Kawash critiques the notion of "freedom" attained.

8. Studies of American ex-slave narratives have burgeoned and developed increasingly nuanced readings since James Olney's "'I Was Born'" and Henry Louis Gates Jr.'s seminal essay "The Trope of the Talking Book" in *The Signifying Monkey.* In their studies, Ashraf H. A. Rushdy, Samira Kawash, and Michael A. Chaney redefine the terms of enslavement and engagement; Sandra Gunning among many

others rethinks the legacy of Harriet Jacobs; and Lindon Barrett reevaluates the framing of "blackness" by an earlier generation of critics.

5. In the Wake of the Memoir Boom

1. An earlier version of this chapter, focused on works by women, was published in *Revista Canaria de Estudios Ingleses* (April 2009).

2. This section on human rights narratives is adapted from Schaffer and Smith's *Human Rights and Narrated Lives* and "Human Rights, Storytelling"; and Smith and Watson's "New Genres, New Subjects."

3. See also http://disstud.blogspot.com/2005/08/simi-linton-promotes-ds-in-village.html.

4. In 1971, Pankejeff questioned many uses to which Freud's psychiatric case study of him had been put and told his own story quite differently. (Incidentally, his version was edited by Muriel Gardiner, herself the author of *Code Name Mary*, from which Lillian Hellman's character "Julia" in *Pentimento* was taken.)

5. The contours of aging are explored by Simone de Beauvoir in *The Coming of Age*. Women's narratives of aging have been studied by Kathleen Woodward, Barbara Frey Waxman, Ruth E. Ray, Margaret Morganroth Gullette, and others.

6. See Ken Plummer's *Telling Sexual Stories* for an overview of many kinds, including antecedents of and British practices of enacting coming-out stories.

7. The series publicity asserts, "autobiography is an essential gay form—a crucial way of reclaiming invisible lives." See http://uwpress.wisc.edu/books/livingout/htm.

8. The book has sold nearly a half-million copies. In 2006, five of her eight siblings told the *Guardian* that much of the book was fantasy, although O'Beirne produced documents arguing the contrary and argues she was vindicated by a lie detector test (see Addley).

9. See the special issue of *a/b: Auto/Biography Studies* (19.1–2) on life writing and the generations. We recommend in particular David Parker's discussion in that volume of the interplay of autonomy and relationality in various kinds of intergenerational narratives, in "Narratives of Autonomy and Narratives of Relationality in Auto/Biography."

10. See the special issue of *a/b: Auto/Biography Studies* (18.2) on adoption narratives; and Marianne Novy's edited collection *Imagining Adoption*.

11. See, for instance, Rocío G. Davis's exploration of Asian North American life writing.

12. Social scientists have used autoethnographic methods to reshape their projects, a practice that Robert Coles emphasized in his use of stories in his studies of education, and Laurel Richardson in both her theorizing and *Last Writes: A Daybook for a Dying Friend*. Carolyn Ellis, for example, in *The Ethnographer's I,*

what she considers a methodological novel, refracts her study through her subjective, diurnal experience. While debates about its value in social-scientific study continue, some new-model projects are manifestly autoethnographic.

13. See also the studies on collaboration in Native American ethnography of Arnold Krupat, Gretchen Bataille and Kathleen Sands, and Hertha D. Sweet Wong.

14. Perreten discusses ecological literary criticism (ecocriticism) that contextualizes his reading of narratives by Annie Dillard, N. Scott Momaday, and Lisa Dale Norton.

6. The Visual-Verbal-Virtual Contexts of Life Narrative

1. Anglophone scholars have for some time understood the complexities of automediality. See Meskimmon; Smith and Watson ("Introduction" to *Interfaces*); Hirsch; Bal; Jones; and Kauffman.

2. For a history of autographics in the United States since 1972, see Jared Gardner's "Autography's Biography."

3. "I wanted to put a few things straight," explains the narrating Marjane from her studio at Place des Vosges, one of the oldest districts of Paris. "When I arrived in France, I met many people who expected me to speak Arabic. So many Europeans do not know the difference between Arabs and Iranians. They don't know anything of our centuries-old culture. They seem to think Iran has always been a country of religious fundamentalists, that Iranian women either have no place in our society or that they are hysterical black crows. In fact, Iranian women are not downtrodden weeds: my mother's maid has kicked out her husband, and I myself slapped so many men who behaved inappropriately in the street. And even during the worst period of the Iranian Revolution, women were carrying weapons" (quoted in Kutschera).

4. See Watson's "Autographic Disclosures" for an extended discussion of *Fun Home*.

5. This section on Emin's installation is drawn from our keynote address presented on July 27, 2000, at the Autobiography and Changing Identities conference, held at the University of British Columbia; and subsequently published in *Biography* (Smith and Watson "The Rumpled Bed").

6. For an extended discussion of Hatoum's project, see Phillipi.

7. See Jennifer Drake for a fuller discussion of Piper's confrontational self-presentations across racialized boundaries.

8. We are indebted to Jim Lane's presentation on this film at the 2006 International Auto/Biography Association meeting in Mainz.

9. Jim Lane has long focused on autobiographical film. In *The Autobiographical Documentary in America from the 1960s to the Present,* he discusses such films as *Roger and Me, Sherman's March,* and *Silverlake Life.* Lane has noted the emergence

of new hybrid kinds of autobiographical documentary film in forms of self-documenting and of multiplying the subjects of documentation. Susanna Egan also explores a range of "thanatographical" films about death and mourning in *Mirror Talk*. See also Renov; and Gaines and Renov.

10. For the material in this section we are deeply indebted to Julia's students in Comparative Studies Honors 203 and H203, Fall 2007, at the Ohio State University and Sidonie's students in English 646, Winter 2006, at the University of Michigan. Their research and group presentations on these sites were perceptive, informative, and cogently articulated—and humblingly instructive. Throughout we have interwoven their responses as our "informant group."

11. See www.youtube.com/user/lonelygirl15.

12. More specifically, SecondLife is an example of "massively multiplayer on-line role-playing games" (MMORPGs). See the discussion by Tracy Wilson in the newsletter from howstuffworks.com (fall 2007) exploring the deep connection between the user and the avatar.

13. For expanded discussion of SecondLife, see Boellstorff; and Ludlow and Wallace.

14. Editors Rachel Fershleiser and Larry Smith collected six-word memoirs from readers and combined them with those of famous people to produce the book *Not Quite What I Was Planning: Six-Word Memoirs by Writers Famous and Obscure* (2008). After its publication, reports on NPR in the United States and the BBC in Britain elicited six-word lives from around the world. The *Smith* Web site constantly updates its listing of memoirs, inviting submissions: "Everyone has a story. Can you tell yours in six words?" See www.smithmag.net/sixwords/.

15. See Bella Brodzki's discussion of acts of bearing witness to the Holocaust, in *Can These Bones Live?* (especially 118–19 ff).

16. A book version titled *Listening Is an Act of Love* was published in 2007 (see Isay).

7. A History of Autobiography Criticism, Part I

1. Misch's study, produced over forty years and translated in part into English only in 1951, did not play a major role in the criticism of life narrative until midcentury. The assumptions of Misch's appear, less fully formulated, elsewhere in early scholarship, as in Anna Robeson Brown Burr's 1909 *The Autobiography: A Critical and Comparative Study,* because the notion of a representative life dominated concepts of textual personhood.

2. As Griselda Pollock argues, in considering the notion of the canon in art history, "Canons may be understood . . . as the retrospectively legitimating backbone of a culture and political identity, a consolidated narrative of origin, conferring authority on the texts selected to naturalise this function. Canonicity refers to both the assumed quality of an included text and to the status a text acquires

because it belongs within an authoritative collection. Religions confer sanctity upon their canonised texts, often implying, if not divine authorship, at least divine authority" (3).

3. The impact of de Man's poststructuralist interrogation of self and author (as well as that of other poststructural theorists) is insightfully assessed in Candace Lang's 1982 "Autobiography in the Aftermath of Romanticism," in which she also historicizes the concept of individualism and frames new terms for conceptualizing autobiographical practices.

8. A History of Autobiography Criticism, Part II

1. In its winter issue *Biography,* a preeminent journal, assembles "The Annual Bibliography of Works about Life Writing," annotating all books, edited collections, special issues of journals, and articles appearing during the previous year.

2. Recent work in this area includes Leigh Gilmore, *The Limits of Autobiography: Trauma and Testimony* (2001); Kay Schaffer and Sidonie Smith, *Human Rights and Narrated Lives: The Ethics of Recognition* (2004); Anne Cubilié, *Women Witnessing Terror* (2005); Gillian Whitlock, *Soft Weapons: Autobiography in Transit* (2007); Joseph Slaughter, *Human Rights, Inc.: The World Novel, Narrative Form, and International Law* (2007); Elizabeth Swanson Goldberg, *Beyond Terror: Gender, Narrative, Human Rights* (2007); Wendy Hesford and Wendy Kozol's two edited collections *Haunting Violations: Feminist Criticism and the Crisis of the "Real"* (2001) and *Just Advocacy? Women's Human Rights, Transnational Feminisms, and the Politics of Representation* (2005); James Dawes, *That the World May Know: Bearing Witness to Atrocity* (2007). Several important essays, notably by Allen Feldman, are published in the winter 2004 issue of *Biography.*

3. See the work of Gillian Whitlock, Philip Holden, and Robert Young, among others, as well as studies of such germinal autobiographical figures as Gandhi.

4. For instance, H. Porter Abbott has been considering the evolutionary "prehistory" of narrative origins ("Evolutionary Origins of the Storied Mind").

5. See the analyses of Carolyn Kay Steedman, Liz Stanley, Simon Dentith, and Regenia Gagnier.

6. More generally, H. Aram Veeser's anthology *Confessions of the Critics: North American Critics' Autobiographical Moves* captures the critical turn in the 1990s to personal modes of engagement with experiences inside and outside the academy. Herman Rapaport, however, notes that, among academic practitioners of autobiographical writing as personal criticism, widely varying critical assumptions inform their work, assumptions about "situatedness, interpellation, typification, group identity, the sharability of experience, and the banality of everyday life" (49).

Bibliography

Primary Works

Abbey, Edward. *Desert Solitaire: A Season in the Wilderness.* New York: Simon and Schuster, 1968.

———. *The Monkey Wrench Gang.* Philadelphia: Lippincott, 1975.

Abelard, Peter, and Héloïse. *The Letters of Abelard and Héloïse.* Translated by Betty Radice. Harmondsworth: Penguin, 1974.

Abu-Jaber, Diana. *The Language of Baklava.* New York: Pantheon Books, 2005.

Abu-Jamal, Mumia. *Live from Death Row.* New York: Harper Perennial, 1996.

Adair, Casey, and Nancy Adair. *Word Is Out: Stories of Some of Our Lives.* San Francisco: New Glide Publications, 1978.

Adams, Henry. *The Education of Henry Adams: An Autobiography.* Boston: Houghton Mifflin, 1918.

Addams, Jane. *Twenty Years at Hull-House: With Autobiographical Notes.* New York: Macmillan, 1910.

Adielé, Faith. *Meeting Faith: The Forest Journals of a Black Buddhist Nun.* New York: Norton, 2004.

Adivar, Halidé Edib. *Memoirs of Halidé Edib.* Introduced by Hülya Adak. Piscataway, N.J.: Gorgias Press, 2005.

Agassi, Andre. *Open: An Autobiography.* New York: Knopf, 2009.

Ahmed, Salma. *Cutting Free: The Extraordinary Memoir of a Pakistani Woman.* New Delhi: Lotus Collection, 2007.

Akhmatova, Anna. *A Poem without a Hero.* Translated by Carl R. Proffer. Ann Arbor, Mich.: Ardis, 1973.

Alexander, Jon. *American POW Memoirs from the Revolutionary War through the Vietnam War: The Autobiography Seminar.* Eugene, Ore.: Wipf & Stock, 2007.

Alexie, Sherman. *First Indian on the Moon.* Brooklyn, N.Y.: Hanging Loose Press, 1993.

Allen, Paula Gunn. "The Autobiography of a Confluence." In *I Tell You Now: Autobiographical Essays by Native American Writers,* ed. Brian Swann and Arnold Krupat, 143–54. Lincoln: University of Nebraska Press, 1987.

Allende, Isabel. *Paula*. New York: Harper Perennial, 1996.

Amaechi, John. *Man in the Middle*. New York: ESPN, 2007.

Ammons, A. R. *Tape for the Turn of the Year*. Ithaca, N.Y.: Cornell University Press, 1965.

Anderson, Laurie. *Stories from the Nerve Bible: A Retrospective, 1972–1992*. New York: Harper Perennial, 1994.

Andrews, William L., ed. *Sisters of the Spirit: Three Black Women's Autobiographies of the Nineteenth Century*. Bloomington: Indiana University Press, 1986.

Angela of Foligno. *Complete Works*. Translated by Paul Lachance. New York: Paulist Press, 1993.

Angela's Ashes. Videorecording. Directed by Alan Parker. Hollywood: Paramount Pictures, 2000.

Angelou, Maya. *The Heart of a Woman*. New York: Random House, 1981.

——. *I Know Why the Caged Bird Sings*. New York: Random House, 1969.

Antin, Mary. *The Promised Land*. Boston: Houghton Mifflin, 1912.

Antoni, Janine. *Gnaw*. London: Saatchi Collection, 1992.

Anzaldúa, Gloria. *Borderlands/La Frontera: The New Mestiza*. San Francisco: Spinsters/Aunt Lute, 1987.

——, ed. *Making Face, Making Soul = Haciendo Caras: Creative and Critical Perspectives by Feminists of Color*. San Francisco: Aunt Lute Foundation Books, 1990.

Apess, William. "The Experience of Five Christian Indians of the Pequot Tribe." In *On Our Own Ground: The Complete Writings of William Apess, a Pequot*, ed. Barry O'Connell, 117–61. Amherst: University of Massachusetts Press, 1992.

——. "A Son of the Forest." In *On Our Own Ground: The Complete Writings of William Apess, a Pequot*, ed. Barry O'Connell, 1–97. Amherst: University of Massachusetts Press, 1992.

Apted, Michael. *Up! Series*. Videorecording. New York: First-Run Features, 2004.

Aptheker, Bettina. *Intimate Politics: How I Grew Up Red, Fought for Free Speech, and Became a Feminist Rebel*. Emeryville, Calif.: Seal Press, 2006.

Arenas, Reinaldo. *Before Night Falls: A Memoir*. Translated by Dolores M. Koch. New York: Penguin Books, 1994.

Arnold, Mary Ellicott, and Mabel Reed. *In the Land of the Grasshopper Song: A Story of Two Girls in Indian Country in 1908–1909*. New York: Vantage, 1957.

Ashbery, John. *Self-Portrait in a Convex Mirror*. New York: Viking, 1975.

Ashbridge, Elizabeth. "Some Account of the Early Life of Elizabeth Ashbridge." In *Journeys in New Worlds: Early American Women's Narratives*, ed. William L. Andrews, 147–80. Madison: University of Wisconsin Press, 1990.

Ashe, Arthur, and Arnold Rampersad. *Days of Grace: A Memoir*. New York: Knopf, 1993.

Ashton-Warner, Sylvia. *Teacher*. New York: Simon and Schuster, 1963.

Augustine, Saint, Bishop of Hippo. *The Confessions of St. Augustine.* Translated by Rex Warner. New York: New American Library, 1963.

Auster, Paul. *The Invention of Solitude.* New York: Penguin, 1982.

Bâ, Mariama. *So Long a Letter.* London: Virago Press, 1982.

Baepler, Paul, ed. *White Slaves, African Masters: An Anthology of American Barbary Captivity Narratives.* Chicago: University of Chicago Press, 1999.

Baldwin, James. *Notes of a Native Son.* Boston: Beacon Press, 1957.

Barnes, Mary, and Joseph Berke. *Mary Barnes: Two Accounts of a Journey through Madness.* New York: Harcourt Brace, 1971.

Barnum, P. T. *The Autobiography of P. T. Barnum: Clerk, Merchant, Editor, and Showman, with His Rules for Business and Making a Fortune.* London: Ward and Lock, 1855.

Barrios de Chungara, Domitila, and Moema Viezzer. *Let Me Speak! Testimony of Domitila, a Woman of the Bolivian Mines.* New York: Monthly Review Press, 1978.

Barry, Lynda. "Interview with Lynn Neary." *Talk of the Nation.* National Public Radio, aired 1 October 2002. http://www.Npr.org/templates/story.php?storyid=1150937

———. *One Hundred Demons.* Seattle: Sasquatch, 2002.

Barthes, Roland. *Camera Lucida: Reflections on Photography.* Translated by Richard Howard. New York: Hill and Wang, 1981.

———. *Roland Barthes by Roland Barthes.* Translated by Richard Howard. New York: Hill and Wang, 1977.

Bauby, Jean-Dominique. *The Diving Bell and the Butterfly.* Translated by Jeremy Leggatt. New York: Knopf, 1997.

Bayley, John. *Elegy for Iris.* New York: Macmillan, 2000.

Beah, Ishmael. *A Long Way Gone: Memoirs of a Boy Soldier.* New York: Farrar, Straus and Giroux, 2007.

Beauvoir, Simone de. *The Coming of Age.* Translated by Patrick O'Brian. New York: Putnam, 1972.

Bechdel, Alison. *Fun Home: A Family Tragicomic.* Boston: Houghton Mifflin, 2006.

Before Night Falls. Videorecording. Directed by Julian Schnabel. New Line Home Entertainment, 2001.

Behar, Ruth. *Translated Woman: Crossing the Border with Esperanza's Story.* Boston: Beacon Press, 1993.

Benjamin, Walter. *Berliner Chronik.* Frankfurt am Main: Suhrkamp Verlag, 1970.

———. *Berliner Kindheit um Neunzehnhundert.* Frankfurt am Main: Suhrkamp Verlag, 1983.

———. *Gesammelte Schriften.* Vol. 6. Edited by Rolf Tiedemann and Hermann Schweppenhuser. Frankfurt am Main: Suhrkamp, 1972–89.

———. *Moscow Diary*. Edited by Gary Smith, translated by Richard Sieburth. Cambridge, Mass.: Harvard University Press, 1986.

Bentley, Toni. *The Surrender: An Erotic Memoir*. New York: Ecco, 2004.

Berkman, Alexander. *Prison Memoirs of an Anarchist*. New York: Mother Earth Publishing Association, 1912.

Bernstein, Harry. *The Invisible Wall: A Love Story That Broke Barriers*. New York: Ballantine Books, 2007.

Berry, Wendell. *The Art of the Commonplace: The Agrarian Essays of Wendell Berry*. Edited by Norman Wirzba. Washington, D.C.: Counterpoint, 2002.

Berzon, Betty. *Surviving Madness: A Therapist's Own Story*. Living Out Series. Madison: University of Wisconsin Press, 2002.

Beyala, Calixthe. *Your Name Shall Be Tanga*. Translated by Marjolijn de Jager. Oxford: Heinemann Educational Publishers, 1996.

Bhutto, Benazir. *Benazir Bhutto: Daughter of the East*. London: Hamilton, 1988.

Biko, Steve. *I Write What I Like*. Edited by Aelred Stubbs. New York: Harper and Row, 1978.

Bird, Isabella. *Collected Travel Writings of Isabella Bird*. Bristol, England: Ganesha Publications, 1997.

Black Elk. *Black Elk Speaks: Being the Life Story of a Holy Man of the Ogalala Sioux as Told to John G. Neihardt*. New York: W. Morrow, 1932.

Blew, Mary Clearman. *All but the Waltz: Essays on a Montana Family*. Norman: University of Oklahoma Press, 1991.

Bok, Edward William. *The Americanization of Edward Bok: The Autobiography of a Dutch Boy Fifty Years After*. New York: Scribner's, 1922.

Bornstein, Kate. *Gender Outlaw: On Men, Women, and the Rest of Us*. New York: Routledge, 1994.

Boswell, James. *Boswell on the Grand Tour: Germany and Switzerland, 1764*. Edited by Frederick A. Pottle. London: W. Heinemann, 1953.

———. *Boswell on the Grand Tour: Italy, Corsica, and France, 1765–1766*. Edited by Frank Brady and Frederick A. Pottle. London: W. Heinemann, 1955.

———. *The Life of Samuel Johnson*. Garden City, N.Y.: Doubleday, 1946.

Bouton, Jim, and Leonard Shecter. *Ball Four*. Twentieth anniversary ed. New York: Colliers, 1990.

Brabner, Joyce, Harvey Pekar, and Frank Stack. *Our Cancer Year*. New York: Four Walls Eight Windows, 1994.

Bradley, Bill. *Life on the Run*. New York: Quadrangle/New York Times Books, 1976.

Breytenbach, Breyten. *The True Confessions of an Albino Terrorist*. London: Faber and Faber, 1984.

Brodkey, Harold. *This Wild Darkness: The Story of My Death*. New York: Henry Holt, 1996.

Brontë, Charlotte. *Jane Eyre.* Edited by Margaret Smith. New York: Oxford University Press, 1998.

Browne, Thomas. "Religio Medici." In *Selected Writings,* ed. Geoffrey Keynes, 5–89. Chicago: University of Chicago Press, 1968.

Broyard, Anatole. *Thanatography: Intoxicated by My Illness.* New York: Ballantine, 1993.

Broyard, Bliss. *One Drop: My Father's Hidden Life—A Story of Race and Family Secrets.* New York: Little, Brown, 2007.

Bugul, Ken (Mariétou M'baye). *The Abandoned Baobab: The Autobiography of a Senegalese Woman.* Translated by Marjolijn De Jager. Brooklyn, N.Y.: Lawrence Hill Books, 1991.

Bunyan, John. *Grace Abounding to the Chief of Sinners.* Edited by Roger Sharrock. Oxford: Clarendon Press, 1962.

Burney, Charles. *Dr. Charles Burney's Continental Travels, 1770–1772.* Edited by Cedric Howard Glover. London: Blackie and Son, 1927.

Burney, Fanny. *The Journals and Letters of Fanny Burney (Madame D'Arblay).* Vol. 3. Edited by Joyce Hemlow. Oxford: Clarendon Press, 1973.

Burroughs, Augusten. *Dry: A Memoir.* New York: St. Martin's, 2003.

———. *Running with Scissors: A Memoir.* New York: Picador, 2002.

Burton, Robert. *Anatomy of Melancholy.* Edited by Holbrook Jackson. London: Dent, 1972.

Byerly, Victoria Morris. *Hard Times Cotton Mill Girls: Personal Histories of Womanhood and Poverty in the South.* Ithaca, N.Y.: ILR Press, 1986.

Byron, George Gordon. *Don Juan.* Edited by T. G. Steffan, E. Steffan, and W. W. Pratt. New Haven, Conn.: Yale University Press, 1982.

Cahun, Claude. *Aveux non avenus.* Paris: Editions de Carrefour, 1930.

Canseco, José. *Juiced: Wild Times, Rampant 'Roids, Smash Hits, and How Baseball Got Big.* New York: HarperCollins, 2005.

Cantú, Norma Elia. *Canícula: Snapshots of a Girlhood en la Frontera.* Albuquerque: University of New Mexico Press, 1995.

Cardano, Girolamo. *The Book of My Life.* Translated by Jean Stoner. New York: Dover, 1962.

Cardinal, Marie. *The Words to Say It: An Autobiographical Novel.* Translated by Pat Goodheart. Cambridge, Mass.: VanVactor and Goodheart, 1983.

Carlyle, Thomas. *Sartor Resartus.* Edited by Archibald MacMechan. Boston: Ginn, 1897.

Carter, Elizabeth. *Letters from Mrs. Elizabeth Carter to Mrs. Montagu between the Years 1755 to 1800.* New York: AMS Press, 1973.

———. *A Series of Letters between Mrs. Elizabeth Carter and Miss Catherine Talbot, from the Year 1741 to 1770.* 4 vols. London: F. C. and J. Rivington, 1809.

Casanova, Giacomo. *History of My Life*. 12 vols. Translated by Willard R. Trask. New York: Harcourt, Brace and World, 1966–71.

Casas, Bartolomé de Las. *Witness: Writings of Bartolomé de Las Casas*. Edited and translated by George Sanderlin. Maryknoll, N.Y.: Orbis Books, 1992.

Cavendish, Margaret. *The Life of William Cavendish, Duke of Newcastle, to Which is Added the True Relation of My Birth, Breeding, and Life*. 2nd ed. Edited by C. H. Firth. London: G. Routledge and Sons, 1903.

Cellini, Benvenuto. *Autobiography of Benvenuto Cellini*. Translated by George Bull. Harmondsworth: Penguin Books, 1956.

Charke, Charlotte. *A Narrative of the Life of Mrs. Charlotte Charke (Youngest Daughter of Colley Cibber, Esq.), Written by Herself*. Edited by Leonard R. N. Ashley. Gainesville, Fla.: Scholar's Facsimiles and Reprints, 1969.

Chernin, Kim. *In My Mother's House: A Daughter's Story*. New York: Harper and Row, 1983.

Chessler Books. Homepage. Accessed 30 April 2009. www.chesslerbooks.com

Child, Julia, Louisette Bertholle, and Simone Beck. *Mastering the Art of French Cooking*. 2 vols. New York: Knopf, 1961.

Child, Julia, and Alex Prud'homme. *My Life in France*. New York: Knopf, 2006.

Clapton, Eric, and Christopher Simon Sykes. *Eric Clapton: The Autobiography*. London: Century, 2007.

Clarke, Austin. *Pig Tails 'n Breadfruit: A Culinary Memoir*. New York: New Press, 1999.

Cleaver, Eldridge. *Soul on Ice*. New York: McGraw-Hill, 1968.

Clemens, Paul. *Made in Detroit: A South of 8-Mile Memoir*. New York: Doubleday, 2005.

Cliff, Michelle. *Abeng: A Novel*. New York: Crossing Press, 1984.

———. *No Telephone to Heaven*. New York: Vintage Books, 1989.

Clinton, Hillary Rodham. *Living History*. New York: Simon & Schuster, 2003.

Coetzee, J. M. *Boyhood: Scenes from Provincial Life*. New York: Viking, 1997.

———. *Diary of a Bad Year*. London: Harvill Secher, 2007.

———. *Doubling the Point: Essays and Interviews*. Edited by David Attwell. Cambridge, Mass.: Harvard University Press, 1992.

———. *Summertime: Fiction*. New York: Viking, 2009.

———. *Youth: Scenes from Provincial Life II*. New York: Viking, 2002.

Colette, Sidonie-Gabrielle. *Earthly Paradise: An Autobiography*. Edited by Robert Phelps. New York: Farrar, Straus & Giroux, 1966.

Collard, Cyril. *Savage Nights*. Translated by William Rodarmor. Woodstock, N.Y.: Overlook Press, 1994.

Columbus, Christopher. *The Diario of Christopher Columbus's First Voyage to America, 1492–1493*. Translated by Oliver Dunn and James E. Kelly Jr. Norman: University of Oklahoma Press, 1991.

Condé, Maryse. *Hérémakhonon: A Novel*. Translated by Richard Philcox. Washington, D.C.: Three Continents Press, 1982.

———. *I, Tituba, Black Witch of Salem.* Charlottesville: University Press of Virginia, 1992.

Cortés, Hernán. *Letters from Mexico.* Edited and translated by A. R. Pagden. New York: Grossman Publishers, 1971.

Crowley, Aleister. *The Confessions of Aleister Crowley: An Autohagiography.* New York: Penguin, 1989.

cummings, e. e. *The Enormous Room.* New York: Modern Library, 1934.

Dangarembga, Tsitsi. *Nervous Conditions.* London: Women's Press, 1988.

Danica, Elly. *Don't: A Woman's Word.* San Francisco: Cleis Press, 1988.

Dante Alighieri. *Dante Alighieri's Divine Comedy.* Translated by Mark Musa. Bloomington: Indiana University Press, 1971.

———. *La Vita Nuova* (The New Life). Translated by Mark Musa. Bloomington: Indiana University Press, 1962.

Danticat, Edwidge. *Brother, I'm Dying.* New York: Knopf, 2007.

David B. *Epileptic.* New York: Pantheon, 2005.

Day, Dorothy. *The Long Loneliness: The Autobiography of Dorothy Day.* New York: Harper Bros., 1952.

DeBaggio, Thomas. *Losing My Mind: An Intimate Look at Life with Alzheimer's.* New York: Simon and Schuster, 2001.

Defoe, Daniel. *The Farther Adventures of Robinson Crusoe; Being the Second and Last Part of His Life, and of the Strange Surprizing Accounts of His Travels Round Three Parts of the Globe.* London: Printed for W. Taylor, 1719.

———. *The Fortunes and Misfortunes of the Famous Moll Flanders, & C. Who Was Born in Newgate, . . . Written from Her Own Memorandums.* 3rd ed. London: Printed for, and sold by W. Chetwood et al., 1722.

———. *A Journal of the Plague Year.* New York: Dutton, 1966.

Delany, Mary. *Letters from Georgian Ireland: The Correspondence of Mary Delany, 1731–68.* Edited by Angélique Day. Belfast: Friar's Bush Press, 1991.

Delbo, Charlotte. *Auschwitz and After.* Translated by Rosette C. Lamont. New Haven, Conn.: Yale University Press, 1995.

De Quincey, Thomas. *Confessions of an English Opium Eater.* Oxford: Woodstock, 1989.

Derounian-Stodola, Kathryn Zabelle, ed. *Women's Indian Captivity Narratives.* New York: Penguin Books, 1998.

Descartes, René. *Discourse on the Method; and, Meditations on First Philosophy.* Edited by David Weissman. New Haven, Conn.: Yale University Press, 1996.

Diawara, Manthia. *In Search of Africa.* Cambridge, Mass.: Harvard University Press, 1998.

Dickens, Charles. *David Copperfield.* Edited by Nina Burgis. New York: Oxford University Press, 1981.

Dickinson, Emily. *The Poems of Emily Dickinson.* Cambridge, Mass.: Belknap Press of Harvard University Press, 1999.

Didion, Joan. *The Year of Magical Thinking*. New York: Knopf, 2005.

Dillard, Annie. *An American Childhood*. New York: Harper and Row, 1987.

———. *Pilgrim at Tinker Creek*. New York: Harper's Magazine Press, 1974.

Dinesen, Isak. *Out of Africa*. New York: Random House, 1938.

The Diving Bell and the Butterfly. Videorecording. Directed by Julian Schnabel. Burbank, Calif.: Touchstone Home Entertainment, 2008.

Djebar, Assia. *Femmes d'Alger dans Leur Appartement: Nouvelles*. Paris: Des femmes, 1980.

———. "Forbidden Gaze, Severed Sound." Excerpted in *Women, Autobiography, Theory: A Reader*, ed. Sidonie Smith and Julia Watson, 337–42. Madison: University of Wisconsin Press, 1998.

Donne, John. *Sermons*. New York: Meridian Books, 1958.

Dostoyevsky, Fyodor. *Notes from Underground*. New York: Signet, 1961.

Doucet, Julie. *My New York Diary*. Montreal: Drawn & Quarterly Publications, 1999.

Douglass, Frederick. *Life and Times of Frederick Douglass*. New York: Collier, 1962.

———. *My Bondage and My Freedom*. New York: Dover, 1969.

———. *Narrative of the Life of Frederick Douglass, an American Slave*. New York: Signet, 1968.

Du Bois, W. E. B. *The Autobiography of W. E. B. Du Bois: A Soliloquy on Viewing My Life from the Last Decade of Its First Century*. New York: International Publishers, 1968.

Duras, Marguerite. *The Lover*. Translated by Barbara Bray. New York: Pantheon, 1985.

Dylan, Bob. *Chronicles*. New York: Simon & Schuster, 2004.

Eagleton, Terry. *The Gatekeeper: A Memoir*. London: St. Martin's Griffin, 2003.

Ebadi, Shirin, with Azadeh Moaveni. *Iran Awakening: A Memoir of Revolution and Hope*. New York: Random House, 2006.

Edwards, Brian. *Helen: Portrait of a Prime Minister*. Auckland, New Zealand: Exisle, 2001.

Edwards, Jonathan. "Personal Narrative." In *Selected Writing of Jonathan Edwards*, ed. Harold P. Simonson, 27–44. New York: Ungar Publishing, 1970.

Eggers, Dave. *What Is the What: The Autobiography of Valentino Achak Deng: A Novel*. San Francisco: McSweeney's, 2006.

Eiseley, Loren C. *The Star Thrower*. New York: Times Books, 1978.

Elaw, Zilpha. "Memoirs of the Life, Religious Experience, Ministerial Travels, and Labors of Mrs. Zilpha Elaw." In *Sisters of the Spirit*, ed. Andrews, 49–160.

Eliot, T. S. *Four Quartets*. New York: Harcourt Brace Jovanovich, 1971.

Ellerby, Janet Mason. *Following the Tambourine Man: A Birthmother's Memoir*. New York: Syracuse University Press, 2007.

Ellroy, James. *My Dark Places: An L.A. Crime Memoir*. New York: Knopf, 1996.

Emecheta, Buchi. *Head above Water*. Oxford: Fontana, 1986.

Emerson, Ralph Waldo. *The Journals and Miscellaneous Notebooks of Ralph Waldo Emerson.* 16 vols. Edited by William H. Gilman et al. Cambridge, Mass.: Belknap Press of Harvard University Press, 1960–82.

Ephron, Nora. *I Feel Bad about My Neck: And Other Thoughts on Being a Woman.* New York: Vintage, 2008.

Equiano, Olaudah. *Equiano's Travels: His Autobiography; The Interesting Narrative of the Life of Olaudah Equiano, or Gustavus Vassa the African.* Edited by Paul Edwards. London: Heinemann, 1967.

Erasmus, Desiderius. *The Praise of Folly.* Translated by John Wilson. Ann Arbor: University of Michigan Press, 1958.

Erauso, Catalina de. *The Lieutenant Nun: Memoir of a Basque Transvestite in the New World.* Translated by Michele Stepto and Gabriel Stepto. Boston: Beacon Press, 1996.

Ernaux, Annie. *Shame.* Translated by Tanya Leslie. New York: Seven Stories Press, 1998.

Fanon, Frantz. *Black Skin, White Masks.* Translated by Charles Lam Markmann. New York: Grove Press, 1967.

Fanshawe, Ann, and Anne Halkett. *The Memoirs of Anne, Lady Halkett, and Ann, Lady Fanshawe.* Edited by John Loftis. New York: Oxford University Press, 1979.

Fearless. DVD. Directed by Peter Weir. Warner Home Video, June 2004.

Feinberg, Leslie. *Stone Butch Blues: A Novel.* Ithaca, N.Y.: Firebrand Books, 1993.

Fershleiser, Rachel, and Larry Smith, eds. *Not Quite What I Was Planning: Six-Word Memoirs by Writers Famous and Obscure: From Smith Magazine.* New York: HarperPerennial, 2008.

Finger, Anne. *Elegy for a Disease: A Personal and Cultural History of Polio.* New York: St. Martin's Press, 2006.

First, Ruth. *117 Days: An Account of Confinement and Interrogation under the South African 90-Day Detention Law.* New York: Stein and Day, 1965.

Flanagan, Bob. *Bob Flanagan: Super-Masochist.* Edited by Andrea Juno and V. Vale. San Francisco: Re/Search Publications, 1993.

Flaubert, Gustave. *Madame Bovary.* Paris: Livre de Poche, 1961.

Flynn, Elizabeth Gurley. *I Speak My Own Piece: Autobiography of "The Rebel Girl."* New York: Masses and Mainstream, 1955.

Fonda, Jane. *My Life So Far.* New York: Random House, 2005.

Foote, Julia A. "A Brand Plucked from the Fire." In *Sisters of the Spirit,* ed. Andrews, 161–234.

Forbidden Lies. Directed by Anna Broinowski. Roxie Releasing, 2007.

Ford, Richard. *The Lay of the Land.* New York: Knopf, 2006.

Fox, George. *The Journal of George Fox.* Cambridge: Cambridge University Press, 1952.

Frame, Janet. *An Angel at My Table: An Autobiography.* Vol. 2. New York: G. Braziller, 1984.

Frank, Anne. *The Diary of a Young Girl.* Translated by B. M. Mooyaart-Doubleday. Garden City, N.Y.: Doubleday, 1952.

Franklin, Benjamin. *The Autobiography of Benjamin Franklin: A Genetic Text.* Edited by J. A. Leo LeMay and P. M. Zall. Knoxville: University of Tennessee Press, 1981.

Franzen, Jonathan. "My Father's Brain." *New Yorker* 10 September 2001.

Fraser, Sylvia. *My Father's House: A Memoir of Incest and Healing.* New York: Harper and Row, 1987.

Freadman, Richard. *Shadow of Doubt: My Father and Myself.* Northcote, Victoria, Australia: Bystander, 2003.

Frey, James. *A Million Little Pieces.* New York: N.A. Talese/Doubleday, 2003.

Fries, Kenny. *Body, Remember: A Memoir.* Madison: University of Wisconsin Press, 2003.

Frost, Robert. *Collected Poems of Robert Frost.* New York: Henry Holt, 1930.

Fusco, Coco. *English Is Broken Here.* New York: New Press, 1995.

Gailhard, Jean. *The Compleat Gentleman, or, Directions for the Education of Youth as to Their Breeding at Home and Travelling Abroad.* London: Thomas Newcomb, 1678.

Gandhi, Mahatma K. *An Autobiography, or, The Story of My Experiments with Truth.* 2 vols. Translated by Mahadev Desai. Ahmedabad: Navajivan Publishing House, 1927–29.

Gandhi, Mahatma K., and Mahadev H. Desai. *Gandhi's Autobiography: The Story of My Experiments with Truth.* Washington, D.C.: Public Affairs Press, 1948.

Gibbon, Edward. *Memoirs of My Life.* Edited by Georges A. Bonnard. London: Nelson, 1966.

Gilbert, Elizabeth. *Eat, Pray, Love: One Woman's Search for Everything across Italy, India, and Indonesia.* New York: Viking, 2006.

Gilman, Charlotte Perkins. *The Living of Charlotte Perkins Gilman: An Autobiography.* Madison: University of Wisconsin Press, 1990.

——. *The Yellow Wallpaper.* New York: Feminist Press, 1973.

Ginibi, Ruby Langford. *Don't Take Your Love to Town.* Edited by Susan Hampton. New York: Penguin, 1988.

Giovanni, Nikki. *Quilting the Black-Eyed Pea: Poems and Not Quite Poems.* New York: William Morrow, 2002.

Girl, Interrupted. Videorecording. Directed by James Mangold. Culver City, Calif.: Columbia Tristar Home Video, 1999.

Gloeckner, Phoebe. *Diary of a Teenage Girl: An Account in Words and Pictures.* Berkeley, Calif.: Frog, 2002.

Glückel of Hameln. *The Memoirs of Glückel of Hameln.* Translated by Marvin Lowenthal. New York: Schocken Books, 1977.

Gobodo-Madikizela, Pumla. *A Human Being Died That Night: A South African Story of Forgiveness.* Boston: Houghton Mifflin, 2003.

Goethe, Johann Wolfgang von. *The Auto-Biography of Goethe. Truth and Poetry: From My Own Life.* 2 vols. Translated by John Oxemford. London: Bell and Daldy, 1872.

———. *The Sorrows of Young Werther and Novella.* Translated by Elizabeth Mayer, Louise Brogan, and W. H. Auden. New York: Modern Library, 1993.

———. *Wilhelm Meister's Apprenticeship.* Translated by R. Dillon Boylan. London: G. Bell and Sons, 1898.

Goldman, Emma. *Living My Life.* Edited by Richard and Anna Maria Drinnon. New York: New American Library, 1977.

Gómez-Peña, Guillermo. *A New World Border: Prophecies, Poems, and Loqueras for the End of the Century.* San Francisco: City Lights Books, 1996.

Goodison, Lorna. *From Harvey River: A Memoir of My Mother and Her Island.* New York: Amistad, 2008.

Gordon, Barbara. *I'm Dancing as Fast as I Can.* New York: Harper and Row, 1979.

Gordon, Mary. *Circling My Mother.* New York: Anchor, 2008.

———. *The Shadow Man: A Daughter's Search for Her Father.* New York: Random House, 1996.

Gore, Albert, and Melcher Media. *An Inconvenient Truth: The Planetary Emergency of Global Warming and What We Can Do About It.* Emmaus, Penn.: Rodale Press, 2006.

Gorky, Maxim. *Autobiography of Maxim Gorky: My Childhood. In the World. My Universities.* Translated by Isidor Schneider. New York: Citadel Press, 1949.

Gornick, Vivian. *Fierce Attachments: A Memoir.* Boston: Beacon Press, 1987.

Gosse, Edmund. *Father and Son: A Study of Two Temperaments.* London: W. Heinemann, 1907.

Grandin, Temple. *Thinking in Pictures: My Life with Autism.* 2nd ed. New York: Vintage, 2006.

Grealy, Lucy. *Autobiography of a Face.* Boston: Houghton Mifflin, 1994.

Green, Hannah (Joanne Greenberg). *I Never Promised You a Rose Garden.* New York: New American Library, 1964.

Grimes, William. *Life of William Grimes, the Runaway Slave.* Edited by William L. Andrews and Regina E. Mason. New York: Oxford, 2008.

Grizzly Man. Videorecording. Directed by Werner Herzog. Santa Monica, Calif.: Lions Gate Home Entertainment, 2005.

Günderrode, Karoline von. "Selected Letters." In *Bitter Healing: German Women Writers from 1700 to 1830, An Anthology,* ed. Jeannine Blackwell and Susanne Zantop, 417–42. Lincoln: University of Nebraska Press, 1990.

Guyon, Jeanne Marie, Bouvier de La Motte. *Madame Guyon, an Autobiography.* Chicago: Moody Press, 1990.

Hadewijch. *The Complete Works.* Translated by Columba Hart. New York: Paulist Press, 1980.

Haizlip, Shirlee Taylor. *The Sweeter the Juice: A Family Memoir in Black and White.* New York: Simon and Schuster, 1994.

Hale, Janet Campbell. *Bloodlines: Odyssey of a Native Daughter.* New York: Random House, 1993.

Halkett, Anne. *The Autobiography of Anne, Lady Halkett.* Edited by John Gough Nichols. Westminster: Camden Society, 1875.

Hamper, Ben. *Rivethead: Tales from the Assembly Line.* New York: Warner Books, 1991.

Harrison, Kathryn. *The Kiss: A Secret Life.* New York: William Morrow, 1998.

Harrisson, Tom, Charles Madge, and Humphrey Jennings. *Mass Observation Project.* 1937/1981. University of Sussex. Accessed on 14 February 2009. http://www.massobs.org.uk/index.htm

Hatoum, Mona. *Mona Hatoum.* London: Phaidon Press, 1997.

———. *Pull.* Live video performance and installation. 1995.

Head, Bessie. *A Question of Power.* London: Heinemann Educational, 1974.

Hensel, Jana. *Zonenkinder.* Rowohlt: Reinbek, 2002.

Henson, Maria Rosa. *Comfort Woman: A Filipina's Story of Prostitution and Slavery under the Japanese Military.* Lanham, Md.: Rowman & Littlefield, 1999.

Hildegard of Bingen. *Hildegard of Bingen: The Book of the Rewards of Life.* Translated by Bruce W. Hozeski. New York: Garland, 1994.

Hill, Jerome. *Film Portrait.* Buffalo, N.Y.: SUNY Buffalo Media Library, 1972.

Hobbes, Thomas. "Considerations upon the Reputation, Loyalty, Manners, and Religion of Thomas Hobbes." In *The English Works of Thomas Hobbes of Malmesbury,* ed. Sir William Molesworth. Aalen: Scientia, 1962.

Hoffman, Eva. *Lost in Translation: A Life in a New Language.* Boston: E. P. Dutton, 1989.

hooks, bell. *Bone Black: Memories of Girlhood.* New York: Henry Holt, 1996.

Hopkins, Gerard Manley. *The Poems of Gerard Manley Hopkins.* 4th ed. Edited by W. H. Gardner and N. H. MacKenzie. London: Oxford, 1967.

Hornbacher, Marya. *Wasted: A Memoir of Anorexia and Bulimia.* New York: Harper Perennial, 1999.

Hurston, Zora Neale. *Dust Tracks on a Road: An Autobiography.* 2nd ed. Edited by Robert Hemenway. Urbana: University of Illinois Press, 1984.

Hutchinson, Lucy. *Memoirs of the Life of Colonel Hutchinson, with the Fragment of an Autobiography by Mrs. Hutchinson.* Edited by James Sutherland. London: Oxford University Press, 1973.

Ignatius of Loyola, Saint. *St. Ignatius' Own Story, As Told to Luis González de Cámara.* Translated by William J. Young. Chicago: Loyola University Press, 1956.

I'm Not There. Videorecording. Directed by Todd Haynes et al. New York: Weinstein Company, 2008.

I Never Promised You a Rose Garden. Directed by Anthony Page. 1977.

In My Country. Videorecording. Directed by John Boorman. Culver City, Calif.: Sony Pictures Home Entertainment, 2005.

Into Thin Air: Deaths on Everest. Directed by Robert Markowitz. Columbia Tristar Television, 1997.

Isaacson, Walter. *Benjamin Franklin.* Thorndike Press, 2004.

Isay, Dave, ed. *Listening Is an Act of Love: A Celebration of American Life from the StoryCorps Project.* London and New York: Penguin, 2007.

Jackson, Phil, and Hugh Delehanty. *Sacred Hoops: Spiritual Lessons of a Hardwood Warrior.* New York: Hyperion, 1995.

Jacobs, Harriet A. *Incidents in the Life of a Slave Girl: Written by Herself.* Edited by Lydia Maria Child and Jean Fagan Yellin. Cambridge, Mass.: Harvard University Press, 1987.

James, Alice. *The Diary of Alice James.* Edited by Leon Edel. New York: Dodd, Mead, 1964.

James, Henry. *Henry James: Autobiography.* New York: Criterion Books, 1956.

———. *Notes of a Son and Brother.* London, Macmillan, 1914.

———. *A Small Boy: And Others.* New York: Scribner, 1962.

Jamison, Kay Redfield. *An Unquiet Mind.* New York: Knopf, 1995.

Jarhead. Videorecording. Directed by Sam Mendes. Universal City, Calif.: Universal Pictures, 2006.

Jemison, Mary. *A Narrative of the Life of Mrs. Mary Jemison.* Edited by June Namias. Norman: University of Oklahoma Press, 1992.

Jesus, Carolina Maria de. *Child of the Dark: The Diary of Carolina Maria de Jesus.* Translated by David St. Clair. New York: E. P. Dutton, 1962.

Johnson, Samuel. *Johnson and Queeney: Letters from Dr. Johnson to Queeney Thrale from the Bowood Papers.* Edited by Marquis of Lansdowne. New York: Random House, 1932.

Johnson, Samuel, and Hester Lynch Piozzi. *The Letters of Samuel Johnson with Mrs. Thrale's Genuine Letters to Him.* Edited by R. W. Chapman. Oxford: Clarendon Press, 1952.

Johnson-Sirleaf, Ellen. *This Child Will Be Great: Memoir of a Remarkable Life by Africa's First Woman President.* New York: Harper, 2009.

Johnston, Jill. *Lesbian Nation: The Feminist Solution.* New York: Simon and Schuster, 1973.

Jolly, Margaretta. *In Love and Struggle: Letters in Contemporary Feminism.* New York: Columbia University Press, 2007.

Jorgensen, Christine. *Christine Jorgensen: A Personal Autobiography.* New York: P. S. Eriksson, 1967.

Joyce, James. *Ulysses.* New York: Modern Library, 1961.

Joyce, James, and Chester G. Anderson. *A Portrait of the Artist as a Young Man: Text, Criticism, and Notes.* New York: Viking Press, 1968.

Juana Inés de la Cruz, Sor. *A Sor Juana Anthology.* Translated by Alan S. Trueblood. Cambridge, Mass.: Harvard University Press, 1988.

Julian of Norwich. *The Shewings of Julian of Norwich.* Edited by Georgia Ronan Crampton. Kalamazoo, Mich.: Medieval Institute Publications, 1994.

Juska, Jane. *A Round-Heeled Woman: My Late-Life Adventures in Sex and Romance.* New York: Villard, 2003.

Kartini, Raden Adjeng. *Letters of a Javanese Princess.* Translated by Agnes Louise Symmers. New York: Norton, 1964.

Kaysen, Susanna. *Girl, Interrupted.* New York: Vintage Books, 1993.

Keller, Helen, with John Albert Macy and Annie Sullivan. *The Story of My Life.* New York: Doubleday, Page, 1903.

Kemal Atatürk. *A Speech Delivered by Mustafa Kemal Atatürk, 1927.* Istanbul: Ministry of Education Printing Plant, 1963.

Kemble, Frances Anne. *Journal of a Residence on a Georgian Plantation, 1838–1839.* Edited by John A. Scott. Athens: University of Georgia Press, 1984.

Kempe, Margery. *The Book of Margery Kempe.* Translated by B. A. Windeatt. London: Penguin, 1994.

Kempis, Thomas à. *Imitatio Christi.* Translated by Leo Sherley-Price. Harmondsworth, England: Penguin Books, 1952.

Khaldūn, Ibn. *At-Ta'rîf bi-Ibn Khaldûn wa-rihlatuh û charban wa-sharqan.* Edited by Muh.ammad Tâwît at.-T.anjî. Cairo: n.p., 1370; 1951.

Khouri, Norma. *Forbidden Love: A Harrowing True Story of Love and Revenge in Jordan.* London: Doubleday, 2003.

Kincaid, Jamaica. *The Autobiography of My Mother.* New York: Plume, 1997.

Kingsolver, Barbara, Steven L. Hopp, and Camille Kingsolver. *Animal, Vegetable, Miracle: A Year of Food Life.* New York: HarperCollins Publishers, 2007.

Kingston, Maxine Hong. *The Woman Warrior: Memoirs of a Girlhood among Ghosts.* New York: Vintage, 1976.

Kittredge, William. *Hole in the Sky: A Memoir.* New York: Knopf, 1992.

Kiyooka, Roy. *Mothertalk: Life Stories of Mary Kiyoshi Kiyooka.* Edmonton, Alberta.: NeWest Press, 1997.

Kleege, Georgina. *Blind Rage: Letters to Helen Keller.* Washington, D.C.: Gallaudet University Press, 2006.

Knapp, Carolyn. *Drinking: A Love Story.* New York: Dell, 1997.

Kollontai, Alexandra. *The Autobiography of a Sexually Emancipated Communist Woman.* Edited by Irving Fetscher. Translated by Salvator Attanasio. New York: Schocken, 1975.

Koolmatrie, Wanda. *My Own Sweet Time.* Broome, Australia: Magabala Books, 1994.

Krakauer, Jon. *Into the Wild.* New York: Anchor, 2007.

———. *Into Thin Air: A Personal Account of the Mount Everest Disaster.* New York: Villard, 1997.

Krog, Antjie. *Country of My Skull: Guilt, Sorrow, and the Limits of Forgiveness in the New South Africa.* New York: Times Books, 1999.

Kuhn, Annette. *Family Secrets: Acts of Memory and Imagination.* London: Verso, 1995.

Kuusisto, Stephen. *Planet of the Blind.* New York: Dell, 1998.

Labé, Louise. *Complete Poetry and Prose.* Translated by Annie Finch et al. Chicago: University of Chicago Press, 2006.

Labumore, Elsie Roughsey. *An Aboriginal Mother Tells of the Old and the New.* Edited by Paul Memmott and Robyn Horsman. Fitzroy, Victoria: McPhee Gribble, 1984.

Ladurie, Emmanuel LeRoy. *Montaillou: The Promised Land of Error.* New York: G. Braziller, 1978.

Lafayette, Madame de (Marie-Madeleine Pioche de La Vergne). *The Princess of Clèves.* Translated by Nancy Mitford. Harmondsworth, England: Penguin Books, 1978.

Langguth, Gerd. *Angela Merkel.* München: DTV Deutscher Taschenbuch, 2005.

Larcom, Lucy. *A New England Girlhood.* Boston: Corinth Books, 1961.

Latifah, Queen, and Karen Hunter. *Ladies First: Revelations of a Strong Woman.* New York: William Morrow, 1999.

La Vie en Rose. DVD. Directed by Olivier Dahan. HBO Home Video, November 13, 2007.

Laye, Camara. *The Dark Child.* Translated by James Kirkup. New York: Noonday Press, 1954.

Lee, Jarena. "Life and Religious Experience of Jarena Lee." In *Sisters of the Spirit,* ed. Andrews, 25–48.

Leiris, Michel. *Manhood: A Journey from Childhood Into the Fierce Order of Virility.* Translated by Richard Howard. New York: Grossman, 1963.

———. *Scraps.* Vol. 2 of *Rules of the Game.* Translated by Lydia Davis. Baltimore: Johns Hopkins University Press, 1997.

———. *Scratches.* Vol. 1 of *Rules of the Game.* Translated by Lydia Davis. Baltimore: Johns Hopkins University Press, 1997.

Leonard, Joanne. *Being in Pictures: An Intimate Photo Memoir.* Ann Arbor: University of Michigan Press, 2008.

Léry, Jean de. *History of a Voyage to the Land of Brazil, Otherwise Called America.* Translated by Janet Whatley. Berkeley: University of California Press, 1990.

Les Nuits Fauves (Savage Nights). Directed by Cyril Collard. Videorecording. New York: PolyGram Video, 1994.

Levi, Primo. *Survival in Auschwitz: The Nazi Assault on Humanity.* Translated by Stuart Woolf. New York: Collier Books, 1993.

Ligon, Glenn. *Some Changes.* Touring exhibition. Wexner Center for the Arts, The Ohio State University, Columbus, 26 January to 15 April 2007.

Lim, Shirley Geok-lin. *Among the White Moon Faces: An Asian-American Memoir of Homelands.* New York: Feminist Press, 1996.

Linton, Simi. *My Body Politic: A Memoir.* Ann Arbor: University of Michigan Press, 2006.

Lomas Garza, Carmen. *Pedacito de Mi Corazón.* Austin, Tex.: Laguna Gloria Art Museum, 1991.

Lorde, Audre. *A Burst of Light.* Toronto: Women's Press, 1988.

——. *The Cancer Journals.* Argyle, N.Y.: Spinsters, 1980.

——. *Zami: A New Spelling of My Name.* Trumansberg, N.Y.: Crossing Press, 1982.

Lowell, Robert. *Life Studies.* New York: Farrar, Straus, and Cudahy, 1959.

——. *Notebook 1967–68.* New York: Farrar, Straus and Giroux, 1969.

Lumumba. DVD. Directed by Raoul Peck. Zeitgeist, 2001.

Mairs, Nancy. *Voice Lessons: On Becoming a (Woman) Writer.* Boston: Beacon, 1997.

——. *Waist-High in the World: A Life among the Nondisabled.* Boston: Beacon, 1996.

Malcolm X, with Alex Haley. *The Autobiography of Malcolm X.* New York: Grove, 1965.

Malcolm X. Videorecording. Directed by Spike Lee. Burbank, Calif.: Warner Home Video, 1993.

Mandela, Nelson. *Long Walk to Freedom: The Autobiography of Nelson Mandela.* Boston: Little, Brown, 1994.

——. *No Easy Walk to Freedom: Articles, Speeches, and Trial Addresses.* London: Heinemann, 1973.

——. *The Struggle Is My Life.* New York: Pathfinder Press, 1986.

Mann, Thomas. Translated by H. T. Lowe-Porter. *Buddenbrooks: The Decline of a Family.* New York: Vintage, 1952.

Manrique, Jaime. *Eminent Maricones: Arenas, Lorca, Puig, and Me.* Living Out Series. Madison: University of Wisconsin Press, 1999.

Martineau, Harriet. *Harriet Martineau's Autobiography.* Edited by Maria Weston Chapman. Boston: James R. Osgood, 1877.

Mathabane, Mark. *Kaffir Boy: The True Story of a Black Youth's Coming of Age in Apartheid South Africa.* New York: Macmillan, 1986.

Maya Deren, Collected Experimental Films. Videorecording. Directed by Maya Deren. New York: Mystic Fire Video, 1986.

McBride, James. *The Color of Water: A Black Man's Tribute to His White Mother.* New York: Riverhead Books, 1996.

McCann, Richard. *Just a Boy: The True Story of a Stolen Childhood.* London: Ebury Press, 2005.

McCarthy, Mary. *How I Grew.* San Diego: Harcourt, Brace, Jovanovich, 1987.

———. *Memories of a Catholic Girlhood.* New York: Harcourt, Brace, 1957.

McCloskey, Deirdre N. *Crossing: A Memoir.* Chicago: University of Chicago Press, 1999.

McCourt, Frank. *Angela's Ashes: A Memoir.* New York: Scribner, 1996.

McCullough, David G. *John Adams.* New York: Simon and Schuster, 2001.

McMichael, James. *Four Good Things.* Boston: Houghton Mifflin, 1980.

McNamara, Robert S. *In Retrospect: The Tragedy and Lessons of Vietnam.* New York: Times Books, 1995.

Meggyesy, Dave. *Out of Their League.* Berkeley, Calif.: Ramparts Press, 1970.

Meir, Golda. *My Life.* New York: Putnam, 1975.

Menchú, Rigoberta. *I, Rigoberta Menchú: An Indian Woman in Guatemala.* Edited by Elisabeth Burgos-Debray. Translated by Ann Wright. London: Verso, 1984.

Merton, Thomas. *The Seven-Storey Mountain.* New York: Harcourt, Brace, 1948.

Mill, John Stuart. *Autobiography.* London: Longmans, Green, Reader, Dyer, 1873.

Miller, Nancy K. *Bequest and Betrayal: Memoirs of a Parent's Death.* New York: Oxford University Press, 1996.

Millet, Catherine. *The Sexual Life of Catherine M.* Translated by Adriana Hunter. New York: Grove Press, 2001.

The Miracle Worker. Videorecording. Directed by Arthur Penn. Culver City, Calif.: MGM/UA Home Video, 1992.

Moaveni, Azadeh. *Honeymoon in Tehran: Two Years of Love and Danger in Iran.* New York: Random House, 2009.

———. *Lipstick Jihad: A Memoir of Growing Up Iranian in America and American in Iran.* New York: Public Affairs, 2005.

Modjeska, Drusilla. *Poppy.* Sydney: Pan Macmillan, 1997.

Momaday, N. Scott. *House Made of Dawn.* New York: New American Library, 1969.

———. *The Names: A Memoir.* New York: Harper & Row, 1976.

Monette, Paul. *Becoming a Man: Half a Life Story.* New York: Harcourt, Brace, Jovanovich, 1992.

———. *Borrowed Time: An AIDS Memoir.* San Diego: Harcourt, Brace, 1998.

———. *Last Watch of the Night: Essays Too Personal and Otherwise.* New York: Harcourt Brace, 1994.

Montagu, Lady Mary Wortley. *The Letters and Works of Lady Mary Wortley Montagu.* Edited by Lord Wharncliffe. New York: AMS Press, 1970.

Montaigne, Michel de. *The Complete Essays of Montaigne.* Translated by Donald M. Frame. Stanford, Calif.: Stanford University Press, 1958.

———. *Les Essais.* 2nd ed. Paris: PUF, 1992.

Montéjo, Esteban. *The Autobiography of a Runaway Slave.* Edited by Miguel Barnet. Translated by Jocasta Innes. New York: Pantheon Books, 1968.

Moore, Thomas. *Care of the Soul: A Guide for Cultivating Depth and Sacredness in Everyday Life*. New York: HarperCollins, 1992.

Moraga, Cherríe. *Loving in the War Years: Lo que nunca pasó por sus labios*. Boston: South End Press, 1983.

Moraga, Cherríe, and Gloria Anzaldúa, eds. *This Bridge Called My Back: Writings by Radical Women of Color*. New York: Kitchen Table Press, 1983.

Morgan, Sally. *My Place*. Freemantle, Australia: Freemantle Arts Press, 1987.

Morris, Edmund. *Dutch: A Memoir of Ronald Reagan*. New York: Random House, 1999.

Mother Jones. *The Autobiography of Mother Jones*. Edited by Mary Field Parton. Chicago: Charles H. Kerr, 1925.

Muir, John. *The Story of My Boyhood and Youth*. Boston and New York: Houghton Mifflin, 1913.

Musil, Robert. *The Man without Qualities*. Translated by Eithne Wilkins. London: Secker & Warburg, 1953.

My Left Foot. Videorecording. Directed by Jim Sheridan. New York: HBO Video, 1990.

Nabokov, Vladimir Vladimirovich. *Lolita*. New York: Putnam, 1955.

———. *Speak, Memory: A Memoir*. Rev. ed. New York: Putnam, 1966.

Nafisi, Azar. *Reading Lolita in Tehran: A Memoir in Books*. New York: Random House, 2003.

———. *Things I've Been Silent About: Memories*. New York: Random House, 2008.

Neal, John. *Wandering Recollections of a Somewhat Busy Life: An Autobiography*. Boston: Roberts Brothers, 1869.

Nestle, Joan, Clare Howell, and Riki Anne Wilchins. *GenderQueer: Voices from Beyond the Sexual Binary*. Los Angeles: Alyson Books, 2002.

Newman, Cardinal John Henry. *Apologia Pro Vita Sua: Being a History of His Religious Opinions*. Edited by Martin J. Svaglic. Oxford: Clarendon Press, 1967.

Nietzsche, Friedrich. *On the Genealogy of Morals and Ecce Homo*. Translated and edited by Walter Kaufmann. New York: Vintage, 1967.

Nin, Anaïs. *Incest: From a Journal of Love: The Unexpurgated Diary of Anaïs Nin, 1932–1934*. New York: Harcourt Brace Jovanovich, 1992.

Norris, Kathleen. *Dakota: A Spiritual Geography*. Boston: Houghton Mifflin, 1993.

Novalis (Friedrich von Hardenberg). *Heinrich von Ofterdingen*. Leipzig: Hesse and Becker, 1903.

Nugent, Thomas. *Travels through Germany: Containing Observations on Customs, Manners, Religion, Government, Commerce, Arts, and Antiquities, with a Particular Account of the Courts of Mecklenburg in a Series of Letters to a Friend*. London: E. and C. Dilly, 1768.

Obama, Barack. *Dreams from My Father: A Story of Race and Inheritance*. New York: Times Books, 1995.

O'Beirne, Kathy. *Don't Ever Tell: Kathy's Story: A True Tale of a Childhood Destroyed by Neglect and Fear.* Edinburgh: Mainstream Publishing, 2006.

O'Brien, Tim. *The Things They Carried: A Work of Fiction.* Boston: Houghton Mifflin, 1990.

O'Casey, Sean. *I Knock at the Door: Swift Glances Back at Things That Made Me.* New York, Macmillan, 1950.

Olds, Sharon. *The Father.* New York: Knopf, 1992.

Ondaatje, Michael. *Running in the Family.* New York: Norton, 1982.

Out of Africa. Videorecording. Directed by Sydney Pollack. Universal City, Calif.: MCA Home Video, 1986.

Palin, Sarah. *Going Rogue: An American Life.* New York: HarperCollins, 2009.

Pamuk, Orhan. *Istanbul: Memories and the City.* Translated by Maureen Freely. New York: Knopf, 2005.

Pankejeff, Sergius. *The Wolf-Man. With the Case of the Wolf-Man, by Sigmund Freud.* Edited by Muriel Gardner. New York: Basic Books, 1971.

Parkman, Francis. *The California and Oregon Trail: Being Sketches of Prairie and Rocky Mountain Life.* New York: T. Y. Crowell, 1901.

Partnoy, Alicia. *The Little School: Tales of Disappearance & Survival in Argentina.* Translated by Lois Athey. Pittsburgh: Cleis Press, 1986.

Pascal, Blaise. *Pensées.* Translated by A. J. Krailsheimer. Harmondsworth: Penguin, 1966.

Pax, Salam. *The Clandestine Diary of an Ordinary Iraqi.* New York: Grove, 2003.

Pekar, Harvey, et al. *The Quitter.* New York: DC Comics, 2005.

Pelzer, David J. *A Child Called "It": An Abused Child's Journey from Victim to Victor.* Deerfield Beach, Fla.: Health Communications, 1995.

———. *The Lost Boy: A Foster Child's Search for the Love of a Family.* Deerfield Beach, Fla.: Health Communications, 1997.

———. *A Man Named Dave: A Story of Triumph and Forgiveness.* Electronic ed. New York: Dutton, 2004.

Pepys, Samuel. *Diary and Correspondence of Samuel Pepys, Esq.* 6 vols. London: Bickers and Son, 1875–79.

Perec, Georges. *W, Or the Memory of Childhood.* Translated by David Bellos. Boston: David R. Godine, 2003.

Performing the Border. Directed by Ursula Biemann. 1999. Switzerland/Mexico.

Persepolis. DVD. Directed by Marjane Satrapi and Vincent Paronnaud. Sony Pictures Classics, 2007.

Petrarch, Francis. "The Ascent of Mount Ventoux." In *Petrarch: A Humanist Among Princes. An Anthology of Petrarch's Letters and of Selections from His Other Works,* ed. and trans. David Thompson, 27–36. New York: Harper and Row, 1971.

The Pianist. Videorecording. Directed by Roman Polanski. Universal City, Calif.: Universal Pictures, 2003.

Pilkington, Doris. *Rabbit-Proof Fence: The True Story of One of the Greatest Escapes of All Time.* New York: Miramax Books, 2002.

Pilkington, Laetitia. *Memoirs of Mrs. Laetitia Pilkington, 1712–1750, Written by Herself.* London: George Routledge and Sons, 1928.

Piper, Adrian. *Cornered.* New York: New Museum of Contemporary Art, 1988.

Plato. *Apology of Socrates.* Translated by Michael C. Stokes. Warminster, England: Arris and Phillips, 1997.

Plutarch. *Plutarch: The Lives of the Noble Grecians and Romans, the Dryden Translation.* Chicago: Encyclopedia, 1990.

Polo, Marco. *The Travels of Marco Polo, the Venetian.* Translated by William Marsden. Edited by Thomas Wright. New York: AMS Press, 1968.

Pound, Ezra. *The Cantos of Ezra Pound.* London: Faber and Faber, 1954.

Price, Reynolds. *A Whole New Life.* New York: Atheneum, 1994.

Prince, Nancy. *A Narrative of the Life and Travels of Mrs. Nancy Prince.* 2nd ed. Boston: Nancy Prince, 1853.

Prosser, Jay. *Second Skins: The Body Narratives of Transsexuality.* Gender and Culture series. New York: Columbia University Press, 1998.

Proust, Marcel. *The Remembrance of Things Past.* 2 vols. Translated by C. K. Scott Moncrieff. New York: Random House, 1932–34.

Pruitt, Ida. *A Daughter of Han: The Autobiography of a Chinese Working Woman.* Stanford, Calif.: Stanford University Press, 1945.

Rabbit-Proof Fence. Videorecording. Directed by Phillip Noyce. Burbank, Calif.: Miramax Home Entertainment, 2003.

Ramirez, José. *Squint: My Journey with Leprosy.* Hattiesburg: University of Mississippi Press, 2009.

Reagan, Nancy. *My Turn: The Memoirs of Nancy Reagan.* New York: Random House, 1989.

Reichl, Ruth. *Comfort Me with Apples: More Adventures at the Table.* New York: Random House, 2002.

———. *Garlic and Sapphires: The Secret Life of a Critic in Disguise.* New York: Penguin Press, 2005.

———. *Not Becoming My Mother: And Other Things She Taught Me along the Way.* New York: Penguin, 2009.

———. *Tender at the Bone: Growing up at the Table.* New York: Broadway Books, 1999.

Rescue Dawn. Videorecording. Directed by Steve Marlton. Beverly Hills, Calif.: 20th Century Fox Home Entertainment, 2007.

Rich, Adrienne. *Diving into the Wreck: Poems 1971–72.* New York: Norton, 1973.

Richardson, Laurel. *Fields of Play: Constructing an Academic Life.* New Brunswick, N.J.: Rutgers University Press, 1997.

Riis, Jacob. *The Making of an American.* New York: Macmillan, 1901.

Rilke, Rainer Maria. *Duino Elegies.* Translated by David Young. New York: Norton, 1978.

———. *The Notebooks of Malte Laurids Brigge.* Translated by Stephen Mitchell. New York: Limited Editions Club, 1987

Ringgold, Faith. *The Change Series: Faith Ringgold's 100-Pound Weight-Loss Quilt.* New York: Bernice Steinbaum Gallery, 1987.

———. *Dancing at the Louvre: Faith Ringgold's French Collection and Other Story Quilts.* Berkeley: University of California Press, 1998.

Robinson, Mary. *Perdita: The Memoirs of Mary Robinson.* London: Chester Springs Peter Owen, 1994 (1895).

Rodman, Dennis. *Bad as I Wanna Be.* New York: Delacorte Press, 1996.

Rodriguez, Richard. *Hunger of Memory: The Education of Richard Rodriguez, an Autobiography.* Boston: D. R. Godine, 1981.

Rogers, Annie G. *A Shining Affliction: A Story of Harm and Healing in Psychotherapy.* New York: Viking, 1995.

Roiphe, Anne. *Fruitful: Living the Contradictions: A Memoir of Modern Motherhood.* Boston: Houghton Mifflin, 1996.

Rosa Luxemburg (Die Geduld der Rosa Luxemburg). Videorecording. Directed by Margarethe von Trotta. New Yorker Video, 1986.

Rose, Gillian. *Love's Work: A Reckoning with Life.* London: Chatto & Windus, 1995.

Rosenthal, Rachel. "My Brazil." In *Rachel's Brain and Other Storms: Rachel Rosenthal: Performance Texts,* ed. Una Chaudhuri, 43–54. London and New York: Continuum International, 2001.

Roth, Philip. *Exit Ghost.* New York: Vintage International, 2008.

Rousseau, Jean-Jacques. *Confessions.* Translated by Angela Scholar. New York: Oxford University Press, 2000.

Rowlandson, Mary. "A True History of the Captivity and Restoration of Mrs. Mary Rowlandson," ed. Amy Schrager Lang. In *Journeys in New Worlds,* ed. William L. Andrews et al., 27–65. Madison: University of Wisconsin Press, 1990.

Rutgers University Department of History. *The Rutgers Oral History Archives of World War II, the Korean War, the Vietnam War and the Cold War.* Accessed on 13 February 2009. http://oralhistory.rutgers.edu/

Ryan, Michael. *Secret Life: An Autobiography.* New York: Pantheon Books, 1995.

Saadawi, Nawal. *A Daughter of Isis: The Autobiography of Nawal El Saadawi.* Translated by Sherif Hetata. London: Zed Books, 1999.

———. *Memoirs from the Women's Prison.* Translated by Marilyn Booth. London: Women's Press, 1986.

———. *Woman at Point Zero.* Translated by Sherif Hetata. London: Zed Books, 1983.

Sage, Lorna. *Bad Blood.* New York: Harper Perennial, 2003.

Said, Edward W. *Out of Place: A Memoir.* New York: Knopf, 1999.

Sales, Saint Francis de. *An Introduction to a Devout Life.* Ilkley, England: Scolar Press, 1976.

Salinger, J. D. *The Catcher in the Rye.* Boston: Little, Brown, 1951.

Sand, George (Aurore Dudevant Dupin). *Story of My Life: The Autobiography of George Sand.* Edited by Thelma Jurgrau. Albany: State University Press of New York, 1991.

Sangtin Writers Collective and Richa Nagar. *Playing with Fire: Feminist Thought and Activism through Seven Lives in India.* Minneapolis: University of Minnesota Press, 2006.

Santiago, Esmeralda. *When I Was Puerto Rican.* New York: Vintage, 1993.

Sappho. *Poems and Fragments.* Translated by Mary Barnard. Berkeley: University of California Press, 1958.

Sarrazin, Albertine. "Journal de Prison, 1959." In *Le Passe-Peine: 1949–1967.* 102–68. Paris: Julliard, 1976.

Sarton, May. *At Eighty-Two: A Journal.* New York: Norton, 1996.

———. *Journal of a Solitude.* New York: Norton, 1973.

Satrapi, Marjane. *Persepolis.* Translated by Mattias Ripa. New York: Pantheon Books, 2004.

———. *Persepolis 2: The Story of a Return.* Translated by Mattias Ripa. New York: Pantheon Books, 2004.

Savage, Dan. *The Commitment: Love, Sex, Marriage, and My Family.* New York: Dutton, 2005.

———. *The Kid: What Happened after My Boyfriend and I Decided to Go Get Pregnant: An Adoption Story.* New York: Plume, 2000.

Sebald, W. G. *Austerlitz.* Translated by Anthea Bell. New York: Random House, 2001.

———. *The Emigrants.* Translated by Michael Hulse. New York: New Directions, 1997.

Sebold, Alice. *Lucky.* New York: Scribner, 1999.

Sedaris, David. *Naked.* Boston: Little, Brown, 1997.

Serano, Julia. *Whipping Girl: A Transsexual Woman on Sexism and the Scapegoating of Femininity.* Emeryville, Calif.: Seal Press, 2007.

Sévigné, Marie de, Rabutin Chantal. *Letters of Madame de Sévigné to Her Daughter and Her Friends.* Translated by Leonard Tancock. Harmondsworth: Penguin, 1982.

Sexton, Anne. *Live or Die.* Boston: Houghton Mifflin, 1966.

Shahnawaz, Jahan Ara. *Father and Daughter: A Political Autobiography.* Lahore: Nigarishat, 1971.

Shakur, Assata. *Assata: An Autobiography.* Westport, Conn.: L. Hill, 1987.

Sheff, David. *Beautiful Boy: A Father's Journey through His Son's Addiction.* Boston: Houghton Mifflin, 2008.

Sheff, Nic. *Tweak: Growing Up on Methamphetamines.* New York: Atheneum Books for Young Readers, 2007.

Sherman, Cindy. *Cindy Sherman: Retrospective.* New York: Thames and Hudson, 1997.

Sigourney, Lydia H. *Letters of Life.* New York: D. Appleton and Co., 1866.

Silko, Leslie Marmon. *Storyteller.* New York: Seaver Books/Grove Press, 1981.

Silverlake Life: The View from Here. Videorecording. Directed by Tom Joslin. Zeitgeist Films, 1993.

Simpson, O. J., Dominick Dunne, and Pablo F. Fenjves. *If I Did It: Confessions of the Killer.* New York: Beaufort Books, 2006.

Slater, Lauren. *Lying: A Metaphorical Memoir.* New York: Random House, 2000.

Smart-Grosvenor, Vertamae. *Vibration Cooking; or, The Travel Notes of a Geechee Girl.* New York: Ballantine, 1992.

Smith, John. *The Complete Works of Captain John Smith (1580–1631).* 3 vols. Edited by Philip L. Barbour. Chapel Hill: University of North Carolina Press, 1986.

Sosa, Sammy, and Marcos Bretón. *Sammy Sosa: An Autobiography.* New York: Grand Central Publishing, 2000.

Souad. *Burned Alive: A Victim of the Law of Men.* Translated by Judith Armbruster. New York: Warner Books, 2004.

Soyinka, Wole. *Aké: The Years of a Childhood.* New York: Random House, 1981.

Spence, Jo. *Putting Myself in the Picture: A Political, Personal, and Photographic Autobiography.* London: Camden Press, 1986.

Spiegelman, Art. *Breakdowns: Portrait of the Artist as a Young %@&*!* New York: Pantheon, 2008.

———. *Maus I: A Survivor's Tale: My Father Bleeds History.* New York: Pantheon Books, 1986.

———. *Maus II: A Survivor's Tale: And Here My Troubles Began.* New York: Pantheon Books, 1991.

Staël, Madame de. *Corinne, or Italy.* Translated and edited by Sylvia Raphael. New York: Oxford University Press, 1998.

Stedman, John Gabriel. *Narrative of a Five Years' Expedition against the Revolted Negroes of Surinam: Transcribed for the First Time from the Original 1790 Manuscript.* Edited by Richard Price and Sally Price. Baltimore: Johns Hopkins University Press, 1988.

Steedman, Carolyn Kay. *Landscape for a Good Woman.* New Brunswick, N.J.: Rutgers University Press, 1986.

Stein, Gertrude. *The Autobiography of Alice B. Toklas.* New York: Harcourt Brace, 1933.

———. *Everybody's Autobiography.* New York: Random House, 1937.

Stendhal (Henri Brulard). *The Life of Henry Brulard.* Translated by Jean Stewart and B. C. J. G. Knight. New York: Noonday Press, 1958.

Stevens, Wallace. *Collected Poems.* New York: Knopf, 1954.

Stewart, Kathleen. *The Space by the Side of the Road.* Princeton, N.J.: Princeton University Press, 1996.

Stewart, Rory. *The Places in Between.* Orlando, Fla.: Harcourt, 2006.

Strachey, Lytton. *Eminent Victorians: Cardinal Manning, Dr. Arnold, Florence Nightingale, General Gordon.* New York: Modern Library, 1933.

Strindberg, August. *The Son of a Servant.* Translated by Claud Field. New York: Putnam's Sons, 1913.

Styron, William. *Darkness Visible: A Memoir of Madness.* New York: Random House, 1990.

Sui Sin Far. "Leaves from the Mental Portfolio of an Eurasian." *The Independent,* 21 January 1909, 125–32.

———. "Sui Sin Far, the Half Chinese Writer, Tells of Her Career." *Boston Globe,* 5 May 1912 (morning edition), 31.126.

Suleri, Sara. *Meatless Days.* Chicago: University of Chicago Press, 1991.

Sultaan, Abida. *Memoirs of a Rebel Princess.* Karachi: Oxford University Press, 2004.

Super Size Me. Videorecording. Directed by Morgan Spurlock. Culver City, Calif.: Columbia TriStar Home Entertainment, 2004.

Swofford, Anthony. *Jarhead: A Marine's Chronicle of the Gulf War and Other Battles.* New York: Scribner, 2003.

Szpilman, Władysław, and Wilm Hosenfeld. *The Pianist: The Extraordinary Story of One Man's Survival in Warsaw, 1939–1945.* New York: Picador USA, 1999.

Tarnation. Videorecording. Directed by Jonathan Caouette et al. Wellspring Media, 2003.

Taylor, Sheila Ortiz, and Sandra Ortiz Taylor. *Imaginary Parents: A Family Autobiography.* Albuquerque: University of New Mexico Press, 1996.

Teresa of Avila, Saint. *Interior Castle.* Translated and edited by E. Allison Peers. Garden City, N.Y.: Doubleday, 1961.

———. *The Life of Teresa of Jesus: The Autobiography of St. Teresa of Avila.* Translated by E. Allison Peers. Garden City, N.Y.: Doubleday, 1960.

Terkel, Studs. *Working: People Talk about What They Do All Day and How They Feel about What They Do.* New York: New Press, 1974.

Thigpen, Corbett H., and Hervey M. Cleckley. *The Three Faces of Eve.* New York: McGraw-Hill, 1957.

Thiong'o, Ngũgĩ wa. *Detained: A Writer's Prison Diary.* London: Heinemann, 1981.

Thoreau, Henry David. *Walden.* Edited by J. Lyndon Shanley. Princeton, N.J.: Princeton University Press, 1971.

Thrale, Hester. *Thraliana; The Diary of Mrs. Hester Lynch Thrale (Later Mrs. Piozzi), 1776–1809.* 2 vols. Edited by Katharine C. Balderston. Oxford: Clarendon Press, 1942.

The Three Faces of Eve. Videorecording. Directed by Nunnally Johnson. 20th Century Fox Home Entertainment, 2004.

Time Like Zeros. Videorecording. Directed by Carol Jacobsen. Forthcoming, 2010.

Timerman, Jacobo. *Prisoner without a Name, Cell without a Number.* Translated by Toby Talbot. New York: Knopf, 1981.

Tolle, Eckhart. *Practicing the Power of Now: Essential Teachings, Meditations, and Exercises from* The Power of Now. New York: New World Library 2001.

Trethewey, Natasha D. *Native Guard.* Boston: Houghton Mifflin, 2006.

Trollope, Frances. *A Visit to Italy.* London: R. Bentley, 1842.

Troyano, Alina, et al. *I, Carmelita Tropicana: Performing between Cultures.* Boston: Beacon Press, 2000.

Twain, Mark. *Life on the Mississippi.* New York: Penguin, 1984.

Twitch and Shout. Videorecording. Directed by Laurel Chiten. Harriman, N.Y.: New Day Films, 1994.

Umutesi, Marie Béatrice. *Surviving the Slaughter: The Ordeal of a Rwandan Refugee in Zaire.* Women in Africa and the Diaspora. Madison: University of Wisconsin Press, 2004.

Urban School of San Francisco. *Telling Their Stories: Oral History Archives Project.* www.tellingstories.org

Valéry, Paul. *La Jeune Parque* (The Young Fate). Translated by Alistair Elliot. Chester Springs, Penn.: Dufour Editions, 1997.

Varnhagen, Rahel. "Selected Letters," trans. Katharine R. Goodman. In *Bitter Healing: German Women Writers from 1700 to 1830,* ed. Jeannine Blackwell and Susanne Zantop, 408–16. Lincoln: University of Nebraska Press, 1990.

Verghese, Abraham. *My Own Country: A Doctor's Story of a Town and Its People in the Age of AIDS.* New York: Simon and Schuster, 1994.

Vico, Giambattista. *Autobiography of Giambattista Vico.* Translated by Max Harold Fisch and Thomas Goddard Bergin. Ithaca, N.Y.: Cornell University Press, 1944.

Vizenor, Gerald. "Crows Written on the Poplars: Autocritical Autobiographies." In *I Tell You Now: Essays by Native American Writers,* ed. Brian Swann and Arnold Krupat, 99–109. Lincoln: University of Nebraska Press, 1987.

Walker, Rebecca. *Black, White, and Jewish: Autobiography of a Shifting Self.* New York: Riverhead Books, 2001.

Warner-Vieyra, Myriam. *Juletane.* Translated by Betty Wilson. London: Heinemann, 1987.

Washington, Booker T. *Up from Slavery.* New York: Doubleday, 1998.

Wexler, Alice. *Mapping Fate: A Memoir of Family, Risk, and Genetic Research.* Berkeley: University of California Press, 1996.

Whitman, Walt. "Song of Myself." In *Leaves of Grass.* New York: Heritage Press, 1950.

———. *Specimen Days.* Vol. 1 of *Prose Works, 1892.* Edited by Floyd Stovall. New York: New York University Press, 1963.

Wideman, John Edgar. *Brothers and Keepers.* New York: Holt, Rinehart and Winston, 1984.

Wiesel, Elie. *Night.* Translated by Stella Rodway. New York: Hill and Wang, 1960.

Wilke, Hannah. *Intra-Venus.* Photography. New York: Ronald Feldman Gallery, 1994.

Wilkomirski, Binjamin. *Fragments: Memories of a Wartime Childhood.* Translated by Carol Brown Janeway. New York: Schocken Books, 1996.

Williams, Donna. *Nobody Nowhere: The Extraordinary Autobiography of an Autistic.* New York: Times Books, 1992.

———. *Somebody Somewhere: Breaking Free from the World of Autism.* New York: Times Books, 1994.

Williams, Gregory Howard. *Life on the Color Line: The True Story of a White Boy Who Discovered He Was Black.* New York: Dutton, 1995.

Williams, Terry Tempest. *Refuge: An Unnatural History of Family and Place.* New York: Vintage Books, 1992.

Wojnarowicz, David. *Close to the Knives: A Memoir of Disintegration.* New York: Vintage Books, 1991.

Wolf, Christa. *Patterns of Childhood.* Translated by Ursula Molinaro and Hedwig Rappolt. New York: Farrar, Straus and Giroux, 1980.

Wolfe, Thomas. *Look Homeward, Angel: A Story of the Buried Life.* New York: Scribner, 1957.

Woodman, Francesca. *Francesca Woodman: Photographic Work.* Wellesley, Mass.: Wellesley College Museum, 1986.

Woodruff, Lee, and Bob Woodruff. *In an Instant: A Family's Journey of Love and Healing.* New York: Random House, 2008.

Woolf, Virginia. "A Sketch of the Past." In *Moments of Being,* ed. Jeanne Schulkind. 2nd ed. New York: Harcourt Brace, 1985.

Woolman, John. *The Journal and Major Essays of John Woolman.* Edited by Phillips P. Moulton. New York: Oxford University Press, 1971.

Wordsworth, Dorothy. *Journals of Dorothy Wordsworth.* 2 vols. Edited by Ernest De Selincourt. London: Macmillan, 1941.

Wordsworth, William. *The Prelude; or, Growth of a Poet's Mind.* Edited by Ernest De Selincourt. Oxford: Clarendon Press, 1959.

Wright, Richard. *Black Boy (American Hunger): A Record of Childhood and Youth.* Restored ed. New York: Harper Collins, 1993.

Wurtzel, Elizabeth. *Prozac Nation: Young and Depressed in America.* Boston: Houghton Mifflin, 1994.

Yale University Library. Fortunoff Video Archive for Holocaust Testimonies. 2005. www.library.yale.edu/testimonies/

Yeats, W. B. *Autobiographies: Reveries over Childhood and Youth and the Trembling of the Veil.* New York: Macmillan, 1927.

———. *A Vision.* London: Macmillan, 1937.

Zitkala-Ša. "Impressions of an Indian Childhood." In *Classic American Autobiographies,* ed. William L. Andrews, 414–32. New York: Mentor, 1992.

Secondary Works

Abbott, H. Porter. "The Evolutionary Origins of the Storied Mind: Modeling the Prehistory of Narrative Consciousness and Its Discontents." *Narrative* 8.3 (October 2000): 247–56.

Adak, Hülya. "National Myths and Self-Na(rra)Tions: Mustafa Kemal's *Nütük,* and Halide Edib's *Memoirs* and the Turkish Ordeal." *South Atlantic Quarterly* 102.2–3 (2003): 509–27.

Adams, Lorraine. "Almost Famous: The Rise of the 'Nobody Memoir.'" *Washington Post,* 10 April 2002.

Adams, Timothy Dow. "Borderline Personality: Autobiography and Documentary in Susan Kaysen's *Girl, Interrupted.*" *Life Writing* 2.2 (2005): 103–21.

———. *Light Writing and Life Writing: Photography in Autobiography.* Chapel Hill: University of North Carolina Press, 2000.

———. *Telling Lies in Modern American Autobiography.* Chapel Hill: University of North Carolina Press, 2000.

Addley, Esther. "Author Accused of Literary Fraud Says: 'I Am Not a Liar. And I Am Not Running Any More.'" *Guardian* 23 September 2006.

Alcoff, Linda Martín, and Laura Gray-Rosendale. "Survivor Discourse." In *Getting a Life,* ed. Smith and Watson, 198–225.

Althusser, Louis. *Essays on Ideology.* London: Verso, 1984.

Andrews, William L. "African-American Autobiography Criticism: Retrospect and Prospect." In *American Autobiography,* ed. Eakin, 195–215.

———. *To Tell a Free Story: The First Century of Afro-American Autobiography, 1760–1865.* Urbana: University of Illinois Press, 1986.

———, ed. *Sisters of the Spirit: Three Black Women's Autobiographies of the Nineteenth Century.* Bloomington: Indiana University Press, 1986.

Andrews, William L., and Regina E. Mason, eds. *Life of William Grimes, the Runaway Slave.* New York: Oxford University Press, 2008.

Appadurai, Arjun. "Disjuncture and Difference in the Global Cultural Economy." In *Colonial Discourse and Post-Colonial Theory: A Reader,* ed. Patrick Williams and Laura Chrisman, 324–39. New York: Columbia University Press, 1994.

Backscheider, Paula R. *Reflections on Biography.* Oxford: Oxford University Press, 2001.

Baena, Rosalia. "Gastro-Graphy: Food as Metaphor in Fred Wah's *Diamond Grill* and Austin Clarke's *Pig Tails 'n Breadfruit.*" *Canadian Ethnic Studies* 38.1 (Spring 2006): 105–16.

Baepler, Paul, ed. "Introduction." In *White Slaves, African Masters: An Anthology of American Barbary Captivity Narratives.* Chicago: University of Chicago Press, 1999.

Bakhtin, M. M. *The Dialogic Imagination: Four Essays.* Edited by Michael Holquist. Translated by Caryl Emerson and Michael Holquist. Austin: University of Texas Press, 1981.

Bal, Mieke. "Autotopography: Louise Bourgeois as Builder." In *Interfaces,* ed. Smith and Watson, 163–85.

Barbour, John D. *The Value of Solitude: The Ethics and Spirituality of Aloneness in Autobiography.* Charlottesville: University of Virginia Press, 2004.

Barrett, Lindon. *Blackness and Value: Seeing Double.* New York: Cambridge University Press, 1999.

Bartkowski, Frances. *Travelers, Immigrants, Inmates: Essays in Estrangement.* Minneapolis: University of Minnesota Press, 1995.

Bataille, Gretchen, and Kathleen Mullen Sands. *American Indian Women Telling Their Lives.* Lincoln: University of Nebraska Press, 1984.

Bauman, H-Dirksen L. *Open Your Eyes: Deaf Studies Talking.* Minneapolis: University of Minnesota Press, 2008.

———. "'Voicing' Deaf Identity: Through the 'I's and Ears of an Other." In *Getting a Life,* ed. Smith and Watson, 47–62.

Beard, Laura J. *Acts of Narrative Resistance: Women's Autobiographical Writings in the Americas.* Charlottesville and London: University of Virginia Press, 2009.

Beaujour, Michel. *Poetics of the Literary Self-Portrait.* Translated by Yara Milos. New York: New York University Press, 1991.

Belsey, Catherine. "Constructing the Subject: Deconstructing the Text." In *Feminisms: An Anthology of Literary Theory and Criticism,* ed. Robyn R. Warhol and Diane Price Herndl, 657–73. Revised ed. New Brunswick, N.J.: Rutgers University Press, 1997.

Benjamin, Jessica. "A Desire of One's Own: Psychoanalytic Feminism and Intersubjective Space." In *Feminist Studies/Critical Studies,* ed. Teresa de Lauretis, 78–101. London: Macmillan, 1988.

Benstock, Shari. "Authorizing the Autobiographical." In *The Private Self: Theory and Practice of Women's Autobiographical Writings,* ed. Benstock, 10–33. Chapel Hill: University of North Carolina Press, 1988.

Bergland, Betty. "Postmodernism and the Autobiographical Subject: Reconstructing the 'Other.'" In *Autobiography and Postmodernism,* ed. Kathleen Ashley, Leigh Gilmore, and Gerald Peters, 130–66. Amherst: University of Massachusetts Press, 1994.

Besemeres, Mary, and Anna Wierzbicka. *Translating Lives: Living with Two Languages and Cultures.* St. Lucia: University of Queensland Press, 2007.

Beverley, John. "The Margin at the Center: On 'Testimonio' (Testimonial Narrative)." In *De/Colonizing the Subject,* ed. Smith and Watson, 91–114.

Bhabha, Homi K. "Introduction: The Locations of Culture." In *The Location of Culture.* London: Routledge, 1994.

Biography. Special Issue on the Biopic. *Biography* 23.1 (Winter 2000).

Boardman, Kathleen, and Gioia Woods. *Western Subjects: Autobiographical Writing in the North American West.* Salt Lake City: University of Utah Press, 2004.

Boelhower, William. "The Making of Ethnic Autobiography in the United States." In *American Autobiography,* ed. Eakin, 123–41.

Boellstorff, Tom. *Coming of Age in Second Life: An Anthropologist Explores the Virtually Human.* Princeton, N.J.: Princeton University Press, 2008.

Bongie, Chris. *Exotic Memories: Literature, Colonialism, and the Fin de Siècle.* Stanford, Calif.: Stanford University Press, 1991.

Bottrall, Margaret. *Every Man a Phoenix: Studies in Seventeenth-Century Autobiography.* Freeport, N.Y.: Books for Libraries Press, 1972.

Bouldrey, Brian. *The Autobiography Box: A Step-by-Step Kit for Examining the Life Worth Living.* San Francisco: Chronicle Books, 2000.

Boustany, Nora. "Judging the Mullahs: The Iranian Human Rights Activist Who Won the Nobel Peace Prize Tells Her Inspiring Life Story." *Washington Post* 18 June 2006.

Bowring, Richard. "The Female Hand in Heian Japan: A First Reading." In *The Female Autograph,* ed. Domna C. Stanton, 55–62. New York: New York Literary Forum, 1984.

Boynton, Victoria, and Jo Malin, eds. *Encyclopedia of Women's Autobiography.* 2 vols. Westport, Conn.: Greenwood Press, 2005.

Braxton, Joanne. *Black Women Writing Autobiography: A Tradition within a Tradition.* Philadelphia: Temple University Press, 1989.

Braziel, Jana Evans. "Alterbiographic Transmutations of Genre in Jamaica Kincaid's 'Biography of a Dress' and *Autobiography of My Mother.*" *a/b: Auto/Biography Studies* 18.1 (Summer 2003): 85–104.

Brett, Guy. *Mona Hatoum.* Interview by Michael Archer; essays by Guy Brett and Catherine De Zegher. London: Phaidon Press, 1997.

Brewster, Anne. *Reading Aboriginal Women's Autobiography.* South Melbourne: Sydney University Press, 1996.

Brockmeier, Jens. "Autobiographical Time." *Narrative Inquiry* 10.1 (2000): 51–73.

Brodkey, Linda. "Writing on the Bias." *College English* 56, no. 5 (September 1994): 524–48.

Brodzki, Bella. *Can These Bones Live? Translation, Survival, and Cultural Memory.* Stanford, Calif.: Stanford University Press, 2007.

———. "Trauma and Transgression." In *Teaching the Representation of the Holocaust,* ed. Marianne Hirsch and Irene Kacandes, 123–48. New York: Modern Language Association, 2004.

Brodzki, Bella, and Celeste Schenck, eds. *Life Lines: Theorizing Women's Autobiography.* Ithaca, N.Y.: Cornell University Press, 1988.

Brophy, Sarah. *Witnessing AIDS: Writing, Testimony and the Work of Mourning.* Cultural Spaces. Toronto: University of Toronto Press, 2004.

Broughton, Trev Lynn. *Men of Letters, Writing Lives: Masculinity and Literary Auto/Biography in the Late-Victorian Period.* New York: Routledge, 1999.

Brueggemann, Brenda. *Deaf Subjects: Between Identities and Places.* New York: New York University Press, 2009.

Bruner, Jerome. "Life as Narrative." *Social Research* 54 (Spring 1987): 11–32.

Bruss, Elizabeth. *Autobiographical Acts: The Changing Situation of a Literary Genre*. Baltimore: Johns Hopkins University Press, 1976.

———. "Eye for I: Autobiography in Film." In *Autobiography*, ed. Olney, 296–320.

Buell, Lawrence. "Autobiography in the American Renaissance." In *American Autobiography*, ed. Eakin, 47–69.

———. *The Environmental Imagination: Thoreau, Nature Writing, and the Formation of America*. Cambridge, Mass.: Harvard University Press, 1995.

Bunkers, Suzanne. "Midwestern Diaries and Journals: What Women Were (Not) Saying in the Late 1800s." In *Studies in Autobiography*, ed. James Olney, 190–210. New York: Oxford University Press, 1988.

Bunkers, Suzanne, and Cynthia A. Huff, eds. *Inscribing the Daily: Critical Essays on Women's Diaries*. Amherst: University of Massachusetts Press, 1996.

Burr, Anna Robeson Brown. *The Autobiography: A Critical and Comparative Study*. Boston: Houghton Mifflin, 1909.

Burt, Raymond. "The Bildungsroman." In *Encyclopedia of Life Writing: Autobiographical and Biographical forms*, vol. 1, ed. Margaretta Jolly, 105. London: Fitzroy Dearborn, 2001.

Buss, Helen M. *Mapping Ourselves: Canadian Women's Autobiography in English*. Montreal: McGill-Queen's University Press, 1993.

Butler, Judith. *Bodies That Matter: On the Discursive Limits of "Sex."* New York: Routledge, 1993.

———. *Gender Trouble: Feminism and the Subversion of Identity*. New York: Routledge, 1990.

———. *Giving an Account of Oneself*. Bronx, N.Y.: Fordham University Press, 2005.

Canby, Peter. "The Truth about Rigoberta Menchú." *New York Review of Books*, 8 April 1999, 28–33.

Carretta, Vincent. "Olaudah Equiano or Gustavus Vassa? New Light on an Eighteenth-Century Question of Identity." *Slavery and Abolition* 20.3 (December 1999): 96–105.

Caruth, Cathy, ed. *Trauma: Explorations in Memory*. Baltimore: Johns Hopkins University Press, 1995.

Catan, Thomas. "Online Anorexia Sites Shut Down Amid Claims They Glorify Starvation." November 22, 2007. *TimesOnline*, 22 November 2007. Accessed on 20 January 2009. http://www.timesonline.co.uk/tol/life_and_style/health/article2916356.ece

Cavarero, Adriana. *Relating Narratives: Storytelling and Selfhood*. New York: Routledge, 2000.

Certeau, Michel de. *The Practice of Everyday Life*. Translated by Steven Rendall. Berkeley: University of California Press, 1984.

Chaloupka, William. "(For)Getting a Life: Testimony, Identity, and Power." In *Getting a Life*, ed. Smith and Watson, 369–92.

Chambers, Ross. *Facing It: AIDS Diaries and the Death of the Author.* Ann Arbor: University of Michigan Press, 1998.

———. *Untimely Interventions: AIDS Writing, Testimonial, and the Rhetoric of Haunting.* Ann Arbor: University of Michigan Press, 2004.

Chaney, Michael A. *Fugitive Vision: Slave Image and Black Identity in Antebellum Narrative.* Bloomington: Indiana University Press, 2008.

Chard, Chloe. *Pleasure and Guilt on the Grand Tour: Travel Writing and Imaginative Geography, 1600–1830.* Manchester, England: Manchester University Press, 1999.

Charon, Rita. *Narrative Medicine: Honoring the Stories of Illness.* New York: Oxford University Press, 2006.

Chester, Suzanne. "Writing the Subject: Exoticism/Eroticism in Marguerite Duras's *The Lover* and *The Sea Wall.*" In *De/Colonizing the Subject,* ed. Smith and Watson, 436–57.

Chodorow, Nancy. *The Reproduction of Mothering: Psychoanalysis and the Sociology of Gender.* Berkeley, Calif.: University of California Press, 1978.

Chow, Rey. *Ethics after Idealism: Theory, Culture, Ethnicity, Reading.* Bloomington: Indiana University Press, 1998.

Chute, Hillary. "The Texture of Retracing in Marjane Satrapi's *Persepolis.*" *WSQ: Women's Studies Quarterly* 36.1–2 (Spring/Summer 2008): 92–110.

Chute, Hillary L., and Marianne DeKoven. "Introduction: Graphic Narrative." *Modern Fiction Studies* 52.4 (Winter 2006): 767–82.

Coe, Richard. *When the Grass Was Taller: Autobiography and the Experience of Childhood.* New Haven, Conn.: Yale University Press, 1984.

Colie, Rosalie L. *Paradoxia Epidemica: The Renaissance Tradition of Paradox.* Princeton, N.J.: Princeton University Press, 1966.

Cook, Kay K. "Medical Identities: My DNA/Myself." In *Getting a Life,* ed. Smith and Watson, 63–88.

Coullie, Judith Lütge, Stephan Meyer, Thengani H. Ngwenya, and Thomas Olver, ed. *Selves in Question: Interviews on Southern African Auto/Biography.* Honolulu: University of Hawai'i Press, 2006.

Couser, G. Thomas. *Altered Egos: Authority in American Autobiography.* New York: Oxford University Press, 1989.

———. "Black Elk Speaks with Forked Tongue." In *Studies in Autobiography,* ed. James Olney, 73–88. Oxford: Oxford University Press, 1988.

———. "Genre Matters." *Life Writing* 2.2 (2005): 123–40.

———. "Introduction: The Some Body Memoir." In *Signifying Bodies: Disability in Contemporary Memoir.* Ann Arbor: University of Michigan Press, 2009.

———. "Making, Taking, and Faking Lives: The Ethics of Collaborative Autobiography." Special issue. *Style on Literary Ethics* (Summer 1998): 334–50.

———. Personal correspondence with Julia Watson, June 20, 2000.

———. *Recovering Bodies: Illness, Disability, and Life Writing*. Madison: University of Wisconsin Press, 1997.

———. *Signifying Bodies: Disability in Contemporary Life Writing*. Ann Arbor: University of Michigan Press, 2009.

———. "Undoing Hardship: Life Writing and Disability Law." *Narrative* 15.1 (2007): 71–84.

———. *Vulnerable Subjects: Ethics and Life Writing*. Ithaca, N.Y.: Cornell University Press, 2004.

Cox, James. *Recovering Literature's Lost Ground: Essays in American Autobiography*. Baton Rouge: Louisiana State University Press, 1989.

Craig, Terrence L. *The Missionary Lives: A Study in Canadian Missionary Biography and Autobiography*. New York: Brill, 1997.

Cubilié, Anne. *Women Witnessing Terror: Testimony and the Cultural Politics of Human Rights*. New York: Fordham University Press, 2005.

Culley, Margo, ed. "Introduction." In *A Day at a Time: Diary Literature of American Women from 1764 to the Present*. New York: Feminist Press, 1985.

Curtis, Bryan. "Capote at the Bat." *New York Times Play Magazine*, November 2007, 34, 36.

Dalziell, Rosamund. *Shameful Autobiographies: Shame in Contemporary Australian Autobiographies and Culture*. Melbourne: Melbourne University Press, 2000.

Damasio, Antonio R. *Descartes' Error: Emotion, Reason, and the Human Brain*. New York: Putnam, 1994.

Danahay, Martin. *A Community of One: Masculine Autobiography and Autonomy in Nineteenth-Century Britain*. Albany: State University of New York Press, 1993.

———. "Professional Subjects: Prepackaging the Academic C.V." In *Getting a Life*, ed. Smith and Watson, 351–68.

Davies, Carole Boyce. *Black Women, Writing, and Identity: Migrations of the Subject*. London: Routledge, 1994.

Davis, Rocío G. *Begin Here: Reading Asian North American Autobiographies of Childhood*. Honolulu: University of Hawai'i Press, 2007.

———. "'A Task of Reclamation': Subjectivity, Self-Representation, and Textual Formulation in Sara Suleri's *Meatless Days*." In *Asian North American Identities: Beyond the Hyphen*, ed. Eleanor Ty and Donald Goellnicht, 117–29. Bloomington: Indiana University Press, 2004.

Dawes, James. *That the World May Know: Bearing Witness to Atrocity*. Cambridge, Mass.: Harvard University Press, 2007.

Deans, Jill R. "The Birth of Contemporary Adoption Autobiography: Florence Fisher and Betty Jean Lifton." *a/b: Auto/Biography Studies* 18:2 (Winter 2003): 239–58. Special Issue on Adoption.

Dekker, Rudolf. *Childhood, Memory, and Autobiography in Holland: From the Golden Age to Romanticism.* New York: St. Martin's, 2000.

Delany, Paul. *British Autobiography in the Seventeenth Century.* London: Routledge and Kegan Paul, 1969.

de Lauretis, Teresa. *Alice Doesn't: Feminism, Semiotics, Cinema.* Bloomington: Indiana University Press, 1984.

———. "Eccentric Subjects: Feminist Theory and Historical Consciousness." *Feminist Studies* 16.1 (Spring 1990): 115–50.

de Man, Paul. "Autobiography as De-Facement." *Modern Language Notes* 94.5 (December 1979): 919–30.

Dentith, Simon. "Contemporary Working-Class Autobiography: Politics of Form, Politics of Content." In *Modern Selves: Essays on Modern British and American Autobiography,* ed. Philip Dodd, 60–80. London: Frank Cass, 1986.

Denton, Andrew. "Ishmael Beah." *Enough Rope with Andrew Denton.* Accessed 12 November 2009. www.abc.net.au/tv/enoughrope/transcripts/s1968333.htm

Deresiewicz, William. "Foes." *The Nation,* 25 February 2008, 29–34.

Derounian-Stodola, Kathryn Zabelle, and James A. Levernier. *The Indian Captivity Narrative, 1550–1900.* New York: Twayne, 1993.

Derrida, Jacques. *The Ear of the Other: Otobiography, Transference, Translation.* Edited by Christie V. McDonald. Translated by Peggy Kamuf. New York: Schocken Books, 1985.

Dilthey, Wilhelm. *Pattern and Meaning in History: W. Dilthey's Thoughts on History and Society.* Edited by H. P. Rickman. New York: Harper & Row, 1960.

———. *Selected Writings.* Edited and translated by H. P. Rickman. New York: Cambridge University Press, 1976.

Douglas, Kate, and Gillian Whitlock. "Introduction." *Life Writing* 5.2 (2008): 139–41. Special Issue on Trauma in the Twenty-First Century.

Drake, Jennifer. "Variations of Negation: Breaking the Frame with Lorna Simpson and Adrian Piper." In *Interfaces,* ed. Smith and Watson, 211–39.

Du Bois, W. E. B. *The Souls of Black Folk: Essays and Sketches.* Chicago: A. C. McClurg, 1903.

Dünne, Jörg, and Christian Moser. "Automédialité. Pour un dialogue entre médiologie et critique littéraire." *Revue d'Etudes Culturelles* 4 (Hiver 2008): 11–20.

Eakin, Paul John. *American Autobiography: Retrospect and Prospect.* Madison: University of Wisconsin Press, 1992.

———. *Fictions of Autobiography: Studies in the Art of Self-Invention.* Princeton, N.J.: Princeton University Press, 1986.

———. *How Our Lives Become Stories: Making Selves.* Ithaca, N.Y.: Cornell University Press, 1999.

———. *Living Autobiographically: How We Create Identity in Narrative.* Ithaca, N.Y.: Cornell University Press, 2008.

———. "Relational Selves, Relational Lives: The Story of a Story." In *True Relations: Essays on Autobiography and the Postmodern,* ed. G. Thomas Couser and Joseph Fichtelberg, 63–81. Westport, Conn.: Greenwood Press, 1998.

———. *Touching the World: Reference in Autobiography.* Princeton, N.J.: Princeton University Press, 1992.

———, ed. *The Ethics of Life Writing.* Ithaca, N.Y.: Cornell University Press, 2004.

Eco, Umberto. *The Role of the Reader: Explorations in the Semiotics of Texts.* Bloomington: Indiana University Press, 1979.

Egan, Susanna. *Mirror Talk: Genres of Crisis in Contemporary Autobiography.* Chapel Hill: University of North Carolina Press, 1999.

———. *Patterns of Experience in Autobiography.* Chapel Hill: University of North Carolina Press, 1984.

———. "'Self'-Conscious History: American Autobiography after the Civil War." In *American Autobiography,* ed. Eakin, 70–94.

Ellis, Carolyn. *The Ethnographic I: A Methodological Novel about Autoethnography.* Walnut Creek, Calif.: AltaMira Press, 2004.

Emberley, Julia V. *Thresholds of Difference: Feminist Critique, Native Women's Writing, Postcolonial Theory.* Toronto: University of Toronto Press, 1993.

Engel, Susan. *Context Is Everything: The Nature of Memory.* New York: W. H. Freeman, 1999.

Feldman, Allen. "Memory Theaters, Virtual Witnessing, and the Trauma-Aesthetic." *Biography* 27.1 (Winter 2004): 163–202.

Felman, Shoshana, and Dori Laub. *Testimony: Crises of Witnessing in Literature, Psychoanalysis, and History.* New York: Routledge, 1992.

Felski, Rita. *Beyond Feminist Aesthetics: Feminist Literature and Social Change.* Boston: Harvard University Press, 1989.

Finke, Laurie. "Mystical Bodies and the Dialogics of Vision." In *Maps of Flesh and Light: The Religious Experience of Medieval Women Mystics,* ed. Ulrike Wiethaus, 28–44. Syracuse, N.Y.: Syracuse University Press, 1993.

Fish, Stanley. "Just Published: Minutiae without Meaning." *New York Times,* 7 September 1999, A19.

Fleishman, Avrom. *Figures of Autobiography: The Language of Self-Writing in Victorian and Modern England.* Berkeley: University of California Press, 1983.

Folkenflik, Robert, ed. "Introduction: The Institution of Autobiography." In *The Culture of Autobiography: Constructions of Self-Representation,* 1–20. Palo Alto, Calif.: Stanford University Press, 1993.

Foster, Frances Smith. *Witnessing Slavery: The Development of Ante-Bellum Slave Narratives.* Westport, Conn: Greenwood Press, 1979.

Foucault, Michel. *The History of Sexuality,* vol. 1. Translated by Robert Hurley. New York: Pantheon Books, 1978.

———. "Technologies of the Self." In *Technologies of the Self: A Seminar with Mi-*

chel Foucault, ed. Luther H. Martin, Huck Gutman, and Patrick H. Hutton, 16–49. Amherst: University of Massachusetts Press, 1988.

Fox, Margalit. "Raymond Federman, Avant-Garde Novelist and Beckett Scholar, Dies at 81." *New York Times,* 12 October 2009.

Franklin, Cynthia G. *Academic Lives: Memoir, Cultural Theory, and the University Today.* Athens and London: University of Georgia Press, 2009.

———. *Writing Women's Communities: The Politics and Poetics of Contemporary Multi-Genre Anthologies.* Madison: University of Wisconsin Press, 1997.

Franklin, H. Bruce. *Prison Literature in America: The Victim as Criminal and Artist.* Westport, Conn.: L. Hill, 1978.

Freadman, Richard. *Threads of Life: Autobiography and the Will.* Chicago: University of Chicago Press, 2001.

Freud, Sigmund. "Fragment of an Analysis of a Case of Hysteria." In *The Standard Edition of the Complete Psychological Works of Sigmund Freud,* ed. James Strachey, 7:3–122. London: Hogarth Press, 1953.

Friedman, Susan Stanford. *Mappings: Feminism and the Cultural Geographies of Encounter.* Princeton, N.J.: Princeton University Press, 1998.

———. "Spatial Poetics and Arundhati Roy's *The God of Small Things.*" In *A Companion to Narrative Theory,* ed. James Phelan and Peter J. Rabinowitz. Malden, Mass.: Blackwell, 2005.

———. "Women's Autobiographical Selves: Theory and Practice." In *The Private Self: Theory and Practice of Women's Autobiographical Writings,* ed. Shari Benstock, 34–62. Chapel Hill: University of North Carolina Press, 1988.

Fuchs, Miriam. *The Text Is Myself: Women's Life Writing and Catastrophe.* Wisconsin Studies in Autobiography. Madison: University of Wisconsin Press, 2004.

Fuchs, Miriam, and Craig Howes. *Teaching Life Writing Texts.* New York: Modern Language Association of America, 2008.

Fuderer, Laura Sue. *The Female Bildungsroman in English.* New York: Modern Language Association of America, 1990.

Gagnier, Regenia. *Subjectivities: A History of Self-Representation in Britain, 1832–1920.* New York: Oxford University Press, 1991.

Gaines, Jane, and Michael Renov. *Collecting Visible Evidence.* Visible Evidence series. Minneapolis: University of Minnesota Press, 1999.

Gardner, Jared. "Archives, Collectors, and the New Media Work of Comics." *Modern Fiction Studies* 52.4 (Winter 2006): 787–806.

———. "Autography's Biography, 1972–2007." *Biography* 3.1 (Winter 2008): 1–26.

Gates, Henry Louis, Jr. *The Signifying Monkey: A Theory of Afro-American Literary Criticism.* New York: Oxford University Press, 1988.

Genette, Gérard. *Paratexts: Thresholds of Interpretation.* Literature, Culture, Theory series. Cambridge and New York: Cambridge University Press, 1997.

Gerschick, Thomas Joseph. "Toward a Theory of Disability and Gender." *Signs: Journal of Women in Culture and Society* 25.4 (Summer 2000): 1263–68.

Gilligan, Carol. *In a Different Voice: Psychological Theory and Women's Development.* Cambridge, Mass.: Harvard University Press, 1982.

Gilmore, Leigh. *Autobiographics: A Feminist Theory of Women's Self-Representation.* Ithaca, N.Y.: Cornell University Press, 1994.

———. "Jurisdictions: *I, Rigoberta Menchú, The Kiss,* and Scandalous Self-Representation in the Age of Memoir and Trauma." *Signs: Journal of Women in Culture and Society* 28.2 (Winter 2003): 695–718.

———. *The Limits of Autobiography: Trauma and Testimony.* Ithaca, N.Y.: Cornell University Press, 2001.

———. "Trauma." In *Encyclopedia of Life Writing: Autobiographical and Biographical Forms,* ed. Margaretta Jolly, 885–87. London: Fitzroy Dearborn, 2001.

Glissant, Edouard. *Caribbean Discourse: Selected Essays.* Translated by J. Michael Dash. Charlottesville: University Press of Virginia, 1989.

Glotfelty, Cheryll, and Harold Fromm, eds. *The Ecocriticism Reader: Landmarks in Literary Ecology.* Athens: University of Georgia Press, 1996.

Gluck, Sherna Berger, and Daphne Patai, eds. *Women's Words: The Feminist Practice of Oral History.* New York: Routledge, 1991.

Goffman, Erving. *Gender Advertisements.* New York: Harper & Row, 1979.

———. *The Presentation of Self in Everyday Life.* Garden City, N.Y.: Doubleday, 1959.

Goldberg, Elizabeth Swanson. *Beyond Terror: Gender, Narrative, Human Rights.* New Brunswick, N.J.: Rutgers University Press, 2007.

Goldman, Anne E. *Take My Word: Autotopographical Innovations of Ethnic American Working Women.* Berkeley: University of California Press, 1996.

González, Jennifer A. "Autotopographies." In *Prosthetic Territories: Politics and Hypertechnologies,* ed. Gabriel Brahm Jr. and Mark Driscoll, 133–50. Boulder, Colo.: Westview Press, 1995.

Goswami, Namita. "Autophagia and Queer Transnationality: Compulsory Heteroimperial Masculinity in Deepa Mehta's *Fire.*" *Signs: Journal of Women in Culture and Society* 33.2 (2008): 342–69.

Green, Barbara. *Spectacular Confessions: Autobiography, Performative Activism, and the Sites of Suffrage.* New York: St. Martin's Press, 1997.

Greenblatt, Stephen. *Renaissance Self-Fashioning: From More to Shakespeare.* Chicago: University of Chicago Press, 1980.

Grewal, Inderpal. *Home and Harem: Nation, Gender, Empire, and the Cultures of Travel.* Durham, N.C.: Duke University Press, 1996.

Grosz, Elizabeth. *Volatile Bodies: Toward a Corporeal Feminism.* Bloomington: Indiana University Press, 1994.

Gullette, Margaret Morganroth. *Declining to Decline: Cultural Combat and the Politics of the Midlife.* Charlottesville: University Press of Virginia, 1997.

———. "No Longer Suppressing Grief: Political Trauma in Twentieth Century America." *Life Writing* 5.2 (October 2008): 253–61.

Gunn, Janet Varner. *Autobiography: Toward a Poetics of Experience.* Philadelphia: University of Pennsylvania Press, 1982.

Gunning, Sandra. "Reading and Redemption in *Incidents in the Life of a Slave Girl.*" In *Harriet Jacobs and Incidents in the Life of a Slave Girl,* ed. Deborah Garfield and Rafia Zafar, 131–55. New York: Cambridge University Press, 1996.

Gusdorf, Georges. "Conditions and Limits of Autobiography." Translated by James Olney. In *Autobiography,* ed. Olney, 28–48.

Haaken, Janice. *Pillar of Salt: Gender, Memory, and the Perils of Looking Back.* New Brunswick, N.J.: Rutgers University Press, 1998.

———. "The Recovery of Memory, Fantasy, and Desire: Feminist Approaches to Sexual Abuse and Psychic Trauma." *Signs: Journal of Women in Culture and Society* 21.4 (Summer 1996): 1069–94.

Hall, Stuart. "Cultural Identity and Diaspora." In *Colonial Discourse and Post-Colonial Theory: A Reader,* ed. Patrick Williams and Laura Chrisman, 392–403. New York: Columbia University Press, 1994.

Hames-Garcia, Michael Roy. *Fugitive Thought: Prison Movements, Race, and the Meaning of Justice.* Minneapolis: University of Minnesota Press, 2004.

Hamilton, Nigel. *Biography: A Brief History.* Cambridge, Mass.: Harvard University Press, 2007.

Hanley, Christine. "Handyman Sentenced to Life in Prison." *Columbus Dispatch,* 14 September 2000, A–10.

Hanscombe, Elisabeth. "Aspects of Trauma: Incest, War and Witness." *Life Writing* 5.1 (April 2008): 117–24.

Hardey, Michael. "Digital Life Stories: Auto/Biography in the Information Age." *Auto/Biography* 12.3 (2004): 183–200.

Harlow, Barbara. *Barred: Women, Writing, and Political Detention.* Middletown, Conn.: Wesleyan University Press, 1992.

———. "From a Women's Prison: Third World Women's Narratives of Prison." *Feminist Studies* 12.3 (1986): 501–24.

———. *Resistance Literatures.* New York: Methuen, 1987.

Hart, Francis R. "Notes for an Anatomy of Modern Autobiography." *New Literary History* 1 (Spring 1970): 486–511.

Hawkins, Anne Hunsaker. *Reconstructing Illness: Studies in Pathography.* West Lafayette, Ind.: Purdue University Press, 1993.

Hayano, David. "Auto-Ethnography: Paradigms, Problems, and Prospects." *Human Organization* 38.1 (1979): 99–104.

Henderson, Mae Gwendolyn. "Speaking in Tongues: Dialogics, Dialectics, and the Black Woman Writer's Literary Tradition." In *Changing Our Words: Essays on Criticism, Theory, and Writing by Black Women,* ed. Cheryl A. Wall, 116–42. New Brunswick, N.J.: Rutgers University Press, 1989.

Henke, Suzette. *Shattered Subjects: Trauma and Testimony in Women's Life-Writing.* New York: St. Martin's Press, 1998.

Hesford, Wendy S. "Documenting Violations: Rhetorical Witnessing and the Spectacle of Distant Suffering." *Biography* 27.1 (Winter 2004): 104–44.

———. *Framing Identities: Autobiography and the Politics of Pedagogy.* Minneapolis: University of Minnesota Press, 1999.

Hesford, Wendy S., and Wendy Kozol. *Haunting Violations: Feminist Criticism and the Crisis of the "Real."* Urbana: University of Illinois Press, 2001.

———. *Just Advocacy? Women's Human Rights, Transnational Feminisms, and the Politics of Representation.* New Brunswick, N.J.: Rutgers University Press, 2005.

Hipchen, Emily, and Jill Deans. "Introduction: Adoption Life Writing: Origins and Other Ghosts." *a/b: Auto/Biography Studies* 18.2 (Winter 2003): 163–70. Special Issue on Adoption.

Hirsch, Marianne. "Editor's Column: Collateral Damage." *PMLA* 119.5 (October 2004): 1209–15.

———. *Family Frames: Photography, Narrative, and Postmemory.* Cambridge, Mass.: Harvard University Press, 1997.

———. "Masking the Subject: Practicing Theory." In *The Point of Theory: Practices in Cultural Analysis,* ed. Mieke Bal and Inge E. Boer, 109–24. New York: Continuum, 1994.

Hogan, Rebecca. "Engendered Autobiographies: The Diary as a Feminist Form." *Prose Studies* 14.2 (September 1991): 95–107. Special Issue on Autobiography and Questions of Gender.

Holden, Philip. *Autobiography and Decolonization: Modernity, Masculinity, and the Nation-State.* Madison: University of Wisconsin Press, 2008.

———. "Other Modernities: National Autobiography and Globalization." *Biography* 28.1 (Winter 2005): 89–103.

Holman, C. Hugh. "Preface." In *A Handbook to Literature,* ed. William Flint Thrall and Addison Hibbard, v–vi. New York: Odyssey Press, 1960.

Hooton, Joy. *Stories of Herself When Young: Autobiographies of Childhood by Australian Women.* New York: Oxford University Press. 1990.

Howarth, William L. "Some Principles of Autobiography." In *Autobiography,* ed. Olney, 84–114.

Howes, Craig. *Voices of the Vietnam POWs: Witnesses to Their Fight.* New York: Oxford University Press, 1993.

Huff, Cynthia. *British Women's Diaries: A Descriptive Bibliography of Selected Nineteenth-Century Women's Manuscript Diaries.* New York: AMS Press, 1985.

Ibsen, Kristine. *Women's Spiritual Autobiography in Colonial Spanish America.* Gainesville: University Press of Florida, 1999.

Isaak, Jo Anna. *Feminism and Contemporary Art: The Revolutionary Power of Women's Laughter.* London: Routledge, 1996.

Jackson, David. *Unmasking Masculinity: A Critical Autobiography.* London: Unwin Hyman, 1990.

Jardine, Alice. *Gynesis: Configurations of Women and Modernity.* Ithaca, N.Y.: Cornell University Press, 1985.

Jay, Paul. *Being in the Text: Self-Representation from Wordsworth to Roland Barthes.* Ithaca, N.Y.: Cornell University Press, 1984.

Jelinek, Estelle C., ed. *Women's Autobiography: Essays in Criticism.* Bloomington: Indiana University Press, 1980.

Jolly, Margaretta, ed. *Encyclopedia of Life Writing: Autobiographical and Biographical Forms.* 2 vols. London: Fitzroy Dearborn, 2001.

———. *In Love and Struggle: Letters in Contemporary Feminism.* New York: Columbia University Press, 2008.

Jones, Amelia. *Body Art/Performing the Subject.* Minneapolis: University of Minnesota Press, 1998.

Juhasz, Alexandra, and Jesse Lerner. "Introduction: Phony Definitions and Troubling Taxonomies of the Fake Documentary." In *F Is for Phony: Fake Documentary and Truth's Undoing,* ed. Alexandra Juhasz and Jesse Lerner, 1–38. Minneapolis: University of Minnesota Press, 2006.

Kaplan, Caren. *Questions of Travel: Modern Discourses of Displacement.* Durham, N.C.: Duke University Press, 1996.

———. "Resisting Autobiography: Out-Law Genres and Transnational Feminist Subjects." In *De/Colonizing the Subject,* ed. Smith and Watson, 115–38.

Kauffman, Linda. "Cutups in Beauty School—and Postscripts, January 2000 and December 2001." In *Interfaces: Women/Autobiography/Image/Performance,* ed. Sidonie Smith and Julia Watson, 103–31. Ann Arbor: University of Michigan Press, 2002.

Kawash, Samira. *Dislocating the Color Line: Identity, Hybridity, and Singularity in African-American Narrative.* Stanford, Calif.: Stanford University Press, 1997.

Keith, Michael, and Steve Pile, eds. *Place and the Politics of Identity.* London: Routledge, 1993.

Kennedy, Rosanne. "Vulnerable Children, Disposable Mothers: Holocaust and Stolen Generations' Memoirs of Childhood." *Life Writing* 5.2 (October 2008): 161–84. Special Issue on Trauma in the Twenty-First Century.

Kennedy, Rosanne, and Gillian Whitlock. Conference announcement for Testimony, Trauma and Social Suffering: New Contexts/New Framings, April 14–16, 2009, Research School of Humanities, Australian National University, Canberra, Australia.

Kermode, Frank. "Fictioneering." *London Review of Books* 8 October 2009, 9–10.

Kline, Kerwin Lee. "On the Emergence of 'Memory' in Historical Discourse." *Representations* 69 (Winter 2000): 127–50.

Knox, Malcolm. "Bestseller's Lies Exposed: Literary Editor Malcolm Knox Uncovers Australia's Latest Hoax Author." *Sydney Morning Herald,* 24 July 2004.

Krailsheimer, A. J. *Studies in Self-Interest: From Descartes to La Bruyère*. Oxford: Clarendon Press, 1962.

Krupat, Arnold. *Ethnocriticism: Ethnography, History, Literature*. Berkeley: University of California Press, 1992.

———. *For Those Who Come After: A Study of Native American Autobiography*. Berkeley: University of California Press, 1985.

———. "Introduction." In *Native American Autobiography: An Anthology*, 3–17. Madison: University of Wisconsin Press, 1994.

Kulbaga, Theresa. "Pleasurable Pedagogies: *Reading Lolita in Tehran* and the Rhetoric of Empathy." *College English* 70.5 (May 2008): 506–21.

Kutschera, Chris. "Iran: Marjane Satrapi's 'Persepolis,' the Iranian Revolution Seen through the Eyes of a 10-Year Old Girl." Chris Kutschera: 30 Years of Journalism (Texts and Photos). Accessed on 20 January 2009. http://www.chris-kutschera .com/A/Marjane%20Satrapi.htm

Lacan, Jacques. *The Language of the Self: The Function of Language in Psychoanalysis*. Translated by Anthony Wilden. Baltimore: Johns Hopkins University Press, 1968.

Landsberg, Alison. *Prosthetic Memory: The Transformation of American Remembrance in the Age of Mass Culture*. New York: Columbia University Press, 2004.

Lane, Jim. *The Autobiographical Documentary in America from the 1960s to the Present*. Wisconsin Studies in Autobiography. Madison: University of Wisconsin Press, 2002.

Lang, Candace D. "Autobiography in the Aftermath of Romanticism." *Diacritics* 12 (Winter 1982): 2–16.

———. *Irony/Humor: Critical Paradigms*. Baltimore: Johns Hopkins University Press, 1988.

Lather, Patti, and Chris Smithies. *Troubling the Angels: Women Living with HIV/ AIDS*. Boulder, Colo.: Westview Press, 1997.

Laudun, John. "Orality." In *Encyclopedia of Life Writing*, ed. Jolly, 680–82.

Leed, Eric J. *The Mind of the Traveler: From Gilgamesh to Global Tourism*. New York: Basic Books, 1991.

Leith, Dick, and George Myerson. *The Power of Address: Explorations in Rhetoric*. London: Routledge, 1989.

Lejeune, Philippe. "The Autobiographical Pact." In Lejeune, *On Autobiography*.

———. "The Autobiographical Pact (bis)." In Lejeune, *On Autobiography*, 119–37.

———. *L'Autobiographie en France*. Paris: Colin, 1971.

———. "Autobiography in the Third Person." In Lejeune, *On Autobiography*, 31–51.

———. "The Autobiography of Those Who Do Not Write." In Lejeune, *On Autobiography*, 185–215.

———. *On Autobiography*. Edited by Paul John Eakin and translated by Katherine Leary. Minneapolis: University of Minnesota Press, 1989.

———. *On Diary,* ed. Jeremy Popkin and Julie Rak, trans. Katharine Durnin. Honolulu: Center for Biographical Research, University of Hawai'i, 2009.

———. "The Practice of the Private Journal: Chronicle of an Investigation (1986–1998)." In *Marginal Voices, Marginal Forms: Diaries in European Literature and History,* ed. Rachel Langford and Russell West, 185–211. Translated by Russell West. Amsterdam: Rodopi, 1999.

Lewis, Jon, ed. *The End of Cinema as We Know It: American Film in the Nineties.* New York: New York University Press, 2001.

Lim, Shirley Geok-lin. *Writing S.E./Asia in English: Against the Grain, Focus on Asian English-Language Literature.* London: Skoob Books, 1994.

Linde, Charlotte. *Life Stories: The Creation of Coherence.* New York: Oxford University Press, 1993.

Lindemann Nelson, Hilde. *Damaged Identities, Narrative Repair.* Ithaca, N.Y.: Cornell University Press, 2001.

Lionnet, Françoise. *Autobiographical Voices: Race, Gender, Self-Portraiture.* Ithaca, N.Y.: Cornell University Press, 1989.

———. "Of Mangoes and Maroons: Language, History, and the Multicultural Subject of Michelle Cliff's *Abeng.*" In *De/Colonizing the Subject,* ed. Smith and Watson, 321–45.

———. *Postcolonial Representations: Women, Literature, Identity.* Ithaca, N.Y.: Cornell University Press, 1995.

Lowe, Lisa. *Immigrant Acts: On Asian American Cultural Politics.* Durham, N.C.: Duke University Press, 1996.

Ludlow, Peter, and M. Wallace. *The Second Life Herald: The Virtual Tabloid That Witnessed the Dawn of the Metaverse.* Cambridge, Mass.: MIT Press, 2007.

Lyotard, Jean-François. *The Postmodern Condition: A Report on Knowledge.* Translated by Geoff Bennington and Brian Massumi. Minneapolis: University of Minnesota Press, 1984.

Marcus, Laura. *Auto/Biographical Discourses: Theory, Criticism, Practice.* Manchester: Manchester University Press, 1994.

Martz, Louis Lohr. *The Poetry of Meditation: A Study in English Religious Literature of the Seventeenth Century.* New Haven, Conn.: Yale University Press, 1954.

Mascuch, Michael. *Origins of the Individual Self: Autobiography and Self-Identity in England, 1591–1791.* Cambridge: Polity Press, 1997.

Mason, Mary G. "Autobiographies of Women Writers." In *Autobiography,* ed. Olney, 207–35.

McHugh, Kathleen. "Lourdes Portillo, Rea Tajiri, and Cheryl Dunye: History and Falsehood in Experimental Autobiographies." In *Women and Experimental Filmmaking,* ed. Jean Petrolle and Virginia Wright Wexman. Urbana: University of Illinois, 2005.

———. "Where Hollywood Fears to Tread: Autobiography and the Limits of Commerical Cinema." In *The End of Cinema as We Know It,* ed. Lewis.

McNeill, Laurie. "Death and the Maidens: Vancouver's Missing Women, the Montreal Massacre, and Commemoration's Blind Spots." *Canadian Review of American Studies* 39.3 (Winter 2008): 375–98.

———. "Diary 2.0? A Genre Moves from Page to Screen." In *New Media and Linguistic Change,* ed. Charley Rowe and Eva Wyss. Cresskill, N.J.: Hampton Press, 2008.

Menand, Louis. "Lives of Others." *New Yorker* 4 August 2007, 64–66.

Meskimmon, Marsha. *The Art of Reflection: Women Artists' Self-Portraiture in the Twentieth Century.* New York: Columbia University Press, 1996.

Milani, Farzaneh. *Veils and Words: The Emerging Voices of Iranian Women Writers.* Syracuse: Syracuse University Press, 1992.

Miller, Carolyn R. "Genre as Social Action." In *Genre and the New Rhetoric,* ed. Aviva Freedman and Peter Medway, 23–42. London: Taylor & Francis, 1984.

Miller, Nancy K. *But Enough about Me: Why We Read Other People's Lives.* Gender and Culture series. New York: Columbia University Press, 2002.

———. "Closing Comments." Presented at the International Auto/Biography Association, Life Writing & Translations conference, Honolulu, Hawaii, 2008.

———. "The Entangled Self: Genre Bondage in the Age of Memoir." *PMLA* 122.2 (2007): 537–48.

———. *Getting Personal: Feminist Occasions and Other Autobiographical Acts.* New York: Routledge, 1991.

———. "Memory Stains: Annie Ernaux's *Shame.*" *a/b: Auto/Biography Studies* 14.1 (Summer 1999): 38–50.

———. "Out of the Family: Generations of Women in Marjane Satrapi's *Persepolis.*" *Life Writing* 4.1 (April 2007): 13–30.

———. "Representing Others: Gender and the Subjects of Autobiography." *differences* 6.1 (1994): 1–27.

———. "Toward a Dialectics of Difference." In *Women and Language in Literature and Society,* ed. Sally McConnell-Ginet, Ruth Borker, and Nelly Furman, 258–73. New York: Praeger, 1980.

———. "Writing Fictions: Women's Autobiography in France." In *Life/Lines: Theorizing Women's Autobiography,* ed. Bella Brodzki and Celeste Schenck, 45–61. Ithaca, N.Y.: Cornell University Press, 1988.

Mintz, Susannah B. "Anxiety of Choice: Teaching Contemporary Women's Autobiography." In Fuchs and Howes, *Teaching Life Writing Texts,* 318–26.

———. *Unruly Bodies: Life Writing by Women with Disabilities.* Chapel Hill: University of North Carolina Press, 2007.

Misch, Georg. *A History of Autobiography in Antiquity.* 2 vols. Trans. E. W. Dickes. London: Routledge & Paul, 1950.

Mitchell, David D., and Sharon Snyder. *Narrative Prosthesis: Disability and the Dependencies of Discourse.* Ann Arbor: University of Michigan Press, 2001.

Mitchell, W. J. T. *Picture Theory: Essays on Visual and Verbal Representation.* Chicago: University of Chicago Press, 1994.

Molloy, Sylvia. *Autobiographical Writings in Spanish America: At Face Value.* Cambridge: Cambridge University Press, 1991.

Mostern, Kenneth. *Autobiography and Black Identity Politics: Racialization in Twentieth-Century America.* Cambridge: Cambridge University Press, 1999.

Mouffe, Chantal. "Feminism, Citizenship, and Radical Democratic Politics." In *Feminists Theorize the Political,* ed. Judith Butler and Joan W. Scott, 369–84. New York: Routledge, 1992.

Myers, Susan. "Precious Moments." Gallery notes. Columbus, Ohio: Hammond Harkins Gallery, 2000.

Nadel, Ira Bruce. *Biography: Fiction, Fact, and Form.* New York: St. Martin's, 1984.

Namias, June. "Introduction." In *A Narrative of the Life of Mrs. Mary Jemison,* ed. James E. Seaver. Norman: University of Oklahoma Press, 1992.

Nelson, Katherine. "The Psychological and Social Origins of Autobiographical Memory." *Psychological Science* 4.1 (January 1993): 7–14.

Neuman, Shirley. "Introduction: Reading Canadian Autobiography." *Essays on Canadian Writing* 60 (Winter 1996): 1–13. Special issue on Canadian Autobiography.

Nichols, Charles Harold. *Many Thousand Gone: The Ex-Slaves' Account of Their Bondage and Freedom.* Leiden: E. J. Brill, 1963.

Nora, Pierre. *Les Lieux de mémoire.* Vols. 1–3. Paris: Gallimard, 1984, 1986, 1992.

Noriega, Chon. Personal communication. 28 July 2002.

Novy, Marianne, ed. *Imagining Adoption: Essays on Literature and Culture.* Ann Arbor: University of Michigan Press, 2001.

Nussbaum, Felicity A. *The Autobiographical Subject.* 2nd ed. Baltimore: Johns Hopkins University Press, 1995.

Oliver, Kelly. *Witnessing: Beyond Recognition.* Minneapolis: University of Minnesota Press, 2001.

Olney, James. "Autobiography and the Cultural Moment." In *Autobiography,* ed. Olney, 3–27.

———. "'I Was Born': Slave Narratives, Their Status as Autobiography and as Literature." In *The Slave's Narrative,* ed. Charles T. Davis and Henry Louis Gates Jr., 148–74. New York: Oxford University Press, 1985.

———. *Memory and Narrative: The Weave of Life-Writing.* Chicago: University of Chicago Press, 1998.

———. *Metaphors of Self: The Meaning of Autobiography.* Princeton, N.J.: Princeton University Press, 1972.

———. "Some Versions of Memory/Some Versions of Bios: The Ontology of Autobiography." In *Autobiography,* ed. Olney, 236–67.

——. *Tell Me Africa: An Approach to African Literature.* Princeton, N.J.: Princeton University Press, 1973.

——, ed. *Autobiography: Essays Theoretical and Critical.* Princeton, N.J.: Princeton University Press, 1980.

Ortner, Sherry B. *Making Gender: The Politics and Erotics of Culture.* Boston: Beacon Press, 1996.

Padilla, Genaro M. *My History, Not Yours: The Formation of Mexican American Autobiography.* Madison: University of Wisconsin Press, 1993.

Panofsky, Erwin. *Tomb Sculpture: Four Lectures on Its Changing Aspects from Ancient Egypt to Bernini.* Edited by H. W. Janson. New York: H. N. Abrams, 1964.

Paquet, Sandra Pouchet. *Caribbean Autobiography: Cultural Identity and Self-Representation.* Madison: University of Wisconsin Press, 2002.

Parker, David. "Narratives of Autonomy and Narratives of Relationality in Auto/Biography." *a/b: Auto/Biography Studies* 19.1–2 (Summer–Winter 2004): 137–55.

Pascal, Roy. *Design and Truth in Autobiography.* Cambridge, Mass.: Harvard University Press, 1960.

Patton, Sandra. "Race/Identity/Culture/Kin: Constructions of African American Identity in Transracial Adoption." In *Getting a Life,* Smith and Watson, 271–98. Minneapolis: University of Minnesota Press, 1996.

Paxton, Nancy. *Writing under the Raj: Gender, Race, and Rape in the British Colonial Imagination, 1830–1947.* New Brunswick, N.J.: Rutgers University Press, 1999.

Peck, Janice. "The Mediated Talking Cure: Therapeutic Framing of Autobiography on TV Talk Shows." In *Getting a Life,* ed. Smith and Watson, 134–155.

Perreault, Jeanne. *Writing Selves: Contemporary Feminist Autography.* Minneapolis: University of Minnesota Press, 1995.

Perreten, Peter F. "Eco-Autobiography. Portrait of Place: Self-Portrait." *a/b: Auto/Biography Studies* 18.1 (2003): 1–22.

Peterson, Linda H. *Traditions of Victorian Women's Autobiography: The Poetics and Politics of Life Writing.* Charlottesville: University Press of Virginia, 1999.

Phelan, James. *Living to Tell about It: A Rhetoric and Ethics of Character Narration.* Ithaca, N.Y.: Cornell University Press, 2004.

——. "Teaching Voice of Authors, Narrators and Audience." In *Teaching Narrative Theory,* ed. James Phelan, Brian McHale, and David Herman. New York: Modern Language Association, forthcoming.

Phillipi, Desa. "Mona Hatoum: Some Any No Every Body." In *Inside the Invisible: An Elliptical Traverse of Twentieth Century Art in, of, and from the Feminine,* ed. Catherine de Zegher, 363–70. Cambridge, Mass.: MIT Press, 1996.

Phillips, Dana. "Ecocriticism, Literary Theory, and the Truth of Ecology." *New Literary History* 30.3 (Summer 1999): 577–602.

Pile, Steve, and Michael Keith. *Geographies of Resistance.* New York: Routledge, 1997.

Plummer, Ken. *Telling Sexual Stories: Power, Change, and Social Worlds.* London: Routledge, 1995.

Pollock, Griselda. *Differencing the Canon: Feminist Desire and the Writing of Art's Histories.* London: Routledge, 1999.

Popkin, Jeremy D. "Historians on the Autobiographical Frontier." *American Historical Review* 104.3 (June 1999): 725–48.

———. *History, Historians, and Autobiography.* Chicago: University of Chicago Press, 2005.

Porter, Dennis. *Haunted Journeys: Desire and Transgression in European Travel Writing.* Princeton, N.J.: Princeton University Press, 1991.

Porter, Roger. *Self-Same Songs: Autobiographical Reflections and Performances.* Lincoln: University of Nebraska Press, 2002.

Poster, Mark. *Information Please: Culture and Politics in the Age of Digital Machines.* Durham, N.C.: Duke University Press, 2006.

———. *What's the Matter with the Internet?* Minneapolis: University of Minnesota Press, 2001.

Pratt, Mary Louise. *Imperial Eyes: Travel Writing and Transculturation.* London: Routledge, 1992.

———. "Mad about Menchú." *Lingua Franca* 9.8 (November 1999): 22.

———. "'Me llamo Rigoberta Menchú': Auto-Ethnography and the Recoding of Citizenship." In *Teaching and Testimony: Rigoberta Menchú and the North American Classroom,* ed. Allen Carey-Webb and Stephen Benz, 57–72. Albany: State University of New York Press, 1996.

Progoff, Ira. *At a Journal Workshop: Writing to Access the Power of the Unconscious and Evoke Creative Ability.* Los Angeles: J. P. Tarcher, 1992.

Prosser, Jay. "No Place Like Home: The Transgendered Narrative of Leslie Feinberg's *Stone Butch Blues.*" *Modern Fiction Studies* 41.3–4 (1995): 483–514.

Quinby, Lee. "The Subject of Memoirs: *The Woman Warrior*'s Technology of Ideographic Selfhood." In *De/Colonizing the Subject,* ed. Smith and Watson, 297–320.

Rak, Julie. "Are Memoirs Autobiography? A Consideration of Genre and Public Identity." *Genre: Forms of Discourse and Culture* 37.3–4 (Fall/Winter 2004): 483–504.

———. "The Digital Queer: Weblogs and Internet Identity." *Biography* 28.1 (2005): 166–82.

———. *Negotiated Memory: Doukhobor Autobiographical Discourse.* Vancouver: University of British Columbia Press, 2004.

Rapaport, Herman. "The New Personalism." *Biography* 21.1 (Winter 1998): 36–49.

Ray, Ruth E. *Beyond Nostalgia: Aging and Life-Story Writing.* Charlottesville: University Press of Virginia, 2000.

Raynaud, Claudine. "'A Nutmeg Nestled Inside Its Covering of Mace': Audre Lorde's *Zami.*" In Brodzki and Schenck, *Life Lines: Theorizing Women's Autobiography,* 221–42.

———. "'Rubbing a Paragraph with a Soft Cloth?' Muted Voices and Editorial Constraints in *Dust Tracks on a Road.*" In Smith and Watson, *De/Colonizing the Subject,* 34–64.

Reed-Danahay, Deborah E. *Auto/Ethnography: Rewriting the Self and the Social.* New York: Berg, 1997.

Renov, Michael. *The Subject of Documentary.* Visible Evidence series. Minneapolis: University of Minnesota Press, 2004.

Renza, Louis A. "The Veto of the Imagination: A Theory of Autobiography." In *Autobiography,* ed. Olney, 268–95.

Rich, Motoko. "Successful at 96, Writer Has More to Say." *New York Times,* 7 April 2007, A21.

Richter, Gerhard. *Walter Benjamin and the Corpus of Autobiography.* Detroit: Wayne State University Press, 2000.

Rimmon-Kenan, Shlomith. *Narrative Fiction: Contemporary Poetics.* London: Routledge, 1983.

Rodriguez, Barbara. *Autobiographical Inscriptions: Form, Personhood, and the American Woman Writer of Color.* New York: Oxford University Press, 1999.

Rooke, Tetz. *In My Childhood: A Study of Arabic Autobiography.* Stockholm: Stockholm University Press, 1997.

Roorbach, Bill. *Writing Life Stories.* Cincinnati: Writer's Digest, 1999.

Rose, Steven P. R. *The Making of Memory: From Molecules to Mind.* New York: Anchor, 1993.

Rotman, Brian. *Becoming Beside Ourselves: The Alphabet, Ghosts, and Distributed Human Being.* Durham, N.C.: Duke University Press, 2008.

Rowbotham, Sheila. *Woman's Consciousness, Man's World.* Harmondsworth: Penguin, 1973.

Rugg, Linda Haverty. *Picturing Ourselves: Photography and Autobiography.* Chicago: University of Chicago Press, 1997.

Rushdy, Ashraf H. A. *Neo-Slave Narratives: Studies in the Social Logic of a Literary Form.* New York: Oxford University Press, 1999.

Sabbioni, Jennifer, Kay Schaffer, and Sidonie Smith, eds. *Indigenous Australian Voices: A Reader.* New Brunswick, N.J.: Rutgers University Press, 1998.

Said, Edward. *Culture and Imperialism.* New York: Vintage, 1994.

Saldívar, José David. *Border Matters: Remapping American Cultural Studies.* Berkeley: University of California Press, 1997.

Saldívar, Ramón. *The Borderlands of Culture: Américo Paredes and the Transnational Imaginary.* Durham, N.C.: Duke University Press, 2006.

———. *Chicano Narrative: The Dialectics of Difference.* Madison: University of Wisconsin Press, 1990.

Saldívar-Hull, Sonia. *Feminism on the Border: Chicana Gender Politics and Literature.* Berkeley: University of California Press, 2000.

Sanders, Mark. "Theorizing the Collaborative Self: The Dynamics of Contour and Content in the Dictated Autobiography." *New Literary History* 25 (1994): 445–58.

Sartwell, Crispin. *Act Like You Know: African-American Autobiography and White Identity.* Chicago: University of Chicago Press, 1998.

Saul, Joanne. *Writing the Roaming Subject: The Biotext in Canadian Literature.* Toronto: University of Toronto Press, 2006.

Saussure, Ferdinand de. *Course in General Linguistics.* Edited by Charles Bally, Albert Sechehaye, and Albert Riedlinger. Translated by Roy Harris. London: Duckworth, 1983.

Sayre, Robert F. *The Examined Self: Benjamin Franklin, Henry Adams, Henry James.* Madison: University of Wisconsin Press, 1988.

Scarry, Elaine. *The Body in Pain: The Making and Unmaking of the World.* New York: Oxford University Press, 1985.

Schacter, Daniel L. *Searching for Memory: The Brain, the Mind, and the Past.* New York: Basic Books, 1996.

Schaffer, Kay. *In the Wake of First Contact: The Eliza Fraser Stories.* Cambridge: Cambridge University Press, 1995.

Schaffer, Kay, and Sidonie Smith. *Human Rights and Narrated Lives: The Ethics of Recognition.* New York: Palgrave Macmillan, 2004.

———. "Human Rights, Storytelling, and the Position of the Beneficiary: Antjie Krog's *Country of My Skull.*" *PMLA* 121.3 (October 2006): 1577–84. Special Section on Human Rights and the Humanities.

Scholes, Robert, and Robert Kellogg. *The Nature of Narrative.* New York: Oxford University Press, 1966.

Scott, Joan W. "Experience." In *Feminists Theorize the Political,* ed. Judith Butler and Joan W. Scott, 22–40. New York: Routledge, 1992.

Secor, Laura. "A Dissenting Voice." *New York Times,* 16 July 2006, Sunday book review section.

Shea, Daniel B. "The Prehistory of American Autobiography." In *American Autobiography,* ed. Eakin, 25–46.

———. *Spiritual Autobiography in Early America.* Madison: University of Wisconsin Press, 1988.

Sheringham, Michael. *Everyday Life: Theories and Practices from Surrealism to the Present.* Oxford: Oxford University Press, 2009.

———. *French Autobiography: Devices and Desires.* Oxford: Clarendon Press, 1993.

Shumaker, Wayne. *English Autobiography: Its Emergence, Materials, and Forms.* Berkeley: University of California Press, 1954.

Siebers, Tobin. *Disability Theory.* Ann Arbor: University of Michigan Press, 2008.

Siegert, Bernhard. *Relais: Literature as an Epoch of the Postal System.* Translated by Kevin Repp. Stanford, Calif.: Stanford University Press, 1999.

Sioui, Georges E. *Autohistory: An Essay on the Foundations of a Social Ethic.* Translated by Sheila Fischman. Montreal: McGill-Queen's University Press, 1992.

Sitney, P. Adams. *Visionary Film: The American Avant-Garde.* 2nd ed. Oxford and New York: Oxford University Press, 1979.

Skura, Meredith Anne. *Tudor Autobiography: Listening for Inwardness.* Chicago: University of Chicago Press, 2008.

Slaughter, Joseph R. *Human Rights, Inc.: The World Novel, Narrative Form, and International Law.* New York: Fordham University Press, 2007.

Smith, Paul. *Discerning the Subject.* Minneapolis: University of Minnesota Press, 1988.

Smith, Sidonie. *Moving Lives: Twentieth-Century Women's Travel Writing.* Minneapolis: University of Minnesota Press, 2001.

———. "Performativity, Autobiographical Practice, Resistance." *a/b: Auto/Biography Studies* 10.1 (Spring 1995): 17–33.

———. *A Poetics of Women's Autobiography: Marginality and the Fictions of Self-Representation.* Bloomington: Indiana University Press, 1987.

———. *Subjectivity, Identity, and the Body: Women's Autobiographical Practices in the Twentieth Century.* Bloomington: Indiana University Press, 1993.

———. "Taking It to the Limit One More Time: Autobiography and Autism." In Smith and Watson, *Getting a Life: Everyday Uses of Autobiography,* 226–48.

Smith, Sidonie, and Julia Watson, eds. *De/Colonizing the Subject: The Politics of Gender in Women's Autobiography.* Minneapolis: University of Minnesota Press, 1992.

———. *Getting a Life: Everyday Uses of Autobiography.* Minneapolis: University of Minnesota Press, 1996.

———. "Introduction: Mapping Women's Self-Representation at Visual/Textual Interfaces." In *Interfaces: Women/Autobiography/Image/Performance,* ed. Sidonie Smith and Julia Watson, 1–46. Ann Arbor: University of Michigan Press, 2005.

———. "Introduction: Situating Subjectivity in Women's Autobiographical Practices." In *Women, Autobiography, Theory: A Reader,* ed. Sidonie Smith and Julia Watson, 3–52. Madison: University of Wisconsin Press, 1998.

———. "New Genres, New Subjects: Women, Gender and Autobiography after 2000." *Revista Canaria de Estudios Ingleses* 58 (April 2009): 13–40.

———. "The Rumpled Bed of Autobiography: Extravagant Lives, Extravagant Questions." *Biography* 24.1 (Winter 2001): 1–14.

———. "Say It Isn't So: Autobiographical Hoaxes and the Ethics of Life Narrative." *Ibidem Studies* (Winter 2007): 15–34.

Sollors, Werner. *Beyond Ethnicity: Consent and Descent in American Culture.* New York: Oxford University Press, 1986.

——. *Neither Black Nor White Yet Both: Thematic Explorations of Interracial Literature.* New York: Oxford University Press, 1977.

Sommer, Doris. *Foundational Fictions: The National Romances of Latin America.* Berkeley: University of California Press, 1993.

Sontag, Susan. *Illness as Metaphor.* New York: Farrar, Straus and Giroux, 1978.

Spacks, Patricia Ann Meyer. *Imagining a Self: Autobiography and Novel in Eighteenth-Century England.* Cambridge: Harvard University Press, 1976.

Spender, Stephen. "Confessions and Autobiography." In *Autobiography,* ed. Olney, 115–22.

Spengemann, William C. *The Forms of Autobiography: Episodes in the History of a Literary Genre.* New Haven, Conn.: Yale University Press, 1980.

Spivak, Gayatri Chakravorty. "Lives." In *Confessions of the Critics: North American Critics' Autobiographical Moves,* ed. H. Aram Veeser, 205–18. New York: Routledge, 1996.

——. "Three Women's Texts and Circumfession." In *Postcolonialism and Autobiography: Michelle Cliff, David Dabydeen, Opal Palmer Adisa,* ed. Alfred Hornung and Ernstpeter Ruhe, 7–22. Amsterdam: Rodopi, 1998.

Sprinker, Michael. "Fictions of the Self: The End of Autobiography." In *Autobiography,* ed. Olney, 321–42.

Stanley, Liz. *The Auto/Biographical I: The Theory and Practice of Feminist Auto/ Biography.* Manchester: Manchester University Press, 1992.

——. "The Epistolarium: On Theorizing Letters and Correspondences." *Auto/ Biography* 12.3 (2004): 201–35.

Stanley, Liz, and Helen Dampier. "Simulacrum Diaries: Time, the 'Moment of Writing' and the Diaries of Johanna Brandt-Van Warmelo." *Life Writing* 3 (2006): 25–52.

Stanton, Domna C. "Autogynography: Is the Subject Different?" In *The Female Autograph: Theory and Practice of Autobiography from the Tenth to the Twentieth Century,* ed. Domna C. Stanton. Chicago: University of Chicago Press, 1987.

Starobinski, Jean. "The Style of Autobiography." In *Autobiography,* ed. Olney, 73–83.

Stelzig, Eugene, ed. *Romantic Autobiography in England.* Oxford: Ashgate, 2009.

Stepto, Robert B. *From Behind the Veil: A Study of Afro-American Narrative.* Champaign-Urbana: University of Illinois Press, 1979.

Stoll, David. *Rigoberta Menchú and the Story of All Poor Guatemalans.* Boulder, Colo.: Westview Press, 1999.

Stone, Albert E. *Autobiographical Occasions and Original Acts: Versions of American Identity from Henry Adams to Nate Shaw.* Philadelphia: University of Pennsylvania Press, 1982.

Stone, Lawrence. *The Family: Sex and Marriage in England, 1500–1800.* London: Penguin, 1983.

Strathern, Marilyn. "The Limits of Auto-Anthropology." In *Anthropology at Home,* ed. Anthony Jackson, 16–37. London: Tavistock Publications, 1987.

Sturrock, John. "The New Model Autobiographer." *New Literary History* 9.1 (Autumn 1977): 51–63.

Suleri, Sara. *The Rhetoric of English India.* Chicago: University of Chicago Press, 1992.

Swindells, Julia. *The Uses of Autobiography.* London: Taylor and Francis, 1995.

Taylor, Thérèse. "Truth, History, and Honor Killing: A Review of *Burned Alive*." Accessed on 2 September 2006. http://www.antiwar.com/orig/ttaylor.php?articleid=5801

Tensuan, Teresa. "Comic Visions and Revisions in the Work of Lynda Barry and Marjane Satrapi." *Modern Fiction Studies* 52.4 (Winter 2006): 947–64.

Thomson, Rosemarie Garland. *Extraordinary Bodies: Figuring Physical Disability in American Culture and Literature.* New York: Columbia University Press, 1997.

———. *Freakery: Cultural Spectacles of the Extraordinary Body.* New York: New York University Press, 1996.

———. "Integrating Disability, Transforming Feminist Theory." *NWSA Journal* 14.3 (2002): 1–32.

Toor, Rachel. "Creating Nonfiction." *Chronicle of Higher Education,* 7 December 2007.

Veeser, H. Aram, ed. *Confessions of the Critics: North American Critics' Autobiographical Moves.* New York: Routledge, 1996.

Verene, Donald Phillip. *The New Art of Autobiography: An Essay on the Life of Giambattista Vico Written by Himself.* Oxford: Clarendon Press, 1991.

Vernon, Alex. *Arms and the Self: War, the Military, and Autobiographical Writing.* Kent, Ohio: Kent State University Press, 2005.

———. "Submission and Resistance to the Self as Soldier: Tim O'Brien's Vietnam War Memoir." *a/b: Auto/Biography Studies* 17.2 (Winter 2002): 161–79.

Voloshinov, V. N., Ladislav Matejka, and I. R. Titunik. *Marxism and the Philosophy of Language.* New York: Seminar Press, 1973.

Wang, Jing M. *When "I" Was Born: Women's Autobiography in Modern China.* Madison, Wis.: University of Wisconsin Press, 2008.

Wang, Lingzhen. *Personal Matters: Women's Autobiographical Practice in Twentieth-Century China.* Palo Alto, Calif.: Stanford University Press, 2004.

Warhol, Robyn, and Helena Michie. "Twelve-Step Teleology: Narratives of Recovery/Recovery as Narrative." In Smith and Watson, *Getting a Life,* 327–50.

Warrior, Robert. *The People and the Word: Reading Native Nonfiction.* Minneapolis: University of Minnesota Press, 2005.

Watson, Julia. "'As Gay and as Indian as They Chose': Collaboration and Counter-Ethnography in *In the Land of the Grasshopper Song*." *Biography* 31.3 (Summer 2008): 397–428.

———. "Autographic Disclosures and Genealogies of Desire in Alison Bechdel's *Fun Home*." *Biography* 31.1 (Winter 2008): 27–58.

———. "Ordering the Family: Genealogy as Autobiographical Pedigree." In *Getting a Life,* ed. Smith and Watson, 297–323.

———. "The Spaces of Autobiographical Narrative." In *Räume des Selbst. Selbstzeugnisforschung transkulturell* (Selbstzeugnisse der Neuzeit 19), ed. Andreas Bähr, Peter Burschel, and Gabrielle Jancke, 13–25. Köln: Böhlau, 2007.

———. "Unspeakable Differences: The Politics of Gender in Lesbian and Heterosexual Women's Autobiographies." In *De/Colonizing the Subject,* ed. Smith and Watson, 139–68.

Waxman, Barbara Frey. *To Live in the Center of the Moment: Literary Autobiographies of Aging.* Charlottesville: University Press of Virginia, 1997.

Weintraub, Karl Joachim. *The Value of the Individual: Self and Circumstance in Autobiography.* Chicago: University of Chicago Press, 1978.

Wells, Susan. "Freud's Rat Man and the Case Study: Genre in Three Keys." *New Literary History* 34.2 (2003): 353–66.

White, Hayden. *The Content of the Form: Narrative Discourse and Historical Representation.* Baltimore: Johns Hopkins University Press, 1987.

Whitlock, Gillian. "Autographics: The Seeing 'I' Of the Comics." *Modern Fiction Studies* 52.4 (Winter 2006): 965–79.

———. "Disciplining the Child: Recent British Academic Memoir." *a/b: Auto/Biography Studies* 19.1–2 (Summer 2004): 46–58.

———. *The Intimate Empire: Reading Women's Autobiography.* New York: Cassell, 2000.

———. *Soft Weapons: Autobiography in Transit.* Chicago: University of Chicago Press, 2007.

Wilson, Tracy. "How MMORPGs Work." Accessed on 20 January 2009. http://electronics.howstuffworks.com/mmorpg.htm

Wimsatt, W. K. "The Intentional Fallacy." In Wimsatt, *The Verbal Icon: Studies in the Meaning of Poetry,* 3–18. Lexington: University of Kentucky Press, 1954.

Wimsatt, W. K., Jr., and Cleanth Brooks. *Literary Criticism: A Short History.* New York: Knopf, 1957.

Wingrove, Elizabeth. "Interpellating Sex." *Signs: Journal of Women in Culture and Society* 24.4 (Summer 1999): 869–93.

Witzling, Mara, ed. *Voicing Today's Visions: Writings by Contemporary Women Artists.* New York: Universe Publishing, 1994.

Wong, Hertha D. Sweet. "First-Person Plural: Subjectivity and Community in Native American Women's Autobiography." In *Women, Autobiography, Theory,* ed. Smith and Watson, 168–78.

———. *Sending My Heart Back across the Years: Tradition and Innovation in Native American Autobiography.* New York: Oxford University Press, 1992.

Wong, Sau-Ling Cynthia. "Immigrant Autobiography: Some Questions of Definition and Approach." In *American Autobiography,* ed. Eakin, 142–70.

Woodhull, Winifred. *Transfigurations of the Maghreb: Feminism, Decolonization, and Literatures in France*. Minneapolis: University of Minnesota Press, 1993.

Woodward, Kathleen. *Aging and Its Discontents: Freud and Other Fictions*. Bloomington: Indiana University Press, 1991.

——, ed. *Figuring Age: Women, Bodies, Generations*. Bloomington: Indiana University Press, 1999.

Woolf, Virginia. *A Room of One's Own*. London: Hogarth Press, 1929.

Yaeger, Patsy. "Introduction: Dreaming of Infrastructure." *PMLA* 122.1 (January 2007): 9–26.

Yates, Frances A. *The Art of Memory*. Chicago: University of Chicago Press, 1966.

Yellin, Jean Fagan. *Harriet Jacobs: A Life*. New York: Basic Civitas Books, 2004.

Young, Michael W., and Noel Stanley. "Sporting Autobiography." In Jolly, *Encyclopedia of Life Writing*, 837–40.

Young, Robert J. C. *Postcolonialism: An Historical Introduction*. Oxford and Malden, Mass.: Blackwell Publishers, 2001.

Zhao, Baisheng. *Zhuan ji wen xue li lun* (A Theory of Autobiography). Beijing Shi: Beijing da xue chu ban she, 2003.

Index

Author photo by Gregory Grieco

SIDONIE SMITH is Martha Guernsey Colby Collegiate Professor of English and women's studies and 2010 president of the Modern Language Association. **JULIA WATSON** is associate dean of Arts and Sciences and professor of comparative studies at The Ohio State University. They have collaborated on *Getting a Life: Everyday Uses of Autobiography* (1996) and *De/Colonizing the Subject: The Politics of Gender in Women's Autobiography* (1992), both published by the University of Minnesota Press.